Identity and Leadership in Virtual Communities:

Establishing Credibility and Influence

Dona J. Hickey
University of Richmond, USA

Joe Essid
University of Richmond, USA

A volume in the Advances in Social
Networking and Online Communities
(ASNOC) Book Series

Information Science
REFERENCE
An Imprint of IGI Global

Managing Director:	Lindsay Johnston
Production Manager:	Jennifer Yoder
Development Editor:	Austin DeMarco
Acquisitions Editor:	Kayla Wolfe
Typesetter:	John Crodian
Cover Design:	Jason Mull

Published in the United States of America by
Information Science Reference (an imprint of IGI Global)
701 E. Chocolate Avenue
Hershey PA 17033
Tel: 717-533-8845
Fax: 717-533-8661
E-mail: cust@igi-global.com
Web site: http://www.igi-global.com

Library of Congress Cataloging-in-Publication Data

Identity and leadership in virtual communities : establishing credibility and influence / Dona J. Hickey and Joe Essid, editors.
       pages cm
  Includes bibliographical references and index.
   ISBN 978-1-4666-5150-0 (hardcover) -- ISBN 978-1-4666-5151-7 (ebook) -- ISBN 978-1-4666-5153-1 (print & perpetual access) 1. Computer networks--Social aspects. 2. Internet--Social aspects. 3. Group identity. I. Hickey, Dona J., editor of compilation.
  HM1017.I34 2014
  302.23'1--dc23
                           2013044136

This book is published in the IGI Global book series Advances in Social Networking and Online Communities (ASNOC) (ISSN: 2328-1405; eISSN: 2328-1413)

British Cataloguing in Publication Data
A Cataloguing in Publication record for this book is available from the British Library.

For electronic access to this publication, please contact: eresources@igi-global.com.

Advances in Social Networking and Online Communities (ASNOC) Book Series

Hakikur Rahman
University of Minho, Portugal

ISSN: 2328-1405
EISSN: 2328-1413

MISSION

The advancements of internet technologies and the creation of various social networks provide a new channel of knowledge development processes that's dependent on social networking and online communities. This emerging concept of social innovation is comprised of ideas and strategies designed to improve society.

The **Advances in Social Networking and Online Communities** book series serves as a forum for scholars and practitioners to present comprehensive research on the social, cultural, organizational, and human issues related to the use of virtual communities and social networking. This series will provide an analytical approach to the holistic and newly emerging concepts of online knowledge communities and social networks.

COVERAGE

- Agent-mediated Knowledge Management
- Broadband Infrastructure and the New Wireless Network Solutions
- Conceptual Role of ICTs in Knowledge Communication and Management
- Distributed Knowledge Management Business Cases and Experiences
- Framework of a Pragmatic Conception of Knowledge
- Knowledge Management Practices and Future Perspectives
- Networks and Knowledge Communication in R&D Environments
- Networks as Institutionalized Intermediaries of KC
- Strategic Management and Business Process Analysis
- Supporting Virtual Communities of Practice and Interest Networks

IGI Global is currently accepting manuscripts for publication within this series. To submit a proposal for a volume in this series, please contact our Acquisition Editors at Acquisitions@igi-global.com or visit: http://www.igi-global.com/publish/.

Titles in this Series

For a list of additional titles in this series, please visit: www.igi-global.com

Identity and Leadership in Virtual Communities Establishing Credibility and Influence
Dona J. Hickey (University of Richmond, USA) and Joe Essid (University of Richmond, USA)
Information Science Reference • copyright 2014 • 321pp • H/C (ISBN: 9781466651500) • US $205.00 (our price)

Harnessing the Power of Social Media and Web Analytics
Anteneh Ayanso (Brock University, Canada) and Kaveepan Lertwachara (California Polytechnic State University, USA)
Information Science Reference • copyright 2014 • 363pp • H/C (ISBN: 9781466651944) • US $215.00 (our price)

Educational, Psychological, and Behavioral Considerations in Niche Online Communities
Vivek Venkatesh (Concordia University, Canada) Jason Wallin (University of Alberta, Canada) Juan Carlos Castro (Concordia University, Canada) and Jason Edward Lewis (Concordia University, Canada)
Information Science Reference • copyright 2014 • 313pp • H/C (ISBN: 9781466652064) • US $195.00 (our price)

Gender and Social Computing Interactions, Differences and Relationships
Celia Romm Livermore (Wayne State University, USA)
Information Science Publishing • copyright 2012 • 343pp • H/C (ISBN: 9781609607593) • US $195.00 (our price)

Virtual Worlds and Metaverse Platforms New Communication and Identity Paradigms
Nelson Zagalo (University of Minho, Portugal) Leonel Morgado (University of Trás-os-Montes e Alto Douro, Quinta de Prados, Portugal) and Ana Boa-Ventura (The University of Texas at Austin, USA)
Information Science Reference • copyright 2012 • 423pp • H/C (ISBN: 9781609608545) • US $195.00 (our price)

Youth Culture and Net Culture Online Social Practices
Elza Dunkels (Umeå University, Sweden) Gun-Marie Franberg (Umea University, Sweden) and Camilla Hallgren (Umea University, Sweden)
Information Science Reference • copyright 2011 • 472pp • H/C (ISBN: 9781609602093) • US $180.00 (our price)

Collaborative Search and Communities of Interest Trends in Knowledge Sharing and Assessment
Pascal Francq (Universite Libre de Bruxelles, Belgium)
Information Science Reference • copyright 2011 • 312pp • H/C (ISBN: 9781615208418) • US $180.00 (our price)

Gender Issues in Learning and Working with Information Technology Social Constructs and Cultural Contexts
Shirley Booth (University of Gothenburg, Sweden) Sara Goodman (Lund University, Sweden) and Gill Kirkup (Open University, UK)
Information Science Reference • copyright 2010 • 350pp • H/C (ISBN: 9781615208135) • US $180.00 (our price)

www.igi-global.com

701 E. Chocolate Ave., Hershey, PA 17033
Order online at www.igi-global.com or call 717-533-8845 x100
To place a standing order for titles released in this series, contact: cust@igi-global.com
Mon-Fri 8:00 am - 5:00 pm (est) or fax 24 hours a day 717-533-8661

Editorial Advisory Board

Table of Contents

Section 1
Identity Formation and Political Potential of Social Media

Section 2
Celebrity, Identity,
and Social Media

Detailed Table of Contents

Section 1
Identity Formation and Political Potential of Social Media

Chapter 1

  Tüge T. Gülşen, Istanbul Bilgi University, Turkey

This chapter examines the use of social media in the protests that led up to the 2013 disturbances in Istanbul and other Turkish cities. The author surveys participants and examines the power and limitations of online approaches to distributed leadership in a revolution.

Chapter 2

  Katherine Bridgman, Florida State University, USA

This chapter focuses on the use of Twitter during the anti-Mubarak protests in Egypt during 2011. The author considers how identities emerged online not possible under the eyes of Mubarak's security services.

Chapter 3

  Nahla Nadeem, Cairo University, Egypt

This chapter looks closely at responses by anonymous posters to an Al Jazeera Website following the suicide of a Tunsian protester. The author considers the unique ways in which solidarity exists among respondents to this event that helped fuel other events in the Arab Spring.

Section 2
Celebrity, Identity,
and Social Media

Chapter 4
Cheri Lemieux Spiegel, Northern Virginia Community College, USA & Old Dominion University, USA

This chapter explores the coy use of social media by Graffitist "Banksy," who has maintained his (or her?) anonymity well despite enormous attention attracted by the artist's political statements and works.

Chapter 5
Thomas J. Mowbray, The Ohio State University, USA

This chapter considers what it means to have a brand associated with one's representation in a virtual world such as Second Life. The author interviews several well-known Second Life residents whose avatars are an established part of the virtual world's social scene or economy.

Section 3
Educators and Digital Media

Chapter 6
Elizabeth Hodges, Virginia Commonwealth University, USA

This chapter looks hard at what may work, or not work so well, for a teacher experimenting with multimodal, multimedia in the classroom when local community and support can be difficult to find.

Chapter 7
Karen Keifer-Boyd, The Pennsylvania State University, USA
Wanda B. Knight, The Pennsylvania State University, USA
Aaron Knochel, State University of New York at New Paltz, USA
Christine Liao, University of North Carolina Wilmington, USA
Mary Elizabeth Meier, Mercyhurst University, USA
Ryan Patton, Virginia Commonwealth University, USA
Ryan Shin, University of Arizona, USA
Robert W. Sweeny, Indiana University of Pennsylvania, USA

This chapter presents the performance art of a team collaborating in both Second Life and experimenting with the notion of distributed leadership.

Chapter 8
Faculty Users on Facebook: What We Can Learn from Women Academics-Mothers' Rhetorical
Methods for Visual Self-Presentation Online 121
Sarah Spangler, Old Dominion University, USA

This chapter shows how the all-pervasive social network influences issues of identity and the work-life
balance of academic participants whose every keystroke or image can influence their careers.

Section 4
Social Values and Ethics in Online Gaming

Chapter 9
Friends and Rivals: Loyalty, Ethics, and Leadership in BioWare's Dragon Age II 145
Kristin M. S. Bezio, University of Richmond, USA

This chapter demonstrates the complexity of ethical choices made possible even in a single-player game,
whenever participants, in the role of a leader, must decide the fate of computer-generated non-player
characters.

Chapter 10
Supporting Visibility and Resilience in Play: Gender-Supportive Online Gaming Communities as a
Model of Identity and Confidence Building in Play and Learning 170
Gabriela T. Richard, University of Pennsylvania, USA

This chapter explores the types of collaboration needed for gender-inclusive gaming online as these
communities attract ever more female players.

Section 5
Building and Sustaining Communities Online

Chapter 11
Internet Past Tense: Trolls, Sock-Puppets, and Good Joes in the Sandbox Newsgroup 188
Joe Essid, University of Richmond, USA

This chapter looks at the rhetorical and management strategies that emerged in an unmoderated online
community of toy collectors, then what happens when that group moves to social networking and moderated forums.

Chapter 12
Firepups at the Lake: Ties that Bind Until They Don't 206
Dona J. Hickey, University of Richmond, USA

This chapter looks at the rhetorical strategies for building social community in a small left-leaning,
moderated, political blog, then what happens to that community when political disagreement cannot
be overcome and after the blog becomes a large umbrella site for multi-authored blogs. At issue is the
nature of community itself and what it means to participants on and off line.

Section 6
Digital Spaces that Influence Socio-Political Discourse

This chapter considers the strategies used online by 2 opposition movements that employed different methods of leadership. The author considers why the Zapatistas succeeded and Occupy failed in the face of governmental backlash to their demands.

Chapter 14 illustrates the power of community building in a setting where traditional media and forms of dissent have been restricted or where physical spaces do not permit the forms of community now possible online.

Preface

The idea of community in computer-mediated communication is self-evident to those who engage it, even among those who acknowledge differences between pixilated and live communities. After all, those of us who have any contact with young people witness, daily, students' "plodding text-walks, heads down, absorbed by their own flying thumbs fluttering above tiny screens" (Lebduska, 2013, p. 41). Life is both lived in the flesh and, as Turkle (1997) already saw at the end of the last century, on the screen. With our contact lists, status updates, and group-gaming sessions, our immersion in the digitized world has only deepened since then. We may, in fact, be as addicted as teenagers who feel that life-events are not valid unless shared with and liked by their Facebook friends (Turkle, 2011). We do not know the long-term societal, psychological, and physical effects of ubiquitous Internet use. Perhaps by the time this anthology of essays is a decade old all of these chapters will seem quaint.

We suspect, however, that will not be the case, since what informs the ideas in this anthology of international authors is less the technologies of networked communities and more the bonds that link them. We also focus on the ways in which some participants craft their identities and leverage them to gain influence. Those are old aspects of human behavior that span many generations of technology, from Socrates' use of rhetoric in Athens Agora, from the transmission of knowledge in written and later printed texts, from the widely republished Gettysburg Address, to JFK's ability to shine on television when Richard Nixon failed, and on to our present stew of social technologies where a new and compelling application seems to bubble to the surface every month.

NEW TECHNOLOGIES AND NEW COMMUNITIES

Today, when one thinks of influence and leadership online, the images evoked may come more from Hollywood than from the Oval Office; for example, the skilled mage in the World of Warcraft who recruits a team to raid and kill a powerful enemy. This leader of the virtual group shares in the glory as everyone "levels up" as better players then trades virtual goods that often can be re-sold for actual-world currency. Team-gaming is, however, only one form of influence a skilled community member can employ. In the streets of Cairo, Tunis, or Istanbul, as Bridgeman in chapter 2, Nadeem in chapter 3, and Gulsen in chapter 1 each shows, for these "assemblages of dissent," the stakes are real, not pixelated violence; the online community becomes the place to organize events in the world of bricks, mortar, teargas, and torture.

Communities that organize online can, however, quickly fracture and fail under pressure. Even widely promoted dissent can end quickly, when such a community does not generate effective real-world leadership and planning. Ramos's chapter 13 considers a stark outcome: the failure of Occupy Wall Street and its offshoots to thrive after evictions from parks and public spaces. While Occupy used the Internet well, it literally had nowhere to go in the flesh, after the police shut down Occupy's encampments. Ramos considers how starkly that model of community differs from the successes of the Zapatistas against the Mexican government. Thus, a coherent set of demands, coupled with both physical and networked communities, means the difference between success and irrelevance.

SMART BOMBS AND SMART PHONES

A failure of civil disobedience in the US should give readers pause, even as the successful use of Twitter, Facebook, and Instagram in Qatar, as Rajakumar demonstrates in chapter 14, should give us hope that open political discourse can flourish online and real-world change follow. These events are still very much unfolding around the Middle East in a time when Hamas and the Israeli Defense Forces "troll" their enemies' Twitter feeds. Perhaps an Arab Winter will follow its Spring; perhaps Turkey will turn more Islamist or more secular as a result of the "Resistanbul" uprising for which Gulsen's chapter provides a introduction. Whatever the final outcome in that part of the world, to an older generation of computer users, we seem to have entered the surrealist narrative of a Vonnegut novel. Where one might find a banality of modern war in drone-strikes directed by young people sitting in trailers in the middle of Nevada, there are even stranger juxtapositions online. When mortal enemies taunt each other online or plan attacks, they might then, without leaving their chairs, use the same technologies to download music, share baby photos, and shop for socks.

This anthology thus charts, in a generation, a seismic shift in technology. With the convergence of military, consumer, and commercial technologies, we are clearly no longer in the era of Cold War missile silos, bomber bases, and Berlin checkpoints between Soviet and Allied arsenals. If the National Security Agency wishes to find the latest terrorist plot, it need not send an operative to Yemen. It might start with or without a warrant, sifting through Facebook posts or shopping habits at Amazon.com by Yemenis or US citizens. What such surveillance means to a foundation of American democracy remains to be seen, as does the reaction of US citizens. Like many of the technologies discussed in the chapters here, the public reaction to data mining is still evolving as this anthology goes to print.

THE NEW INTERNET: ART AND COMMERCE COLLIDE

Beyond what often may appear an absurdist version of geopolitics, though in close conversation with it, lies the world of political art. This collection of essays includes, in Spiegel's chapter 4, explorations of the graffiti by street artist and muralist "Banksy," whose work questions the underlying assumptions of free-market capitalism regarding workers and the environment. In Keifer-Boyd and her co-authors' chapter 7, performance art in the virtual world of Second Life raises real-world issues about race, gender, sexual orientation, and economic status. Such online spaces were scarcely imaginable when many academics working today began their careers, yet the arts are being transformed by creative individuals such as these. At the same time, as the writers herein discuss at length, the arts struggle to manifest themselves online in the more commercial format of what Essid in chapter 11 calls the "New Internet," where targeted advertising and IP-tracking by service-providers have monetized the experience of going online.

The latest generation of Internet users may not be able to imagine a not-too-distant past when an older form of Internet access enabled anonymity and freedom from marketers, often at the price of flame-wars and "trolling" by malicious geeks. Facebook's digital tsunami swept many older communities before it, though many who remembered BBS systems and USENET resisted or subverted the social-media giant's insistence that only real identities be linked to profiles. Other users, less concerned with anonymity and more with the vitality of their established networks of online friends, made difficult transitions to new online spaces. The communities Essid and Hickey explore, The Sandbox of chapter 11 that has made the transition to social media and moderated blogs, and Firedoglake of chapter 12 that has evolved from a small moderated blog to a large, multi-authored one, have lost some of the old sense of playfulness along the way. As Hickey examines changes in community, playful diversion from arguments among like-minded people can help to mend fissures, but when disagreement strikes at the heart of the community's origins, some of the old community ties may break irrevocably.

TRANSHUMANIST PLAY

As the Internet evolves, so has our sense of play, both serious and casual, by the games we play, games that become ever more responsive to player input. Readers will find that Bezio in chapter 13 analyzes in depth how a player's sense of ethics informs decisions made when interacting with the in-game, non-player characters of *Dragon Age II*. Given the possible directions that artificial intelligence and human enhancement could take in coming decades, Bezio's work may guide future discussions of ethics for transhuman people and humanistic machines. Bridgeman's chapter 2 and Richard's chapter 10 extend this discussion, showing us the need to make such transhuman communities gender-inclusive. Gender and other markers of our flesh may persist, whatever Raymond Kurzweil might predict about a future of disembodied and immortal former humans, their uploaded intellects like ghosts in the global data-net. Even if an avatar wears a different gender from its creator, or none at all, we already live in a time when one's avatar can be profitably branded, as Mowbray discusses in chapter 5. Ours is simultaneously an era when women in academia cannot escape cultural and professional expectations placed upon them by their peers; female academics must cultivate a certain type of Facebook profile to avoid censure from some colleagues, as Spangler shows in chapter 8.

Where Spangler's work suggests more studies about a thriving online community, Mowbray's chapter also prompts future research about communities in decline. The two chapters in this collection that focus on Second Life do not consider the very real decline in size and influence of that virtual world between 2008 and 2013. Second Life generated a great deal of hyperbole as the next generation of Web use not so long ago, yet it has declined in size, profitability, and academic use from a combination of high prices, poor customer service, sudden changes in terms of service, lagging technology, and user fatigue. All of these have resulted in a once-revolutionary and widely discussed virtual world never quite living up to its disruptive potential (Essid, 2011). Certainly, follow-up studies to Mowbray's and Keifer-Boyd's will have to consider what users do with their friends lists, intellectual property, performance art, and avatarian brands when the platform of choice loses prominence or vanishes. Several notable and briefly popular virtual worlds, such as Sims Online, Glitch, and Metaplace have all gone into the recycling bin of cyber-history. Where did their communities go? To diaspora worlds online? Into oblivion?

The editors find Hodges' chapter 6 particularly instructive here. In the story of one faculty member's struggle to reach the horizon of ubiquitous computing that transforms teaching, the editors see a perfectly cautionary tale for a utopian dream lost. The very real hurdles educators face all stymie good pedagogy: lack of support for cutting-edge applications, snobbery about operating systems, departmental and other administrative fiefdoms, inflexible attitudes about budgeting. Though Hodges' focus is on her personal and intellectual adjustments for teaching with technology, the impact is bigger. Outside of campus borders, a transformation unfolds in how we connect to each other. If wearable computing and other technologies right out of science fiction become common, how will those of us, weaned on what Cynthia Selfe (qtd. in chapter 6) calls "alphabetic texts" make the leap?

THE NEXT BIG THINGS?

You hold a text still firmly rooted in that tradition, one honored since the age of Gutenberg. The impulses that drive us to make and maintain contact with others, as well as the need to be popular and influential, are older still. As editors, we feel that the authors herein continue a lively discussion as all of us move forward into an era of ubiquitous computing and networked communities in the Academy and, most certainly, outside it. As was the case for the first generation of texts about personal computing technology and education in the late 1980s and early 90s, the editors find it instructive to end with several large questions that unite the diverse range of issues raised by our authors. These questions include but are not limited to:

- How will global geopolitics shift when billions come online via relatively cheap smart phones and tablets?
- Can governments control or suppress online communities that go global?
- What sorts of new communities may emerge if users decide that the big social networking sites are too big?
- What happens to communities that decline or vanish? Where do old friends and friendships go?
- If the current form of Internet use follows Tim Wu's (2010) cycle of consolidation common among earlier telecommunications, what will happen to voices of dissent? To the online commons?
- Will the gaming communities online make ever-greater space for women, people of color, and older gamers?
- How is the very nature of community changing, resisting any one definition whether that be person-to-person, or avatar-to avatar?
- How do the various online communities affect the way we see and engage each other in person, in groups?
- What will be the fate of anonymous and pseudonymous users in the next generation of online communities? With increased surveillance by governments and pressure by corporations to track user preferences, will such concealment even be possible?

We invite readers to take a look outside their office windows, in the breaks between classes, to see that reality unfold, one smart phone or tablet at a time.

Dona J. Hickey
University of Richmond, USA

Joe Essid
University of Richmond, USA

REFERENCES

Essid, J. (2011). *A failure to disrupt: Why second life failed*. [Web log post]. Retrieved from http://www.vwer.org/2011/01/14/a-failure-to-disrupt-why-second-life-failed/

Lebduska, L. (2013). Profession of letters. *College Composition and Communication, 65*(1), 40–42.

Turkle, S. (1997). *Life on the screen*. New York, NY: Simon and Schuster.

Turkle, S. (2011). *Alone together: Why we expect more from technology and less from each other*. New York, NY: Basic Books.

Wu, T. (2010). *The master switch: The rise and fall of information empires*. New York, NY: Alfred A. Knopf.

Acknowledgment

The editors wish to thank Austin DeMarco of IGI Global for guidance with innumerable questions as this anthology came to press. Our efforts would have all been for naught, however, without the members of our editorial advisory board, who made many creative and helpful suggestions to each of our authors. Finally, we wish to thank the students we have taught over the past 20 years, as technology firmly and permanently entered our classrooms. Their questions about the Internet and intellectual struggles adapting it to daily use have inspired us, even as we both wonder where adaptation will end, if ever.

Dona J. Hickey
University of Richmond, USA

Joe Essid
University of Richmond, USA

Section 1
Identity Formation and Political Potential of Social Media

Chapter 1
Turkish Youth's (Re) Construction of their Political Identity in Social Media, before "Resistanbul"

Tüge T. Gülşen
Istanbul Bilgi University, Turkey

ABSTRACT

This chapter explores the political potential of social media widely used as a means of communication by Turkish young people and examines how they perceive social media as alternative social environments, where they can manifest their political identities. In addition, the study conducted aims at understanding whether the political situation in Turkey before the "Resistanbul" events, beginning toward the end of May 2013, created fear among young people that could cause them to hesitate to express their political thoughts or feel the need to veil their political identities. The results of the survey reveals that Turkish young people, despite having a high sense of freedom, tend to be politically disengaged in social media, and they seem to be hesitant to reveal their political identities in this alternative democratic social space, but they do not mind "others" manifesting their political identities.

DOI: 10.4018/978-1-4666-5150-0.ch001

INTRODUCTION

The motivation behind this study conducted derived from the growing authoritarianism that the state practices in society, and the current policies that restrict the freedom of expression and freedom of assembly of young adults who want to pronounce their criticisms concerning the state and the ruling party Justice and Development Party (AKP). On December 18, 2012, prior to the Prime Minister's arrival on the Middle East Technical University (METU) campus, where he went to watch the launch of a Turkish earth observation satellite into the orbit aboard a Chinese rocket, students had gathered to protest the new government policies that affect higher education in Turkey. The peaceful protesters who were chanting slogans against the government were met by 3,000 police officers and approximately 100 armored vehicles. Police forces fired tear gas and water cannon to disperse the protest at the university. The rector declared that the university supported their students' freedom of expression and freedom of assembly and put the responsibility of the excessive police force targeting the students and the faculty on the police forces' and the Internal Affairs Minister's shoulders. On December 20, the academics at METU boycotted classes to protest police violence on METU campus. On December 21, 12 students were arrested, and then they were released. Following the Prime Minister's statements saying "What a shame! Shame on the professors who raised those students! Instructors first have to teach their students how to be respectful" targeting METU students and academics and the initiation of investigations by both the police and the Higher Education Council, the rectors of several universities including Galatasaray University, Istanbul Technical University, Yıldız Technical University, Mimar Sinan University, Marmara University, and Hacettepe University condemned the "student violence" at METU. As a response, students and faculty members in many of these universities protested their rectors, issued public statements and press releases in support of students and academics at METU, condemned their own rectors' statements as unrepresentative of their university. Academics from some other universities like Ankara University, Bosporus University, and Istanbul Bilgi University issued declarations to express their concerns regarding the violations of the right of freedom of speech in Turkey mainly through social media. University students protested the violation of their rights of freedom of expression in universities in different cities like Adana, Mersin, Eskisehir, Izmir, Trabzon, and Kocaeli. The labor unions like KESK, Sosyal-Is, some branches of Turkish Bar Association, the Association of Academics condemned both these some rectors' and the government's approach to the events at METU. Also, the METU Academic Personnel Association, the METU Alumni Association Council, the Education and Science Employees Union and METU students, issued a joint declaration.

The Deputy Prime Minister's statements made on December 27, 2012 on a TV program unveiled the government's approach to universities and students in Turkey: "Such events are likely to accelerate. There is potential danger in universities," (Arinc, "There is danger in universities," 2012) which foreshadowed the recent "Resistanbul" events. The events accelerated, and on May 31, 2013 when a peaceful protest that started to stop the demolition of Gezi Park in Taksim Square, the only remaining green area in the heart of Istanbul, was met by excessive police force, it triggered the ongoing nationwide protests. Hundreds of protesters including mainly university students, academics, white-collars chanted, "Everywhere is Taksim, everywhere is resistance," "Together against fascism," "Tayyip resign." And yes, the Deputy Prime Minister was right; there was a potential danger for *them* because things would not be as easy as they were before. There are now thousands of people marching against the government in the streets.

During the events in METU, social media played a fundamental role in the communication of news because the mainstream visual and print media were censored. The event was significant in the sense that the public could largely witness how the government could manipulate media corporations and make people see and believe what the authorities want them to. News about the protests in different universities nationwide to support METU students and academics, letters from protesters, petitions, political jokes and cartoons in defense of students' rights of freedom of expression and freedom of assembly were posted and shared on social media Websites after the events while the government's growing political pressure on mainly the opposing groups was protested. Today, it is unfortunately seen that the government's being increasingly authoritarian still leads to public unease in Turkey; the excessive police force targeting unarmed young people who simply use their rights of freedom of expression clearly shows us that the authorities still perceive them as "potential danger." They still manipulate media corporations to make their voters believe that the protesters in the streets are "vandals" or "terrorists," and they even make them fire the opposing journalists. However, young people continue to use social media to communicate realities and use it even as a tool to push the authorities to take actions by sharing an enormous amount of information about the events.

The events that started in METU and accelerated since then renewed debates concerning the number of students in jail in Turkey. The Justice Minister declared in response to a Parliamentary question posed by a deputy of the main opposition People's Republican Party (CHP) that 2,824 students were still imprisoned as of January 31, 2012. The Minister also provided further details with respect to the situation of arrested students in Turkey in his response: there were 1,046 convicted and 1,778 arrested students in prisons across Turkey, 609 students arrested were facing charges of "membership in an armed terrorist organization," and courts had convicted 178 students on the charge of "membership in a terrorist organization." The figures must be even more alarming today because hundreds of people, including almost 60 lawyers who protested the government in Istanbul Caglayan Courtyard, have been detained during the recent protests. Who are those university students that are claimed to be "members of terrorist organizations?" What did they do? Here are just two examples:

In February 2010, Cihan Kirmizigul, a student in Galatasaray University, was detained on charges of membership of the terrorist Kurdistan Workers' Party (PKK), possession of explosives and damaging property while he was walking in the street in Istanbul. The prosecution was based on his wearing a *poshu*[1], and some other protesters nearby also wearing *poshu,* allegedly PKK sympathizers, threw Molotov at a shop. He was held in pre-trial detention in Tekirdag F-Type Prison, where people convicted of being members of armed organizations, drug offences or organized crimes, and those sentenced to aggravated life imprisonment are kept, for 25 months. On the day when he was released, his father Vahap Kırmızıgul said, "I just want them to leave my boy alone!" Another student detained on charges of membership of a terrorist organization is Duygu Kerimoglu, a 22-year-old university student. Her house was raided in May 2012 as part of an operation against a socialist hacker group RedHack[2] because she followed the group in social network, shared their updates, and commented on news about this hacker group on Facebook. She was held in pre-trial detention for 9 months and then released. The Kerimoglu case shows that mainly following, liking, sharing, posting, tweeting, and commenting in social media could also cause young people to face charges of "membership in a terrorist organization" in Turkey.

Social media could function as a non-violent but powerful tool for Turkish young people to show resistance and opposition against the status quo while it is at the same time the reason for the oppression. The vicious circle in Turkey is that when the government becomes increasingly authoritarian with changes in legislation or current public policies, young people show resistance using social media. When they do show resistance through social media, authorities track the ones actively opposing online, open investigations into their online acts, and prosecute. Young people are tried for being members of terrorist organizations, or the authorities simply issue declarations to threaten people that they will block access to social network sites. Then, resistance restarts and accelerates because this is exactly what young people are opposing.

Public demand is something very simple in fact; Turkish people do not want the state to interfere with their individual lives. They do not want the Prime Minister to comment on how many children they will have, at what time they can buy alcoholic drinks, what they can and cannot wear. They do not want the parliament to legislate about their everyday practices. When the authorities do not recognize their demands, groups organize events and demonstrations via social media, people following those events gather in squares and streets, protest the government and recent policies. Then, the police use excessive force against people regardless of age, sex, social class, and occupation. During the recent Gezi Park protests, for instance, even some deputies of opposing parties were exposed to police violence. While the author is writing these lines, thousands of protesters still protest the demolition of Gezi Park in Taksim Square for a shopping mall to be built. As the events accelerated, as a result of social media participation, more and more protesters including artists, musicians, deputies, academics gathered in the park. The peaceful protesters who were singing songs and reading books in the park to say no to the demolition were attacked by the police forces at 5 a.m. while sleeping in tents in the park on May 30 and 31, 2013. The police fired tear gas and water cannon to disperse the activists, burnt their tents, beat them violently.[3]

On the following days, the tension and the consequent resistance simultaneously grew, and the police used the Mass Incident Intervention Vehicle (TOMA) to disperse the unarmed peaceful demonstrators, fired tear gas and plastic bullets. Many young people were injured and 5 people were killed as a result of police intervention. The 14-year-old boy Berkin Elvan who was shot in the head with a teargas canister while going to the bakery shop has been in coma since June 15. There have been numerous reports claiming that the police have used even Agent Orange, which is considered to be a chemical weapon and its use is banned by the United Nations, to disperse the protesters. There are photos of used capsules and scenes showing orange colored smoke in different parts of Istanbul, and many protesters report the significant difference between their experience with tear gas and that orange smoke. Even if that gas had not been Agent Orange, people know that it is a different kind of chemical that targeted people in the streets. Moreover, the water used in water cannons included chemicals. There have been a great number of people who had serious burns on their skins and were treated in hospitals or by volunteer doctors, who are now facing lawsuits for helping protesters. The Mayor of Istanbul denied that the police used "chemicals" but interestingly admitted that there was "medicine" in the water fired by water cannons. Volunteer doctors warned people of the dangers of exposure to the chemicals used and informed them about the ways to protect themselves on Facebook and Twitter.

Slogans like "stay vigilant, stay united, stay informed, protect your fellow countrymen, do not trust the media" are being shared on social media, and the tension in Turkey is rising continuously. Social media today are the only means of communication for protesters except for two opposing TV channels, because the government has censored other television reporting. People actively use Twitter and Facebook as a means of resistance and political engagement. Facebook and Twitter are being used to share lifesaving information, protests, petitions, and so forth while all TV channels, except for only two opposing ones, show entertainment programs or documentaries as if nothing was happening in the streets. Social media have become such a powerful tool among protesters that the state started blocking Facebook, ordered mobile phone companies to block 3G connections in order to stop people communicating with each other via social media. The Prime Minister even announced that social network sites are "menace to society" while he also actively used his Twitter account. However, after the warnings circulated through social media, people started changing their DSN applications on their computers to access to Facebook and Twitter, and many succeeded. Turkish users spread news about the "Resistanbul" events globally and gained support from other countries. Turkish people living abroad in collaboration with locals have organized demonstrations all over the world to support the protesters. They chanted slogans like "Resist Turkey, London is with you!" Everything started with the trees of Gezi Park, but nothing will be same as before. Millions of people all over the world are now familiar with the slogan "one tree falls, one nation rises" through social media participation.

This paper is an attempt to understand how young people perceive social media in such a tense social and political context in Turkey. The research questions central to this study are,

a.   Do young people in Turkey worry about the consequences of expressing their political thoughts in social network sites?
b.   Do young people in Turkey use social media to manifest their political identity?

There are two dimensions in the analysis that are the sense of security and insecurity, which are the pillars of freedom of speech. These dimensions will help us see whether young people have a sense of security or not and consequently if they worry about the consequences of being

politically engaged in social media and manifest their political identities in these new alternative spaces for communication.

BACKGROUND

The Use of Social Media

With the rise of the computer-mediated communication in the 21st century, communication patterns have changed, and people have shifted from face-to-face, landline telephone and postal communication to digital communication that enables users to stay online all the time. The mobile phone technologies that also offer Internet connection have changed the communication patterns of primarily the Millennial generation, the members of whom are between 18 and 33 (Pinchot et al., 2011, pp. 1-9). The mobility of the new age elevated by mobile communication systems have also given rise to the use of social network sites which have gained popularity merely among the members of the new postmodern techno-literate generation. Social network sites, as Boyd and Ellison (2007) also define, are the Web pages that provide users with the opportunity to create their public or semi-public profiles and add friends to their lists so that both parties could build connections with each other, see and explore their social network (p. 211). Users of social network sites can upload their photos, publicize their personal information like their interests, birthdays, hometowns, the languages they speak, their educational and professional background, and so on.

A recent survey covering 21 nations was carried out from March 17 to April 20, 2012 by the Pew Research Center as part of the Global Attitudes Project. The survey revealed that the number of the Internet users using social network sites has increased. In the US, 63% of the Internet users were using social networks as the results in Spring 2012 demonstrated while the rates were 60% in Spring 2011 and 57% in Spring 2010. In Turkey, on the other hand, as of Spring 2012, 81% of the Internet users were using social networks while the rates were 76% in Spring 2011 and 68% in Spring 2010. The results also showed that people between 18 and 29 were using these sites considerably more than the other age groups. Among 21 countries, the results in 17 countries revealed a gap of 50 points or more in social network use between those younger than 30 and 50 or older. In Turkey, 69% of the social network users are those between 18 and 29. 67% of the smart phone users, 49% of whom are between the ages of 18 and 29 in Turkey, have access to social network sites.

The rise of social networking that enables users to publicize themselves in a vast community has brought debates regarding the privacy and security issues. Privacy in social media refers to the right of users to control the information that they share with other users and regulate their online relationships, and security measures will ensure users' privacy and sense of safety. They can choose to share everything they post with the "friends" on their lists, or they can restrict some users' access to their profiles. Besides the security measures available, users build their own tactics and strategies to ensure their security. Because of religious concerns and anxiety, the female Qatari Facebook users' being cautious about uploading their actual photos as their profile pictures is a good example to such strategies that could enable individuals to neither fight with the current social order nor refuse the existence of the new means of communication (Rajakumar, 2012, pp. 125-134). Moreover, social network today appear to be the alternative means of media that is used quite differently from the traditional media. As Bennett (2003) puts it, "new media provide alternative communication spaces in which information can develop and circulate widely with fewer conventions or editorial filters than in the mainstream media" (p. 161). Social media then are more liberated form of media that cannot be easily manipulated and censored by the power groups in contrast to visual and print media. The governments could

certainly cut access to social network sites locally, which means they cannot censor a site abroad but they can block the access of the users within their borders. During "Resistanbul" events, the Turkish government has threatened people that they would restrict their access to Facebook and Twitter as the Prime Minister stated Twitter was a "menace to society." Following these statements, a lot of people have changed their DSN applications on their computers so that they could reach their social network accounts from other countries' Internet links. Fortunately, the Turkish government could not go that far, but there are numerous reports and also tweets from people in authority that they are tracking people who support protesters. Thus, unless local interventions are made to block access to social network sites, such sites offer more democratic social and political platforms where people can share information and news, initiate and participate in discussions, forums, and offline events.

In countries like Turkey, where the state could enforce serious restrictions and censorship in conventional means of media, social media appear to be the one that contribute to the circulation of news that people could not follow from any other means of media. The media censorship enforced by the Turkish state with the claim that "the psychology of the public could be negatively influenced" after the terrorist attack in a small town Reyhanli near the Syrian border on May 16, 2013 is a good example to see how social media could function free of censorship in Turkey. While none of the TV channels were allowed to show scenes from the town including public protests against the government, the Internet users could watch videos recorded by some media agencies and citizens and follow news that never appeared in traditional media. Social media also functioned as alternative social spaces where certain political activist groups could initiate and organize offline protests against the government's policies regarding the Syrian conflict.

Research on Social Media

Millions of people all around the world use social network for different purposes, and they share their views on different topics. The survey conducted by Pew Research Center revealed that social network users share views on music and movies (67%), community issues (46%), sports (43%), politics (34%) and religion (14%). The results specifically concerning Turkey show that people share music and movies (78%), community issues (63%), sports (61%), politics (57%) and religion (53%) on social network sites. The survey covered mainly the use of the sites Facebook, Twitter and MySpace. In Turkey, these sites are quite popular like in other countries. However, it is worthy to note that there are some national social network sites like *Eksi Sozluk, ITU Sozluk, Inci Sozluk* (*sozluk* means "dictionary" in Turkish, and there is a group of social network sites named as *sozluk* in Turkey) where numerous users (they call themselves *writers)* share their views with others and follow the current events in the country from these *writers'* entries.

Social network sites, as the new form of communication, have been the interest of social-science researchers who investigated the phenomenon from different aspects. Research indicates that while all other media are mainly used for emotional and social needs, social media are used for all four categories which are emotional, cognitive, social, and habitual needs but are distinguishingly driven by emotional and cognitive needs rather than social and habitual needs (Wang et al., 2012, pp. 1829-1839). Referring to previous research that focused on the role of the Big Five (openness to experience, conscientiousness, extraversion, agreeableness, neuroticism), self-esteem, and narcissism in the use of social network, Utz et. al. (2012) identify "need for popularity" as a better predictor of social network use since its main objective is social acceptance online and predicts social behavior on social network (p.41), but the number of *friends* in users' lists indicates popularity on the surface but does not really initiate friendships in the real sense, and research also shows that the popularity gained on a social network site "is not necessarily the same as being attractive as a real friend" (Utz, 2010, p. 328). Also, Facebook, one of the most popular social network sites also in Turkey, is used as a tool for self-affirmation that heals individuals' egos wounded by everyday offline incidents and helps them "preserve self-worth and self-integrity" (Toma & Hancock, 2013, p. 329).

The popularity of social network sites also makes educators to rethink alternative ways to teach using these sites to initiate learning (Kelm, 2011; Silius et al., 2011; Denton & Wicks, 2013) while they are cautious about the negative effects of social media on young people like cyber-bullying that leads to serious consequences in young people's lives (Bhat et al., 2010; Steffgen et al., 2011; Oravec, 2012) because "socially-mediated publicness may be a source of support and empowerment while simultaneously posing conflict and risk" (Baym & Boyd, 2012, p.325). Studies have also investigated why young people use social media and how online communication affects their offline relationships and their identities. Social network sites that offer fast and easy communication to college students are increasingly used by the youth, and they "create new ways of communication with friends and family and also influence individual's self-concept" (Sponcil & Gitimu, n.d, p. 11), which contributes to young people's identity construction as all other social communication patterns do.

Moreover, social network sites are explored as a new powerful tool to circulate information and initiate activism. Although Theocharis (2013) does not deny the impact of social network on protest action organization in the sense that such sites provide activists with the opportunity to have better organization and coordination online, he states that they do not fully attain mobilization. The coordinative potential of social media and the political power, which will have long-term effects in political change in both democratic and repressive countries as Shirky (2011) asserts, are utilized by major organizations like Amnesty International and Greenpeace to organize protests, boycotts, and issue petitions. Other than such well-known organizations, some other social initiatives can organize protests like the one held first in September 2012 in Turkey. Thousands of people who were solely informed that there would be protests against the government's new legislation that could allow the state to kill street animals gathered in specified locations on the same day at the same time in eleven different cities in Turkey, and said "No!" to the legislation, and they made the government step back. Moreover, the "Resistanbul" events demonstrated that when both print and visual mainstream media are censored by the government, social media becomes the only channel through which people get informed, keep others updated, call for help, initiate offline protests and strengthen the resistance. Contemporary forms of protests are organized, announced, commented on via social media, and the scenes and news from the actual offline protests are also circulated, and the evaluation of the effectiveness of them on the groups targeted is also made via social media. The ones who are informed about protests but do not make presences in the streets can also follow what is happening with the help of social media.

Cyber-Identities

Erikson (1997) explains the stages in psychosocial development as fidelity (identity vs. identity confusion) in adolescence and care (generativity vs. self absorption) in adulthood (p.55). The participants of the study in this paper are primarily the ones at the stage of late adolescence that is prolonged by college education and delays the construction of identity (Erikson, 1995a, pp. 633-634). According to Erikson (1995a), identity construction starts early in childhood when "an individual develops images of himself, evokes images in others, and experiences continuities,

and dis-continuities in these images" (p. 635). Identity construction is directly linked to others' confirmation and appreciation of one's self image in the social environment, but it also involves "a continuous conflict with powerful negative identity elements: what we know or fear or are told we are but try not to be or not to see; and what we consequently see in exaggeration in others" (Erikson, 1995b, pp. 489-490). Before the emergence of social media, all elements that are involved in identity construction were from the offline social environment. However, today young people in late adolescence, who have already delayed their construction of identity, have both online and offline connections with others starting from early ages, which contributes to their identity construction. Thus, their identity formation includes not only their actual offline social environment including their families, peers, teachers, neighbors etc. but also their online friends in "friends lists" or lists of their "followers." Their struggle is still to become individuals in a collective social environment where they need the sense of belonging to cyber-groups. They can belong to multiple social groups where they can create their cyber-identities, and they can create more than one online identity if they want. Social networks give the users the opportunity to create their own avatars and be the ones that they wish to be.

The individual identity defines one's uniqueness among all others while the affiliative identity defines one's connectedness with others. While social network users' profile pictures, the information regarding their interests, the location where they live, their education and work display their uniqueness, they are important to show one's connectedness to thousands of other users at the same time. Social media users' individual comments, postings, shares, and so forth all serve their need to belong to masses online. Whatever they share with other users on their profile pages shows how much devoted they are to the alumni, fan clubs, consumers of certain brands, for example. When one has a quick look at an active user's profile and check his/her recent activities on a social network site, they can figure out whether he/she is a vegetarian, environmentalist, rock music listener, romantic movie lover, republican, liberal, conservative, and so forth. One could also see which political party one user supports and another user's approach to certain social and political issues. In brief, you are what you post by all means, and users attribute importance to their individual identities through allowing other users to consume what they share on their profiles. Their need for approval is fed by the number of "likes," "shares," "comments," "retweets."

Things are not always what they seem on social network sites. On such sites, there are numerous fake accounts that users create for different purposes. Also, users can choose pseudonyms as their usernames, and one can create an identity, or identities, to participate in the online activities of certain groups. There could be various reasons behind such users' hiding their actual names and identities and creating different avatars on social network sites. As the main focus of this paper is the political participation of young social network users in Turkey, it is essential to note that some of them hide their actual names and use pseudonyms to hide themselves when they want to make political comments online, and the authorities also use social network to counterattack, provoke young people, and retaliate for their anti-government protests. During the "Resistanbul" events, first of all, there appeared some distinct users whose posts have been shared and commented on continuously. People do not know who they actually are, but they recognize these certain names, and in everyday offline discussions one can hear young people asking each other if they had seen the last tweet or post of user X or an online political group. Also, many users have reported online that some users intend to provoke protests. For example, such users reported some fake incidents that a pro-government group had firearms to shoot protesters in streets, which could inevitably lead to chaos. As protesters mainly communicate

through social network during protests, posts and tweets of that kind could harm the peaceful protests demanding simply more democracy and a less authoritarian government, and there have been online rumors that these users provoking protests were actually from the government or the police forces. Moreover, people in authority used mainly Twitter to "warn" anti-government users, and some of them have already threatened these users that the police were tracking them and they would "pay for what they state online." In addition, it revealed that thousands of "followers" of people in authority including the Prime Minister were in fact fake accounts, so the government intended to create a false impression that they have gained the support of masses and the protesters belong to a small minority. In brief, cyber-identities could liberate young people who want to express themselves more freely hiding their actual identities to protect themselves; however, they can also be used as weapons to counterattack them. Thus, the "Resistanbul" events have taught young people to approach what they see online more critically than before.

Social Media as New Platforms for Political Practice

There are also a considerable number of studies that assess the political potential of social network sites and the nature of political activities in social media stating that the social network sites have become alternative mechanisms that are also used by governments, organizations, societies and NGOs. The discussions that revolve around the online political engagement of Internet users derive from in ways in which social network sites enable individuals to reach masses. Collin (2008) focuses on the spontaneity of political engagement of young people in "everyday politics" and identifies the Internet as "a new platform for the realization of project oriented political identities" where young people can identify the current political issues, get informed about these issues and integrate their online participation into their offline lives (p. 539). There is a promising potential of social network as new venues to increase young people's political involvement (Utz, 2009), and political engagement of the youth has become more instant and mobile with the rise of social media.

Social media have certainly changed the nature of political activities, discourse and forms of individuals' political engagement. After the launch of Facebook, a new term was brought into the literature, which is "mass interpersonal persuasion" (Fogg, 2008), combining the power of persuasion with the capacity to reach masses. The power of persuasion that used to be centralized will be decentralized, and not only the power groups and organizations but also individuals will also have the power of persuasion because they are capable of reaching masses now (Fogg, 2008). Thus, social media could enable "democratization of persuasion" (Fogg, 2008, p. 12). Nevertheless, Fenton and Barassi (2011) see the practices on social network liberating but not necessarily democratizing, and points to the "practices of domination that are ever deeper embedded in the means of communication" which is not generally identified by the users (p. 194). Similarly, Boyd (2008) maintains that "social network sites create cavernous echo chambers" where users who are already politically engaged connect to others alike, and "given the typical friend overlap in most networks, many within those networks hear the same thing over and over until they believe it to be true" (p. 243). According to Boyd (2008), social network sites do not play a critical role in politically engaging users; however, "they can make visible whether or not political operatives are succeeding in getting their message across" (p. 244). Still, these "echo chambers" play a considerable role in users' political engagement in the way that users can find an alternative terrain where they can spontaneously share their political ideas, which is not actually possible offline. Social network sites create a sense of freedom of association in users.

While some researchers assert that the role of social media in political acts is overemphasized, others believe that the power of social media must not be underestimated. Bennett (2012) describes the manifestation of political identities in social media as "large-scale individualized collective action" (p. 37). On social network sites, although users seem to act individually, they take part in a collective action that can be shared and followed by huge digital networks. This is the reason why political groups also use social media to reach masses. Today, political parties, deputies, politically engaged organizations have their official accounts on social media sites, and they use social media to reach masses and make them politically engaged. Kushin and Yamamoto (2010) come to the conclusion that online expression of political thoughts concerning the 2008 election in the US was in relation with "situational political involvement but not political self-efficacy," and they state that "as young adults go online to express opinions, discuss issues, or share information, they become more cognitively involved in the election" (p. 624). Similarly, Valenzuela et. al. (2009) present data that show a relationship between the intensity of Facebook use and participation in civic and political activities among college students. Social media alone certainly does not shape young people's political identity or make them politically more active and engaged in political acts. However, the impact of social media on political practice cannot be denied either. Bennett et. al. (2008) state that "personal level digital communication networks may help account for the scale and speed of mobilization of recent transnational protests" (p. 285). Vargas (2007) finds out that Mexican youth "became aware, involved, and motivated to participate in May 1st protest activities through social networks," and suggests that both identity and social network are evaluated together because although the power of identity is central to individuals' political engagement, if social network did not exist, they could not be given the opportunity to learn about and participate in political activities (p.19). As in "Occupy Wall Street" protests, demonstrations, and finally in the "Resistanbul" events, social media could take an active role in organizing and activating people to protest offline, march in streets and turn their "virtual" reactions into real ones.

Social Media as a Tool for Resistance in Turkey

Hofstede et. al. (2010) define power distance as "the extent to which the less powerful members of institutions and organizations within a country expect and accept that power is distributed unequally" (p. 61). In Turkey, where the "power distance" is high, the society is dependent, hierarchical, and superiors are not often accessible. Also, communication is indirect, and the information flow is selective. Turkish society, in terms of "individualism," is a collectivistic society. This means that "I" is not important but "we" is, and people belong to groups who take care of each other in exchange for loyalty. This cultural profile of the country certainly brings expectations that using social media as an everyday practice enables individuals to be involved in groups that they can socially, culturally and ideologically identify themselves with. With the use of social media, a virtual sense of solidarity has mainly become part of the real lives of young people. No matter how (in)effective it could be, individuals can get the feeling that they can make themselves heard if they post a comment to or tweet someone in authority. The non-hierarchical structure of the · Internet allows individuals of a highly hierarchical society to have more space to communicate their identities.

Compared to the past generations, the Millennial Generation, as described in the US, demonstrates a lower level of trust in the societies, institutions, and the governments people elected (Halstead, 1999, p. 33-42), and young people do not consider themselves to be politically engaged or active as the 2006 youth survey conducted by

Harvard University, Institute of Politics demonstrated. Similarly, in Turkey a survey conducted by KONDA in 2010 revealed that as the educational level and income of individuals increase, their level of trust in constitutional state surprisingly decreases. According to a more recent survey conducted by KONDA in 2011, 32.7% of young people do not trust any institutions in Turkey, 20.9% of young people trust the army, 16.9% trust the police, 13.7% of them trust the parliament, and 10.3% of them trust the law. The current political and social situation in Turkey specified above brings numerous academic questions concerning the youth in Turkey, their political identity, the role of social media in the construction and (re)construction of their political identities, and even the multiplicity of their political identities. Certainly, when young people see that 2,824 students, over 300 serving and retired army officers, over 100 journalists, many academics, former rectors, deputies, lawyers are jailed in Turkey on charges of "membership of terrorist organizations," a new survey to be conducted would most probably display even a lower level of trust in the political institutions and also the justice system today. This situation also influences the way young people construct their political identities in Turkey, and since the most common social space where they prefer expressing themselves is the social media, it is worthy to examine whether they see social media as democratic platforms where they can freely express their political thoughts, and if they are politically engaged online.

As online technologies develop, the social space where individuals communicate their views has taken new forms and created a new means of communication. Turkish young people today, like many others worldwide, know that social media offer them powerful tools that they can use across borders in order to make themselves seen and heard. Moreover, while social media break the norms of offline hierarchy in society, make superiors accessible and emerge as alternative platforms where young people can express themselves more freely, in terms of individualism social media feed their need for belonging to groups where they feel secure and content. Social media have become the means of individual collectivist resistance for Turkish young people who sometimes remain online but sometimes find their presence in the street. On May 25, 2013, demonstrators in the city of Ankara, Turkey, staged a "kiss protest" against a warning for passengers to "act in accordance with moral rules" because the security cameras caught a young couple kissing each other in a subway station. The demonstration, which was organized through social media, brought locals together at the subway station specified online, and couples started kissing each other to protest the local authority's intervention with their public rights.

On the other hand, the protests could be passive and remain solely online in the sense that users actively and continuously share, tweet and post comments about political issues, change their profile pictures with political signs and actors to manifest their political identity, but they do not take part in actual protests or turn their online reactions into offline protests. For example, the Turkish government's attempts to delete the abbreviation "T.C." (the Republic of Turkey) from the official documents, signs on official buildings were recently protested in social media by users adding "TC" before their profile names. Thus, social network sites enable users to get activated, but this does not mean that they could make politically disengaged people engaged in political activities. Rather they may help individual find ways to manifest their political identities.

It is evident that all these events that happened in Turkey have taken new forms and meanings in virtual spaces, mainly in social media. The Internet has become both the cause and the result of these political events that directly influence young people. Young people both get informed about current events through social media and show their reactions again through social media. In this new social space, also new discussions concerning identity emerge because social media are seen as "a powerful tool to create space to represent ideologies" (Fauziah et al., 2012, p. 75). Academics accept "cyberspace as an alternate reality, an immaterial universe where time and distance cease to matter and disembodied minds are free to (re) fashion their identities at will" (Carpenter, 2012, p. 200). Although cyberspace seems to be a social space where individuals can (re)construct their identities, in countries like Turkey where people strive to build a sound democracy that ensures human rights, individuals develop new strategies to protect themselves because it seems that they have become the main actors of George Orwell's *Nineteen Eighty Four,* and they believe *the big brother is watching them.* As a result, Internet users sometimes veil their identities, create avatars or display cyber-identities that *the big brother* would not mind or hopefully could not track because "a user expressing controversial political views on a friend's wall may serve as a criminal informant when that friend is flagged as a violent extremist" (Trottier, 2012, p. 422). The social pressure that they experience manifests itself on their construction of new identities online. As the "Resistanbul" events started, so far the protesters have not been detained because of their online political activities maybe because the government is very much busy with retaliating the actual users who are artists, academics, musicians, actors, actresses, etc. There is a common belief that it is not possible to track thousands of anti-government social network users and detain them; also, constitutionally it is not a crime to express one's political ideas in Turkey unless they provoke people and instigate violent protests, so they maintain that the government is simply threatening people to create fear in public and make them step back.

When it comes to the use of social media and political acts, the relationship is quite complex (Vitak et al., 2011, pp. 107-114). There are certain questions that need to be addressed in this study. Do social media sites appear to be alternative spaces where young people could participate in political activities online? Do young people find it safe to publicize their political activities, thoughts, and inclinations in social media? To what extent do young people take part in political activities in social media, and what defines their limits? Then, how could the political order influence young people's activities in social media?

THE STUDY[4]

For this research, a survey was given to 81 Turkish university students both male (n=34) and female (n=47). The participants were mainly born in 1993 (24.7%), 1992 (23.5%), and 1991 (16%), studying in two different foundation universities in Istanbul. The participants were selected among the ones who study Communication Sciences: Cinema and TV (32.1%), Television Reporting and Programming (22.2%), Radio and Television Programming (17.3%), Media and Communication Systems (16%), New Media (11.1%), Media and Communication Technologies (1.2%). 46.9% of the participants were in their first year of study, 25.9% of them were in their second year, and 21% of them were in their third year of study. The participants were all social media users; 38.3% of them were using both Facebook and Twitter, and 40.7% of them were using Facebook, Twitter, and other social network sites such as Instagram, Foursquare, Pinterest, YouTube, etc.

The survey consisted of 32 questions. The first 5 questions aimed at collecting demographical data regarding the participants' sex, age, year of study, department, and the social media sites that they generally use. The next 4 questions were designed on Likert-scale (a. always, b. often, c. sometimes, d. rarely, e. never) to identify the participants' intention to use social network sites. 7 questions in the survey were designed to measure the participants' tendency to fear due to postings, tweets and comments with political content, and they were asked to check a. yes, b. no, and c. hesitant. 14 questions were designed on a yes/no scale. There was 1 question asking

participants to define social media in their own words, which was not included in the analysis of this study, but it was thought to bring insights for further research.

Method

The data obtained was processed following these steps[5]:

- **Step 1:** A reliability test was applied for each question in the survey, and it was seen that all questions addressed to the participants were reliable.
- **Step 2:** All questions were grouped under the following research questions;
  - Do young people in Turkey worry about the consequences of expressing their political thoughts in social network sites?
  - Do young people in Turkey use social media to manifest their political identity?
- **Step 3:** For each question grouped under these research questions, a frequency test was applied, and percentages were obtained.
- **Step 4:** Based on the valid percentages obtained, data was interpreted and conclusions were drawn.

Results

The results obtained from the survey bring new insights to academics interested in social media, youth, and political engagement. The results revealed that Turkish young people have different approaches to their political engagement and manifestation of their political identity in social media than those of other users. There seems to be a clear distinction between "me" and "others."

The results showed that while 37% of users "always" followed social media sites, 45% of them used these sites "often" and 14.8% of users used them "sometimes." As the analysis of Likert-scale allows, if we take the categories of "often" and "sometimes" together in the analysis, we can see that 59.8% of the users were "on-and-off" social media users. However, while 37% of users stated that they were "always" online, there were only 14.8% of the users who "always" used social media "to read news." The users who stated that they were "on-and-off" social media users at the same time claimed that they "often" (40.7%) or "sometimes" (38.3%) used it "to read news." The implications of these results could be that the highest percentages of social media users who do not always follow social media claim that they use these sites "to read news," yet when users are on-and-off, they cannot really follow current news and stay updated. Because of the fact that the fluidity of social media allows users to follow current news fast and spontaneously, the users must be online at all times so that they can get into the current events happening worldwide. These results bring doubts over their understanding of *news* then. It can be possible, for instance, that these users take status updates, tweets about everyday incidents, event announcements, photos or cartoons shared by their "friends" as *news* as well, which could be a significant research topic for future study which could investigate what users are following as *news* like "national news," "regional news," "celebrity news," "sports news," or "news from friends." Thus, the always-online users do not often read news in the real sense online, and they might participate in different activities.

While reading news in social media is a receptive and passive activity, the question whether they use social media "to comment on news" showed us to what extent these users were actively engaged in social media. The social media users who were "always" online (37%) and used it "to read news" (14.8%) were quite hesitant to "comment on news" because the results showed that only 1.2% of these users "always" made comments online. Thus, we can conclude that the users who were always online were not actively engaged in

politics in social media. These results can also show us another aspect of the situation that the always-online users can have such a high level of awareness of social media use that they might be consciously choosing not the comment on news because they consider the potential danger of social network and protect themselves since they have already build a sense of insecurity. There was also a decline in the active participation when we consider on-and-off users; while 59.8% of the users were on-and-off, 79% of the users stated that they were reading news online, yet 64.2% (18.5% say "often" and 45.7% say "sometimes") of the users expressed that they commented on news in social media. The assumption that their understanding of news could be different from that of ours mentioned above might have influenced the results here, too. The ones who commented on "news" like a friend's wedding or a new baby born posted online might have stated that they "often" or "sometimes" commented on "news."

When it comes to "sharing news" in social media, the results indicated that 32.1% of the users were sharing news "often," 43.2% of the users were doing it "sometimes," and 14.8% of them were "rarely" sharing news, but only 2.5% of the users were "always" involved in sharing information with other users. Regardless of their understanding of "news," the on-and-off users seemed to share news without commenting on, and this type of social media participation does not really make them actively engaged in politics in social media.

Turkish young people, as the results showed, had a high sense of freedom. 65.4% of the participants stated, "people in social media are free to express their political thoughts in social media," 96.3% of them expressed that they believed, "social media sites must not block users making political comments," and 77.8% of them asserted, "they can express their political thoughts in social media freely," 88.9% of them stated that "social media sites must not ban political thoughts." Moreover, they (86.4%) thought, "users who make political comments must not get into trouble with the police." However, as the results displayed, the contradiction is in their belief in the possibility of getting into trouble with the police if they make political comments themselves in social media because 48.1% of the participants admitted this danger. They asserted that the police must not interfere with people making political comments online in principle, but they cannot fully ignore the risk. When we look at Turkish young people's approach to their political identity, the results showed that 92.6% of the participants believed, "their political thoughts cannot change because of the political comments in social media," so they are stick to their political identity, and they are not open to changes in their political thoughts. 53.1% of the participants also asserted, "political comments do not change people's political thoughts in social media." They seemed to be more confident in their political thoughts while they considered the possibility of "others" possibly being affected by online political comments.

Participants' high sense of freedom of speech is contradictory to the results showing the degree of their political engagement in social media. 79% of the participants stated, "the friends of their friends must be allowed to see their political comments in social media," and also 71.6% of them stated, "their friends must be allowed to see their own political comments in social media." However, 53.1% of them stated, "they don't make comments about political implementations." Thus, the results revealed that young people were in fact passive in using social media to express their political thoughts, but "others" (whoever they are) can make comments, and they can simply follow them. Referring back to Utz et al. (2012), the participants in this study seemed to be seeking popularity. Because they do not want to make political comments themselves, their responses to the questions that aimed at identifying if they feel secure by asking whether their friends or even friends' friends could see their comments showed us that they felt secure themselves, but

they thought that it was secure for "others." It is all about following others' comments so that users could feel that they belong to a popular community and show others that they are also there. This was also demonstrated by the results concerning another question in the survey asking if "they use social media to announce political events." 87.7% of the participants stated that "users should use social media to announce political events," but 76.5% of them stated that they were not using social media for this purpose. Similar to their approach to making political comments in social media, they do not organize and announce political events, but they do not mind "others" doing that. In fact, they support "others" doing that so that they could follow them. Thus, we can come to the conclusion that the majority of these young people are "passive observers" of politics in social media.

Young people who seemed to have "high sense of freedom of speech" in Turkey according to the research results believed, "social media should be used to support political groups" (85.2%). As they (76.5%) did not organize and announce political events using social media, 71.6% of the participants stated, "they do not support groups that are close to their political thoughts" though. This shows a similar result that they do not mind "others" supporting political groups, but they do not prefer to do it themselves. There were two items in the survey that were attributed great importance in the analysis. The first item aimed at understanding whether these social media users were "members of the groups of the political parties that they supported in social media." The results showed that only 24.7% of the participants were members, so they did not hesitate to label and publicize their political identity in social media. However, 72.8% of the users were not members. The second item asked the participants whether they would state which political party they would vote for in the next general election in 2015 in social media. While 35.8% users stated that they could share the political party that they would vote for with other users, 55.5% of the users stated that they would not, and 8.6% of them stated that they would hesitate to do this. Thus, we can conclude that Turkish young people with "high sense of security" believe that "others" can manifest their political identity in social media through organizing and announcing political events, supporting political groups they feel closer to, making political comments online, and become members of the political parties that they support. However, they are hesitant to be involved in any of these online activities, and they do not want to publicize the political party they are going to vote for probably due to the possibility of getting into trouble with the police embedded deep down in their minds. Beside the well-known cases showing that young people, like Duygu Kerimoglu, can be detained because of their online activities in Turkey, the recent protests revealed that such a danger existed. The statements of the Major of Istanbul confirmed these doubts after the Gezi Park protests started. He declared that the police had started investigations to discover the social media users who *instigated* the protests using these digital platforms. Right after this declaration, in Izmir 27 people were detained for using Twitter and other social media sites to "spread untrue information" and incite people to join demonstrations, but they were released.

The results also showed that young people in Turkey made a clear-cut distinction between social events and political implementations. 92.6% of the participants stated that "comments should be made about social events in social media," and 60.5% of them said that they used social media to share their comments about social events. However, as discussed earlier, they do not want to make comments about political implementations. Then, they probably make comments about domestic violence in Turkish society for example, but they do not make comments about the government's policies to prevent domestic violence. There is also the possibility that the participants took the word "comment" as merely negative criticisms, which is quite common in Turkish society. From this perspective, while answering the questions in the survey, they might not have considered making comments about how effective the policies of the Ministry of Family and Social Policies were while they could make comments about a specific incident revealed in media. Thus, the uneasiness that young people feel when they attempt to express their oppositions to the government was revealed by these results. Besides, what they consider as social events cannot be explained using the data obtained, but interestingly they distinguish social events from political implementations.

Observers, Not Activists

The results of the survey manifested an interesting portrait of young people in Turkey. The participants of the study appeared to be mainly observers of political activities in social media rather than being activists who are politically engaged. It is significant that while the majority of the participants are "passive observers/followers" of politics in social media, 84% of them at the same time claimed, "they were sincere in their political comments in social media" while 51.9% of them believed, "political comments in social media reflected people's political identities genuinely." It is rather contradictory that these young people who accepted that they preferred to be passive in manifesting their political identity in social media simultaneously expressed that they were publicizing their political identity *sincerely*. This inconsistency in their thought pattern could be because of their perception of "being actively engaged" in social media. They may think that *liking* a page on Facebook or *following* some people or institutions simply makes them politically engaged, which is not true. The conclusion drawn from the results of the survey might sound rather puzzling; they do not mind users sharing their political comments and they inevitably *follow* them, but they do not let other users affect *their* political identity, nor do they take others' comments seriously. They may call this "political engagement," which might make them look cool, trendy, or updated in this virtual community.

As mentioned earlier, according to a survey conducted by KONDA in 2011 in Turkey, 32.7% of young people do not trust any institutions while 16.9% of them trust the police forces, which is a higher percentage compared to their level of trust in the parliament (13.7%). The survey in this study also revealed significant points. While the participants (86.4%) think that social media users must not get into trouble with the police because of their political thoughts ideally speaking, they (48.1%) consider this danger for themselves and they (53.1%) at the same time do not make any comments about political applications. It seems that the participants do not actually perceive the police forces as a threatening authority that can restrict their freedom of speech; they seem to be romanticizing the police as the "protective authority," but they are afraid of being monitored by the authorities (but they do not mind others' political comments and activities) because they might be associating the government with the court and imprisonments because of the current political situation in Turkey. Since they do not want to make the government angry, they take a passive role in social media use as political entities. They appear to be politically passive followers/observers in social media and avoid being activists, which might not be quite different after the "Resistanbul" events.

FUTURE RESEARCH DIRECTIONS

There are certain limitations in this study that could lead academics to further research. The major limitation is that this survey was conducted before the anti-government protests started on May 30, 2013 in Taksim Square in Istanbul. Thus, new research must be conducted to explore whether young people's political engagement in social media and their perception of police forces and the government have changed or not and whether there is a difference in their manifestation of their online political identities and the level of their political engagement after the "Resistanbul" events. Moreover, while conducting the survey, Ferhat Boratav, an instructor in the Department of Television Reporting and Programming in Istanbul Bilgi University, raised an issue whether these participants have accounts in social network sites that they actively use with their actual names or pseudonyms. The survey given did not explore this, but further research with a specific focus on the nature of their user names in relation to their sense of security and insecurity can add new dimensions to the issue. Also, if interviews had been held with focus groups among the participants, more detailed data regarding their worry and fear could have been obtained, and this can also be further researched.

CONCLUSION

Worry can be a positive factor that enhances motivation, but when the level of worry increases, and worry turns into anxiety, individuals tend to control their environments so that they could protect themselves from the threats that lead to anxiety. As it is mostly challenging to control others and all other factors in the social environment that cause anxiety in individuals, they generally start to control themselves, which is easier. In Turkey, where power distance is high, individuals mostly comply with the rules and regulations implemented by the authority without really questioning them. Even if some people question the state's policies, they do not have access to social and political mechanisms that could allow them to activate public awareness and take democratic actions for the well-being of the community. In such a collective society with very little trust in institutions, this may result in "collective obedience." As citizens cannot control the threats that create anxiety in them, they regulate their own actions in order to avoid getting into trouble with the government. Thus, not everybody wants to take the responsibility because most people disbelieve the power of every citizen that can contribute to a dramatic change in society if they take on their individual responsibilities and fulfill them.

The result is that they mostly become politically disengaged because they do not believe that they are the most important actors of the political system. In a country like Turkey, it is very likely that many young people cannot complete the construction of their political identities, nor can they really define who they are and where they stand politically. Their offline political identities as responsible citizens of Turkey are usually not clear even to themselves, and because of the highly authoritarian AKP government, their level of anxiety increases, and the way that they manifest their political existence in social media can also be vague. Young people feel the need to be self-controlled because, pure and simple, they cannot always use their civic rights to protect themselves from the threats coming from the police and other governmental agencies. As a result, they read but do not comment on politically loaded posts; they share but do not participate in discussions online in case *the big brother is watching* them and their activities in social media.

In Turkey, the ruling party AKP increased its votes to 49.9% in the last general election in 2011. While the AKP government claims that they make investments in the projects that will empower young people and they secure their well-being, the Prime Minister mentions about strengthening and enabling the rise of a "religious and revengeful youth," which revealed their tendency to impose their Islamic values on Turkish society. Then, young people's well-being depends on their commitment to being a member of *their* young population. However, it is not easy to define and adopt a tailor-made political identity as *them* and *us*. Unless these 81 participants who took part in this study are supporters of opposing parties' by coincidence, the fact that they do not want to publicize their political identity reveals that AKP's so-called youth policies do not increase

young people's sense of security, and they do not help them create a public image that they ensure freedom of speech and democracy for *all people*.

The current political situation in Turkey that is likely to create anxiety in young people prevents people from perceiving social media as alternative democratic platforms where they can be politically engaged. They are hesitant to state which political party they support and who they are going to vote for in the next elections because they do not want *the big brother* to hear them. What happens if they do? They are concerned since they do not want to be compartmentalized or labeled by the government while they fail to consider that having a political stand is their constitutional right. This is because the AKP government unfortunately segregates people as *them* and *us* for so long that they fear to belong neither of these segments of society because when they create an impression that they belong to *them,* they will be out of the *game*; on the other hand, when they are labeled as members of *us,* they are being criticized of being "Islamist." Sometimes anti-government criticisms may lead to serious problems such as police investigations, lawsuits, and imprisonment. The results of this study can bring academics, administrators and policymakers different insights into Turkish university students' political (dis)engagement together with their use of social media despite its limitations. The political situation in Turkey now, as the study demonstrates, has created young individuals who are "politically passive followers/ observers" in social media although you can see that the majority of them check social media sites regularly in daily life. They avoid being activists because they cannot deny the possibility of getting into serious trouble with the governmental agencies, so they control their political presence in social media.

Nevertheless, the anti-government protests that started in May 2013 in Gezi Park in Taksim Square, the "Resistanbul" events, must have made a considerable impact on young people's understanding of politics, democracy, and media. We can take this paper as an analysis of young people's political identity construction "before *Resistanbul*," and young people's perception of themselves as political entities, their understanding of social media use and how secure or insecure they might feel while using social media "after *Resistanbul*" should be further analyzed. This was the first time for the majority of young people that they stood up for more democratic rights and freedom of speech and protested peacefully. This was the first time that they felt they had to overcome their fear and anxiety to claim more democracy no matter which political ideology they were influenced by. This was also the opportunity for young people to experience what their parents experienced in the 60s and 70s and find a common ground that they can share with their parents. They also realized that the gatekeepers could more easily manipulate the conventional means of media than social media, and they used social media sites in such an active way to communicate their ideas and build solidarity that they had never used before.

It is time for young people to redefine politics and democracy in Turkey, and they will not be the same people as they were before. Certainly, Turkish society will keep on experiencing the consequent changes that result from *Resistanbul* and learning lessons from these events to build a sound democracy for future generations.

REFERENCES

Arinc. (2012, December 28). *Internethaber*. Retrieved from http://www.internethaber.com/arinc-universitelerde-tehlike-var-489378h.htm

Baym, N. K., & Boyd, D. (2012). Socially mediated publicness: An introduction. *Journal of Broadcasting & Electronic Media*, *56*(3), 320–329. doi:10.1080/08838151.2012.705200

Bennett, W. L. (2003). Communicating global activism: Strengths and vulnerabilities of networked politics. *Information Communication and Society*, *6*(2), 143–168. doi:10.1080/1369118032000093860a

Bennett, W. L. (2012). The personalization of politics: Political identity, social media, and changing patterns of participation. *The Annals of the American Academy of Political and Social Science*, *644*(20), 20–39. doi:10.1177/0002716212451428

Bennett, W. L., Breunig, C., & Givens, T. (2008). Communication and political mobilization: Digital media and the organization of anti-Iraq war demonstrations in the U.S. *Political Communication*, *25*, 269–289. doi:10.1080/10584600802197434

Bhat, C. S., Chang, S.-H., & Linscott, J. A. (2010). Addressing cyberbullying as a media literacy issue. *New Horizons in Education*, *58*(3), 34–43.

Boyd, D. (2008). Can social network sites enable political action? *International Journal of Media and Cultural Politics*, *4*(2), 241–244. doi:10.1386/macp.4.2.241_3

Boyd, D. M., & Ellison, N. B. (2008). Social network sites: Definition, history and scholarship. *Journal of Computer-Mediated Communication*, *13*, 210–230. doi:10.1111/j.1083-6101.2007.00393.x

Carpenter, R. (2012). Virtual places in the physical world: Geographies of literacy and (national) identity. In B. Williams, & A. A. Zenger (Eds.), *New media literacies and participatory popular culture across borders* (pp. 193–212). New York, NY: Routledge.

Collin, P. (2008). The internet, youth participation policies, and the development of young people's political identities in Australia. *Journal of Youth Studies*, *11*(5), 527–542. doi:10.1080/13676260802282992

Denton, D. W., & Wicks, D. (2013). Implementing electronic portfolios through social media platforms: Steps and student perceptions. *Journal of Asynchronous Learning Networks*, *17*(1), 123–133.

Erikson, E. H. (1995a). Late adolescence. In S. Schlein (Ed.), *A way of looking at things: Selected papers from 1930 to 1980* (pp. 631–643). New York, NY: Norton.

Erikson, E. H. (1995b). Psychoanalysis and ongoing history: Problems in identity, hatred and nonviolence. In S. Schlein (Ed.), *A way of looking at things: Selected papers from 1930 to 1980* (pp. 481–496). New York, NY: Norton.

Erikson, E. H. (1997). *The life cycle completed*. New York, NY: Norton.

Fauziah, A., Kee, C. P., Normah, M., & Ibrahim, F., Mahmud & Dafrizal, W. A. (2012). Information propagation and the forces of social media in Malaysia. *Asian Social Science*, *8*(5), 71–76.

Fenton, N., & Barassi, V. (2011). Alternative media and social networking sites: The politics individuation and political participation. *Communication Review*, *14*(3), 179–196. doi:10.108 0/10714421.2011.597245

Fogg, B. J. (2008). Mass interpersonal persuasion: An early view of a new phenomenon. In *Proceedings of Third International Conference on Persuasive Technology*. Retrieved from http://www.bjfogg.com/mip.html

Halstead. (1999). A politics for generation X. *Atlantic Monthly, 284* (2), 33-42.

Harvard University, Institute of Politics. (2006). *Youth survey*. Retrieved from http://www.iop.harvard.edu/fall-2006-youth-survey

Hofstede, G., Hofstede, G. J., & Minkov, M. (2010). *Cultures and organizations*. New York: McGraw-Hill.

Kelm, O. R. (2011). Social media: It's what students do. *Business Communication Quarterly*, *74*(4), 505–520. doi:10.1177/1080569911423960

KONDA. (2010). *Law and justice – Perceptions and expectations*. Retrieved from http://www.konda.com.tr/tr/raporlar.php?tb=2

KONDA. (2011). *Turkish youth survey*. Retrieved from http://www.konda.com.tr/tr/raporlar.php

Kushin, M. J., & Yamamoto, M. (2010). Did social media really matter? College students' use of online media and political decision making in the 2008 election. *Mass Communication & Society*, *13*, 608–630. doi:10.1080/15205436.2010.516863

Oravec, J. A. (2012). Bullying and mobbing in academe: Challenges for distance education and social media applications. *Journal of Academic Administration in Higher Education*, *8*(1), 48–58.

Pew Research Center. (n.d.). *Social networking popular across globe: Arab publics most likely to express political views online*. Retrieved from http://www.pewglobal.org/files/2012/12/Pew-Global-Attitudes-Project-Technology-Report-FINAL-December-12-2012.pdf

Pinchot, J. L., Douglas, D., Paullet, K. L., & Rota, D. R. (2011). Talk to text: Changing communication patterns. In *Proceedings of Conference for Information Systems Applied Research*. Wilmington, NC: EDSIG.

Rajakumar, M. (2012). Faceless Facebook: Female Qatari users choosing wisely. In B. Williams, & A. A. Zenger (Eds.), *New media literacies and participatory popular culture across borders* (pp. 125–134). New York, NY: Routledge.

Shirky, C. (2011). The political power of social media: Technology, the public sphere, and political change. *Foreign Affairs*, 1.

Silius, K., Kailanto, M., & Tervakari, A. M. (2011). Evaluating the quality of social media in an educational context. *International Journal of Emerging Technologies in Learning, 6*(3), 21–27.

Sponcil, M., & Gitimu, P. (n.d.). Use of social media by college students: Relationship to communication and self-concept. *Journal of Technology Research, 4,* 1-13.

Steffgen, G., König, A., Pfetsch, J., & Melzer, A. (2011). Are cyberbullies less empathic? Adolescents' cyberbullying behavior and empathic responsiveness. *CyberPsychology. Behavior & Social Networking, 14*(11), 643–648. doi:10.1089/cyber.2010.0445

Theocharis, Y. (2013). The wealth of (occupation) networks? Communication patterns and information distribution in a Twitter protest network. *Journal of Information Technology & Politics, 10*(1), 35–56. doi:10.1080/19331681.2012.701106

Toma, C. L., & Hancock, J. T. (2013). Self-affirmation underlies Facebook use. *Personality and Social Psychology Bulletin, 39*(3), 321–331. doi:10.1177/0146167212474694 PMID:23359086

Trottier, D. (2012). Policing social media. *Canadian Review of Sociology, 49*(4), 411–425. doi:10.1111/j.1755-618X.2012.01302.x

Utz, S. (2009). The (potential) benefits of campaigning via social network sites. *Journal of Computer-Mediated Communication, 14,* 221–243. doi:10.1111/j.1083-6101.2009.01438.x

Utz, S. (2010). Show me your friends and I will tell you what type of person you are: How one's profile, number of friends, and type of friends influence impression formation on social network sites. *Journal of Computer-Mediated Communication, 15,* 314–335. doi:10.1111/j.1083-6101.2010.01522.x

Utz, S., Tanis, M., & Vermeulen, I. (2012). It is all about being popular: The effects of need for popularity on social network site use. *Cyberpsychology, Behavior, and Social Networking, 15*(1), 37–42. doi:10.1089/cyber.2010.0651 PMID:21988765

Valenzuela, S., Namsu, P., & Kee, K. F. (2009). Is there social capital in a social network site? Facebook use and college students' life satisfaction, trust, and participation. *Journal of Computer-Mediated Communication, 14,* 875–901. doi:10.1111/j.1083-6101.2009.01474.x

Vargas, R. (2007). Are you going to the March? How Mexican-American youth in Oakland and Richmond California became politically active on May 1st. In *Proceedings of American Sociological Association.* American Sociological Association.

Vitak, J., Zube, P., Smock, A., Carr, C. T., Ellison, N., & Lampe, C. (2011). It's complicated: Facebook users' political participation in the 2008 election. *Cyberpsychology, Behavior, and Social Networking, 14*(3), 107–114. doi:10.1089/cyber.2009.0226 PMID:20649449

Wang, Z., Tchernev, J. M., & Solloway, T. (2012). A dynamic longitudinal examination of social media use, needs, and gratifications among college students. *Computers in Human Behavior, 28,* 1829–1839. doi:10.1016/j.chb.2012.05.001

KEY TERMS AND DEFINITIONS

Gezi Park: The only remaining green area in Taksim Square, the main entertainment center of Istanbul, which environmentalists, city planners and architects insist on preserving. The Ottoman-era military barracks to be rebuilt as a mall in the park are also an ideological symbol in Turkish history, for on March 31, 1909 the Islamic-minded soldiers at the barracks rebelled against the modernist movements of Sultan Abdulhamit

II and claimed for Sharia law. The barracks were demolished in 1940.

Justice and Development Party (AKP): The current ruling party that was first elected in 2002 and has been in power since then. During campaigns, they promoted the party as a center-right conservative party; however, it aims at maintaining the tradition of Islamism, which manifests itself in its major policies, implementations, and political discourse.

Resistanbul: The peaceful anti-government protests that started on May 30, 2013 in Istanbul to stop the demolition of Gezi Park to build a mall instead and has led to nation nationwide protests.

Resistance: The peaceful online and offline anti-government protests that follow the main principles of *passive resistance*.

ENDNOTES

1   *Poshu* is a traditional scarf in Turkey worn by merely Kurds, which is also seen as a political symbol associated with PKK.

2   RedHack is a socialist hacker group that is popular among young people because of their anti-government acts. For example, after learning that journalists who support them were threatened, the RedHack group leaked a file containing the identities of Turkish police informants, or they hacked the Website of Student Selection and Placement Center after it revealed that university entrance exam questions were leaked to some students before the exam date, but the exam was not cancelled. After the event in METU, they announced that they would take the revenge of those students exposed to excessive police force, and they leaked a series of documents from the Higher Education Council Website and publicized documents proving a number of irregularities and corruption in several universities in Turkey.

3   For details of events http://edition.cnn.com/2013/05/30/world/meast/istanbul-protests/index.html, http://edition.cnn.com/2013/06/01/world/europe/turkey-protests

4   The survey was prepared and the data obtained from the survey was processed in colloboration with Elif Canan Onat, the head of the Deapartment of Modern Languages in Bahcesehir University in Istanbul, where she also made it possible to conduct the survey among a number of students from Faculty of Communication.

Chapter 2
Assemblages of Dissent:
The Emergence of Online Identities during the Egyptian Revolution

Katherine Bridgman
Florida State University, USA

ABSTRACT

This chapter examines the online identities of protestors and their transnational audiences that emerged across social media platforms during the Egyptian Revolution of 2011. Using the framework of assemblage theory, the author argues that these online identities emerged as a result of the assemblages of dissent that formed between protestors and their audiences. In particular, she argues that, as protestors and their transnational audiences came together in assemblages of dissent, both gained emergent online identities as activists in the transnational mediatized event of the revolution. Protestors initiated these relationships through petitions for audiences to join the Facebook page "We are All Khaled Said" and follow the Twitter hashtag #Jan25; their catalogue of grievances against Mubarak's regime; and, finally, their digital assertions of lived experiences of violence. As transnational audiences took up these texts as invitations to participate in the doing of this mediatized event, they responded by "liking," commenting, retweeting, and creating new texts of their own. As a result, both protestors and their audiences around the globe gained online identities as activists in the revolution.

DOI: 10.4018/978-1-4666-5150-0.ch002

INTRODUCTION

While the Egyptian Revolution of 2011 was reported across traditional news venues by global media outlets, protestors also reported on the Revolution using social media platforms such as Twitter and Facebook. Many of these protestors transmitted social media texts from the streets of Egypt during moments they experienced police brutality and within scenes of unified force among anti-Mubarak protestors. As these protestors used social media to provide real-time reports of events as they unfolded, they participated in the formation of online identities for both themselves and audience members around the globe who were tuning in through social media. This chapter seeks to understand these online identities and their formation as a result of the discursive strategies employed by activists to engage transnational audiences witnessing the Revolution through digital screens in coffee shops, bus stops, and office break rooms around the globe. Using the framework of assemblage theory, I argue that the online identities of protestors and their audiences emerged from the assemblages of dissent that formed between them as a result of their exchanges across social media platforms such as Facebook and Twitter.

Events such as the Revolution of 2011 underscore John Tomlinson's observation in *Globalization and Culture* (1999) that most people will experience globalization through extended mediated experiences rather than actual physical mobility. Stig Hjarvard (2008) defines mediatization as "a double-sided process of high modernity in which the media on one hand emerge as an independent institution with a logic of its own" and are, on the other hand "an integrated part of other institutions like politics, work, family, and religion as more and more of these institutional activities are performed through both interactive and mass media" (p. 1). In the global mediatized event of the Revolution, the logic of social media facilitated the formation of an event that was characterized by the open and participatory logics

of social media (Shirky). As a result of this logic, the Revolution was woven through the "institutions" of people's daily lives as a) updates about the Revolution were interspersed between and among other, more locally oriented updates about family, friends, work, and religion across social media platforms and b) social media enabled these streams of information to be interjected whenever and wherever people checked updates from personal cell phones, portable computers, and the like. As social media has been integrated throughout the "institutional activities" of people's daily lives, it has also contributed to what Sasha Costanza-Chock (2003) has suggested are the primary goals of "electronic civil disobedience:" "to bring together groups of people in collective action" and facilitate "changes in social norms, behaviors, and ways of thinking among a public that extends beyond movement constituents or beneficiaries" (p. 178). Similarly, those participating in the mediatized global event of the Egyptian Revolution of 2011 extended beyond national borders to include transnational audiences located around the globe.

Transnationalism turns our attention to how the "electronic civil disobedience" of Egyptian protestors across social media extended beyond the local context of the Revolution and enabled this movement to reach a much broader audience around the world. Exploring the Revolution with an emphasis on these transnational audiences turns our attention to the discursive strategies used by protestors as a means of connecting their local experiences of the Revolution to transnational audiences around the globe. Steven Vertovec (1999) writes that transnationalism describes "a condition" wherein despite distance and intervening borders, "certain kinds of relationships have been globally intensified and now take place paradoxically in a planet-spanning yet common – however virtual – arena of activity" (p. 3). Transnationalism highlights the ways in which this "arena of activity" remains provocatively rooted in the local contexts of those who are participating in it. As Sidney Tarrow (2005) points out, "even as they make transnational claims, [transnational activists] draw on the resources, networks, and opportunities of the societies they live in" (p. 2). Highlighting the ways that transnational activists connect the local and the global, Michael Howard (2011) claims that transnationalism is "essentially about humans creating boundaries and then crossing them" (ch. 1). In the case of the Egyptian Revolution, transnationalism offers an opportunity to explore the unique role of social media in connecting the physical locations of protestors in Egypt to audiences scattered across the globe. Through social media platforms such as Twitter and Facebook, these distant audiences were able to connect and respond to the local experiences of protestors and, by doing so, participate as activists in the Revolution as it was mediatized across these platforms. Describing this role of media in transnational protest, Simon Cottle and Libby Lester (2011) write:

Though physically enacted in particular locales, cities, countries or indeed on different continents, it is by means of contemporary communication networks and media systems that [transnational protests] effectively become coordinated, staged for wider audiences and disseminated around the world. (p. 17)

Thus, "as [an] ethico-political imaginary (of what should be) and as collective political action (the struggle to bring this about)" (p. 5), protest movements such as the Egyptian Revolution "effectively become transnationalized" as a result of their "communicative enactment" across social media (p. 17). It was through this communicative enactment that protestors and their audiences around the world engaged each other to form assemblages of dissent from which each gained online identities as activists in the Egyptian Revolution.

For Tarrow, the kinds of relationships that are facilitated by transnational activism such as this chapter explores in the context of the Egyptian Revolution are not suitable for an examination through the framework of globalization. He writes: "Although globalization is a powerful source of new actors, new relationships, and new inequalities, as an orienting concept for understanding transnational activism it leaves much to be desired" (p. 5). Globalization for Tarrow is "the increasing volume and speed of flows of capital and goods, information and ideas, people and forces that connect actors between countries" (p. 5). He juxtaposes globalization to what he refers to as internationalization. For Tarrow, internationalization is the "opportunity structure" within which transnational activism occurs. Internationalization has three primary characteristics: the "increasing density of relations across states, governmental officials, and nonstate actors," "increasing vertical links among the subnational, national, and international levels," and "an enhanced formal and informal structure that invites transnational activists and facilitates the formation of networks of nonstate, state, and international actors" (p. 8). Tarrow uses the term internationalization to describe contexts such as we see in the case of social media use during the Egyptian Revolution. Focusing on these audiences as transnational rather than global turns our attention to the ways in which these social media users around the world were potentially implicated in the events of the Revolution as protestors across the streets of Egypt used social media as a means of inviting, informing, and inscribing their physical experiences for others to see and respond to. As transnational audiences responded to these authors' texts, both emerged with online identities as activists in the Revolution.

The value of this argument for our understanding of online identities is two-fold. First, it moves us toward a framework that demystifies the influential identities that protestors in the Arab Spring established through their work online. In particular, this argument nuances our understandings of the role played by social media in the Egyptian Revolution and the role of the transnational support that was garnered through protestors' uses of social media platforms. Second, this argument enables us to understand where identities within worldwide digital contexts come from and the complex ways that these identities negotiate the intersections of the local and global.

This chapter begins with a discussion of the framework that I use to explore the emergence of these online identities in a transnational context: assemblage theory. Next, I discuss the role of assemblages in the formation of emergent identity. Then, I discuss the Revolution as a mediatized event that both developed as a result of and provided a context for the assemblages of dissent that I examine between protestors and their audiences around the world. These assemblages of dissent were the generative relationships that formed between protestors and their audiences as a result of discursive exchanges manifesting both parties' dissent of the Mubarak regime and their desire for Revolution. Finally, this chapter's analysis will turn to three discursive strategies that facilitated the creation of these provocative relationships between protestors and their audiences: protestors' petitions for audiences to join the Facebook page "We are All Khaled Said" and follow the Twitter hashtag #Jan25; protestors' catalogue of grievances against Mubarak's regime; and, finally, protestors' digital assertions of their lived, protesting bodies. These three discursive strategies reflect protestors' *doing* of a mediatized event of the Revolution, a *doing* that was taken up by many transnational audiences as an invitation to themselves participate in the Revolution. Once this occurred, assemblages of dissent formed between protestors and their audiences and, as a result of these assemblages, their online identities as activists in the Revolution emerged.

IDENTITY AS AN EMERGENT CAPACTY OF ASSEMBLAGES

Assemblage theory provides a robust framework for understanding the hybrid and emergent formation of socially mediated transnational activist identities. The strengths of assemblage theory align with the challenges of examining the transaction among local and global stakeholders as well as the discursive flows of information that maintained transnational support over multiple incidents. Specifically, assemblage theory provides a means of tracking identity through wholes, rather than discrete parts that are subject to cause and effect chains as well as a framework through which to approach the online identities of activists and their audiences as one of many, overlapping identities.

The online identities that formed between protestors in the streets of Egypt and their transnational audiences around the globe emerged from what Manuel DeLanda has called assemblages. DeLanda defines assemblages in *A New Philosophy of Society* (2006) as "wholes whose in properties emerge from the interactions between parts" ("Introduction"). These "parts" can be anything from the fork and spoon in a place setting to bodies in a classroom. In this chapter, the parts being examined are protestors and their social media audiences from around the world. As the parts of assemblages are removed from one assemblage and entered into another, they have different interactions with the parts of these new assemblages. For example, in this context protestors have different interactions with other local protestors in the streets of Egypt than they do with their online audiences from around the world. In other words, DeLanda (2006) explains, "component parts can never explain the relations which constitute a whole" ("Introduction"). Rather, the capacities of an assemblage, here the emergent online identities of protestors and their social media audiences, form as a result of the interacting capacities of the assemblage's component parts, the protestors who were risking their lives in the streets of Egypt *and* the transnational audiences who engaged these texts by recirculating them, increasing their visibility, and creating new texts in response. Capacities such as the online identities that I examine here are defined by DeLanda as "what [social entities] are capable of doing when they interact with other social entities." These capacities transpire as the result of flows of what DeLanda describes in *A Thousand Years of Nonlinear History* (1997) as "matter-energy" (p. 26). These flows are the "structure generating processes" that bring together and maintain the parts of an assemblage. They can take any number of forms; flows can be organic or inorganic, material or immaterial, discursive or nondiscursive (DeLanda, 1997, p. 135). This chapter's investigation of the online identities of protestors and their audiences will focus on the discursive "matter-energy flows" that brought protestors and their audiences into assemblages with each other. These flows took shape through discursive exchanges in which protestors used social media platforms such as Facebook and Twitter to invite audiences to join the revolutionary effort online, to catalogue their grievances, and to document their physical experiences of the Revolution. As audiences responded to these texts and entered into relationships with their authors, a key emergent capacity of these assemblages was the online identities that each gained.

Geographer Doreen Massey (2005) also approaches identities as the products of assemblages. She highlights identities as emergent from wholes rather than discrete parts. Her use of assemblage theory turns our attention to the political nature of identities as they emerge through embedded practices:

In place of an individualistic liberalism or a kind of identity politics which makes those identities as already, and for ever, constituted, and argues for the rights of, or claims to equality for, those already-constituted identities, this politics takes the constitution of the identities themselves and the relations through which they are constructed to be one of the central stakes of the political. 'Relations' here, then, are understood as embedded practices. Rather than accepting and working with already-constituted entities/identities, this politics lays its stress upon the relational constructedness of things. (p. 10)

This emphasis on the "relational constructedness of things" points to the ways in which identities emerge as capacities of the relationships that protestors formed with their transnational audiences. Here, identity is framed as emergent from collective, shared practices that facilitated generative relationships between individuals and groups such as we saw in the Egyptian Revolution. For example, in an interview with Robert Mackey of *The New York Times* blog *The Lede* on January 27, 2011 (two days into the protests that began on January 25, 2011), anti-Mubarak protestor Gigi Ibrahim described her use of social media to initiate some of the discursive exchanges with audiences around the world that this chapter will investigate in more detail:

So, I tweet a lot while I'm in the protest, I'm telling everybody the security situation or how many people there [are] at the protest, if any arrests are happening, I'm reporting it [...] pretty much I'm trying to spread information, accurate information, and relate and paint the picture at the ground to people who aren't there via twitter and Facebook. And I record videos and take pictures as well.

Here, Ibrahim describes the creation of texts that, within DeLanda's framework, initiate the discursive flows that brought protestors and their online audiences together into assemblages of dissent. In particular, as Ibrahim and her fellow protestors created these texts, they formed powerful relationships with their social media audiences as activists in the Revolution. These online identities were maintained, however, only so long as protestors continued to create texts that invited the responses of their social media audiences and these audiences indeed took up these texts as invitations to respond and participate in the Revolution through "liking," commenting, retweeting, and creating new texts of their own. Once these discursive flows subsided, once protestors stopped posting and their audiences stopped responding, the assemblages of dissent between them fragmented and the emergent identities of protestors and their audiences as activists in the Revolution vanished.

While Massey explores identity in terms of embedded practices, Jasbir Puar frames identity in terms of the co-creation of relationships across which identities are plural and overlapping. Her approach to identity as emergent from assemblages reiterates the multiple and overlapping identities inherent to the transnational context of this phenomenon and continues to challenge the boundaries of identity by denying the existence of a "structural container" of identity that encases difference (Puar, 1997, "Conclusion"). In her discussion of identities as assemblages, Puar describes identities as the results of "interwoven forces that merge and dissipate time, space, and body against linearity, coherency, and permanency" ("Conclusion"). Arguing that online identities are the results of assemblages enables this chapter to move away from an intersectional model of identity, one presuming that "components – race, class, gender, sexuality, nation, age, religion – are separable analytics and can thus be disassembled" (Puar, 1997, "Conclusion").

The emergence of religious and secular identities as capacities of the assemblages that formed among protestors unifying in the streets provides a particularly powerful illustration of Puar's description of identities as plural and overlapping. A powerful backdrop to the identities that this chapter will be examining, the (re)negotiation of secular, Coptic, and Muslim identities among protestors was periodically played out for audiences around the world across social media platforms such as Twitter. For example, on February 1, 2011, as Coptics and Muslims came together in Tahrir square, @ORHamilton tweeted "A priest and an imam stand, hands together, aloft as the crowd chants "WE ARE AS ONE HAND" #Jan25 #Egypt." Retweeted by followers from the Netherlands, Indonesia, Whales, and the US, this tweet references an event that was widely covered by foreign press outlets. A woman in the crowd named Rana told Reuters: "All Egyptians, regardless of whether they are Christian or Muslim, want change, liberty, and justice for all people" (Cole, 2011). Later, @NevineZaki posted an image of two young Christian men holding hands in a human chain protecting Muslims during their prayers. These human chains became common sights as two groups who were historically at odds with each other, Coptics and Muslims, negotiated new identities as they formed new relationships through the protests. In the context of this chapter, this scene illustrates the ways in which the online identities that were gained by protestors in the streets were one of many, overlapping identities that emerged from the myriad of relationships that formed during the Egyptian Revolution of 2011.

Turning our attention to identities as emergent from wholes rather than cause and effect relationships between discrete parts at the same time that identites are plural and overlapping, assemblage theory enables this chapter to explore the *doing* of transnational activism that was taken up by protestors who put their lives on the line in the name of freedom from Mubarak's authoritarian regime. Through the texts that they created and the discursive flows of information that formed as audiences around the world took up these texts, protestors and their social media audiences emerged with online identities as activists in the Revolution.

THE TRANSNATIONAL MEDIATIZED EVENT OF THE EGYPTIAN REVOLUTION

Throughout the revolutionary protests that began on January 25, 2011, social media played a central role in protestors' *doing* of the Revolution. Writing for the *Huffington Post*, Raymond Schillinger (2011) suggests that "channels of social media" were at the roots of the Arab Spring, or what he defines as a "rising spirit of protest [that has] spread like wildfire." This suggestion is underscored by headlines such as "Social Media Sparked, Accelerated Egypt's Revolutionary Fire" (Gustin, 2011) and "Egypt's Revolution by Social Media: Facebook and Twitter let the people keep ahead of the regime" (Crovitz, 2011) that position social media as a key force behind the revolutions of the Arab Spring. In the midst of these headlines, however, protestors such as Wael Ghonim highlighted the contested role of social media in the Egyptian Revolution. In his memoir, *Revolution 2.0* (2012), Ghonim describes how it was the power of the people that made the revolution happen. "The power of the people," he writes, "will always be stronger than the people in power" (p. 294). Ghonim's sentiment is echoed in an interview reported on the *Hope140* blog in February of 2011 where protestor @alya1989262 describes the ways that protestors in the Egyptian Revolution had already been using Twitter as a means of organizing body power on the streets of Egypt long before the January 25 protests began:

We use [Twitter] to campaign and spread the word about protests/stands–hashtags are invaluable in that respect, and to share news quickly and efficiently, with our own 140-char commentary on them, and subsequently have conversations with random people/complete strangers. But most importantly, it allows us to share on the ground info like police brutality, things to watch out for, protestors getting arrested, etc. (para. 5)

The texts @alya1989262 describes in this passage facilitated more than communication between protestors or "conversations with random people/complete strangers," these texts also facilitated the relationships from which protestors and their online audiences around the world would gain online identities as activists in the Revolution.

Sean Aday, Director of the Institute for Public Policy and Global Administration at George Washington University, and a team of researchers (2010) state that protestors were, more often than not, aware of the transnational audiences who were watching them organize and communicate with one another across social media platforms (p. 12). Aday et al suggest that, at the same time protestors were communicating with each other, they were also keenly aware of audiences that were watching them from afar. This is emphasized in the multi-layered framework of analysis that Aday and his colleagues have developed; the fifth layer of which is "garner[ing] international attention" (p. 3). In line with Aday and his fellow researchers, Paolo Gerbaudo (2012) agrees that the primary role of social media "was thus mainly as a means of eliciting" this external attention ("Chapter 2"). These observations are affirmed by Christopher Wilson and Alexandra Dunn (2011) who describe protestors' use of social media "as a key resource for getting information to the outside world, perpetuating the feeling that the world was watching, which was an important factor for morale and coordination on the ground" (p. 1252).

Indeed, these audiences were watching the Revolution and their support often extended beyond mere sentiment and was manifested through supportive action. For example, a constant struggle for protestors within Egypt during the Revolution was maintaining communication links with the outside world. We see a clear expression of these frustrations when protestor Gigi Ibrahim tweeted on February 3, 2011: "I wanna say: fuck you @ vodafone." Cartoon artist Carlos Latuff captured these frustrations in an image of a dying protestor with Jan25 written on his shirt surrounded by blood. The man kneeling at his side has a panicked look on his face as he looks at his mobile phone to the right of which we see a large pair of scissors cutting his wireless connection that form the "V" of Vodafone. When this image was posted to the Facebook page "We are All Khaled Said," it was accompanied by text reading:

During the Egyptian revolution, Mobile Operators: Vodafone Egypt (largest network), Mobinil & Etisalat have cut off all mobile phones in Egypt. This has meant that many protesters & elderly people died because they couldn't call for help wherever they were.

In response to these mass disconnections, many individuals and activist groups around the world stepped up to help protestors circumvent these communication blockades. For example, on hearing that social media sites were being blocked by the Egyptian government, UCLA doctoral student John Scott-Railton began calling those he knew in Egypt, first on their cell phones and then through landlines, and tweeting their accounts of the Revolution under the Twitter username @jan25voices. In a live phone call that Scott-Railton tweeted on February 8, 2011 the caller reported: "When I crossed the checkpoints into the square, it was like crossing the border into a new Egypt." In addition to these efforts by individuals, larger organizations such as telecomix, a loosely organized collective of Web activists, also came forward to help. In addition to receiving communications from activists using Morse code and ham radios, telecomix assembled a list of Internet Service Providers (ISPs) around the world that activists could access via dial-up. These ISP addresses were then distributed through a variety of means including Facebook and Twitter posts such as one that appeared on Gigi Ibrahim's Facebook page on January 29, 2011: "To bypass government blocking of Websites, use numerical IP addresses: Twitter '128.242.240.52' Fb '69.63.189.34' Google '172.14.204.99'. A French

ISP offers free dial up Internet access ~ +33 1 72 89 01 50 password: toto. Please pass this on and share." This mobilization of transnational audiences within a global sphere of action illustrates the complex exchanges between local and global that occurred throughout the Egyptian Revolution of 2011 and reminds us that at the same time transnational audiences were forming online identities as activists in the Revolution, so too were many enacting these identities offline through a variety of supportive actions.

The next three sections return our attention to the online identities of protestors and their audiences around the globe by tracing three discursive strategies that sparked the relationships from which each gained online identities as activists in the Revolution. In the following three sections I will examine protestors' texts from the January 25, 2011 protests as well as the months and days leading up to them. In particular, I will examine texts posted to the English language Facebook page "We are All Khaled Said" as well as texts posted to Twitter with the hashtag #Jan25. The English language Facebook page "We are all Khaled Said" was set up by administrators on July 19, 2010. With explicit intentions of reaching transnational audiences, this Facebook page currently has over 337,000 members from around the world. Later, in January of 2011, Twitter's role in the Revolution was solidified by the introduction of the hashtag #Jan25. This hashtag became the most commonly used hashtag during the early months of the Revolution and the eighth most popular hashtag used on Twitter during 2011.

Petitions to Join with Protestors

In a blog post dated May 4, 2011, protestor Ramy Raoof describes one of the first tents erected in Tahrir Square during the January 25 protests: the media tent. Staffed by bloggers, human rights defenders and political activists among others, Raoof writes:

[M]ost of us were there with our personal laptops, cameras, memory-readers, hard-disks, cables and devices that we might need [...] the main thing we did was gathering all kind of multimedia from demonstrators in Tahrir Square then making the content available online once its possible. For me, gathering content from people and making it available online via different means was very important because i believed that making those pictures and videos public will help everyone to really understand whats happening on the ground, follow-up the situation and be able to judge, as well as have an overview of what happened in different cities in Egypt as those people who had pictures or videos were not only from Cairo.

Like Raoof and others working in the media tent in Tahrir Square, many of the activists who took to the streets during the Egyptian Revolution of 2011 were familiar with the use of social media as a means of organizing and publicizing their efforts. With a long history of use in Egyptian protests, social media had become for many inseparable from what it meant to *do* activism in Egypt. As protestors took to the streets, they used social media platforms not only to communicate among each other, but to also communicate with social media audiences around the world and petition these transnational audiences to join with them on sites such as the Facebook page "We are All Khaled Said" and the Twitter hashtag #Jan25. These invitations to join the Revolution initiated what DeLanda refers to as a discursive flow of information that brought protestors such as Raoof together with online audiences around the world. As relationships formed between these groups and assemblages of dissent emerged in disapproval of Mubarak, each gained online identities as activists in the Revolution.

The tone of protestors' invitations to join the Facebook page "We are All Khaled Said" was both urgent and direct. This tone underscores the degree to which protestors' were counting on an audience that was paying attention to what they had to say. Within Facebook's infrastructure, only once these users joined a Facebook page, would they see the texts posted by administrators as part of their local newsfeeds. In other words, within this economy of circulation, page administrators were reliant on the simple click of a button by online audiences if they wanted their message to circulate through Facebook at all.

Administrators bolstered these invitations to join the Facebook page "We are All Khaled Said" by drawing direct comparisons between the international support of this Revolution and the international support that helped end apartheid in South Africa. On July 20, 2010 – the second day of the page's existence – administrators wrote: "The world support and international protestors' pressure ended the apartheid system. We hope that your support will end injustice, torture and police brutality in Egypt." Later that same day administrators reiterated this invitation posting: "Please invite your friends to this page. We need people from all over the world to join us in our struggle to end Police brutality in Egypt." Seven days later, this invitation was again repeated:

Please Please invite all your friends to this page if you have not already done so. We need the support of all individuals worldwide. Don't under estimate [sic] the power of individuals, your support can and does make a difference. This is the first act of support you can do to help our cause at this stage. End emergency law in Egypt. End Police brutality and torture in Egypt.

Although this strategy of starting a Facebook page and inviting individual audience members to join it may seem fairly straightforward now that the page touts a following of over 337,000 members and Mubarak has been removed from power, turning to social media as a means of building relationships with transnational audiences in support of the Revolution was not always so obvious.

As "We are All Khaled Said" built its base of support with audiences around the world, many questioned the page's effectiveness since its distribution of protestors' messages was dependent on getting one follower at a time to join the page. Administrators addressed this doubt on August 3, 2010, reiterating the comparison between Egypt's overthrow of Mubarak and South Africa's overthrow of apartheid:

Once again, I have received few messages from Egyptians "not sure" about what we are trying to do on this page. The Apartheid system in South Africa ended by the support of INDIVIDUALS and human rights protestors from all over the world. We want individual supporters from all over the world to support us in our struggle to end torture in Egypt and end the emergency law. This Facebook page is about raising awareness.

Thus, as protestors used this social media platform to raise awareness, they were charged with the task of getting Facebook users around the world to become members of the page so that the updates and other texts posted by protestors would appear as part of local newsfeeds around the world.

While posts petitioning users to "join" the Facebook page reflect protestors' *doing* of the Revolution, the assemblages of dissent that would eventually form between protestors and their transnational audiences required these audiences to take up these invitations and respond to protestors' requests for support. Although the comments and "likes" that posts attracted early during the page's development show that the first audiences to come to this Facebook page were primarily English speaking Egyptians and members of the Egyptian Diaspora living outside of Egypt, after just a few months, this appeared to be changing. In August 2010 administrators posted an update that things were starting to turn around:

Some stats for facebook page: 2000 of our members are from 19 different countries other than Egypt. About 2800 members have joined us in the past 10 days alone. It's a good rate but we can definitely do better. Please invite your friends to join us. We want the whole world to be aware of our anti-torture campaign.

This breakdown of where users were from was followed up the next day with a post celebrating the relationships between protestors and audiences that were forming as a result of these invitations. Audiences wanting to assert their online identities as activists through the *doing* of Revolution offline had contacted page administrators. Beginning with "[o]ur message is reaching the world," administrators described how they were being contacted by journalists looking for more information about torture victims who also wished to be put in touch with them. Later in August, administrators posted that two international human rights lawyers had contacted them through the Facebook page and also wanted to help. This report was followed up with the reassertion: "Our efforts will make a difference." The difference that was made by these efforts was reliant on audiences around the world such as these human rights lawyers taking up protestors' call to join the Revolution by responding to their texts and embracing their online identities as activists in the Revolution.

As new members joined the Facebook page, they began to develop their own voices of dissent through the comments they posted to the page. For example, in response to the second status update posted in July of 2010, a member posting from the Philippines commented:

not jst those criminals nd also those have animal-hearted nd who treat ppl like an animal thy dont realy belong frm anywhre in ths world,,thy dont hve any right to cut anyones life,,mostly innocent ppl,,like wht th've done to khaled but only him fr those all forgoten brutality cases,nd killing ppl

*nd mostly the youth!!!!!!!animal ppl who treated
inhumanly must be treated as animally nd burn
them in fires of hell!!!!!! [sic]*

Later that month, another member of the page
posting from Madrid, Spain, posted the text of a
poem entitled "Sweet Freedom" and followed this
with the comment: "from Madrid we share all of
you the heay sadnesss [sic]. God bless all of you."
These nascent voices of dissent from around the
world also took shape as members of the page
came together to write paragraphs in many different languages that summarized the cause of the
page and its goals. Translations include French,
German, Finnish, Norwegian, Bangla, Russian,
and Danish. Through these activities that brought
transnational audiences into powerful relationships with protestors, each gained online identities
as activists in the Revolution.

In many ways, the long-time anonymity of the
primary administrator of the Facebook page "We
are All Khaled Said," Mohamed Ibrahim, highlights the dangers that came with the open invitations to join the Revolution that were also issued
by protestors posting to Twitter from the streets
of Egypt. Ibrahim anonymously coordinated this
Facebook page and worked with protestors in the
streets of Egypt from London during the January
25 Revolution of 2011. On July 7, 2012, Ibrahim
posted to his personal Facebook page saying, "I
have been anonymous for so long and it's time you
know more about my story." Describing his work
with Wael Ghonim (a protestor and administrator
of the Arabic language Facebook page of the same
name), Ibrahim writes:

*[f]or security reasons, we worked together
anonymously for almost a year and throughout
the revolution day (he was arrested [during] the
revolution). I have since preferred not to appear
much on the media, first because i [sic] enjoy my
privacy and secondly because I do not see benefit
to Egypt in that. It will also affect my career which
has nothing to do with politics or human rights.*

Ibrahim ended his anonymous administration
of the page when he won the Best Social Activism
Campaign category of the 2011 Best of Blogs
(BOBs) awards hosted by the German international
broadcasters, Deutsche Welle. In an interview after
he won this award, Ibrahim pointed out:

*The absolute minimum really is that people who
are not happy about what is happening in their
country, they need to start writing about it. Writing
a blog or starting a Facebook page like we did in
our case or even if you start a Twitter account and
write 140 characters to explain how you feel about
it. It's as simple as 140 characters. As time goes
by, you'll find other people starting to read what
you're saying, other people are listening to you
and that's where you'll start to make difference.
Other people will start doing like you. Tweeting
and Facebooking or blogging about what they
want to say.*

In addition to Facebook, Twitter was a popular social media platform that protestors used to
petition audiences around the globe to join the
movement by following the hashtag #Jan25. While
Twitter had been used earlier by administrators
of the Facebook page "We are All Khaled Said"
and other protestors, the full force of Twitter as a
tool to reach audiences around the world did not
surface until just days before the January 25 protests when @alya1989262 tweeted #Jan25 for the
first time on January 15, 2011: "http://on.fb.me/
fBoJWT over 16000 of us are taking to the streets
on #jan25! join us: http://on.fb.me/fQosDi#egypt
#tunisia #revolution." With two links that led
back to Facebook, this tweet is emblematic of
the ways that protestors' discursive relationships
with transnational audiences reinforced each other
across both Facebook and Twitter.

Hashtags were a powerful way that protestors
in the Egyptian Revolution secured the visibility of
their tweets in the context of a worldwide audience.
This is because hashtags such as #Jan25 function
within Twitter as a means of "annotat[ing] tweets

with metadata" (Conover, Ratkiewicz, Francisco, Goncalves, Flammini, & Menczer, 2011, Sec. 2). The inclusion of this metadata increases the visibility of a particular tweet and the conversation it is participating in by connecting the tweet to a broader, ongoing conversation with a topical marker that enabled users around the world to follow and to contribute (boyd, Golder, & Lotan, 2010, p. 1). As the significance of #Jan25 expanded to the naming of a transnational event, #Jan25 began to be attached to a variety of actions connected to the Egyptian Revolution. This is evidenced in the use of #Jan25 as a way of marking actions both within and outside of social media. For example, Brazilian cartoon artist Carlos Latuff who penned what have been referred to as "some of the most acerbic political cartoons of the Egyptian Revolution" (Biel) included #Jan25 in some of his most famous images. In one, a figure wearing and plain gray hooded sweatshirt and who is clearly Khaled Said dangles a tiny Hosni Mubarak out in front of him. Written in large white letters across Said's gray sweatshirt is "#Jan25." These cartoons circulated across the Web and even appeared on signs carried by protestors well beyond January 25, 2011.

During the days and moments leading up to the January 25 protests, protestors advertised #Jan25 as the hashtag for protests that were scheduled in coordination with National Police Day, January 25. Although the protests were in response to a variety of abuses, their coordination with National Police Day signaled the unification of protestors in response to the police's abuse of power that had helped to keep Mubarak in office for so long and was mentioned repeatedly on the "We are All Khaled Said" Facebook page after Said's death. While this local significance was not lost on Egyptians and many transnational audiences, #Jan25 quickly became a rallying cry for the protests that lasted beyond January 25, 2011 and eventually led to the removal of Hosni Mubarak from power.

Protestors used this particular hashtag both to invite fellow protestors to post updates from the demonstrations using the hashtag #Jan25 and to advertise this hashtag to transnational audiences, letting them know that they could follow the protests as they unfolded using this hashtag. For example, on January 20, 2011 @midoo0 tweeted: "ok this is our hashtag #Jan25." Later, on January 24, just hours before protestors took to the streets, @RamyRaoof tweeted: "Dear Friends, in case if u don't know, tomorrow #Jan25 demonstrations will take place in #Egypt against unemployment, corruption, and torture." While these tweets petitioning transnational audiences to follow the hashtag #Jan25 reflect protestors' *doing* of the Revolution, they required the response of transnational audiences in order for each to gain and maintain online identities as activists in the Revolution. Although these tweets from @RamyRaoof and @midoo0 were primarily retweeted by Egyptian audiences, other protestors, such as @weddady, a particularly involved protestor on Twitter throughout the Revolution, were more explicit in their invitations and successful in eliciting responses from transnational audiences: "Follow the hashtag #Jan25 to keep track of the protest day in #Egypt tomorrow #sidibouzid #mideat #Arabprotest." This tweet by @weddady was responded to by transnational audiences, many of whom retweeted it continuing its circulation and contributing to the visibility of these protests online. These 24 audience members who retweeted @weddady's original tweet report being from Romania, America, London, France, Peru, Canada, and Cardiff among other locations. By retweeting this text, these users contributed to the circulation of @weddady's tweet and helped it to appear at least 22,000 more times across the news feeds of their followers. @Dima_Khatib also tweeted: "Tomorrow: protests are planned in Egypt. We will be using #Jan25 + if you can: #sidibouzid too." Retweeted 34 times by both Egyptian and other audience members from around the world, this tweet was recirculated by Twitter users who report being from the Netherlands,

Sweden, the United States, the UK, Paris, and Venezuela among other places. Together, these 34 users helped @Dima_Khatib's tweet to appear over 300,000 more times on the newsfeeds of their followers around the world. Tweets such as these illustrate the ways in which protestors' invitations for transnational audiences to join the movement sparked relationships that were maintained across social media interfaces and afforded both protestors in the streets of Egypt as well as their audiences scattered across the globe with online identities as activists in the Egyptian Revolution.

Catalogues of Grievances

In addition to petitioning audiences around the world to join the Revolution, protestors also used social media platforms such as Facebook and Twitter to catalogue their grievances. This collaborative effort to catalogue Mubarak's abuses for audiences around the world provided many with their first glimpses behind the heavily monitored façade of Egyptian state media. As protestors posted a variety of images and accounts of their experiences, audiences around the world took up these texts as invitations to respond to and participate in the Revolution through their online identities as activists in the Revolution.

In many ways, the interface designs of Facebook and Twitter facilitated the use of these platforms as shared spaces for this collaborative catalogue of grievances that invited the response of transnational audiences. As administrators of the Facebook page "We are All Khaled Said" increased their number of followers by petitioning audiences to join, status updates were exceptionally well-suited for the "breaking news" posts that administrators frequently used to create this catalogue as they posted about the unfolding events surrounding Khaled Said's death. As administrators catalogued protestors' grievances of the Mubarak regime through updates that appeared on followers' newsfeeds, Facebook's interface facilitated the immediacy of these nascent relationships

between transnational audiences and protestors working in the streets of Egypt. In 2010, Kristin Arola wrote that Facebook's newsfeed:

[e]ncourages us to understand others through their actions in Facebook. It also encourages us to understand ourselves in relations to the actions of others. In the case of both the profile view and the home view, the design template encourages an understanding of self and others in part through our image and in large part through actions taken within the space of Facebook. (p. 8)

Once transnational audiences began to see themselves in this way and then took up administrators' texts as invitations to "like" or comment on them, they entered into relationships with protestors from which both gained online identities as activists in the Revolution.

Twitter's interface invites a similar kind of interrelation among users through both the home feed as well as the ability that users have to follow hashtags such as #Jan25. Here, it is important to clarify that following a hashtag such as #Jan25 was an important way that transnational audiences were able to read texts created by users whom they did not already follow. danah boyd, Scott Golder, and Gilad Lotan (2010) describe this unique dynamic of Twitter writing that "[b]ecause Twitter's structure disperses conversation throughout a network of interconnected actors rather than constraining conversation within bounded spaces or groups, many people may talk about a topic at once, such that others have a sense of being surrounded by a conversation" (p. 1). In this digital context, protestors' use of the hashtag #Jan25 to catalogue their grievances enabled them to open up their conversations about the Revolution and transport their local experiences within Egypt into the mediatized event of the Revolution once transnational audiences responded to these texts by tweeting or retweeting. These responses from audiences point to how Twitter's interface, similar to that of Facebook, enabled protestors to put their local experiences of the Revolution in conversation with the local experiences of audiences all over the world.

Another benefit of social media interfaces such as Facebook and Twitter for protestors, was that these platforms encouraged audiences to leave breadcrumb trails, or signs for others that they had read and (most often) responded affirmatively to a post. Within Facebook, breadcrumb trails primarily took the form of "liking" or commenting on a post. Within Twitter, breadcrumb trails most often took the form of reweeting. boyd, Golder and Lotan (2010) write that retweeting "contributes to a conversational ecology in which conversations are composed of a public interplay of voices that give rise to an emotional sense of shared conversational context" (p. 1), an emotional sense that Aday et al point out was critical to protestors' use of social media during the Revolution. While these responses do not reflect how many people may have actually read a post, they do give a glimpse of who was reading and what their responses were. Aside from signaling affirmative responses, "liking," commenting, and retweeting also lent visibility to the grievances that were catalogued on this page by administrators.

Protestors' catalogue of grievances across social media platforms such as Facebook and Twitter served several functions as the Revolution unfolded across social media. First, this was a strategy that increased the international visibility of the conditions in Egypt – a central element in gaining international support since Mubarak's regime had successfully inhibited the free circulation of this information. Secondly, this cataloguing of grievances operated as a rallying cry, reiterating for Egyptians just how much they had endured and for how long they had endured this. Ultimately, and most importantly, these catalogues of protestors' grievances unified their experiences of Mubarak's abuses. While each of the experiences catalogued was unique, these experiences were brought together into a cohesive

whole that would eventually lead to the mobilization of a Revolution. More immediately, however, these catalogues created a cohesive impression of the conditions under Mubarak that was taken up by transnational audiences as an invitation to respond to and participate in this cataloguing by participating in the *doing* of this mediatized event through recirculating activists' texts and helping to make these texts more visible by "liking," commenting, and retweeting.

As its name suggests, the Facebook page "We are All Khaled Said" was sparked by the brutal death of 28-year-old Khaled Said at the hands of Egyptian police. Allegedly in possession of a video that incriminated some police as participants in a corrupt drug deal, Said entered an Internet café with intentions of posting this video to the Internet when police dragged him out into the street and beat him to death. Drawing attention to Said's death within the broader context of Mubarak's abuses of power enabled protestors to expose individual atrocities while simultaneously highlighting the shared unity of these experiences. Here, "we are" becomes a way of both highlighting these individual experiences and presenting a unified front – one that was solidified through social media texts that brought together protestors and audiences around their shared dissent of Mubarak's regime.

As a form of digital memorialization of Khaled Said, this Facebook page started out cataloguing the grievances of administrators through updates about events related to Said's death. For example, the second post to the page provided a link to a webpage that had "[a]ll the latest details about Khaled Said torture [sic] in Egypt." The next day, administrators posted more updates reporting that a policeman convicted of "torture and sexual torture" who had recently been released from jail had been allowed to return to work after three years of imprisonment and that Khaled Said's friend, Tamer ElSayed who had been a witness to Said's brutal death, had also been beaten up by the police and was hospitalized. In December of 2011 we read that Said's trial had been postponed for a fifth time.

Status updates, however, were not the only way that administrators created catalogues of their grievances. They also did so visually through the creation of photo albums. For example, administrators posted the first album on July 20, 2011 – the day after the page was started. Titled "Police Brutality in Egypt," the album contains 46 graphic photos of police violence – one of which is of the battered face of Khaled Said after police had beaten him to death. Posted early in the page's history, this album only received 58 likes. However, among these likes are members of a transnational audience spanning from North Carolina to the Philippines and Canada among other places. Despite what may initially appear to be a failure to attract audiences around the world, this early album shows that this Facebook page was beginning to play a role in raising awareness about the conditions in Egypt as these audiences took up protestors' catalogues of grievances as invitations to respond to protestors' texts and, by doing so, continue a critical discursive flow that established and maintained the relationships that formed between protestors and their audiences around the world.

Six days after posting the photo album "Police Brutality in Egypt," administrators posted another album titled "Police Brutality against Menoufia University Students." This album features images from a student protest that had drawn the violent response of state police earlier that April. In their description of this album, administrators wrote:

The police has [sic] once again used thugs and criminal gangsters to help them attack the Egyptian public. What other police force in the world uses criminals in their attacks rather than arrest those criminals themselves? This has become a norm and quite common to take place in Egypt these days.

This album received more "likes" and "comments" than the previous album featuring images of police brutality that was posted only days earlier. For example, one reader from the UK responded to this catalogue of grievances writing on July 27, 2010: "It happens in England too, just not so obviously! Doesn't it happen in the US also? There are so many ways to abuse the law and the public!" The closer posts get to the January 25 protests, the more transnational audiences respond to protestors' cataloguing of grievances and affirm their online identities as activists in the Revolution. For example, on December 27, 2010 administrators posted an update alerting followers that Said's court case had been postponed a fifth time. Within hours, one member responded: "I can only hope that his good name is restored & justice in its truest sense prevails in 2011. Best wishes to all." In this exchange transnational audiences and protestors came together around the *doing* of the Revolution and gained online identities as activists as a result.

Less than a year after the Facebook page "We are All Khaled Said" was set up, Twitter became a prominent social media platform hosting protestors' texts. As many transnational audiences had become more familiar with the conditions in Egypt by the weeks and days leading up to the January 25 protests, Twitter became a useful tool for synthesizing the catalogue that had been started by protestors through online venues such as the "We are All Khaled Said" Facebook page. Given the restriction of tweets to 140 characters, Twitter was particularly effective for breaking down large pieces of information into small pieces of text that reiterated the urgency of the Revolution. Thus, while the earlier use of Facebook sought to inform audiences of the broader context of Egyptians' experiences under Mubarak, Twitter enabled protestors to issue urgent rallying cries during the weeks and days preceding the protests of January 25. The catalogues produced by protestors using the hashtag #Jan25 underscore both the immediacy of these conditions and the pressing need for a Revolution to end them.

On January 24, 2011, the day before the January 25 protests were scheduled to begin, protestor Mona Eltahawy included #Jan25 in a series of five tweets that, beyond cataloguing the abuses of the Mubarak regime, connect these abuses to the urgency of #Jan25. Her first tweet in this series, "#Egypt riot police&hired thugs r experts at sexually assaulting women protesters to discourage, shame. Fuck the security thugs #Jan25," underscored the long history of oppression and fear that the Mubarak regime used to control Egyptians and women in particular. Seven minutes later, Eltahawy connected this oppression to the long history of Western occupation that continued to plague Egypt even after the 1952 removal of the British: "Shame on #Mubarak & security thugs. #Egyptian women&men 2gether will liberate #Egypt, protest 2gether as did vs #British occupation #Jan25." Six minutes later, Eltahawy clarified the connection that she was making when she asked: "How did #Egypt police go from helping to end #British occupation to helping maintain #Mubarak occupation? 29 years of Emergency Law #Jan25." Although Eltahawy continued to tweet throughout the day, her next tweet that included #Jan25 came later that evening at 9:58pm: "In past 8 days at least 12 #Egyptians set themselves on fire out of desperation: unemployment, poverty, corruption. #Jan25 #Egypt protest." Twenty-seven minutes later she continued her catalogue of the conditions under 29 years of Emergency Law: "Imagine being 25: no job, no freedom, no money, same dictator all your life, robbing your country blind. What would you do? #Egypt #Jan25." This particular catalogue illustrates one tactic used by protestors to reach their transnational audiences. Here, Eltahawy's texts highlight the ways that protestors often used the relationships they formed with audiences around the world to confront Western audiences in particular with their complicity in the violence to which they were being asked to respond. For example, among the 11 retweets of Eltahawy's original tweet were followers from the United

States, Canada, and Northern Europe. These catalogues of protestors' grievances provide glimpses of how transnational audiences responded to these texts by recirculating them and increasing their visibility. As audiences in Egypt and around the world took up these invitations and expressed their responses though liking, commenting, and retweeting, powerful relationships formed from which each gained online identities as activists in the Revolution.

Assertions of Lived Bodies of Activism

The final step of this analysis looks at how protestors engaged in the *doing* of the Revolution by creating texts that asserted the experiences of their lived, protesting bodies across the streets of Egypt. This final discursive strategy that I will examine highlights the embodied connections between the voices through which protestors invited audiences around the world to participate in the Revolution and the events of the Revolution itself. Protestors made these embodied connections through texts that highlighted their physical experiences of violence under Mubarak's regime by vividly representing these experiences across social media platforms such as Facebook and Twitter. This reassertion of protestors' lived, protesting bodies served two purposes. First, these digital representations of protestors' local embodied experiences reiterated for transnational audiences the ways in which their activities as protestors were not limited to social media. Instead, the work of protestors online, as mentioned earlier by @alya1989262, worked in tandem with their other local, offline efforts as protestors. Second, these digital representations of abuse underscored the constant threat of violence experienced by protestors as they took to the streets of Egypt. As protestors asserted their physical experiences of Mubarak's rule, audiences who encountered the protests online often responded by establishing their own protesting bodies. A primary way that they did so was through the numerous solidarity protests that were held leading up to and in connection with the January 25 protests. Like activists protesting in the streets of Egypt, activists protesting around the world depicted these protests through texts online as a means of maintaining their relationships with protestors in Egypt and their mutual online identities as activists in the Revolution.

Underscoring the physical violence inflicted by Mubarak, the first profile image for the Facebook page "We are All Khaled Said" was a portrait of Said taken before he was beaten to death by the police. This image functioned as a reminder to audiences of the disfigurement that Said experienced at the hands of authorities. In this image, Said directly faces viewers with a slight smile and wears a simple gray hooded sweatshirt that would become iconic, remediated into satirical cartoons, signs held by protestors in the streets of Cairo, and even a painting that was done on two pieces of the Berlin wall. His casual gray sweatshirt with a white t-shirt under it and his clean-shaven face highlight how young Said looked when he died at just 28 years old. This image of youth presents a powerful juxtaposition to the event that is commemorated by this Facebook page: Said's brutal death at the hands of Egyptian police. Although the image of Said's battered face was never made the profile picture for this Facebook page, this image was posted both as a status update by page administrators and within the photo album "Police Brutality in Egypt." Both posted on July 20, 2010, these two images in conjunction with the profile image suggesting Said's hopeful youthfulness powerfully underscore the physical brutality that was endured by Egyptian citizens living under Mubarak's rule and the embodied experiences of violence that linked protestors' catalogue of grievances with their online voices of dissent.

Another way that administrators of the Facebook page "We are All Khaled Said" reiterated their lived experiences of physical violence under Mubarak was through a variety of posts that went beyond alerting audiences to the violence that had occurred and, instead, provided transnational audiences with details and graphic images of this violence. For example, of the 46 images in the photo album "Police Brutality in Egypt," over half of these images show bodies that were either bleeding and disfigured or bodies that were being beaten by the police. Nearly six months after this album was posted, one viewer responded to the images writing: "[…] can't believe what i [sic] see we should be all one and not against each other…" The day after page administrators posted the image of Said's battered face, administrators posted "breaking news" that Said's friend, Tamer ElSayed, "was beaten by the witnesses that Police used to say that Khaled swallowed Marijuana!" Although administrators do not include an image of ElSayed with this post, they do tell us that he was hospitalized. Administrators of the page also underscore the immediacy of this violence within their lived experiences by posting about the threats of violence they had received as a result of their work: "Our team members have received death threats and torture threats from people saying they are members of the Egyptian Police forces."

While these posts asserting suffering bodies reflect an element of protestors' *doing* of the Revolution, they implicitly invite responses from audiences as online protestors that would continue this work. An example of audiences doing this came on July 21, 2010 when page administrators posted: "Press Release: 'We are All Khaled Said' facebook page calls for a worldwide silent stand in solidarity with torture victims in Egypt on Friday the 23rd July. Please join us from wherever you are. Please like." Posted on only the third day of the page's existence, this post received 26 likes. At the behest of what seems to be another protestor, administrators created a Facebook "Event" "in order to have an organized calendar of protests." When administrators did this they put the following as the location of the event: "Individuals and groups in their home towns any where in the world if they live outside Egypt. Cairo, Alexandria and every where in Egypt if you live in Egypt [sic]."

Among those who responded that they would attend were individuals from North Carolina, Arkansas, Texas, Jordan, Cardiff, and Jakarta.

Audience responses to this invitation to hold Silent Stands around the world illustrate the ways in which these transnational audiences built relationships with protestors by developing their own protesting bodies and then digitally representing these bodies online. As digital representations of these bodies were passed on to page administrators, they posted images such as one of two men from Sydney, Australia, doing their silent stand and holding computer printouts of the profile picture discussed above with the text "28 years-old Khaled Said was bashed to death by Egyptian Police." Other images of these Silent Stands were posted in an album titled "International Support and Supporters" that features images of individuals taking silent stands in Newcastle, UK; Budapest, Hungary; Colorado, US; the River Itchen, UK; and Michigan, US.

The imagery of brutalized bodies continued to dominate the Facebook page "We are All Khaled Said" during the months and weeks leading up to the January 25 protests. For example, on July 27, 2010 administrators posted: "Khaled Said's case is postponed till 25th of September! Peaceful protestors got beaten up by Security forces. Photos and Videos are going to be published today!" Later that day, administrators posted an image of a man laying facedown on the pavement as police stood by and watched while he was stomped. This image was accompanied by text reading: "Even if he was a serial killer he doesn't deserve that treatment let alone a law abiding citizen participating in a peaceful demonstration like in this case." As transnational audiences responded to these accounts of protestors' embodied experiences of violence under Mubarak, many began to participate in the *doing* of the Revolution and gained online identities as activists in the Revolution.

While the physical experiences of police brutality and the solidarity protests that were taken up by audiences were advertised across Facebook during the months preceding the protests of January 25, 2011, many protestors turned to Twitter as a means of advertising solidarity protests in coordination with these protests. The popularity of the hashtag #Jan25 illustrates the potential it had to facilitate powerful relationships between protestors and transnational audiences – a potential that protestors were eager to take advantage of as many, like @Gsquare86, used the hashtag to both get word out about the protests beyond local audiences in Egypt and to mobilize the bodies of both local and global audiences. On January 22, 2011, she tweeted: "It doesn't matter where you go on #jan25, just be the street!!!" Mona Eltahawy also gestured toward the mobilization of bodies when she quoted @Elshaheed in a tweet posted on January 24, 2011: "Trending on #Twitter isn't impt. It's more impt to trend on the streets! says @Elshaheed, one of the organizers of #Jan25 #Egypt protests."

Powerful manifestations of this activity by transnational audiences, solidarity protests that coincided with January 25, 2011 were held around the world. While the Silent Stand Facebook event that was posted in July of 2010 had only 317 guests, an event that was crossposted on both the Twitter hashtag #Jan25 and the "We are All Khaled Said" Facebook page for January 28, 2011 reported over 5,000 people "in attendance." Although these numbers are inevitably inaccurate, they reflect a developing trend of solidarity protests that became increasingly visible during the months leading up to the January 25th protests as well as audiences' awareness of the physical lived reality of protestors' experiences of violence under Mubarak and the violence they were about to endure as they sought to overthrow him.

Many of the solidarity protests that were advertised on Twitter during the days leading up to the #Jan25 protests were held within the Western world. For example, @Cer tweeted "A protest in Toronto, Canada on #Jan25 in solidarity with Egyptians protests (via @FarahFilasteen)." Egyptian protestor Mona Eltahawy who was in

New York City during the January 25 protests was among the most active voices online advertising these solidarity protests. She tweeted: "On #jan25, #Egyptians in #NYC will protest in front of Office of #Egypt's Permanent Rep. to #UN in solidarity w Egypt nationwide protests." Later she posted: "Any #Egyptians in #Chicago who will/want to rally on #Jan25? Let @litfreak know." And finally: "#Egyptians in #NYC, #Jan25 rally 1pm-2pm in front of #Egypt Permanent Mission to UN, 44th St. between 1st and 2nd Ave. See you there!" As transnational audiences showed up to these protests and circulated visual texts that reflected their experiences, they reiterated both their relationships with protestors in the streets of Egypt and their online identities as activists in the Revolution.

Emergent Identities

As we read these texts and think back to early invitations by the administrators of the Facebook page "We are All Khaled Said," we are struck by the evolution from invitations to join a Facebook page in July 2010 to invitations to join solidarity protests in January 2011. This shift illustrates the ways in which many transnational audiences responded to protestors' texts by continuing the discursive flows that were initiated by these texts and entering into assemblages of dissent with protestors. Through this process of initiating and maintaining these relationships between transnational audiences and protestors in the streets of Egypt, both engaged in the *doing* of building a mediatized event of the Revolution in response to the abuses of the Mubarak regime. As a consequence of this *doing* and the assemblages that formed as a result, both protestors and their transnational audiences developed online identities as activists in the transnational mediatized event of the Egyptian Revolution that were woven through both the physical and digital realities of activists' lives.

These emergent online identities as activists authorized the *doing* of protestors and their audiences. For example, protestors' emergent online identities as activists authorized their dissent in the context of an audience around the world that was watching the Revolution unfold from a distance. Audiences' responses to protestors' online texts lent public authorization to their grievances as warranting the Revolution they called for. Similarly, the emergent identities of transnational audiences as activists in the mediatized event of the Revolution authorized their responses to protestors' texts through "liking," commenting, retweeting, and creating new texts of their own. This emergent identity authorized these responses as part of the *doing* of this mediatized event by endorsing the relationships that audiences entered into with protestors as foundational to assemblages of dissent within the mediatized event of the Revolution. While these assemblages of dissent resulted in the capacities of each as activists, these assemblages were also key elements in the broader, transnational mediatized event that brought the Revolution global visibility, an event that audiences helped to create through the responses to protestors' texts that I have examined here.

Emerging from the intertextuality of the local and global, the online identities of activists in the Egyptian Revolution also (re)connected them to both global spheres of action such as the mediatized event of the Revolution as well as local spheres of action that formed on the streets of Egypt and other cities around the world. Although dependent on the assemblages of dissent from which they emerged, these online identities were never isolated from the lived experiences of protestors and their audiences around the world. We began to see this as many of the texts discussed in this chapter also served as communications between activists participating in the Revolution on the streets of Egypt as well as activists engaging in other local acts of transnational protest through the solidarity protests and silent stands that took place around the world.

FUTURE RESEARCH DIRECTIONS

While this chapter has taken an optimistic view of the relationships that formed between protestors and their audiences during the Egyptian Revolution, future research directions should include more critical perspectives of this phenomenon. For example, while I have focused on three discursive formations in particular, questions remain about what other strategies – both discursive and nondiscursive – were working alongside the three that I have indentified here. For example, what other nondiscursive "structure generating processes" contributed to the relationships that formed between protestors and audiences around the world such as race, class, gender, and nationality? Another area of research to be taken up addresses what other assemblages formed as a result of these flows and the identities that emerged from them. For example, what identities emerge when audiences do not respond to protestors' texts or respond in ways other than those that I have discussed here? What identities emerge in the case of audiences' voyerism or perhaps their spectatorship of images of death and violence that have also circulated from the Revolution? Third, while this chapter highlights the potential of these digital texts, what are the limitations of this form of activism?

Just over two years after the removal of Hosni Mubarak, his successor Mohamed Morsi was also removed from power. This subsequent wave of protests revealed a number of fractures among the seemingly once unified force of protestors seeking the removal of Mubarak and leaves us asking, has the solidarity of the earlier movement been shattered? And, if it has, what has this meant for the transnational audience that came out in support of the Revolution in 2011? These events raise questions not only about the limits of social media in terms of garnering meaningful support for a movement such as the Egyptian Revolution of 2011, but also the limits of social media as a means of exploring nuance in contexts such as the one that unfolded in Egypt following the removal of Mohamed Morsi.

Finally, in his discussion of the new comparatist approach of American Studies, John Rowe has written "different cultures are transformed by their contact and interaction with each other" (Rowe, 2002, p. 25). Assemblage theory offers a powerful tool to begin to understand the transformative power of interactions between cultures such as we saw during the Egyptian Revolution of 2011. The emergent online identities that have been explored in this chapter cannot be relegated to the digital and treated as existing separately from the historically rooted political, social, and economic dynamics that inform the lived experiences of transnational audiences and protestors in the Revolution. Rather, we must also turn to look at the ways in which these identities potentially transformed the cultural identities of both protestors and their transnational audiences. We are reminded of this when Jasbir Puar describes assemblages "as a series of dispersed but mutually implicated and messy networks" (Conclusion). It is to this messiness that we must continue to attend. While here I have addressed one thread of this messiness in the emergent online identities of protestors and their audiences, this is only one small glimpse at a broader picture of "interwoven forces that merge and dissipate time, space, and body against linearity, coherency, and permanency" and that give rise to the emergent and overlapping identities of protestors and their audiences.

CONCLUSION

As protestors turned to social media platforms such as Twitter and Facebook during the Egyptian Revolution of 2011 to invite transnational audiences to join the Facebook page "We are All Khaled Said" or follow the hashtag #Jan25, catalogue their grievances, and assert their lived experiences of violence, they engaged in the *doing* of a transnational mediatized event that expanded the local event of the Egyptian Revolution into homes and coffee shops around the world. Initiating these discursive flows, protestors reached out to a transnational audience that took up these texts as invitations to also participate in the *doing* of Revolution. As these audiences did so by "liking," commenting, retweeting, and creating new digital texts of their own, they entered into assemblages of dissent with protestors. It was through these assemblages that protestors and their audiences gained online identities as activists in the Revolution.

REFERENCES

Aday, S., Farrell, H., Lynch, M., Sides, J., Kelly, J., & Zuckerman, E. (2010). *Blogs and bullets: New media in contentious politics.* Retrieved from http://www.usip.org/files/resources/pw65.pdf

Agha, A., & Naveen, N. (2011, Jul 12). *Social media activist Mohamed Ibrahim talks to gawaahi. com.* Retrieved from http://www.youtube.com/watch?v=w4Rh497KJ4c

Arola, K. (2010). The design of web 2.0: The rise of the template, the fall of design. *Computers and Composition, 27*, 4–14. doi:10.1016/j.compcom.2009.11.004

Biel, E. (n.d.). The guerilla cartoonist of Rio. *The Cairo Review of Global Affairs.* Retrieved from http://www.aucegypt.edu/gapp/cairoreview/pages/articleDetails.aspx?aid=157#

boyd, d., Golder, & Lotan. (2010). *Tweet, tweet, retweet: Conversational aspects of retweeting on twitter.* Retrieved from http://www.danah.org/papers/TweetTweetRetweet.pdf

Cole, J. (2011, February 7). *Christians, Muslims one hand in Egypt's youth revolution.* [web log post]. Retrieved from http://www.juancole.com/2011/02/christians-muslims-one-hand-in-egypts-youth-revolution.html

Conover, M., Ratkiewicz, J., Francisco, M., Goncalves, B., Flammini, A., et al. (2011). Political polarization on twitter. In *Proceedings of the 5th Intl. Conference on Weblogs and Social Media.* AAAI. Retrieved from http://www.aaai.org/ocs/index.php/ICWSM/ICWSM11/paper/download/2847/3275

Costanza-Chock, S. (2003). Mapping the repertoire of electronic contention. In A. Opel, & D. Pompper (Eds.), *Representing resistance* (pp. 173–191). Westport, CT: Praeger Publishers.

Cottle, S., & Lester, L. (2011). *Transnational protests and the media.* New York, NY: Peter Lang.

Crovitz, L. G. (2011, February 14). Egypt's revolution by social media: Facebook and twitter let the people keep ahead of the regime. *The Wallstreet Journal.* Retrieved from http://online.wsj.com/article/SB10001424052748703786804576137980252177072.html

DeLanda, M. (1997). *A thousand years of nonlinear history.* Brooklyn, NY: Zone Books.

DeLanda, M. (2006). *New philosophy of society: Assemblage theory and social complexity.* Retrieved from www.amazon.com

@ev and @biz. (2011, Feb 16). #Jan25: One tweet, one story. [blog post]. *Hope140.* Retrieved from http://hope140.org/blog/?p=127

Gerbaudo, P. (2012). *Tweets and the streets: Social media and contemporary activism.* New York, NY: Pluto.

Ghonim, W. (2012). *Revolution 2.0*. Retrieved from www.amazon.com

Gustin, S. (2011, February 11). Social media sparked, accelerated Egypt's revolutionary fire. *Wired*. Retrieved from http://www.wired.com/business/2011/02/egypts-revolutionary-fire/

Hesford, W., & Schell, E. (2008). Introduction: Configurations of transnationality: Locating feminist rhetorics. *College English*, *70*(5), 461–470.

Hjarvard, S. (2008). The mediatization of society. *Nordicom Review*, *29*, 105–134.

Howard, M. (2011). *Transnationalism and society*. Jefferson, NC: McFarland and Company, Inc.

Kozlowski, L. (2011, February 1). *Egypt: Capturing voices with Twitter and a cellphone*. [web log post]. Retrieved from http://latimesblogs.latimes.com/babylonbeyond/2011/02/egypt-twitter-voices-jan25-cell-phones-egyptians.html

Mackey, R. (2011, January 27). *Video chat interview with Gigi Ibrahim*. Retrieved from http://thelede.blogs.nytimes.com/2011/01/27/interview-with-an-egyptian-blogger/

Madlena, C. (2011, July 7). Telecomix: Tech support for the Arab spring. *The Gaurdian*. Retrieved from http://www.theguardian.com/technology/2011/jul/07/telecomix-arab-spring

Massey, D. (2005). *For space*. Los Angeles, CA: Sage.

Puar, J. K. (2007). *Terrorist assemblages: Homonationalism in queer times*. Durham, NC: Duke UP. doi:10.1215/9780822390442

Raoof, R. (2011, May 4). *About the media tent in Tahrir Square*. Retrieved from http://ebfhr.blogspot.com/2011/05/media-tent-in-tahrir-square.html

Rowe, J. C. (2002). *The new American studies*. Minneapolis, MN: University of Minnesota Press.

Schillinger, R. (2011, October 20). *Social media and the Arab spring: What have I learned?* [Blog Post]. Retrieved from http://www.huffingtonpost.com/raymond-schillinger/arab-spring-social-media_b_970165.html

Shirky, C. (2010). *Cognitive surplus: How technology makes consumers into collaborators*. New York: Penguin.

Tarrow, S. (2009). *The new transnational activism*. New York: Cambridge UP.

Tomlinson, J. (1999). *Globalization and culture*. Chicago, IL: University of Chicago Press.

Vertovec, S. (1999). Transnationalism and identity. *Journal of Ethnic and Migration Studies*, *27*(4), 573–582. doi:10.1080/13691830120090386

Wilson, C., & Dunn, A. (2011). Digital media in the Egyptian revolution: Descriptive analyses from the Tahrir data set. *International Journal of Communication*, *5*, 1248–1272.

ADDITIONAL READING

Arola, K., & Wysocki, A. F. (Eds.). (2012) composing(media)=composing(embodiment). Logan, UT: Utah State University Press.

Barnes, S., & Bohringer, M. (2011). Modeling use and continuance behavior in microblogging services. *Journal of Computer Information Systems*, *51*(4), 1–10.

Berry, P., Hawisher, G., & Selfe, C. (Eds.). (2012). *Transnational literate lives in digital times*. Logan, Utah: Computers and Composition Digital P/Utah State UP.

Cockburn, A., St. Clair, J., & Sekula, A. (2000). *5 days that shook the world*. New York: Verso.

Discursive Flows of Energy. The discursive "structure generating processes" (DeLanda, 1997, p. 26) that were initiated by protestors' creation of a variety of discursive texts to garner the support of transnational audiences for the Egyptian Revolution of 2011.

Drucker, J. (2003). Visual Studies. *Afterimage*, *31*(1), 4–5.

Drucker, J. (2011). Humanities approaches to interface theory. *Culture Machine 12,* 1-20. Retrieved from: http://www.culturemachine.net.

Dunlap, J., & Lowenthal, P. (2009). Tweeting the night away. [Available from ProQuest.]. *Journal of Information Systems Education*, *20*(2), 129–135.

Dyan, D., & Kataz, E. (1992). *Media events: The live broadcasting of history*. Cambridge, MA: Harvard UP.

Farman, J. (2011). *Mobile interface theory: Embodied space and locative media*. New York, NY: Routledge.

Greer, C., & Ferguson, D. (2011). Following local television news personalities on twitter. *Electronic News 5 (145)*, 145-157. Available from http://www.sagepub.com/.

Grewal, I., & Kaplan, C. (2001). Global identities: Theorizing transnational studies of sexuality. *Glq*, *7*(4), 663–679. Available from http://muse.jhu.edu/ doi:10.1215/10642684-7-4-663

Hargittai, E., & Litt, E. (2011). The tweet smell of celebrity success. *New Media & Society*, *13*(824), 824–842. Available from http://www.sagepub.com/ doi:10.1177/1461444811405805

Hesford, W. (2004). Documenting violations: Rhetorical witnessing and the spectacle of distant suffering. *Biography*, *1*(27), 104–144. Available from http://muse.jhu.edu/ doi:10.1353/bio.2004.0034

Hesford, W. (2006). Global turns and cautions in rhetoric and composition studies. [Web]. *PMLA*, *121*(3), 787–801. Available from http://www.jstor.org/ doi:10.1632/003081206X142887

Hesford, W. (2010). Cosmopolitanism and geopolitics of feminist rhetoric. In E. Schell and K.J. Rawson, Rhetorica in motion [Kindle file] (ch. 3). Pittsburgh, PA: University of Pittsburg Press. Available from amazon.com.

Hesford, W. (2011). *Spectacular rhetorics*. Durham, NC: Duke UP.

Hesford, W., & Kozol, W. (Eds.). (2005). *Just advocacy?: Women's human rights, transnational feminisms, and the politics of representation*. New Brunswick, NJ: Rutgers UP.

Honeycutt, C., & Herring, S. (2009). Beyond microblogging: Conversation and collaboration via twitter. Proceedings of the Forty-Second Hawai'i International Conference on System Sciences.

Java, A., Finin, T., Song, X., & Tseng, B. (2007). Why we twitter: Understanding microblogging usage and communities. Proceedings of the Joint 9th WEBKDD and 1st SNA-KDD Workshop. Published by the University of Maryland.

Leiber, A. (2010). A virtual veibershul: Blogging and the blurring of public and private among orthodox Jewish women. [Available from JSTOR.]. *College English*, *72*(6), 621–637.

Nunns, Alex & Idle, N. (2011). *Tweets from Tahrir*. New York, NY: OR Books.

Queen, M. (2008). Transnational feminist rhetorics in a digital world. *College English*, *70*(5), 471–489. Available from http://www.jstor.org/

Wall, M., & Zahed, S. (2011). 'I'll be Waiting for You Guys': A YouTube Call to Action in the Egyptian Revolution. [Retrieved from ijoc.org.]. *International Journal of Communication*, 5, 1333–1343.

KEY TERMS AND DEFINITIONS

Arab Spring: Defined by Raymond Schillinger (2011) as "a rising spirit of protest [that] has since spread like wildfire across the Middle East, communicated primarily through the channels of social media."

Assemblages of Dissent: The generative relationships that developed from interactions between protestors and audiences as a result of the discursive flows of energy manifesting both parties' dissent of the Mubarak regime and their desire for revolution.

Emergent Capacities: Defined by Manuel DeLanda (2006) as "what [social entities] are capable of doing when they interact with other social entities" (Introduction).

Emergent Identities: Products of the assemblages of dissent that formed between protestors and their transnational audiences as a result of their interactions across the social media platforms of Twitter and Facebook in the transnational mediatized event of the Egyptian Revolution of 2011.

Transnationalism: A phenomenon that is dependent on the very borders that it crosses, dissolves, and resurrects through what Steven Vertovec describes as "a planet-spanning yet common – however virtual – arena of activity." Central to this chapter's discussion of this phenomenon has been the role of media through which social movements are transacted and the ways in which media, such as social media, facilitate what Libby Lester and Simon Cottle refer to as both an "ethico-political imaginary" as well as "collective political action" within a shared arena of activity that is realized across multiple local contexts.

Chapter 3
The Emergence of Politicized Collective Identity in Online News Commentaries as a Form of Social Capital

Nahla Nadeem
Cairo University, Egypt

ABSTRACT

This chapter explores how online news commentaries as a platform for social interaction can be considered a form of social capital that later led to the Arab Spring Revolutions. In the study, social capital is conceptualized as consisting of two linguistically measurable variables: a) the emergence of the posters' politicized collective identity (Simon & Klandermans, 2001; Simon, 2004) that emerges in the data through the foregrounding of certain shared aspects of the posters' identity, mainly their Arab nationality; and b) the collaborative performance of face attacks and solidarity acts in the posting content. The data used are responses written to an article posted on the Al Jazeera Website describing the aftermath of the tragic suicide of the Tunisian Bouazizi. Drawing on contemporary theories of sociolinguistics, pragmatics, and social identity, the study provides empirical evidence that such online communication should be considered a social and political capital that can foster social and political activism.

DOI: 10.4018/978-1-4666-5150-0.ch003

INTRODUCTION

Online interaction on Al-Jazeera Website played a prominent role before, during and after the Tunisian Revolution. Since Arab governments exercise control over all forms of traditional media, (e.g. Al-Jazeera TV. Channel was banned in Tunisia at the time the commentaries were posted), the Website gives Arabs access to updated news about the political events as they occur and a chance to post their views and commentaries on the news stories and articles published. The engagement in an online interaction that fosters the collective identity of Arab participants (Simon & Klandermans, 2001) and the "relative" freedom of expression experienced in those responses particularly in making attacks against Arab governments and/or showing solidarity to other Arabs later led to a number of revolutions in the Arab World (AW) in what is known as the Arab Spring. Howard and Hussain (2013) state:

Social protests in the Arab World have spread across North Africa and the Middle East, largely because digital media allowed communities to realize that they shared grievances and because they nurtured transportable strategies for mobilizing against dictators. (p. 3)

Such online social interaction through the Al-Jazeera Website can be seen as a source of social and political capital since it offers empirical examples of how the posters' collective display of their identity and the face attacks (insults, curses, blame and accusations, henceforth, FAs)[1] and/or acts of solidarity (SAs) they perform can tie in with the emergence of what is called a politicized collective identity (PCI) that later led to social and political activism. The main aim of the present study is to explore how the emergence of the PCI in this online setting represents the enactment of social capital and gives empirical evidence of how this form of social capital materializes in the language used among the interactants. It is

believed that such an analysis can contribute to the existing body of knowledge in social capital, social identity theories and sociolinguistics as it will contribute to a better understanding of the sociolinguistic aspects of social capital and its role in social and political activism.

In what follows, I will give a brief summary of an article posted on Al Jazeera Website on which the posters comment and a brief description of the computer-mediated data used in the analysis. Then, the method of analysis will be described and the research questions stated. Section II will briefly review the sociolinguistic aspects of social capital through making links between the emergence of the posters' PCI and its linguistic manifestations through the identity signals picked and the speech acts[2] performed. Section III will present the analysis where samples of identity markers along with tokens of FAs and SAs are analyzed. The analysis will then be followed by a discussion of online interaction as a form of social capital and conclusions will be drawn.

A Brief Note on the Article and the Data Used

The online article that is the focus of this study, "Tunisia Attacks Al-Jazeera and the Protests Expand all over the Country" was written after the suicide of the Tunisian Bouazizi, which was the initial spark that led to the Tunisian Revolution[3]. Bouazizi was an unemployed university graduate who was working as a street vendor. He set himself on fire in December 2010, in protest of the confiscation of his wares and the harassment and humiliation that he suffered at the hands of a municipal official and her aides. In the article, the Tunisian parliament and other political parties attack the Al- Jazeera channel for broadcasting YouTube videos of demonstrations and riots in the Tunisian town of Sidi Bouzid- Bouazizi's hometown- where crowds were protesting against unemployment, economic conditions and political corruption. The political parties and opposition describe the Al- Jazeera's TV news coverage of the protests as interference in the Tunisian internal affairs and the article samples the mixed opinions towards the Al-Jazeera's news coverage of the protests that spread in Tunisia at the time.

At the end of the published article, a commentary option is located through which the readers can post their responses. The article was on top of the list of "the most commented upon" as it received 245 commentaries on the same day of its publication. These computer- mediated commentaries are all asynchronous messages that will serve as a corpus of data for this study. They mainly represent the posters' opinion on the article or a related issue; mainly, Al-Jazeera's role in the region, the state of political, economic and social corruption in the AW, the suicide incident or the mass protests in Tunisia. The commentaries themselves are updated and increase in number as the editor receives them. The whole data set was retrieved in one day since many of the published articles and commentaries undergo constant change and update depending on the top news stories. The article was published just before the Tunisian Revolution broke out as a clear indication of how digital media played a central role in carrying inspiring stories of protest across the AW and in creating a public sphere for the oppressed people to share their grievances and wish for change.

Judging by the content of the postings, names and nicknames, the commentaries all appear to have been written by Arabs from several Arab countries. The headings and content suggest a mixture of Arab nationalities; Arab immigrants, men and women (see Table 1 representing different nationalities of the posters). They vary in length (from one line to a maximum of five lines) and are mostly written in Modern Standard Arabic (MSA) which facilitates communication among the Arab posters (except for few instances of dialectal Arabic especially Egyptian and Tunisian). Those who chose to respond to this article did so with mixed identity representations and a mixture of face attacks (Brown & Levinson, 1987) and solidarity

Table 1. The ratio of the different nationalities of posters

Nationalities	Number	Percentage
Tunisian	71	28.98%
Unknown	39	15.92%
Tunisian/ Immigrant	23	9.39%
Immigrant	23	9.39%
Egyptian	21	8.57%
Algerian	18	7.35%
Libyan	13	5.31%
Morrocan	12	4.90%
Yemani	9	3.67%
Saudi	8	3.27%
Sudanese	2	0.82%
Lebanese	2	0.82%
Jordanian	1	0.41%
France	1	0.41%
Syrian	1	0.41%
Palestinian	1	0.41%

acts as shown in the speech acts used in the segments analyzed and the lexical choices made by the contributors. For this reason, their responses are considered appropriate data for analyzing the emergence of the posters' PCI and its linguistic manifestations as a form of social capital.

METHOD OF ANALYSIS AND RESEARCH QUESTIONS

The core question in this study is how social capital is linguistically manifested in the emergence of the posters' PCI and the FAs and SAs performed in those online postings. The conceptualization of social capital and the analytical framework adopted in this study are based on the insights of several fields of linguistic study; namely, pragmatics studies of politeness, discourse analysis besides work on discursive identity in social psychology. The researcher adopts a mixture of quantitative and qualitative methods: to confirm the PCI hypothesis, a quantitative survey of the identity markers used by the posters is offered; mainly percentages of the different nationalities represented in the data, percentages of the FAs and SAs performed and their target entities besides the ratio of the Tunisians and non- Tunisians making the attacks against the Tunisian government and opposition. To provide further evidence of the emergence of the posters' PCI, excerpts of the data are qualitatively analyzed using a speech act and a discourse analysis approach following Brown and Levinson's work (1987) and Leech's maxims of politeness (1983). By examining numerous segments of those online commentaries, the analysis explores how the posters' performance of certain speech acts and their lexical choices work as discursive resources to develop this PCI- e.g. insults, dispraise, disagreements, accusations of theft and looting are used as FAs to out-group entities (mainly Arab governments, heads of states and opposition) while using agreement, greetings, prayers, praise as SAs to in-group entities (mainly Tunisian rebels and other oppressed Arabs across the AW). It is argued that these linguistic behaviors represent a form of social capital. Since the postings are all in MSA, translations of the examples cited are done by the researcher and added underneath the cited commentary. The paper mainly attempts to answer the following questions:

1. What linguistic evidence is there for the emergence of the posters' PCI in the data?
2. How can the emergence of the posters' PCI be considered a form of social capital?

To answer the main research questions, the researcher has to examine the following sub-questions:

3. How do the commenters discursively construct and display their identity i.e. what are the identity markers selected and foregrounded in the data?

4. How can the collaborative performance of face attacks and solidarity acts provide further evidence of the emergence of the posters' PCI?

THEORETICAL FRAMEWORK: SOCIAL CAPITAL AND POLITICIZED COLLECTIVE IDENTITY

Social capital, in its simplest form, is social interaction that has productive benefits. The variety of definitions identified in the literature stem from the highly context specific nature of social capital and the complexity of its conceptualization and operationalization. The definition adopted in the present study is that social capital refers to the value of social networks in bonding similar people and bridging between diverse people, with norms of reciprocity (Dekker & Uslaner, 2001; Uslaner, 2001). "Its effects flow from the information, influence, and solidarity it makes available to the actor" (Adler & Kwon, 2002, p. 23). Dekker and Uslaner (2001) posit that social capital is fundamentally about how people interact with each other in a way that enables and encourages mutually advantageous social cooperation. If online news commentaries on the Al-Jazeera Website are to be considered a form of social capital, it is worth investigating how it linguistically operates through examining the way the posters choose to reveal their identity, who they considered their allies or their enemies and how this relates to the emergence of a PCI online.

According to Goffman (1967), identity construction is not a static phenomenon but it arises in the flow of events in the social encounter. It involves self- presentation in encounters: how interactants pick the relevant self-aspects to be displayed and foregrounded in a particular social interaction. Latest theories of social psychology maintain that though people may differ in the degree to which they differentiate their various attributes; different self- representations appear in different contexts and social settings. A useful model in this respect is Simon's (2004) Self-Aspect Model of Identity. His theoretical framework distinguishes between individual and collective (social) identities. According to his framework, individual identity results "whenever self-interpretation is based on a more comprehensive set or configuration of different, non-redundant self-aspects," and collective identity results "whenever self-interpretation is based primarily on a single self-aspect that one shares with other, but not all other, people in the relevant social context," (pp. 49-50).

The model (2004) proposes that a person's self-concept comprises beliefs about that person's own attributes or self-characteristics. These can be varied and include elements such as: personality traits (e.g. sociable), abilities (e.g. athletic), physical features (e.g. curly hair, slim), behavioral characteristics (e.g. usually gets up early), ideologies (feminist, democrat), social roles (e.g. project manager), language affiliation(s) (e.g. English, Chinese) and group memberships (e.g. female, academic). The model offers insights into the discursive display of identity in social interaction. When social (collective) identity becomes salient in certain contexts or culture, "the similarity or interchangeability of oneself with other people sharing the same self-aspect moves into the psychological foreground," while other self-aspects become irrelevant; as a consequence "perceived ingroup homogeneity" is promoted (Simon, 2004, p. 49). The point made here about the foregrounding of a particular shared self aspect is similar to Schlenker and Ponatri's argument that while attributes of an individual's identity always remain active, they may be placed either in the background or in the foreground. In other words, what theories of social psychology seem to suggest is that picking an identity signal (whether individual or shared) in a particular social context is not haphazard since it shows how the interactant is integrating himself/ herself into the immediate social milieu.

According to Simon (2004), identity construction has five main functions and there are various social psychological factors that determine the foregrounding of specific identity signals in an interactional context. The five functions, which Simon (2004) associates with both individual and collective identity, manifest themselves in (1) validating the place of individuals in a given community, (2) defining and reinforcing their distinctiveness i.e. what they have in common and their distinctiveness from those other social places (or people) to which one does not belong, (3) acquiring their respect, (4) achieving a view of their social world from which they can derive a meaningful understanding of the world and their place in it; and (5) allowing them to recognize themselves as important social agents. While individual identity traits foster one's distinctiveness, "collective identity signals that one is not alone but can count on the social support and solidarity of other in-group members so that, as a group, one is a much more efficacious social agent ("Together we are strong")" (Simon & Klandermans, 2001, p. 321). It can be seen as a source of social capital since it helps establish their membership as a "group" who like each other, thereby promoting mutual respect, and support. This membership is not shared or enjoyed by those who they consider as "out-group" members.

A sub-type of collective identity is what Simon & Klandermans (2001) call "politicized collective identity" or PCI. They note that when people become aware of shared grievances, and understand that these grievances can be addressed by influencing other members of society, they will come to develop a form of identity that incorporates explicit motivations to engage in a struggle for power. In such a case, they often present themselves as being representative or aligned with dominant, positively valued social categories such as "nations." Simon and Klandermans (2001) claim that PCI might lead unprivileged groups of people to perform social actions such as protesting or revolting against what they see as an oppressive power or authority. In this case, their communication and later action depends on this collective identity as a form of social capital through which they attain power as an "in-group." In Spencer-Oatey's (2007) work on face and identity, she notes that speakers' sense of who they are (i.e. their identity) can influence how they behave linguistically, which implies that some aspects of identity that may not always be actively present can be activated and made central in interactional situations.

Thus, collective identity as group affiliation (i.e. which aspect of identity one shares with other interactants in a given context) can certainly be considered a source of social capital as it relates to the negotiation of relationships with others. It ties in with who those participants are (i.e. which identity signals they pick during the online interaction) and who they regard as "in-group" or "out-group" members. For example, the verbal strategies the posters use are largely explained and predicted through the identity representations they choose to single out in this particular online context. These identity markers relate to the commenters' politicized collective identity as Arabs (McGarty et al., 2009) and directly relate to the FAs and SAs performed in the data. So far, I have offered a review of the theoretical framework on which the analysis is based, in what follows, I shall give further linguistic evidence of how the posters' PCI emerged in the data.

LINGUISTIC MANIFESTATIONS OF THE POSTERS' PCI: DATA ANALYSIS AND DISCUSSION

In the data, the posters use a mixture of strategies to reveal their identity online. In most cases, identity is revealed through providing a name (whether first or full)/ a pseudonym, gender (reflected through the name), nationality/ country of residence and an 'intro' statement. In the case of anonymity, some use revealing pseudonyms such as. "آهات" "صوت الحق"- "voice of truth"- and "انسان"- "a cry of pain from a fellow- human being." Others also use introductory statements that

indicate the poster's standpoint on an issue and often predict the FAs and/or SAs used. Of all the identity markers picked by the posters, nationality is observed to be the most prominent in the data. It is explicitly stated next to the posters' names or pseudonyms and it functions as a key parameter in creating a "politicized collective identity" among the posters. In fact, most Arab nationalities are explicitly represented but the highest percentage is Tunisians 29.98% and Tunisian immigrants 9.39%- which is understood since the article itself is about events that happened in Tunisia (see Table 1). When the poster's nationality is not mentioned, the variety used is another key identity signal. Using MSA is an important signal of the posters' collective identity as it is the most widely used variety among educated Arabs especially if they want to communicate across country boundaries.

Generally speaking, identity construction in news commentaries certainly places less demand on the posters' revelation of their individual identity traits if compared to other forms of social media e.g. Facebook and Twitter. So, another device the posters use for identity construction is using introductory statements as headings for their posts. They are significant since they reveal the posters' ideological and political stand on various issues and therefore, can help identify the entities they consider their enemies or allies. The online context provides them with an interactional setting that enables them to express themselves freely, often anonymously, and share their views of the state of oppression across the AW and not just in Tunisia. In the statements below, stressing shared self –aspects mainly, being an Arab is highlighted and foregrounded since it gives the posters the opportunity to express shared grievances and collaboratively attack what they regard as forces of corruption. For example, the introductory statements below show the open attacks the posters make against the Tunisian government, opposition, other Arab regimes and the Al-Jazeera. The speech acts used in making the attacks are: assertions of the state of corruption not just in

Tunisia but across the AW, call for action, threats to Arab regimes, direct accusations, insults and blame of the opposition for not acting on behalf of the oppressed people, - e.g.:

1. **Insults and blame of opposition for publicly attacking the Al-Jazeera's coverage of the demonstrations instead of supporting the uprising:**

هذه هي أحزاب العا ر

These (opposition) are parties of shame.

2. **Accusing Arab regimes of corruption and using insults:**

لم يعد يخفى ظلمكم يا ظالمين

Your (Arab regimes') oppression and injustices are no longer a secret.

قذارة الانظمة العربية الناهبة لخيرات الشعوب

Dirty Arab regimes that rob the countries' bountiful resources.

3. **Using threats and insults against the Tunisian government and other Arab regimes:**

إلى الزوال يا حكومة العار

Out! You shameful government

إنتهى زمن الخوف و الكذب و التدجيل

Time for fear and fraud has ended.

The statements- as shown above- represent strong attacks against the entities the posters regard as oppressive powers that they need to align against. They use lexical items such as: 'injustices', 'oppression', 'dirty Arab regimes', 'rob', 'shameful', and 'fraud to describe those entities and such terms are generally shared and agreed upon in the data. What this online interaction offers to those angry posters is not just a public space where they can exchange their views, but it seems to generate a sense of common purpose; a sense of "together we are strong" and this was not possible before the Internet. This makes forming allegiances as Arabs and stressing the shared pain and the need to take action feasible. SAs are reflected in the speech acts performed and the subtle lexical choices used in the headings. For example, some tend to introduce the rebels as a new generation of Arab youth who call for change and reform while others stress shared goals and common grievances. In this case, the speech acts used tend to show support and sympathy with the Tunisian rebels and other fellow- sufferers in the AW, sharing prayers, praise and/ or greetings. In contrast to the curses, threats, insults and accusations made against the enemies, terms of endearment and affiliation are used with the allies (e.g. the occurrence of words such as: 'Arabs," "brothers' and 'champs' to describe the rebels in Tunisia). Below are examples of intro statements that reflect SAs in the data: - e.g.

4. **Forming allegiances through foregrounding a shared self-aspect and stressing common pain and goals:**

عــربي مكبّـــل

An Arab in Chains

عربي متلهف للحرية والكرامة

An Arab aspiring for freedom and dignity

ابو سعد ثورة الجياع والغاضبين.

Abu Saad: "A revolution of the hungry and frustrated peoples."

5. **Praise and greetings to Arab youth and the Al-Jazeera for exposing the state of corruption in the AW:**

العرب الجدد

العرب الجدد هم فئة من الشباب المثقف الذي يسعى للإصلاح والتغيير ، فتحية خاصة للشباب العرب

The new Arabs are a group of cultured youth who aspire for change and reform. Special greetings to the new Arab youth!

الجزيرة وكيليكس العرب

Al-Jazeera- Arabs' WikiLeaks

الجزيره تدعم النضال

Al-Jazeera supports the fight for rights

6. **Making assertions about future change and stressing common goals:**

الثورة اتية على كل وطن عربي

The revolution is certainly coming in all Arab countries.

7. **Exchanging prayers with the Tunisian rebels:**

دعوه من القلب

Prayers from the heart

إدعوا لإخوانكم

Pray for your brothers (and sisters) in Tunisia.

8. **Showing support through sharing greetings and praise of the uprising:**

مصــــــــــر التى تغبط شعب تونس

Egypt feels happy for the Tunisian uprising

تحيه من اليمن للأبطال

Greetings from Yemen to the champs

Hence, the poster's discursive display of identity strongly ties in with group affiliation "being an Arab" and is linguistically manifested in the exploitation of various speech acts and the use of MSA as a tool of communication. The word "Arab" with its many derivations is significantly repeated and stressed in the data. It functions as a superordinate term under which all other Arab nationalities are subsumed. The evolving sense of a collective Arab identity is manifested not only in the selection of a shared identity trait but in the consciousness of common pain and goals, as well. It matches what (Simon & Klandermans, 2001) describe as a PCI where shared grievances and pain get people to align together around a dominant, positively valued identity marker; namely, being part of a nation and thus, engage in a struggle against those who represent an oppressive power. The evolving PCI and the call for action also seem to override any local sensitivities or considerations. For example, posters from different Arab nationalities equally and collaboratively attack the Tunisian regime and head of state "Ben Ali." The data analysis does not reveal any significant difference in the percentage of non- Tunisians making attacks against the Tunisian government- 51.80% of all respondents (including anonymous posters) compared to Tunisians 48.20%. Therefore, it can be reasonably said that the online interaction brings to the surface elements of shared identity aspects, a sense of group solidarity and a consciousness of unity and common interests.

FURTHER EVIDENCE OF THE POSTERS' PCI IN THE MESSAGE CONTENT

As for the content of the postings, the same verbal strategies are employed: FAs are manifested in the use of insults, blame, accusations, curses and threats with certain entities; mainly, the Tunisian government and opposition, Ben Ali and his family, other Arab regimes and heads of state and the Al-Jazeera TV channel. Bearing in mind that the article and commentaries are mainly related to the Al-Jazeera's coverage of the uprising that took place in Tunisia, the attacks made against other Arab countries and heads of state are relatively big. In percentage, attacks of Arab countries and heads of state make 26.53% of all attacks in the data and they come only next in percentage to the attacks made against the Tunisian regime (40.88%). The other target entities of the attacks are the Al Jazeera TV channel (6.12%), other contributors (4.08%) or non-applicable (22.39%). Though the postings mainly tackle the posters' evaluation of the Al-Jazeera's coverage of the protests occurring in Tunisia at the time; the posters seize the chance to highlight shared pain and common sufferings.

Incidents of FAs among contributors (mainly disagreements) are minimal and they do not reflect major differences in opinion regarding entities generally seen as oppressive powers that need to be attacked (except for one example of praise of the Tunisian government and Ben Ali (post number 202). Apart from this, the posters mainly seem to differ in their attitude towards Al-Jazeera's role and its political agenda. However, they generally tend to praise rather than attack: 34.29% of the data include praise of Al Jazeera whilst only 6.12% represent attacks against its political agenda, biased and unbalanced coverage. For example, the poster below uses threats, name-calling and curses as FAs against Ben Ali and other Arab heads of state and call on those oppressed to rise and revolt:

وليد محمد

اذهبوا اين شئتم سنأتي بكم أذلاء من بين أحضان اوروبا.....
لا مفرّ لكم اليوم من غضب الشعب...وليتحضّر حسني مبارك..
فالدور عليك بعد الانتهاء من بن علي وازلامه وكل من خان
الشعب التونسي. الويل لك يا بن علي..الويل لك يا بن علي..
الويل لك يا بن علي

Go wherever you (Arab rulers) want, we'll get you. (Literally humiliated from the arms of Europe). No way can you escape from the anger of your people, and you Hosni Moubarak, get ready once we are done with Ben Ali and his gang, we'll get you too. You and everyone who betrayed the Tunisian people. Blows and curses on you Ben Ali, blows and curses on you Ben Ali, Blows and curses on you Ben Ali. (Waleed Mohammed)

Apart from the curses and anger shown in the message, the poster's attack against Hosni Mubarak as someone who betrayed the Tunisian government is quite revealing. Not only does he put him and Ben Ali in the same pack as traitors but he accuses him of betraying the Tunisian government- an accusation that can only be interpreted if the poster's PCI is taken into consideration. In a literal sense, Hosni Mubarak did not betray the Tunisians; according to the poster, he betrayed his own people and thus betrayed Tunisians and all Arabs. The following excerpt shows the same strategies of threatening and cursing against Ben Ali, his family and other Arab heads of State intermixed with the solidarity call to rise and revolt. Adel from Tunisia wrote:

عادل / تونس
الثورة العربية بفضل الجزيرة
ليطمئن بن علي، عصابة الطرابلسية و الحلاقة، الثورة و
التمرد لن تهدأ، ...سنحاكمكم ياسفلة، كم من حاكم خائن في الوطن
العربي يجب سحقه، هذا يقول خادم الحرمين و حساباته بالمليارات
و الموتى في كل هطول امطار بالمئات، ذاك و رثها عن ابيه، و
ذاك يستعد ان يرث ابيه و كأن الدول اصبحت حدائق و الشعوب
مجرد عبيد لهؤلاء الانذال، كل حر شريف عربي عليه أن يثور.

Thanks to Al- Jazeera- An Arab revolution is taking place. Rest reassured Ben Ali, Al Tarabolsia gangster and Alhalaka (Ben Ali and his wife's families), the revolution and the uprising will never cease, we'll bring you to trial you scoundrels. Many Arab rulers are just traitors who must be cracked down. The custodian of the two Holy mosques has billions of dollars in his accounts while his people fall dead in hundreds with every pouring of rain. Other Arab rulers simply inherited the rule from their fathers while others are still waiting to inherit it. For those villains, Arab countries are like gardens and the peoples are like slaves. Every free and honest Arab should revolt (Adel/Tunisia)

In contrast to the curses and name calling cited above. SAs are manifested in the praise offered, the thanks given, the prayers exchanged and the shared empathy among the posters. The growth in participation in news commentaries as a new form of digital media particularly after dramatic events such as the death of Bouazizi show how this new media was attracting more and more participants across the AW (e.g. This article receives 245 commentaries within one day of its publication). It gives those Arab posters a sense of a collective leadership identity that fills the gap they feel between their social, economic and political aspirations and the despicable reality they live in. Aday et al. (2012) writes:

Activists across the region, from Tunisia and Egypt to Bahrain and Yemen, seemed to demonstrate remarkably similar attributes. Most were young, well-educated, and urban. Most were drawn to street protest and distinctive forms of political action that were not widely distributed through other sectors of society. Most shared a common political vocabulary, a common disdain for both regimes and established opposition elites, and a broad pan-Arab political identity. They followed one another's political struggles on the Internet and in real life. And most demonstrated an almost unbelievable courage in challenging entrenched, violently repressive regimes. (p.6)

In the data, the same posting very often includes tokens of FAs and SAs. The strategies used in showing solidarity and the target recipients are as follows: praise and thanks to the Al-Jazeera channel for exposing the corruption (34.29%), showing empathy and solidarity to the Tunisian rebels (25.71%), and fellow Arabs who share similar economic and political conditions (19.85%) and one instance of praise of the Tunisian government (0.41%) or non- applicable (19.74%). The following commentaries are excellent examples of many of the strategies used to show solidarity in a collective sense i.e. mainly to Tunisian protestors and other Arabs who share the same conditions. This is done through sharing prayers and praise, stressing common pain and urging fellow Arabs to rise and revolt:

يمنى مغترب

بلاد الغربة

كان الله معكم مؤيدًا ونصيرًا. ونشكر الجزيرة على تغطيتها للأحداث كما هي. ليست تونس من تجب عليها الانتفاضة فأجزم أن في الدول العربية الظلم الكثير.

Away from my homeland. May God be with you and support you (Tunisians). Thanks to Al-Jazeera for its accurate coverage of the events. Tunisia is not the only Arab country that should revolt; surely other Arab countries suffer from a lot of injustices, too (A Yemeni- from abroad)

Another poster stresses shared oppression and common goals. Mohammed Ali- an Arab immigrant writes from Istanbul:

محمد على ولي / استانبول

ما يحدث في تونس هو صورة عن ما حدث و يحدث و سيحدث في كل أرجاء الوطن العربي, صورة لما حدث في لبنان و سوريا و العراق و مصر و ليبيا و الجزائر و الأردن و فلسطين المحتلة و السعودية و اليمن و البحرين و الامارات و غيرها . المطرقة جاهزة دائما لتنهال فوق أي أي رأس يفكر أن يرتفع أو يثور على ما يحيط به من ظلم و عدوان و لتسحق أي فكر آخر. اذا لم يدعم كل الشرفاء إخواننا بتونس فسيكون مصيرهم مصير

من سبقهم و اذا نجحوا بالتغيير فسيكونوا مثلا لإخوانهم في باقي
أرجاء هذا الوطن.

*What happens in Tunisia is a copy of what hap-
pened and is still happening in all parts of the
Arab world including Lebanon, Syria, Iraq, Egypt,
Libya, Algeria, Jordan, the occupied land of Pal-
estine, Saudi Arabia, Yemen, Bahrain, Emirates
and many more. The hammer is always ready to
fall on any head that dares to think, rise, or revolt
against the injustice we see around us. If we do not
support our brothers in Tunisia, their destiny will
be the same as those who tried to rebel before; but
if they succeed to bring change, they will be a role
model to all the other rebels (their brothers) in
the Arab World. (Mohammed Ali Wally/Istanbul)*

Here, the shared pain and oppression gives
a sense of unity and hope. There are feelings of
solidarity subtly invoked through the long list of
Arab countries and the repeated use of the aligned
"we" and "our brothers." Throughout the data,
there are growing sentiments of Arab nationalism
that connects the posters together as fellow sufferers and strong anti- Arab regimes' sentiments,
too. Though the postings are asynchronous, the
interactants seem to pick up on the same sentiments
and word choice; e.g. words such as "free Arabs,"
"rebels" and "oppressed citizens" are reinforced
through constant repetition. Solidarity acts are
also subtly invoked through the shared grievances: e.g. whenever the posters make reference
to the political corruption in Tunisia, reference
to the corruption in other Arab countries almost
always immediately follows. A female Algerian
poster wrote:

عربية جزائرية
هذه هي الحكومات العربية دائما تلصق التهم في الآخرين و
ما يحدث في تونس سيحدث في باقي الدول العربية فالفقر و الفساد
و انتشار البطالة قد بلغ ذروته في الدول العربية و الإسلامية و
تحية لقناة الجزيرة.

*This is what Arab governments typically do! They
always accuse others of their own faults! What
happens in Tunisia will surely happen in the rest
of the Arab countries! Poverty, corruption and
unemployment have reached their peak in the Arab
and Islamic world but they still dare blame it on
Al-Jazeera! Thanks Al-Jazeera for the coverage!
(An Arab Algerian (female))*

Through the analysis, there is data driven
evidence that the identity signals picked and foregrounded in these e-commentaries are discursively
constructed and closely aligned to the posters'
collective identity, which – in turn- is observed
to affect the verbal strategies used by the posters.
Being an Arab citizen who shares the grievances
and oppression suffered in the AW at large has
been observed to be the central identity marker that
is brought to the foreground and defines in-group
and out-group members (Simon & Klandermans,
2001). It also determines the direction of the FAs
and SAs performed in the data: most postings
include at least one type of FA (e.g. name-calling,
insults, curses, accusations and threats) targeting
what the posters define as an "out-group"- "the
oppressive power/s that they need to align against."
Such FAs are usually loaded with the use of abusive
language and direct insults to governments and
heads of state (e.g. سفلة, خائن, عصابة حرامى,)
(bastards, gang, traitor, and thief). On the other
hand, acts of solidarity are typically shown in the
support and warm prayers the posters exchange
with the rebels in Tunisia and the oppressed people
across the AW. More importantly, the emergence
of the posters' PCI is subtly shown in the general
agreement the posters share of 'who the allies and
the enemies are' and the persistent call for action.
It is reflected in the verbal strategies used (e.g.
praise of the Al-Jazeera's news coverage, sharing
greetings, heart-felt prayers and praise of Arab
rebels who call for change). In such case, those
acts are particularly used with those who are

regarded as "in-group" members and are loaded with terms of endearment (e.g. "our brothers," "champs" and the repeated use of "we" and "us."

CONCLUSION AND DIRECTIONS FOR FURTHER RESEARCH

In conclusion, online interaction through the Al Jazeera Website along with other forms of social media (Twitter & Facebook) has certainly provided and is still providing a platform for the development of such social and political capital. It has helped the posters build extensive networks beyond their local territories and thus given rise to a new form of collective leadership that was not possible before the advent of digital media. It has succeeded to turn these localized individuals into social agents of change through the collective consciousness of shared grievances and wish for reform. However, the emergence of PCI as social capital and this form of collective leadership still need further investigation. In the process of democratization that is taking place in the Arab Spring countries now, online interaction continues to provide a political and public sphere for those Arab activists to share their views about the fast pace events. Therefore, it is worth investigating whether online interaction through digital media is still evolving in the direction of a PCI and regional diffusion or other processes of digital interaction are emerging. In the data, the in-group affiliation and out-group conflict seem to fall among Arab rebels and against the corrupt Arab regimes; yet, it might be the case now that other forms of polarization might arise. Political differences might focus more on internal ideological strife, as in the case of Egypt, Tunisia, Libya and Syria and there might be radically different identity narrative in those online environments from the one observed in the data under study.

Thus far, the analysis has indicated that the social psychological theories of identity- e.g. Simon's self- aspect model (2004) and sociolinguistic methods of analysis can be useful in gaining a deeper understanding of the concept of social capital. The present study aims to add to the existing approaches through the attempt to conceptualize the concept of social capital linguistically using a multi-disciplinary approach and this is seen as the main contribution of the present study. However, since the scale of the present study is relatively small, there is a need for getting more empirical data from different contexts to investigate the concept even further.

REFERENCES

Aday, S., Farrell, H., Lynch, M., Sides, J., & Freelon, D. (2012). *Blogs and bullets II: New media and conflict after the Arab spring. PeaceWorks, 80*. Washington, DC: The American Institute.

Adler, P., & Kwon, S.-W. (2002). Social capital: Prospects for a new concept. *Academy of Management Review, 27*, 17–40.

Brown, P., & Levinson, S. (1987). *Politeness: Some universals in language use*. Cambridge, UK: Cambridge University Press.

Dekker, P., & Uslaner, E. (2001). Introduction. In E. Uslaner (Ed.), *Social capital and participation in everyday life* (pp. 1–8). London: Routledge.

Goffman, E. (1967). *Interaction rituals: Essays on face-to-face behavior*. Garden City, NY: Anchor.

Howard, P., & Hussain, M. (2013). *Democracy's fourth wave? Digital media and the Arab spring*. Oxford, UK: Oxford University Press. doi:10.1093/acprof:oso/9780199936953.001.0001

Leech, G. (1983). *Principles of pragmatics*. London: Longman.

McGarty, C., Bliuc, A.-M., Thomas, E., & Bongiorno, R. (2009). Collective action as the material expression of opinion-based group membership. *The Journal of Social Issues, 65*(4), 839–857. doi:10.1111/j.1540-4560.2009.01627.x

Schlenker, B., & Pontari, B. (2000). The strategic control of information: Impression management and self-presentation in daily life. In A. Tesser, R. Felso, & J. Suls (Eds.), *Psychological perspectives on self and identity* (pp. 199–232). Washington, DC: American Psychological Association. doi:10.1037/10357-008

Simon, B. (2004). *Identity in modern society: A social psychological perspective.* Oxford, UK: Blackwell. doi:10.1002/9780470773437

Simon, B., & Klandermans, B. (2001). Politicized collective identity: A social psychological analysis. *The American Psychologist, 56*(4), 319–331. doi:10.1037/0003-066X.56.4.319 PMID:11330229

Spencer-Oatey, H. (2007). Theories of identity and the analysis of face. *Journal of Pragmatics, 39*(4), 639–656. doi:10.1016/j.pragma.2006.12.004

Tunisia Attacks Al-Jazeera and the Protests Expand all over the Country. (2010, December 28). Retrieved from http://www.aljazeera.net

Uslaner, E. (2001). Volunteering and social capital: How trust and religion shape civic participation in the United States. In E. Uslaner (Ed.), *Social capital and participation in everyday life* (pp. 104–117). London: Routledge. doi:10.4324/9780203451571_chapter_8

KEY TERMS AND DEFINITIONS

Arab World (AW): The Arab World consists of the Arabic-speaking countries and populations in North Africa and the Middle East comprising the 22 countries of the Arab League. In the data, the sentiment of Arab nationalism arose through the collaborative performance of solidarity acts among the Arab posters as well as the face attacks against Arab regimes and heads of state. It is argued that these sentiments are reawakening during what is called the Arab Spring Revolutions.

Face Attacks (FAs): "Face" (as in "save face and lose face") refers to a speaker's sense of linguistic and social identity. Face attacks are speech acts that are generally marked as impolite.

Modern Standard Arabic (MSA): Modern Standard Arabic is the standardized and literary variety of Arabic used in writing and in most formal speech. It is based on the classical language (fusha) and it is the most widely used variety among educated Arabs as the vehicle of communication especially if they want to overcome differences in the regional dialects of Arabic.

Politicized Collective Identity (PCI): According to Simon and Klandermans (2001, p. 319), politicized collective identity revolves around 3 conceptual triads. The first triad consists of collective identity, the struggle between groups for power, and the wider societal context. It is proposed that people evince politicized collective identity to the extent that they engage as self-conscious group members in a power struggle on behalf of their group knowing that it is the more inclusive societal context in which this struggle has to be fought out. Next, 3 antecedent stages leading to politicized collective identity are distinguished: awareness of shared grievances, adversarial attributions, and involvement of society at large.

Solidarity Acts (SAs): The performance of solidarity acts is seen an important aspect of social capital. SAs show the value of social networks in bonding similar people and are linguistically performed through the speech acts of agreements, sharing prayers and showing empathy and support to Tunisian rebels and other oppressed people in the Arab World.

ENDNOTES

1. "Face" (as in "save face and lose face") refers to a speaker's sense of linguistic and social identity. Face attacks are speech acts that are generally marked as impolite.
2. See Searle, John R. (1969). *Speech acts: An essay in the philosophy of language.* Cambridge: Cambridge University Press, Cambridge 1969 & Austin, John L. (1962). *How to do things with words*?, Clarendon, Oxford: Oxford University Press.
3. See the link below for relevant background information on Bouazizi's suicide incident-thttp://en.wikipedia.org/wiki/Mohamed_Bouazizi

Section 2
Celebrity, Identity, and Social Media

Chapter 4
Constructions of Banksy:
Issues of Identity in the Age of Social Media

Cheri Lemieux Spiegel
Northern Virginia Community College, USA & Old Dominion University, USA

ABSTRACT

This chapter examines how multiple, often competing, identities of the street artist Banksy are constructed through a variety of media. It uses actor network theory and activity theory to trace and analyze the contexts, or networks, wherein Bansky's identity is constructed. Banksy's identity is of particular interest because he is an anonymous figure, and he actively abstains from social media. This examination of how he is constructed online sheds light on the agency that individuals have in constructing their identity in digital spaces. The insight from this investigation should be of great relevance for all professionals as they consider the non-professional writing they do, or chose not to do, beyond their office walls, within the public domain.

INTRODUCTION

In the age wherein businesses and teenagers alike regularly share their Twitter names and suggest that others "Facebook" them, the understanding of private and public selves is becoming notably blurred. Furthermore, issues of identity construc-

DOI: 10.4018/978-1-4666-5150-0.ch004

tion in this age of social media have become more important than ever. For one, identity construction in digital spaces gives space for individuals to mediate the disconnect between who they are and who they wish they could be. As Sherry Turkle (2011) explains, "These days, insecure in our relationships and anxious about intimacy, we look to technology for ways to be in relationships and protect ourselves from them at the same time" (p.

xii). Additionally, corporations are allegedly monitoring employee social media pages (Liebowitz, 2012); while multiple employees have been fired for their confessions on social media (Pike, 2011); and scholars use Twitter to self promote, network, and distribute resources with students, as well as share student work with the online community (Veletsianos, 2012).

These activities all shape their user's perceived identity in the online domain. This fact ought to give social media users pause when they consider the material they share, comment upon, re-tweet and "like" in these public venues. The question of which social media to participate in, to what degree, under what name or alias, and with whom is of great concern for all professionals as they consider the non-professional writing they do within the public domain. A number of scholars have begun to wrestle with these issues. They have explored how cultural identity is formed in social media (Sullivan, 2010), how corporations can use social media to successfully market their brand (Volmar, 2010), and how social lives and relationships have been reshaped as a result of the use of this kind of media (Brown, 2011). Most of these authors assume participation in social media. One question that research into these platforms has yet to fully explore is: what happens when one purposefully abstains from social media in an effort to control the way he or she is constructed online?

It is this question that this chapter explores, by tracing the online identity construction of a public figure who purposefully elects to abstain from social media. It works to explore the identity construction of an individual whose identity is considered elusive, even offline, and whose ethos is already associated with criminal behavior: Banksy. The infamous street artist Banksy is known only by this name, which is certainly an alias. This alias presumably stands in for a real-life person. Great research and speculation have gone into attempting to identify Banksy. These efforts have not been fruitful. Collins (2007) reported in *The New Yorker* a summary of what we do know

about Banksy's identity in real life: "Banksy likes pizza, though his preference in toppings cannot be definitively ascertained. He has a gold tooth. He has a silver tooth. He has a silver earring. He's an anarchist environmentalist who travels by chauffeured S.U.V" (para. 1). This list goes on and contains many contradictions as it continues.

It is quite difficult to make definite claims about the identity of the real-life Banksy. However, the real-life Banksy is not the one of greatest concern in this chapter. Instead, this chapter is concerned with the multiple identities of the street artist Banksy that are constructed in the online environment. These identities are largely articulated without the input of the real-life figure himself. Instead, they originate from experiences throughout the digital world. As Turkle (1995) explains, "in the story of constructing identity in the culture of simulation, experiences on the Internet figure prominently, but these experiences can only be understood as part of a larger cultural context" (p. 10). For this reason, this chapter uses actor network theory (ANT) and activity theory to trace and analyze the contexts, or networks, wherein Banksy's identity is constructed. The examination of how he is constructed online sheds light on the agency that an individual has in constructing his or her own identity in digital spaces, even when he or she elects not to self-compose an identity in certain social media spaces.

BACKGROUND

ANT, as Callon (1999) explains, "was developed to analyse situations in which it is difficult to separate humans and non-humans, and in which the actors have variable forms and competencies" (p. 183). It proves useful in this chapter's exploration precisely because ANT provides a means for separating human and non-human agents. To understand the means in which identity is crafted, one needs to be able to separate the individual whose identity is under construction from the identity itself, as well as from the other actors that contribute to the formation of this identity and also artifacts created by the individual being examined. This separation is important because the individual does not act alone in this construction, nor is the individual necessarily the most important actor in his or her own identity construction.

Another reason that ANT is useful here is that it allows for the associations to be assembled, but not fixed indefinitely. This relates well to the construction of identity by the toy collectors discussed in this anthology by Joe Essid and the political bloggers explored by Dona J. Hickey. Such identity might be well understood through Bahktin's concept of unfinalizability. Bahktin (1984) says, "nothing conclusive has yet taken place in the world, the ultimate word of the world and about the world has not yet been spoken, the world is open and free, everything is still in the future and will always be in the future" (p. 166). This fluidity speaks well to the Turkle (1995) conception of the flexible self; she says, "the essence of this self is not unitary, nor are its parts stable entities. It is easy to cycle through its aspects and these are themselves changing through constant communication with each other" (p. 261). Since identity itself can be said to be fluid and change with time, ANT allows for actors to be assembled for a particular instance of identity construction and reassembled for another. This chapter examines multiple instances of identity construction: ones wherein the artist assumes a role as an agent in his identification and another wherein only the artist's artifacts and other outsiders are actors in co-constructing his identity.

While ANT is useful in this chapter for assembling non-human and human actors in a network for a specific instance, it is not useful for explaining why these networks exist at any given moment. ANT must be brought in conversation with activity theory in a way that is not typical in order to account for the difference in the two types of networks that are being explored here.

This paper brings these two theories together in a vein similar to that of Potts and Jones (2011): the goal here is not to "reengage the debate between these two theories," but instead to use ANT "to survey the assemblage of actors and connections," while using "Activity theory's distinction between operations and actions" (p. 345). While Potts and Jones (2011) use this distinction to identify how systems allow participants to work within a network, this chapter uses operations and actions to justify creating two types of networks. Potts and Jones (2011) draw from Kaptelinin and Nardi to explain the difference between operations and actions. Operations "do not have their own goals; rather, they provide an adjustment of actions to current situations" while actions "are conscious, and different actions may be undertaken to meet the same goal" (as cited in Potts & Jones, 2011, p. 345).

This present chapter explores one type of network that might be said to result from action and another that develops as a result of operations. The network that develops as a result of action is the one described above as the situations wherein the artist assumes a role as an agent in his identification. When the artist works as an agent in these spaces, he has the goal of controlling his own identification; his relationship with his identity construction appears to be active, or conscious. However, when others, outsiders, construct his identity, it does not seem to be for the purpose of actively constructing his identity specifically; that is: these occasions seem to have other goals than identity development. As a result of the two different goals in these instances of identity creation, differing networks (and thus identities) are formed—one wherein the artist himself is an actor, and one where he is not. Many public figures might be said to exist in separate identity construction networks in similar ways. As another example of this duality, one might consider the contrast between the Marxist figure Ernesto "Che" Guevara presented through his writing and actions as compared to the persona and values his identity is co-opted to stand for when it is placed on T-shirts sold at popular stores at malls across the country.

The conception of the artist-formed network that develops as a result of action relates well to the Burgess and Ivanic (2010) concept of how identity works as a discoursal construction, if the street artist's work is perceived not only as art, but discourse as well, and thus the man not as only an artist, but also a kind of writer. These scholars explain that "[p]eople are positioned by the discourses they participate in: by the possibilities for selfhood that they take up and the ones they reject" (p. 237). Thus, it follows that Banksy's identity is inscribed in the works he produces and the contexts wherein he chooses to (and not to) circulate his work. Burgess and Ivanic go on to consider how "[d]iscourses, and the 'possiblities for selfhood' inscribed in them, are likely to be multiple, diverse and contradictory, even within a relatively clearly defined social space" (p. 237). These authors think carefully about how discourse actors elect to engage in shaping the formation of selfhood.

However, they give little emphasis to identities created in the absence of the writer. While they present a number of identity models in their timescale progression, only one of their notions looks outside of the writer: an identity they term "the perceived writer" (p. 241). This identity is formed through the reader's impressions upon reading a writer's text. Burgess and Ivanic (2010) explain that the "perceived writer is, therefore, likely to be a relatively long-term 'identity' for the writer" (pp. 241-242). This perceived writer might better align with how Banksy is constructed in his own absence. What the present chapter seeks to examine further is how the author's constructed self compares to a self that might be considered as the next step in a writer's identity progression through time--as it takes place after the text has been consumed by a reader. Instead, this self is formed when the readers seek to construct their own version of the self not only based upon the perceived writer, but also upon their own writing about the original author in contexts where the writer himself elects not to participate.

BANKSY'S "BANKSY"

Banksy seems to have a conception of his own identity; he operates as an actor in the networks wherein this instance is constructed. In this chapter, the term of Banksy's "Banksy" is used to refer to the identity of the artist that is constructed through his direct assistance. The network necessary to construct the idea of Banksy's "Banksy" is diagrammed in Figure 1. A darkened arrow between the person who is Banksy and Banksy's "Banksy" is used to reiterate that this diagram depicts the conception of Banksy in which he is an actor. It is not meant to indicate greater agency. In addition to the individual himself, four types of artifacts represented in this construction are notable actors: his artwork, self-published books, film, and Website. Each of these operates in connection with the others and the person using his alias to make his constructed identity possible.

Figure 1. The network of Banksy's "Banksy"

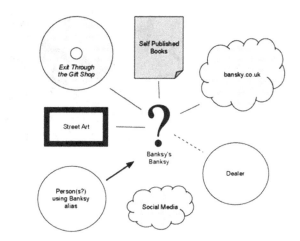

Also noted on the diagram is Banksy's art dealer. While Banksy himself does acknowledge a dealer (in his film in particular), in other places multiple dealers are discussed. Further research into the dealer is needed to appropriately understand his or her (or their) role in the network; therefore, the dealer is connected to the artist's identity only by way of a dotted line on the map. One entity remains on the map, unconnected. There is no evidence that social media plays a role in Banksy's own conception of Banksy; instead, Banksy insists that he is not present in this arena. The sections that follow explore the role each actor from the Bansky's "Banksy" diagram plays in the construction of that identity.

Artwork

Banksy's own art aids in the construction of his identity. First of all, it must be noted that his artwork is what is often described as guerilla art or as vandalism, depending on what population you ask. This terminology paints the image of someone who is politically motivated and who operates outside the confines of government regulation. He is an opinionated criminal.

The nature of his political beliefs and his sarcastic sense of humor can often be observed through his art as well. Take, for example, the Boston, Massachusetts "installation" shown in Figure 2 below. Situated in the United States, this piece demonstrates the artist's jaded outlook on the American Dream, but (especially since the artist is British) likely points to the artist's greater suspicion of promise of the corporate world and capitalism as a whole. This same sad painter from Figure 2 has been pictured in another work by Banksy—in that one he's engaged in pasting up rows of posters with a bright yellow smiling face upon them, each identical and reminiscent of the Wal-Mart smiley face logo. Much of his work presents themes related to social stratification, governmental control/surveillance, environmentalism, labor issues, and consumerism. He often satirizes and criticizes advertising. The work he paints on the streets introduce these themes and he develops his perspective regarding them through other media—his books, film and Website, in particular.

Figure 2. Banksy's "Follow Your Dreams Cancelled" photo © Eric Spiegel

Self-Published Books

Banksy self-published three books that have since been republished into one volume called *Wall and Piece*. This collection contains multiple samples of Banksy's artwork, which is helpful in expanding the reach of his work. The characteristics of himself that can be observed in his artwork have a greater reach as a result of this volume, as individuals do not have to travel to London, for example, to see his work and learn more about who he is. Instead, his identity can be constructed on the page from wherever the reader might be.

In addition to expanding the scope of who would have the opportunity to see Banksy's work, the book itself helps construct Banksy's "Banksy" because Banksy adds his own narrative throughout each section of the book. These short clips convey quite a bit of information about Banksy. One repeated theme, for example is Bansky's great concern for equality. For example, he asks the reader to imagine a city where graffiti isn't illegal; he says that this city would feel "like a party where everyone was invited, not just the estate agents and barons of big business" (Banksy, 2006, p. 97). Repeated throughout his book are sentiments that illustrate distaste for those in power, particularly law enforcement, advertising agencies and others who control the aesthetic of the streets. He presents law enforcement agents in positions that might be considered taboo by a conservative public—one urinating in public and others engaging in a homosexual romance while on the job, for example. One image allegedly attributed to the artist paints over a billboard and says, "the joy of not being sold anything."

Another trend in his work that is shown in the volume is his usage of the rat. He comments directly on the rat, saying "they exist without permission. They are hated, hunted and persecuted. They live in quiet desperation amongst the filth. And yet they are capable of bringing entire civilizations to their knees. If you are dirty, insignificant and unloved then rats are the ultimate role model" (Banksy, 2006, p. 95). This selection rings of Marxist thinking—standing almost as a call to order for the proletariat, while also implying a certain vulnerability. Since Banksy uses the rat so often in his work, might the rat be his own role model? Making the artist himself one who feels dirty, insignificant and unloved?

Film

In 2010, *Exit Through the Gift Shop* was released at the Sundance Film Festival. It is described as "A Banksy Film." This film begins by focusing on a curious man named Thierry Guetta who went through life filming everything he saw. This man eventually became involved in the street art community and filmed the work of street artists such as Invader, Shepard Fairey and of course, Banksy. Eventually, Banksy comes to determine that "Thierry wasn't actually a film maker, and he was maybe just someone with mental problems who happened to have a camera" and resolves to take over the filmmaking process, while Thierry, at Banksy's suggestion, resolves to become a street artist himself (Banksy, 2010).

Within the film, Banksy narrates and appears on screen. Of course, he does not do so in a straightforward nature. He adds to the intrigue of his persona by having his voice distorted when he speaks and having his face silhouetted in such a way that he cannot be identified. These choices add to the idea that Banksy is mysterious. Other actions of Banksy also assist in the construction of his identity throughout the film. For example, through his discussion of Guetta's art, he begins to convey his own artistic point of view. He explains in the film that he used to encourage everyone he knew to make art, until he encouraged Guetta to; now he doesn't do that any longer. He's frustrated by Guetta, who goes by the artist name of "Mr. Brainwash" because he indicates that the work he creates is empty, devoid of true expression: "Warhol repeated iconic images until they became meaningless, but there was something iconic about them. Thierry really makes them meaningless" (Banksy, 2010).

Bansky demonstrates that he believes in art's ability to convey a message and that he believes this message is vital to the worth of the art. The film demonstrates a resistance toward art for profit and a dedication to art for expression's sake. One thing about Banksy that can be taken away from this depiction is that he is not a vandal simply for the sake of misbehaving; his vandalism aims to convey meaning.

Website

Banksy posts his work on a Website that contains his pseudonym as its domain[1]. The site consists of three sections: outdoor art, indoor art, and a "shop." The site's outdoor art and indoor art sections assist in helping him to establish identity through his artwork. This establishment is possible because when Banksy posts a piece of work to his site, he is claiming it as his work. Since so much of his work is not signed (and pieces he hasn't done sometimes are attributed to him), this site is helpful in identifying which pieces should aid in constructing his identity and which ones should not.

There is very little text on Banksy's Website. Of the text he does use, tiny bits do make specific claims relevant to his identity. On the shop page is the following statement: "You're welcome to download whatever you wish from this site for personal use. However, making your own art or merchandise and passing it off as 'official' or authentic Banksy artwork is bad and very wrong" (Banksy, n.d.). From this statement, one learns a few things about the identity of Banksy. Through this statement he essentially refrains from claiming copyright to the images on his Website; however, he also limits who is able to make use of his work, which implies a limited copyright-like agreement; in other words, he does request that his work is not used for a commercial purpose. What is interesting in the way that he conveys this is that he chooses to use the phrase "bad and very wrong" for using his work in a commercial sense. Despite his having

anarchist principles by and large, this statement conveys a guiding moral principle that assumes individuals have responsibility to one another.

An older version of the shop page contained the following claim: "Banksy neither produces or profits from the sale of greeting cards, mugs or photo canvases of his work. He is not represented by any of the commercial galleries that sell his paintings second hand and cannot be found on facebook/twitter/myspace etc." (Banksy, n.d.). The newest version of the site does not contain this clause, but instead says, "I am not on facebook or twitter." (Banksy, n.d.). Social Media, Banksy argues through this text, is not an actor in the network of Banksy's "Banksy."

The Questions page further adds to the construction of Banksy's self-controlled identity creation. On this page, which works as a Frequently-Asked-Questions page, the artist poses two particularly important questions for himself. First, he asks his own opinion of auction houses selling street art, and then he asks what he thinks when people claim that his method of expression is "dumb and simplistic" (Banksy, n.d.). To the first question he responds with a quote from Henri Matisse: "I was very embarrassed when my canvases began to fetch high prices, I saw myself condemned to a future of painting nothing but masterpieces" (as cited in Banksy, n.d). To the second question, he responds, "Well duh" (Banksy, n.d.). These two simple answers tell their reader much about Banksy's view of the art world and how he would like to be perceived. First, he responds to one question by positioning himself within the art community by quoting a high brow artist; then, he positions himself outside of this realm of privilege by using colloquial language to position himself as dumb and simplistic. However, Banksy's "duh" seems to actually be a rhetorical move by which he positions himself as being anything but simple. Instead, he seems more likely to be jabbing at those who pose such questions of him and indicating that those folks might be the less bright, as they have missed the point of his work.

Overall, the artifacts explored in this section of this chapter show the traits of Bansky's identity that are revealed through media that the artist consciously sanctions for public viewing. The artist has purposefully distributed theses artifacts to the public. In this way, he controls how his identity is shaped. He carefully controls the way in which he is presented to the world; he hides his "true" identity, masks his face and voice; he avoids sharing intimate personal details about his life or background. Essentially, Bansky paints an identity through his artwork and perspectives surrounding art and culture alone. In addition, he constructs his identity without requesting or sharing substantive feedback. While many creative types might have critic's opinions of their books on their back covers, or allow comments on their Websites, Banksy only has this quote from a Metropolitan Police spokesperson on the back of his book: "There's no way you're going to get a quote from us to use on your book cover" (Banksy, 2006). The use of this quote reinforces the notion that Banksy is rebellious and unaccepting of authority.

However, the way the artist elected to use the quotation once again puts him in control of how his identity is constructed—he is able to self-identify even when his likely critics refuse to aid in his identity construction. Outside opinions of Banksy are shared in the network of Banksy's "Banksy" within his film but even those opinions are conveyed in a film he directed, one wherein he was able to have active control over what made the final cut and what did not. Overall, Banksy seems to be quite careful and meticulous about maintaining how his identity is constructed and what of his actual identity is shared publicly. However, his participation is limited to these arenas that he can act as the primary agent, controlling the details through editing, not sharing substantive comments on his work, and not allowing commenting on the site where he maintains his Web presence.

SOCIAL MEDIA'S "BANKSY"

Banksy claims that he is not present on social media. Given the anti-corporate, anti-advertising stance of the author, this position is not surprising. Most social media spaces contain quite a bit of self-promotion and actual advertising. Artists and writers who do use the media typically do so as an avenue for self-promotion. Additionally, the social media companies are representative of corporations who continuously gain more cultural influence, something that Banksy would find problematic. It is likely that the artist elects to abstain from being active in these domains because doing so might be in contrast with the identity he has composed for himself. Additionally, however, a presence in these domains might led to stronger connections to his *actual* self, which would be problematic for the artist's legal status.

However, claiming he is not *present* on social media is actually problematic. Banksy is quite present on these sites. However, this "Banksy" is not one that is consciously constructed by the artist himself. Social Media constructs its own Banksy through multiple networks that might be said to be constructing Social Media's "Banksy." This network is one that social media users most likely act in unconsciously, without actively acknowledging their goal as constructing Banksy's identity. While the artist himself may actively elect not to be present in these networks, it does not mean that this version of himself is not in existence. This section explores the means in which social media constructs the identity of the artist in his absence and without his control.

This network is represented in Figure 3. A darkened arrow between Social Media and Social Media's "Banksy" is used in the network diagram to reiterate that this diagram depicts the conception of Banksy in which Social Media is a direct actor. There are similar artifacts in this network as in Banksy's "Banksy": Banksy's art, film related to the artist, and books. These, however, are represented in lighter lines in this network because

Figure 3. Network of social media's "Banksy"

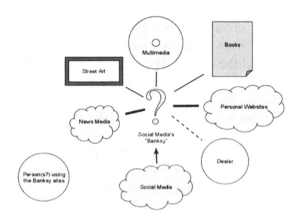

they play less central roles in the operations in the network. In this network, images of the art are circulated, references to Banksy's books are made, and his film is explored. These items are discussed through social media, news media and personal Websites. For that reason, these entities are depicted with darker lines.

Admittedly, these personal Websites are often blogs, which are commonly considered social media themselves. Additionally, news media sites often contain a comments section that create a social media-like presence. Both these personal sites and news sites play specific roles in how other social media forms operate to construct Banksy. As a result, it is useful to examine them separately to observe their role in the network productively.

In the sections that follow, this paper explores the means in which social media constructs the identity of Banksy and the claims that are made through this construction. As a result of the endless nature of the Internet, this network can easily be framed in such a way as to make it unwieldy for analysis. Therefore, for the sake of creating a manageable scope for this task, the following sections look at a narrower instance of identity construction. Specifically, this investigation looks at two particular Twitter-based cases related to Banksy's identity. The first case examines tweets

surrounding the night of the 2010 Oscars, wherein Banksy's film was up for nomination. The second case looks at the tweets of a Twitter account attributed to Banksy (despite his insistence that he is not on social media) that was established after Banksy rose to popularity.

Tweets of February 27, 2010

On February 27, 2010, ABC aired the 83rd Academy Awards ceremony. Like many major media events in the age of Twitter, the social media platform buzzed with activity that night as users "live tweeted" the events. Banksy was a major subject of the tweets that night because *Exit Through the Gift Shop* was nominated for the category of Best Documentary Film. Much hype surrounded this event, in part, because the Academy Awards announced a week before that they had denied Banksy's request to attend the event in disguise (Kemp, 2011). The evening's tweets on the subject of Banksy create a snapshot into the identity of the artist, a very schizophrenic snapshot.

The Website Topsy.com was used to collect data to construct this snapshot of Bansky's identity. Topsy is a Web search engine that specializes in social media. The Topsy search engine allows specific searches to be conducted surrounding specific social media sites, specific dates, and specific usernames. For the purposes of this project, a search was conducted for use of the keyword "Banksy" during the hours of 8 pm and midnight on February 27, 2010. The results were sorted for date, rather than relevance so that the data would be confined to the date in question. Ten pages, with a total of 96 tweets spread over them resulted from this search. It should be noted that Topsy is not perfect and does, at times, miss some relevant pieces of information. However, the resulting data provides a rich pool from which a representative sample can be drawn.

After the data was collected it was examined for patterns. One dominant pattern quickly arose: claims about specific people or entities that Banksy is and claims that assert which specific person Banksy is not. Over the course of these 96 tweets, numerous claims were made about who Banksy is; Table 1 lists the individuals and other entities that Twitter users claimed to be Banksy.

Of all the individuals named as Banksy that evening, Oprah was speculated to be the artist far more than any other. She is referenced in 14 of the 96 tweets from that evening, nearly 15%. These 14 tweets were re-tweeted a total of 370 times. The tweets about Oprah as Banksy come in three basic forms. Essentially, most twitter users either question whether Banksy is Oprah or confirm it. A small group of individuals seems to insist that Banksy was not Oprah herself, but rather one of her breasts. What is interesting throughout all these claims and questions is that no one opposed this speculation. Not one of the 96 tweets refuted the idea that Oprah was Banksy. This observation is particularly interesting in light of the fact that the tweet stream only demonstrates resistance to the idea that Banksy might be one person: Justin Timberlake.

Five tweets address the idea of Banksy being Justin Timberlake. Two simply report it as fact, likely the result of Justin Timberlake announcing

Table 1. Individuals and entities referenced as Banksy on February 27

Individuals	Objects
Jean-Luc Godard	Reese Witherspoon's Weave
James Franco	Mila Kunis's Breasts
"A Singer On Stage"	What's in Oprah's Bra
Teresa (?)	Oprah's left Breast
Kurt Douglas	Woody (from *Toy Story*)
Justin Bieber	
"Guy accepting *Inside Job* Award"	
Asian Woman on Stage	
Justin Timberlake	
Oprah Winfrey	

it on stage that night. Two others acknowledge Timberlake's admission as a joke, not even entertaining whether he could, in fact, be the artist. The fifth directly stated the musician was not Banksy, then asked who was.

Looking at just this narrow selection of tweets, we can draw certain conclusions. First, Twitter followers seem more comfortable likening Banksy to a boob than they are connecting him to a flashy musician. This slang term for breast is used here to allow room for play on words. Might it be that Banksy is characterized as a "stupid person" or "boob" when he is likened to a breast? If so— why allow for this characterization and not one as Timberlake? More importantly, why does the network seem most comfortable constructing him as the famous talk show host? Banksy's identity within this social space is fluid and a source of entertainment. As this network presents not what activity theory would refer to as actions, but operations—the goal is not to form identity, but most likely to place within a space where there is some question of the artist's identity. As a result, the game of "who is Banksy" is more important than who the artist actually is.

Banksy's "Banksy" and Banksy as Oprah may share some traits—activism and interest in the telling the stories of those who are less fortunate, for example—the contrast between the two is great. Oprah is greatly tied to advertising, with shows glorifying consumerism each year. She is a rule follower. She is not lowly and unwanted; she is the queen of the realm of social code. She is what Banksy argues he is not. Perhaps these users allow this speculation to remain uncorrected because of the sheer absurdity of it. Oprah effectively stands for what Banksy opposes—her name itself is a brand. Alternatively, allowing Banksy to stand as equal to Oprah might also stand as a criticism of the artist. Many have accused the artist of selling out over speculations about sales of his work. Identifying him as Oprah might also be a means in suggesting that he is not more divorced from capitalism than celebrity icon who almost seems to stand for consumerism. However, he is not a member of this network and cannot respond to this characterization.

Tweets of @Banksy

The Twitter account with the name "banksy" provides little information about the user. It attaches the name Banksy to the account, gives "Brizzle" as the user location and provides a profile image which is a black and white image of a man in jeans walking away from the camera while pulling off a sweater or jacket of some form. At the time that this was written, "banksy" had 1,746 followers, 28 tweets and was following zero other users. The account has not earned a Verification Badge. As Twitter's FAQs explain, "Verification is currently used to establish authenticity of identities on Twitter" (Twitter Help Center, n.d.). Naturally, the @banksy account was not been vetted by Twitter's verification process because the authenticity of his identity is so mysterious.

None of the tweets posted by the "banksy" account is original in content. Instead, each one pushes content directed at the "banksy" account to the followers of "banksy" through the Twitter mechanism called a re-tweet. Of the 28 re-tweets from the account, half of them contained some discussion of whether the account was authentic, or whether Banksy uses Twitter at all. One of these posts, from I_Am_Banksy, implied that the account was fake because *they* were the real Banksy. Five of the posts discussed issues related to following the "banksy" account, including wondering why they were following it at all. The first tweet listed in the history of the user's account, in fact, speaks about how many people were following the account even though the account seemed inactive. That tweet, by GrumpyCiara (2011), says "I love how @banksy follows nobody and has tweeted nothing and still has 372 followers #respect."

While the account only re-tweets 28 mentions of its username, there are many additional mentions of the name by other Twitter users. In fact,

within the first two weeks of June 2013 alone, the "banksy" account was mentioned 18 times. The user would have received notification each time these mentions occurred. Thus, the user has elected to contribute to shaping Banksy's identity by forming this online presence but abstaining from creating original content and only quite selectively pushing commentary from others about Banksy to the public.

The perspectives put forth by these tweets add in some ways to the notion of Banksy's identity that the artist has already established. Most notably they contribute to the hype around his mysteriousness and anonymity by continuing the discussion of who he is and speculation about what would be within his character. For example, KeithCore88 (2013) asked this question, which was re-tweeted by the @banksy account: "It would make sense for @banksy to be on twitter, but would @banksy be @banksy or would being @banksy be too obvious. Or would it not?" Clearly this user has come to consider Banksy's character and is unsure about whether having a user account with this pseudonym would be within that character or not. The user of the account pushes this message forward, along with 13 others that question whether Banksy is or is not the user of the account.

While these tweets continue to aid in making Banksy mysterious, they might also make the claim that he has made (that he is not a Twitter users) less credible. Banksy himself noted that things could be repeated to the point of becoming meaningless. Perhaps the more Twitter users see tweets repeating that Banksy does not have a Twitter account, the more meaningless this statement might appear. If nothing else, this account and its choice of re-tweets might make users question the artist's honesty when he claims on his Website that he does not have an account. Perhaps he does not, or perhaps claiming he does not adds to the mystery surrounding him.

One thing these tweets bring to the construction of Social Media's Banksy that the artist's rendition does not highlight is direct criticism and praise of the artist. Two of these tweets directly criticize the artist, while one praises him. The user quotemyroomies (2013) says "just show your face dude! You're not even a prolific in the gallery world. Trust me you're dead in the street art world. #Usedtobegood." Another, by CapEff (2013) says, "I normally respect artist, but that dude @banksy is a fucking lame. He's just mad he couldn't make it in the graffiti world." These characterizations of Banksy are distinctly different from those that he allows to be shared about himself through the network he works within actively. These tweets paint the artist as having become irrelevant to the art scene. They suggest he's a thing of the past and that his work was not strong enough to make it in the art scene, or specifically, the graffiti art scene at present. This characterization is in contrast with statements about the artist we see in his network because the only insults seen in that context are those which seem double-sided--he allows insult to himself only when it further does damage to those he dislikes, such as the police department or those that describe his art as simplistic.

FUTURE RESEARCH DIRECTIONS

While this investigation shows the manner in which Banksy has lost control in adding to how he is constructed in the social media realm by abstaining from participation, it is far from an exhaustive treatment of identity construction online. Additionally, this chapter focuses on the identity creation of a notorious figure, rather than a common working professional. It has been the author's intention to shed light on the way in which abstaining from social media does not guarantee a protected online identity. However, further investigation into the effects of abstaining from social media by figures of less media attention would help the professionals further understand how social media shapes online identity regardless of participation. A future study might, for example, examine the means in which scholars within academe are treated through social media platforms that they participate in actively, passively or not at all.

CONCLUSION

While both Banksy and social media can be said to orchestrate networks that construct the identity of the artist, these two identities are decidedly different. The construction of Banksy in his own network might be considered rather tidy. Banksy seems to meticulously control the construction of his identity in this realm.

The identity of Banksy on Twitter is rather unpredictable; anything goes, whether or not there is a foundation for proving its truth. Banksy has no control here. While he claims he is not present in this domain, fans and critics alike bring him to life and craft narratives about who he is.

What is fascinating about this social media network is that there is little dialogue between the participants. What brings them together is momentary attempts at constructing Banksy. Still, no one is operating to correct the miss-aligned images of Banksy that might be crafted in this space. Is Banksy Oprah? We don't know for sure, but no one has told us otherwise. All we can do is weigh the multiple constructions of Banksy we have in comparison to each other.

While other social media sources give users the ability to report or remove content posted about themselves by others, Twitter stays out of making judgments about what content is offense and which is not and refrains from giving users the power to have content removed. Therefore, everything is left to remain as "truth" unless another user challenges it. Truth is constructed through the negotiation of knowledge between users on Twitter. One issue with Banksy's absence from Twitter is that he cannot respond to claims that are made about him.

We're left with what tweets claim about him. He is on Twitter. He is not on Twitter. He is Oprah; but he is also Jean-Luc Goddard and James Franco. But for some reason, he is not Justin Timberlake. Nearly everyone imaginable has been named Bansky—or claimed they were Banksy himself. Perhaps Twitter user yourfriendmitch (2010) was right when he said, "You know we're ALL Banksy, right?" If nothing else, like Banksy, we should all give consideration to how we are constructed online through social media.

So much material is distributed on Twitter about Banksy's identity that it's almost rendered useless. This fact may contribute to why Banksy does not concern himself with controlling this domain of his identity. However, what does this mean for those of use who are not celebrities? Who are only being constructed on social media by a handful of individuals? What if our potential bosses have hackers that break into Facebook to look for us and find, not pages that we've made for ourselves, but only those college party pictures posted by our roommate? What happens when a jaded significant other airs their grievances about us on their Twitter account for the world to see?

We have heard accounts of individuals losing their jobs for sounding off about their boss or company on a social media outlet. However, few people discuss the means by which the boss's reputation is altered in the aftermath of such public stories.

The root issue that this chapter explores is that there is no fact-checking in social media. Online identities, like Banksy's rats (Banksy, 2006, p. 95), may exist within the social media realm without our permission. This fact need not be one to cause alarm, but rather contemplation. Before we conclude that avoiding social media is the best way to ensure that our identities are not tainted as a result of our private lives going public, we may wish to consider what security this abstinence really provides. Perhaps our only hope in controlling our identity construction within these domains is by being present, by being connected, and by being active—if only active as a lurker.

REFERENCES

Bakhtin, M. (1984). *Problems of Dostoevsky's poetics*. Minneapolis, MN: University of Minnesota Press.

Banksy. (2006). *Wall and piece*. London: Century.

Banksy (Director). (2010). *Exit through the gift hop*. [Motion Picture]. United Kingdom: Paranoid Pictures.

Banksy. (n.d.). *Banksy*. Retrieved from http://banksy.co.uk

Brown, A. (2011). Relationships, community, and identity in the new virtual society. *The Futurist*, *45*(2), 29–34.

Callon, M. (1999). Actor network theory--The market test. In J. Law, & J. Hassard (Eds.), *Actor network theory and after* (pp. 181–185). Oxford, UK: Wiley-Blackwell.

CapEff. (2013, January 13). *I normally respect artist, but that dude @banksy is a fucking lame. He's just mad he couldn't make it in the graffiti world*. [Twitter post]. Retrieved from https://twitter.com/CapEff/status/290610859053572096.

Collins, L. (2007). Banksy was here: The invisible man of graffiti art. *The New Yorker*. Retrieved from http://www.newyorker.com/reporting/2007/05/14/070514fa_fact_collin

GrumpyCiara. (2011, November 8). *I love how @banksy follows nobody and has tweeted nothing and still has 372 followers #respect*. [Twitter post]. Retrieved from https://twitter.com/GrumpyCiara/status/132239489262292992

KeithCore88. (2013, April 11). *It would make sense for @banksy to be on twitter, but would @banksy be @banksy or would being @banksy be too obvious? Or would it not?* [Twitter post]. Retrieved from https://twitter.com/KeithCore88/status/322332524175048706

Kemp, S. (2011). Banksy request to appear at the Oscars in disguise rejected. *Hollywood Reporter.* Retrieved from http://www.hollywood-reporter.com/news/banksy-request-at-oscars-disguise-159736

Latour, B. (2008). *Reassembling the social: An introduction to actor-network-theory.* New York, NY: Oxford University Press.

Liebowitz, M. (2012, May 31). *Huge spike expected in employer Facebook snooping.* Retrieved from http://www.nbcnews.com/id/47636375/ns/technology_and_science-security/t/huge-spike-expected-employer-facebook-snoop-ing/https://twitter.com/quotemyroomies/sta-tus/303074529842974720

Pest Control Office. (n.d.). *What is pest control?* Retrieved from http://www.pestcontroloffice.com/whatispco.html

Pike, G. H. (2011). Fired over Facebook. *Information Today, 28*(4), 26.

Potts, L., & Jones, D. (2011). Contextualizing experiences: Tracing the relationships between people and technologies in the social web. *Journal of Business and Technical Communication, 23*(3), 338–358. doi:10.1177/1050651911400839

quotemyroomies. (2013, February 17). *@Banksy just show your face dude! You're not even a prolific in the gallery world. Trust me you're dead in the street art world. #Usedtobegood.* [Twitter post]. Retrieved from https://twitter.com/quote-myroomies/status/303074529842974720

Sullivan, R. (2010). The problem with WHOIS. *Spectator: The University of Southern California Journal of Film & Television, 30*(2), 57–64.

Turkle, S. (1995). *Life on the screen: Identity in the age of the internet.* New York, NY: Simon and Schuster.

Turkle, S. (2011). *Alone together: Why we expect more for technology and less from each other.* New York, NY: Basic Books.

Twitter Help Center. (n.d.). *FAQs about verified accounts.* Retrieved from https://support.twitter.com/groups/31-twitter-basics/topics/111-features/articles/119135-about-verified-accounts

Veletsianos, G. G. (2012). Higher education scholar's participation and practices on twitter. *Journal of Computer Assisted Learning, 28*(4), 336–249. doi:10.1111/j.1365-2729.2011.00449.x

Volmar, P. (2010). How to use social media to forge corporate identity. *Public Relations Tactics, 17*(6), 20.

yourfriendmitch. (2010, February 26). *You know we're ALL Banksy, right?.* [Twitter post].

KEY TERMS AND DEFINITIONS

Actor Network Theory: A theory used to describe networks wherein not all agents are human. This network allows objects agency.

Activity Theory: A theory used to analyze motives for human action.

Identity: A constructed sense of a person developed over time. It is that which makes an individual distinguishable and memorable from others.

Re-Tweet: When a Twitter user quotes another user's quote, with or without adding his or her own words and pushes that content to his or her own users.

Social Media: Virtual networks wherein users share information within a social group or groups.

Twitter: A social media platform wherein users micro blog content in 140 characters or less. Users follow one another to create a feed of content.

ENDNOTES

[1]   While there is no way to be completely certain that this site is authentically associated with the artist because of the nature of his anonymity, the author of this chapter has elected to approach this Website as an artist endorsed text because much of writing on the site is done from the perspective of the artist. In fact, the newest version of the site contains a Question page which is written in first person. Additionally, the overall Website is ran by an organization called Pest Control. According to their own site, "Pest Control is a handling service acting on behalf of the artist Banksy" (Pest Control Office, n.d.). They describe their purpose as twofold: "We answer enquiries and determine whether he was responsible for making a certain piece of artwork and issue paperwork if this is the case. This process does not make a profit and has been set up to prevent innocent people from becoming victims of fraud" (Pest Control Office, n.d.).

Chapter 5
Virtual World Avatar Branding

Thomas J. Mowbray
The Ohio State University, USA

ABSTRACT

Avatar branding is the process of creating a virtual personality, establishing a well-known virtual identity, and immersing oneself as an active participant in virtual society. In virtual worlds such as Second Life and the many Opensim worlds, avatar branding is an essential capability for many kinds of virtual world users, such as fine artists, musicians, poets, writers, deejays, athletes, actors, fashion designers, and other kinds of virtual celebrities. This chapter discusses the process of avatar branding and covers several examples of famous branded avatars.

A NEW LIFE

When you enter a virtual world as a new user, you are establishing a new life, a new identity. You have no friends, no money, and no belongings other than default clothing and body parts that come with your avatar's inventory. Many of us in virtual worlds have had this experience multiple times. In fact, with the proliferation of worlds based upon the OpenSimulator technology (henceforth, OpenSim), it is not unusual to restart your virtual life dozens of times, as each new virtual world poses the same existential challenges. In Open-Sim, it is wise to re-establish you avatar identity in as many virtual worlds as possible (proactively,

before someone else assumes your identity). This is a very basic form of avatar branding, essentially you can proliferate your avatar name into many virtual worlds by creating new free accounts with the same usernames.

AVATAR BRANDING: INTRODUCTION

The term "brand" is inherited from the traditional practice of burning a unique symbol into cattle to distinguish them from other herds. Branding, as adopted by mass marketing, creates a public image of a product line which can have human qualities, such as warmth, sexiness, joy, or friendliness. Because marketing technologies, such as social

DOI: 10.4018/978-1-4666-5150-0.ch005

networks, Web sites, and email lists, are available to individual citizens, we have arrived into an era of personalized branding. As Essid (2011) states, it is commonplace for today's students to devote vast energies into personally branding their real lives through social networking.

An avatar is a computer graphic representation of a person. Avatars are used widely in social networking, blogging, and advertising as iconic representations of brand images, whether personal or corporate. Your avatar picture can stand in as a thumbnail representation of you, your personality, and a brand image that you want to promote. As Sherman (2009) indicates, people who use the default image in social networking are becoming the exception and may even be viewed with suspicion.

In virtual worlds, we have avatars that we can reshape, dress, communicate, move about, and friend other avatars. We can play music, recite poetry, and have discussions. Virtual worlds are real-time three dimensional (3D) simulations of what happens in other social media, but in an intensely immersive way. In fact, we can photograph our avatars and use the image for other forms of Internet interactions, e.g. social networks.

When we promote our avatar and their activities for business or personal reasons we are personally branding a representation of ourselves. Many techniques of personal branding in social networks and avatar branding in virtual worlds are interchangeable, as evidenced by the author's own success on LinkedIn, which led to a cyber security book contract and an executive job opportunity in higher education. For example, Beard (2007) describes how to surf Digg sites of friends to discover other friends that you can friend. In virtual worlds and on LinkedIn, we can do the same with group memberships.

This chapter explains approaches for avatar branding in virtual worlds such as Second Life and Opensim worlds. The next section establishes some basic assumptions about the scope of avatar branding, the economics of virtual worlds, and the advertising environment. The succeeding sections cover the avatar branding process from inception of the avatar's virtual life. After that, several examples of famous branded avatars are discussed.

BACKGROUND

For the purposes of this chapter, the scope of virtual worlds includes Second Life and the numerous Opensim worlds (http://opensimulator. org). Second Life (SL) is the social and economic center of virtual worlds, so the focus on avatar branding primarily applies to this world. Branded avatars have an increasing presence in Opensim worlds; for example, numerous SL musicians are available to play concerts in Opensim.

Opensim and Second Life share a common technology base; Opensim is the open source release of SL technology. Some essential SL features were held back by Linden Research, in particular the in-world events listings. Which is interesting: it indicates that Linden Research understands that the core of SL society revolves around outstanding advertising infrastructure. Avatar branding will use and benefit from this infrastructure.

At the time of this writing, virtual world economies appear reasonably stable. SL hosts extensive free economies (e.g. freebie stores and communities) as well as commerce for goods. Almost all live music and theatrical performances are free for the public in SL, as are most other activities such as poetry, deejay parties, sports, etc. Education is an emerging commercial industry in SL, particularly for natural language instruction; however, many other kinds of instruction, such as building skills and clothing design, are available free to the public. Most Opensim worlds have nascent but emerging economies; however they are more heavily reliant on free economies.

Advertising is an interesting economic phenomenon in virtual worlds (VW), and particularly important to avatar branding. Many forms of VW advertising are free, such as group notices, group instant messages, subscriber groups, email lists, and event listings. These kinds of advertising are also available in Opensim, although event listings are typically hosted on a Website calendar rather than in-world.

The advertising situation is changing in SL. Linden Research, the company that owns SL, posts curated event advertisements prominently in its new viewer, via an in-world tool called the Destination Guide. The new viewer does not keep group notices persistent on the screen, but only displays them a few seconds (called a toast time). This reduces the advertising effectiveness of group notices; even though, group notices can also broadcast to users' email accounts, but only when their avatar is offline. Technology changes have rendered obsolete many of the alternative viewers, so the new Linden Research advertising ecosystem is predominating.

FIRST CHOICES: CREATING THE NEW YOU

In virtual worlds, there are many options and few constraints. What sex will the new you be? What kind of shape? How tall? How fit? Which skin? What will you wear? Will you be human, humanoid, animal or other? (e.g. a flying spaghetti monster)

The initial resources you have available include the Library folder in inventory and freebies. Numerous freebie stores are scattered around virtual worlds, and are easily located via the in-world search or simply by asking, for example, on a volunteer user help group.

It is a simple fact of social engineering that people like to help other people. Some users even make virtual careers out of helping others by volunteering at orientation gateways, volunteering their time to help groups, and teaching. In Second Life, there are several free schools set up to help new users develop virtual world skills; find these classes in the in-world Events search, Education

category. Many in-world businesses offer freebies to new avatars, such as hair, skins, and clothing. These can be located through help groups. Hair is a particularly valuable early acquisition, as high quality hair is expensive, particularly for a new user starting from scratch.

For a modest real-world investment (e.g. US$10), users can purchase substantial virtual currency, more than enough to outfit an avatar in high quality fashion.

INITIAL ACTIVITIES

In this section and the next, we discuss the context for avatar branding. What do people do in virtual worlds? How can one find other virtual people and interact with them? In this section, we consider what new avatars, without established social relationships, can do. If you are avatar branding among new users, this section is relevant. In the next section, we develop more of a social model for avatar activities, introducing generic avatar communities for recurring interaction. In that case, these are opportunities for branding among experienced users whom you will encounter multiple times.

New users in virtual worlds are called newbies. It is not a derogatory term; at some point, everyone in virtual worlds was a newbie. A common newbie question is: what do we do here? The SL Destination Guide is a direct corporate response to this need, where Linden Research hand picks activities for users and provides actionable advertisements (teleport links) for their recommendations.

In general, the types of activities new users can engage in include:

- **Freebie Shopping:** Newbies can locate freebies (free merchandise and clothing) in the in-world search and through help groups. Shopping is a major avocation in virtual worlds. Many commercial stores also offer a small (sometimes large) selection of freebies. These stores can brand themselves by requiring group membership to obtain the freebies. In this way, new users are drawn into the Fashion Community (see next section). Announcing a new Freebie of the Month is a common advertising technique.

- **DJ Dance Parties:** There are hundreds of free avatar dance parties daily throughout the virtual world of Second Life, as well as, on Opensim worlds. See the events listings under live music and nightlife in Second Life and the community calendars on Opensim registration Websites.
- **Free Education:** Education is a very popular activity in virtual worlds; it is possible to learn all about virtual worlds and related technologies, such as 3-D building, animating, and fashion design. Check the education events online or in-world in Second Life.
- **Games:** Gaming in the virtual world is a popular pastime, for example at casino regions. Many clubs also provide a game in the nearby chat called a sploder.

OVERVIEW OF VIRTUAL COMMUNITIES

This section covers the major categories of virtual world communities. Communities are an opportunity for recurring interaction, and for avatar brand building among users with similar interests. The next section discusses some specific Second Life Communities. These categories are informally ordered from most to least levels of user activity.

Note that roughly 70% of SL users spend most of their time on their own virtual land and rarely participate in communities. For example, many users who purchase virtual horses, dogs, or fantasy animals called Meeroos, actively engage in the husbandry of these virtual life forms on their own land.

- **Musical Communities:** Live musical performances are extremely popular in virtual worlds; there are thousands of active musicians and hundreds of free shows daily. Musicians actively brand themselves for every performance by advertising in music groups and using their friends list to setup an impromptu chat.
- **Educational Communities:** There are several types of educational communities in virtual worlds. One type is a form of professional networking; many of the professional societies for real-world educators also have virtual world branches and are very active. Another type of educational community is formed around the free schools discussed in the previous section, which teach primarily virtual world skills of all kinds. Virtual worlds are nearly ideal platforms for foreign language training. Students from anywhere with Internet access can experience realistic role plays, and practice language skills in context. Most of the foreign language institutes are for-profit.
- **Fashion Communities:** There is a saying among virtual world researchers and consultants that "you can buy anything in Second Life." Certainly, with regards to fashion, vibrant communities of fashion designers, store owners, and retail customers thrive throughout Second Life and also on Opensim worlds, although the Opensim economies are nascent.
- **Adult and Role Playing Communities:** A few years ago Linden Research took steps to segregate purely adult activities away from the mainstream regions. Lindens created a new Second Life continent called Zindra, where all adult-rated activities were relocated. There are also extensive role-playing communities with adult themes and content. For example, approximately 400 regions in Second Life are de-

voted to Gor, where users role-play a culture derived from a series of anti-feminist fantasy novels (Norman, 1997).

- **Gaming Communities:** There are many casino-like regions and specialty groups devoted to gaming in-world. Gaming activities called hunts are organized by alliances of retail stores and often borrow their themes from real-world holidays.
- **Poetry and Storytelling Communities:** Poets and storytellers are active in virtual worlds on a daily basis. Most events are open microphone, but there are also some standalone-type events with very accomplished poets.
- **Fine Arts and Theater Communities:** Virtual worlds are worlds of art: the user-generated content parallels real-world art-forms, such as painting, sculpture, plays, fine arts dances, and architecture.
- **Active Citizenship Communities:** Professional networking occurs in the education domain, but also in a handful of other disciplines such as disability rights, sustainability, and nonprofits.
- **Spiritual Communities:** There are both formal and informal spiritual communities in virtual worlds. All it takes is a leader willing to organize events.
- **Sports Communities:** Virtual worlds are less than ideal platforms for sports, e.g. lag, but there are enthusiasts who practice a wide range of sports primarily for their own entertainment.

COMMUNITY PROFILES

Second Life is the social center of the virtual worlds. SL hosts some intriguing communities that we will discuss now. These communities are easy to locate and contact by using the Second Life group search function. Another strategy is to locate a resident with long SL history and open

the groups pages from their in-world profile. Most community groups also have Websites with event calendars.

The *Virginia Society for Technology in Education* (VSTE) is a very active and vibrant community of K-16 teachers. Most, but not all, members of this free-to-join community are teachers in the state of Virginia, but it's fair to say that VSTE's reach is global. VSTE has a professional staff who produce a real-world newsletter as well as host weekly events in SL. There is a companion community based upon the International Society for Technology in Education (ISTE). Other education communities in SL include: Virtual Worlds Education Roundtable (VWER), EDUCAUSE, ARVEL, and Virtual Pioneers. There is also free education in SL that teaches in-world skills, at schools such as New Citizens Inc, Builders Brewery, Rockcliffe University, Happy Hippo Builders School (HHBS), and Caledon Oxbridge University.

The SL community *Etopia* is the virtual epicenter of environmentalism and sustainability in the virtual worlds. Most Etopia citizens are either environmental scientists or avid practitioners of sustainable living. Etopia citizens have a great deal of knowledge to share and a burning passion for sustainability. Etopia's regions are a showcase of sustainable technologies, including many working demonstrations, e.g. solar power, wind power, and recycling. Etopia hosts drum circles on its main island, writers' workshops with award-winning authors, poetry open mikes, dance parties, and regular events such "The Bored Meating." The Bored Meating is a fun weekly Etopia discussion; at Bored Meatings, citizens bring up inane topics just for a laugh. But not without purpose, for communing with others at Etopia reinforces the resolve to improve the environment, even if members are surrounded by negative influences in real life. You can join the groups at Etopia or even rent a storefront or apartment on the Etopia islands. There are other locations for science and environmentalism throughout Second Life (such as the Better World region); a list of these locations is circulating in the SL/Real Life (henceforth, RL) education community.

Nonprofit Commons is a professional networking community for non-governmental organizations (NGOs) and educators. NPC attracts dozens of these professionals to every weekly meeting. The meetings include short courses and invited speakers, usually one of the peer NGO representatives or an outside expert. NPC also hosts weekly social dance party events and special events. NPC is a initiative of TechSoup, a company that aggregates volume discounts and other benefits for its NGO members. Nonprofit groups who are TechSoup members can obtain a free storefront on one of the NPC regions in SL.

Feed a Smile is an RL charity, but also an SL community that hosts frequent events: live music, drum circles, poetry, and storytelling. Entertainers donate their time and talent, and bring their own fans to celebrate with the Feed a Smile regulars. For only 100 Linden dollars (less than ½ US dollar) SL residents can buy a meal for a child in Kenya. Compared with major charities that waste up to 75% of donations on overhead expenses, Feed a Smile has no overhead. That efficiency enables the Feed a Smile SL community to have real impact in the lives of RL school children.

Cybernetic Art Research Project (CARP) is a community of artists, fashion designers, actors, and fine-arts dancers that host gallery shows, SL rock operas, and other events such as IMAGINE PeaceFest. For example CARP rock operas have included The Wall, The Rings, The Change, and Metropolis. Versions of the rock operas are on YouTube. CARP also participates in real-world art shows where CARP hosts mixed-reality SL and real-life events. The CARP founders have cataloged in-world art and artists and produced a series of electronic books which comprise a comprehensive history of the SL fine art's community.

Four Bridges is a community of NGO activists in SL, organized by an official representative to the virtual worlds from Amnesty International. Four Bridges hosts many festival themed activist events such as Human Rights Festival, Earth Week SL, and IMAGINE PeaceFest. Many of these communities are overlapping, so CARP members are also members of Four Bridges and attend NPC meetings. Four Bridges hosts the weekly Amnesty International Poetry Hour, an open mike event.

Virtual Abilities Inc. (VAI) is a community for people with disabilities in SL and other people who support disability rights. VAI hosts frequent invited speaker engagements, bringing world class disability rights experts and researchers into SL. VAI has a Linden Prize award-winning community gateway, a place where new SL residents can learn all the basics needed to survive and thrive in virtual worlds. Another notable community gateway is at Caledon Oxbridge University, a Victorian steampunk community, which offers a generous array of Victorian clothing to new SL residents.

AVATAR BRANDING STRATEGY

Suppose we are setting up a new avatar and preparing a branding campaign. Some first steps include finding events and other avatars in the desired branding domain. We might next build up a list of group memberships by opening the groups in other avatar's profiles. Once we have a critical mass of groups, start attending events in our branding domain. Be an active participant, for example, by volunteering to lead events.

Notecards are a built-in virtual world tool to contain text and other content and can be trasfered from user to user, advertising a brand. Keep trying different advertising ideas until you figure out what works best with your audience. Your brand is established and maintained via regular events that you will lead or actively engage. Every advertisement is a market test and re-asserts your brand in your communities.

AVATAR BRANDING CASE STUDIES

The New York Times documented a branded avatar artist who makes his living through virtual worlds in Corbet (2009) and McCabe (2010) covers a virtual world researcher who studies and interviews financially self-supporting avatars. The selection of virtual world users and their avatars in this chapter's case studies represent a cross section of online activities: musical composition, theater, musical performance, education, facilitation, philosophy, research, poetry, fiction writing, journalism, and celebrity talk show hosting. These case studies provide intriguing insights into the user's mind of branded avatars.

The following avatar branding case studies are presented in an informal interview format, and coded as follows: the *italicized text* denotes verbatim quotations, which are copy edited for minor clarifications. The subheadings (bold text) are the interview prompts (questions). As in virtual world chat, the speakers use many acronyms, marketing English (emphatic incomplete sentences), and texting conventions, such as SHOUTING (capitalization) for emphasis, and smileys to indicate humor.:-) See the final section of this chapter for Key Terms and Definitions.

Note that the speakers very fluently switch contexts between real life (RL) and Second Life (SL), or RL and virtual worlds (VW), even within a single sentence. This is very commonplace and indicative of the way people who use VWs think about them and RL.

CASE STUDY INTERVIEW: JUNIVERS STOCKHOLM

In this first case study, Junivers Stockholm is a very accomplished and famous branded avatar. Junivers is the composer and star of three major rock opera productions in SL: *The Wall, The Rings,* and *The Change* (Figure 1).

How did you get started in SL?

I saw a TV program about Virtual Worlds 2006. I'm very interested in future technology and everything else that is futuristic. I downloaded the VW the TV program suggested. I soon realized it was an online game in which you built up fake skills by paying for different tools and using them - a cyclic cost that developed fake skills only useful in a specific game. But now I was turned on.

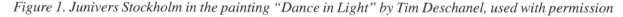

Figure 1. Junivers Stockholm in the painting "Dance in Light" by Tim Deschanel, used with permission

I did additional research and found SL. In SL it was your RL skills that counted. You could use any RL skill (more or less) and make something of it in SL.

What motivates you to keep coming back into SL? What do you enjoy most about your SL experiences?

The fact that my RL skills counted was the number 1 reason I stayed in SL. I could even develop some of my RL skills. Also I needed to extend some of my RL skills into VW. So I developed additional skills because of VWs. SL is a great platform for international collaboration too. VW platforms have many things in common with RL. Sometimes I feel there is no difference, but of course there are. I enjoy SL so much because my RL became extended and became richer (experience wise).

Why did you choose to be Junivers Stockholm, musician and rock opera composer?

Like in RL you need/want something to do. I started to do research in SL about things I worked with in RL. TV/Audio/Media were things I wanted to see if and how they were developed in SL. But I was also very interested in what happened in the world of non-governmental organizations (NGO). I realized NGOs had perhaps even more challenges in SL than RL – for example, to cultivate people's interest to be volunteers or donate money. So my SL life got more and more involved with people that also wanted to "Change the World!"

And before I knew it ALL my SL life was about changing the world. So it wasn't a conscious choice to become a composer and musician. But sure, the path was there all the time. It was more like: "Well somebody has to do it" and I did because I was asked to.

What are some of the best choices or opportunities you have undertaken that have really strengthened your avatar brand and enriched your virtual life?

To be part in events, and sometimes to create them, with the aim to spread awareness and change has been very fulfilling. To work so closely with international people with great skills in many fields of endeavor. People that I love and respect... my virtual life has been very rewarding. My choices have never been about anything to do with branding. I'm not a guy that shouts out about how great I am. I dislike being in situations in which I constantly have to prove how good and skilled I am. I don't want to be stressed out. I guess that is my brand now:) That's what I hope. I refuse to try to be something I'm not.

CASE STUDY INTERVIEW: PAMALA CLIFT

Pamala Clift is a virtual world educator, founder, and facilitator of The Roadside Philosophers, a very popular discussion group in SL, attracting dozens of avatars at each bi-weekly meeting in the underwater grotto at Rockcliffe University. Pamala is also the author of a popular book about SL relationships, the *Virgin's handbook on virtual relationships* (Clift, 2012), which is a significant virtual world research treatise in its own right (Figure 2).

Note that Pamala uses emoting notations in her interview responses. For example: [rolls eyes] and [pulls hair out]. Pamala is a very experienced discussant and talented writer who exuberantly expresses her personality and humor in text.

How did you get started in SL?

Figure 2. Pamala Clift

I started SL because I live in a small town of about 2000. My need is "more input" with greater diversity. My husband is a gamer, which left my evenings without challenge. I do not enjoy following constraints predetermined for me in games, so after hearing about SL through a couple of business and computer magazines, I downloaded it and gave it a try.

What motivates you to keep coming back into SL? What do you enjoy most about your SL experiences?

I come back into SL for people and challenges. New projects, and ways to visualize my thinking so others may also know what I see in my mind.

Why did you choose to be the avatar Pamala Clift and become the leader of the Roadside Philosophers?

Pamala came about because my real life initials are PAM. So I tried for some version of Panama,

Pamela was taken, so to be unique, I put the name with all A's. Clift was the first C surname in the list when I joined. My maiden name starts with a C.

I still need more input, and the added platform of at least a global perspective. People and researchers have not yet put into practice what I have envisioned for education, so I work slowly to orient others to see & understand the possibilities of more experiential learning.

The Roadside Philosophers was originally just the result of trying out all the menu items while exploring this medium. The Roadside Philosopher was part of the name of the never ending novel that I am writing. The first members were just the guys fighting over Pam, and I thought it would be entertaining to see them battle intellectually. Then other people found the group that I didn't even know. I originally thought I knew it all and would help clarify things for all the loss souls, [rolls eyes]

It took me two long years of drama and pain because people were Not getting what I was trying to tell them, before I actually shut up and started to listen. All people have valid reasons for their perception. I now had a large group that I could pose any question my little mind would ponder and get multiple perceptions. Since I always have questions, and the group is so eager to share, I now have a 600 person cabinet for my inquiries.

I feel very blessed to have worked out a method that everyone seems to get, for such a large international eclectic group to discuss civilly very touchy topics. I would like to see a similar virtual world offshoot of the United Nations. Then if parties get mad at each other they can fight it out with pig guns in world instead of real life wars.

What are some of the best choices or opportunities you have undertaken that have really strengthened your avatar brand and enriched your virtual life?

The Roadside Philosophers is all mine and the title I wear above my head as I travel the Metaverse in other areas besides SL, FB, twitter, social media, It is unique enough to be solo on the internet search engines. If you put in Pamala Clift in almost everything, what comes up is related to me.

Because of the philosophers I was invited, when my sim closed, [I wanted] to bring my group and join other organizations. The end result was joining Rockcliffe University Consortium, which works with educational institutions. I have now worked with multiple professors, and doctoral students around the world in their research, setting up the constructs and narrowing down focus. The virtual culture has to be recognized as a culture and first be understood prior to trying to label it, so I work on orientation.

The immersive component of this medium, is extremely valuable for learning but also very dangerous. I was losing my researchers to hiccups with interpersonal relationships. [Pulls hair out]

So my next step was try and figure out a construct that would make sense, so a best practice approach could be established in engaging online. Thankfully I had my philosophers to contribute enough of b their experiences and perception that I developed my famous State of Being lecture that has been given to thousands over the last three plus years. It tells in a light entertaining way the conflicts of engagement, and presents a method of volume control for those online.

The researchers and professors loved it, but wanted more concrete references. So first I set up a website, then started a business, Virtual Handhold LLC, but that was still not enough. They wanted Library of Congress authentication. So that meant either a white paper or a book. Well since few read white papers and the stringent guide lines would bore me to tears, I decided to put my State of Being lecture inside a mass marketable book called Virgin's handbook on virtual relationships That took over a year to write, then start a Kickstarter project to fund the publishing. It is currently undergoing both a reedit, and an audible book.

CASE STUDY INTERVIEW: J. L. MORIN

J. L. Morin is a novelist and adjunct faculty at Boston University in RL. J. L. did significant real world branding for her books *Sazzae* (Morin, 2009a), *Above ground* (2009b), and *Traveling light* (Morin, 2011) before branding in virtual worlds.

J. L.'s decision to brand her avatar and her next book, *Trading dreams* (Morin, 2012), in virtual worlds led to her book's success in reaching

Number 1 in Political Fiction on Amazon's Kindle Store during mixed reality branding campaigns, including advertising and events in RL and SL (Figure 3).

J. L. continues to actively brand in Second Life and in real world media, for example via her Huffington Post blog. Using her leadership roles in both Harvard and Boston University alumni groups (as well as in-world publicity), J. L. promotes a weekly Second Life event that brings very talented, leading-edge authors in-world for readings, poetry, and drum circle fun.

How did you get started in SL?

I discovered SL when Occupy Virtual Worlds asked me to do a book talk on my Occupy novel Trading dreams during the 1-year anniversary of the Occupy movement in October of 2012. I was impressed with the idyllic venue on Etopia Island, and enjoyed reading and talking with folks

at the drum circle. I kept coming back for more every Sunday to hear more literary readings, read more of my fiction, poetry and song lyrics, and I eventually became a drum circle leader.

What motivates you to keep coming back into SL? What do you enjoy most about your SL experiences?

I love the open-mindedness and independent thinking of the community, especially the healthy, anti-corporate orientation, and the music and lyrics are great. People aren't afraid to express their views, probably because they have avatars with fictional names, so I feel at home with them, since I'm hung up on the truth and speaking my mind even in the real world.

Why did you choose to be the avatar jlmorin and become a Poetric Drum Circle leader?

Figure 3. The cover of J. L. Morin's novel Trading dreams, which reached #1 in Political Fiction on Amazon due to mix reality branding campaigns

I wanted my avatar to represent my book, already published under my name J. L. Morin. Trading dreams had already received a lot of rave reviews from Publishers Weekly and the likes, and I've won two book awards, written two other novels, am a Library Journal literary critic and blog for the Huffington Post, so it would have been a waste to re-brand my work in SL under another name.

What are some of the best choices or opportunities you have undertaken that have really strengthened your avatar brand and enriched your virtual life?

Being a Drum Circle leader has been a phenomenal opportunity to connect regularly with like-minded people from all over the world and make culture happen, something that seems rare in the real world, which is more and more controlled by media moguls and big business trying to sell their junk rather than heal the planet or transmit any truth. I keep the drum circle open to those who want to read, so it functions like an open mic, but I also invite special guest authors to present their new works.

CASE STUDY INTERVIEW: NETERA LANDAR

Netera Landar is a celebrity talk show host in Second Life and on Opensim in the virtual community 3rd Rock Grid (Figure 4). Through her series of interviews and discussions, Netera has befriended numerous musicians, authors, artists, intellectuals, and other celebrities, as well as captured the imaginations of her audiences. Netera is also a prolific writer for virtual world periodicals including The Metaverse Tribune and her own virtual magazines, as well as in real life as novelist Denise Fleischer, author of *The guardian* (Fleischer, 2003), *Altar of freedom* (Fleischer, 2007), and *Deadly reservations* (Fleischer, 2013).

In the interview, Landar discusses IMVU.com, a Web-based virtual world where avatars are much less customizable than Second Life. One user of both worlds colorfully describes IMVU avatars as: "ugly, too skinny, has man-shoulders, meatpaws and flipper feet, and no curves whatsoever(for female)."

How did you get started in SL?

Figure 4. Netera Landar onstage with her celebrity guest at her show The Netera Landar Chat

After using IMVU for a year, I grew restless. I wanted to have virtual explorations and challenges. I had been a AOL writer's community leader for years and knew SL was the most advanced of the virtual worlds. I just needed the courage to hop in world and try it out.

What motivates you to keep coming back into SL? What do you enjoy most about your SL experiences?

My primary motivation is getting published and getting paid. I consider myself a professional writer. A writer writes every way she can.

Why did you choose to be the avatar Netera Landar and produce the Netera Landar Chats?

That goes back to my AOL Community Leader days. I interviewed authors back then. That's who I began interviewing in a new virtual world after being a host on an early romance virtual world. Since I'm a newspaper writer in RL, I knew I could continue what I do using SL as a vehicle of communication.

What are some of the best choices or opportunities you have undertaken that have really strengthened your avatar brand and enriched your virtual life?

Switching from a coffee shop chat to a studio-based chat show was a more effective arrangement that expanded my audience. Writing for SL magazines as well for newspapers, that is how I met the many musicians I hosted on Netera Landar Chats.

SEXISM AND AVATAR BRANDING

The study of virtual worlds is an interdisciplinary activity that involves elements of computer science, psychology, sociology, communications and other disciplines. In science communications, Knobloch-Westerwick (2013) informs us that there are measurable sexual identity biases. Males acting as researchers are perceived as producing higher quality work than their female counterparts, even when submitting identical research abstracts. These biases can have dramatic affects on career outcomes, and are largely due to unconscious processes. Coincidentally, the author encountered a similar affect when researching this chapter.

Conducting the preceding interview survey rapidly evolved into an impromptu experiment concerning avatar sexism. Two avatars, a male and a female, solicited the interview surveys from 4 celebrity users each. In each case, 3 female users and 1 male user were solicited in exactly the same way, with the same words. All 8 users are famous virtual celebrities whom the author considers friends. Within 12 hours, the male avatar had all 4 of the preceding interviews, completely populated, and double checked by the interviewees.

In stark contrast, the female avatar got nothing in return. Two of the female celebrities totally ignored the request; the remaining female celebrity literally snarled at the request. The one male asked by the female avatar agreed to participate in the interview, but that he was too busy and that it would take a week or so. No interview surveys were ever received by the female researcher.

This anecdotal research is one of many instances where the treatment of male avatars was noticably different than the female ones. The author does not believe that these people are overtly sexist; in fact, these are a selection of some of the finest progressive minds in the virtual worlds. It is an interesting situation and one that deserves future research.

FUTURE RESEARCH DIRECTIONS

Implicit bias is an expanding research domain, with groundbreaking studies such as Knobloch-Westerwick (2013). Virtual worlds are a nearly ideal environment for conducting this type of research. Traditional implicit bias research, e.g. Molloy (1988), uses photographs or static electronic displays for comparisons. Virtual worlds add multiple new research dimensions, including body shape, 3D viewing, 3D motion, time, and interaction. For example, instead of simply viewing a static image, research subjects could virtually meet and interact with the alternative characters being evaluated. With virtual worlds, new research questions might involve:

- How does implicit bias correlate with body shapes? Or the shape and size of specific body parts?
- How does implicit bias correlate with behaviors such as different behavioral styles during a job interview? Or a different walking gait? Or alternative sitting postures?

Avatar branding is a social capability with many potential applications. Research into avatar branding could further systematize the practice to make it a teachable skill with predictable outcomes. For example, outcomes such as maximizing number of friends, number of interactions, duration of interactions, event popularity, and number of product purchases. Applications of an optimized practice of avatar branding might include:

- Assisting K-16 students in social development such as meeting people, making friends, and conducting meaningful conversions
- Assisting adults in professional development such as public speaking or group facilitation
- Helping a new musician launch their musical career
- Facilitating a government agency to promote a new international campaign with branded human representatives
- Advising a corporation on how to optimize its brand and outreach campaigns or maximizing sales of a new product
- Guiding an NGO to brand its field agents in a new social benefits awareness campaign

CONCLUSION

A few questions arise about avatar-branding research:

- What conclusions does one draw from the work with the case studies?
- What are the ways in which it is possible to brand oneself in virtual space?
- How might virtual world branding be important if virtual worlds become mainstream one day?

Conclusions about the Case Studies

The case studies illustrate the adage that "where there is a will there is a way." Each of the case study subjects displays world-class talent and strong ambition, but with different purposes. Junivers used his many musical and organizational talents to enrich peoples' awareness of social and environmental issues. Pamala used her facilitation talents to build community, conduct social relationships research, and convert her vision into a book. J. L. brought her books and writing talents into the virtual worlds to build community and market her books. There is also an altruistic side to J. L.'s work in virtual worlds because her book readings address women's empowerment and social justice. Netera, at the time of the interview, was highly motivated to use her writing talents to be a productive writer and to raise money. Observing Netera outside of the interview context, she has contributed to virtual society in many ways beyond those narrow motivations.

To the author, Netera's almost shocking focus on money suggests a fundamental weakness of the interview survey technique: the responses are highly dependent upon the subject's state of the mind on the day of the interview. The classic consulting technique to overcome the weakness of interviews is to conduct a large number of interviews (e.g. 50 for a reengineering project), then assessing a wide range of opinions to discover the facts. An alternative, more reliable consulting approach, is to deconstruct documentation to discover the facts. Documentation is typically the product of multiple people and represent a persistent organizational consensus, rather than a temporal state of mind.

There is another key difference between the 4 case studies. Three of the subjects largely found their own way, guided themselves, made all their own discoveries, conducted their own social experiments, found their own in-world friends, and made their virtual life choices independently. Also, these subjects were not widely real-world branded in the specialties they expressed in-world. For them, it took many years of trial and error to fully realize their potential.

In J. L.'s case, she was already real-world branded as a famous book author; she entered the virtual world to perform a book reading, invited by very experienced event organizers, i.e. experts in branding and advertising. By J. L.'s second week in SL, her book-author brand was very widely disseminated, with multiple announcements sent to more than a dozen SL groups. Simultaneously, J. L. was conducting a free give-away promotion of her new book in the Amazon Kindle Store. Her in-world advisors used that event as a key element of the promotion. As a result of the RL and SL campaigns, her book skyrocketed to Number 1 in Political Fiction on Amazon, an amazing branding achievement. Six months later the campaign was repeated in-world with equivalent results. The campaign's real-world value was not a fluke. Before reaching her first year in SL, J.L. was leading public in-world events: poetry hours, drum circles, and writers workshops. The lesson learned from J. L.'s overnight success is that branding can be dramatically accelerated (from years down to weeks), if the results of branding research are systematically applied.

Modes of Avatar Branding

The case studies also display a wide range of branding techniques. J. L.'s approach, discussed just prior, involved advertising primarily in music, fine art, and NGO groups. J.L. also conducted real-world advertising, in particular to friends and alumni groups, and brought in new users to her events as invited guest speakers, e.g. real world novelists. Junivers branded primarily through the advertising of live theater productions. As the lead star of the shows and musical composer, Junivers got top billing as the foremost creative talent in each production. Junivers' productions were advertised on a wide range of music, fine arts, and NGO groups in-world. Pamala branded by conducting academic events, in particular the Roadside Philosophers group. Through an in-world higher education institution, Rockcliffe University, Pamala used the university's faculty and student SL groups, as well as the Rockcliffe Website, to invite participants. Word-of-mouth from her students certainly contributed to her branding efforts. Eventually, she built the Roadside attendance to several dozen regular attendees, making it the largest discussion forum in the virtual worlds. Netera branded in multiple ways: She built up an audience following her Netera Chat talk and musical variety shows, as well as, publishing articles as a reporter for major in-world newspapers. Netera also published and branded her own in-world magazine.

Importance of Avatar Branding to the Mainstream

Avatar branding research can offer real-world value through virtual worlds. Avatar branding is akin general branding. A key element of general branding is the association of human personality attributes to a product, service, organization, or person. So in this section, let's consider virtual world branding (or virtual branding) as a generalization of avatar branding. The value of virtual world branding comes in several forms:

1. Predictable and repeatable success in branding campaigns
2. Rapid launch, ramp-up, and dissemination of the brand
3. Generation of real-world brand popularity
4. An opportunity to pivoting the brand into long term branding engagements with recurring re-branding value

Predictable success means that investments in virtual branding campaigns are secure and worthwhile. A typical branding campaign requires very little time and money, and can be executed part-time by a handful of volunteers.

Rapid launch, ramp up, and dissemination means that major campaigns can easily be planned and launched within a week. A full campaign can be completed within 2 weeks from planning inception through campaign ramp-down. These qualities strongly imply another essential mainstream capability: agility. Agility (or maneuverability) is the goal of real-world strategic planning. If you have a powerful branding capability that can be launched in a heartbeat; that is a truly valuable asset for a mainstream entity, such as a musician, a government agency, an NGO, or a business.

Virtual world branding can and does influence the real world. The users of virtual worlds are real-world people and real-world purchasers of goods and services. They in turn with influence other real-world or virtual users through word-of-mouth. Virtual world campaigns also enter the real world through Internet channels: Websites such as in-world newspapers, online videos, blogs, micro-blogs, social networks, and email. Virtual world branding campaigns are a form of viral marketing, word-of-mouth advertising which is disseminated widely and rapidly through all kinds of Internet channels. The real-world impact of virtual branding is enhanced if the brand is linked to a real-world product, such as a book for sale.

Once a virtual brand is established, the residual goodwill can be readily leveraged into ongoing engagements. The activities of the virtual communities discussed earlier in this chapter are examples of the possible kinds of long-term engagements, with recurring advertising and branding benefits.

All of these in-world and real-world values were realized in J. L. Morin's book campaign discussed in the previous subsection. J. L.'s success was predictable from inception because she engaged experienced organizers who had done numerous similar campaigns before. J. L. repeated the campaign 6 months later and realized comparable real-world value. J. L.'s in-world campaign was launched and disseminated virtual-world-wide within a week of her arrival in SL, an achievement that would be unbelievably rapid by real-world standards. J. L.'s virtual campaign boosted the popularity of her book to Number 1 in her category on Amazon, in other words, the virtual campaign generated unmistakable real-world value to her book product and author brand. J. L. then pivoted her initial branding into long term engagements leading in-world events that regularly generate publicity for her brands.

It is this author's contention that avatar branding is a valuable technology-driven approach to branding, that will deliver mainstream value, should the virtual worlds ever mature into a popular platform for everyone.

REFERENCES

Beard, A. (2007). *How to find the Digg friends you never knew you had*. Retrieved April 16, 2013 from http://andybeard.eu/730/digg-friends.html

Clift, P. (2012). *Virgin's handbook on virtual relationships*. Createspace Independent Publishing Platform.

Corbett, S. (2009). Portrait of an artist as an avatar. *New York Times Magazine.* Retrieved April 17, 2013 from http://www.nytimes.com/2009/03/08/magazine/08fluno-t.html?pagewanted=all&_r=1&

Essid, J. (2011). Playing in a new key: In a new world: virtual worlds, millennial writers, and a 3D composition. In *Teaching and learning in virtual worlds: Pedagogical models and constructivist approaches.* Hershey, PA: IGI Global. doi:10.4018/978-1-60960-517-9.ch010

Fleischer, D. (2003). The guardian (paranormal adventures). Port Town Publishing. Fleischer, D. (2007). Altar of freedom. Port Town Publishing.

Fleischer, D. (2007). *Deadly reservations.* Port Town Publishing.

Knobloch-Westerwick, S., Glynn, C. J., & Huge, M. (2013). The Matilda effect in science communication: An experiment on gender bias in publication quality perceptions and collaboration. *Science Communication.* Retrieved online on May 7, 2013 from http://scx.sagepub.com/content/early/2013/01/24/1075547012472684

McCabe, B. (2010). Blurring the lines between real and virtual, art and work. *CityPaper.* Retrieved April 29, 2013 from http://www2.citypaper.com/news/story.asp?id=20086

Molloy, J. T. (1988). *New dress for success.* New York, NY: Warner Books.

Morin, J. L. (2009a). *SAZZAE.* Hollywood, CA: Harvard Square Ed.s.

Morin, J. L. (2009b). *Above ground.* Hollywood, CA: Harvard Square Ed.s.

Morin, J. L. (2011). *Traveling light.* Hollywood, CA: Harvard Square Ed.s.

Morin, J. L. (2012). *Trading dreams.* Hollywood, CA: Harvard Square Ed.s.

Norman, J. (1997). *Tarnsman of Gor.* Masquerade Books.

Sherman, A. (2009). *6 tips for better branding using avatars.* Retrieved April 16, 2003 from http://gigaom.com/2009/07/16/6-tips-for-better-branding-using-avatars/

KEY TERMS AND DEFINITIONS

AOL: America Online is an Internet Service Provider.

Avatar: A digital representation of a human user's presence. In virtual worlds, avatars are 3 dimensional, move, and communicate according to the user's commands.

Avi: An avatar.

FB: Facebook.com

IMVU: A Web-based virtual world.

In-World: Inside a virtual world.

Log: Usually means logout, but can also refer to logging in.

Marketing English: The use of incomplete sentences, to reduce wordiness, and increase emphasis, without losing clarity.

NGO: A Non-Governmental Organization, for example: Amnesty International.

Relog: Logging out of the virtual world and logging back in. This redundant operation is frequently required because the technology of virtual worlds is buggy (inherently unreliable).

RL: Real life. RL can be used in several ways. RL can refer to the real world. RL can refer to the virtual world user, for example "My RL became extended and became richer (experience wise)." RL can refer to someone's real life partner or spouse, for example "I have to log 'cause my RL just came home." RL can also refer to some generic event or errand that requires real life attention, for example "I have to log because of RL."

SL: Second life.

Teleport: Transporting an avatar immediately from location to location, possibly over great distances.

TV: Television.

VW: Virtual World.

Section 3
Educators and Digital Media

Chapter 6
Going Digital:
A Beginner's Cautionary Tale

Elizabeth Hodges
Virginia Commonwealth University, USA

ABSTRACT

The author reflects on an exploration into the genre of multimodal writing, examining issues of the genre's accessibility for herself and her students and its relevance to writing pedagogy. She examines, too, the need to establish a broadly accessible digital community in sites that seek to foster rich and purposeful multimodal abilities.

INTRODUCTION

In the summer of 2006, I acted on my decision that it was time I learned more about digital writing and, in car fully packed, drove from Richmond, Virginia, to Columbus, Ohio, where I unpacked my car into the carts I had often watched students at my school use to move into their dorms and moved into a dorm room of my own for the two weeks of the summer course I'd registered for. What I recount here are my thoughts about writing during and after this digital boot camp immersion and my experiences working to implement what

I learned that summer in writing workshops the following academic year.

Thoughts on writing first: I am going to start with a premise that is fundamental to everything I think about style in writing: the best writing, regardless of genre, results when form and content are so inexorably wedded that a writer's stylistic choices, minute or grand, become a performance of meaning.

When this premise began to form, I am not sure, but the moment I articulated it I had just finished reading Wesley McNair's poem, "The Abandonment" in *The Atlantic Monthly* in the spring semester of 1989:

DOI: 10.4018/978-1-4666-5150-0.ch006

Climbing on top of him and breathing
into his mouth this way she could be showing her
desire except when she draws back
from him to make her little cries
she is turning to her young son
just coming into the room to find his father my
*   brother*
on the bed with his eyes closed and the slightest
smile on his lips as if when they
both beat on his chest as they do now
he will come back from the dream he is enjoying
so much he cannot hear her calling his name
louder and louder and the son saying get up
get up discovering both of them discovering
for the first time that all along
he has lived in this body this thing
with shut lids dangling its arms
that have nothing to do with him and everything
they can ever know the wife listening weeping
at his chest and the mute son who will never
forget how she takes the face into her hands now
as if there were nothing in the world
but the face and breathes oh
breathes into the mouth that does not breath back.

The poem, twenty-three lines, one sentence of 192 words, no punctuation, tells the story of McNair's sister-in-law trying to resuscitate her husband, McNair's brother, with their young son as witness. Unlike long sentences that work because the sentences have a logic as well as places for readers to breathe, McNair's single-sentence poem works because its enjambment and lack of punctuation leave a reader quickly out of breath, accomplishing both that physical reality and logic of the wife's and child's staggering, resistant, mental denial of the fact of death that lies so clearly before them. The poem leaves readers gasping in some shock, I suspect, about the narrative, but gasping also because of McNair's evoking of an authentic mix of physiological and emotional confusion. The sum of McNair's stylistic choices,

thus, perform his content, drawing readers in as can any exceptional enactment of meaning.

I use McNair to exemplify my premise because I have been thinking about form and content in what Cynthia Selfe calls "alphabetic texts" for a long time and am articulate, I hope, when I discuss how such texts do what they do with other writers or when thinking about my own writing (72). In the summer of 2006, I participated in Selfe's and Scott Lloyd DeWitt's two-week Digital Media and Composition Institute (DMAC) at Ohio State University, going there to start learning about multimedia writing (aka "going digital") with the anticipation of designing and teaching a course in multimodal composition.[1] I did not anticipate that learning to write differently would be balancing act that I was perceptually ill-prepared for. In the end, I came full circle in a way that made complete sense and in fact brought my thinking about multimodal writing into a dialogue with what I was know of writing alphabetic texts. I am a good reader and writer, processing texts on many levels, but as a writer, breaking out of the constraints of the written word forced me to think modally in ways that alphabetic texts allow, but do not necessarily compel. No reader, for example, is compelled to supply visual and auditory realities that writers might work to evoke through words any more than a reader is required to imagine touch, taste or scent. While the common convention of children's books is to tell stories through multiple modes—with images, 3-Ds, tactile elements like faux fur, with scratch and sniffs, sometimes with words that are nonsense, and sometimes with no words at all—once readers graduate to solely to the one-dimensional, linear world of alphabetic texts, they are on their own and at the mercy of their senses because "Language turns out to be a perceptual medium of sounds or signs which, by itself, can give shape to very few elements of thought. For the rest it has to refer to imagery in some other medium" (Arnheim, 2004, p. 240).

One can be locked into or out of textual production depending on what different modes demand of us. Going digital as a writer, I found myself needing to think concretely in shapes and relationships and time frames in ways alphabetic writing never asks me to.

THE BEGINNER'S TALE

Before DMAC began, I received a packet of readings, the course assignment, and a list of what to bring and what to think about, not unlike a list one might received before a group trip; beyond a few devices and gadgets, most of the list suggested all manner of artifacts, visual and audio, that would help us write our digital essays. My artifacts included photographs that spanned over fifty years. That my parents' home videos had been lost somewhere along the years never perturbed me until DMAC began and I found myself greedy for more visual and audible bits of my past. I had reel-to-reel and cassette tapes from when I had musical aspirations as a singer/songwriter in the late 60s, early 70s. Searching through them, relearning how to work the old Roberts 16-track reel-to-reel, I felt how brittle tapes and photos become over what seems like a really short time. As a nonfiction writer always struggling about the frailties of memory, I had not really considered how tenuous and fragile is the past we try to archive through technology. I had photos professionally copied and tapes professionally transferred to CDs lest they be lost forever, which may prove unavoidable at the pace our technologies age.

For a writer in alphabetic mode, these artifacts have worked as reminders, as triggers; as a writer moving into multimodal mode, I knew I was going to have to *do* something with them and could not imagine what that might be. I added stuff to my box—diaries, old copyrights for songs wrote in my Joni Mitchell period, piano music, totem books, letters, whatever seemed remotely appropriate. Because I was driving, I had the writerly opportunity to collect far more data than I could possibly use, the writing habit of mine that transferred most easily from words on the page to digital writing.

Clearly the collecting of artifacts was a major bit of prewriting, brainstorming, but only a start. The first three days of the institute were crammed with learning to use the technology available to us while contemplating our projects, where to start, how to even think about starting. I had expected the technological part of our work to be more problematic it was, but it's a set of writing technologies, like a pen or word-processing software, that one learns to handle in order to get on with the business of writing. Technology takes time and repetition, trial and error. It's frustrating at times and rewarding in others. For some of us, like me, it takes perhaps a little more patient support than others. But the real challenge was the multidimensionality of multimodality. I remember early on feeling that I was, in a sense, juggling in a dark room.

My third night at DMAC I fall into a level of writing anxiety totally unfamiliar to me. Days are speeding by and I don't know where to begin. Whether to start with visuals or audio is a dilemma. All the possibilities paralyze me—did I pack any useful visuals? Can I think in layers of audio? Where to start? How? As a writer, the metaphor of "pulling threads through or across" a piece of writing is quite important to me--lines of thought, strands of ideas, conceptual angles, that stretch across a work, some more dominant than others, but all working to weave the elements of content into a larger textual fabric together through some form of ink and paper that catch thoughts through strings of words that do their best to make my invisible worlds visible to readers in meaningful ways. I imagine these threads rather like the clotheslines of my childhood, a semiotic of carefully pinned flags flapping out in semaphore clues about inhabitants of a certain house. While I cannot say my metaphor was changed by DMAC, writing through a cohesive collection tangible images and real sound, in some cases, devoid of words at all, I can testify that those images and sounds demand their right to participate in the shaping of a text in ways that their alphabetic counterparts never do.

So on this third night at DMAC I plow through my boxes of artifacts, sorting them into piles and then re-sorting them into different piles, looking for a story and seeing none. I go to bed around four in the morning with the dread sense that I haven't brought anything I can use. I page through Temple Grandin's *Thinking in Pictures*, freezing when I read, "It wasn't until I went to college that I realized some people are completely verbal and think only in words" (10). I close the book and push it off the bed where it lands with a hollow clunk on the dorm room floor. I come from a family rich in visual artists. I've often worried that I lack visual imagination. I can see what I've seen, but I am not a person who can mentally visualize so far as imagine worlds of people, or hobbits like Tolkien did. I have long known that is for me a bridge too far. I wonder if I can even do what I have set out to do here, and I suddenly hear the voices of many years of student writers I have worked with repeating the same words: "I don't have anything to say." I have always known what they were saying. Now I feel their pain. But perhaps, also like my students, the fact that DMAC is a three-credit course forces me past the panic to the point where I just tell myself, "I have to do this. I have no choice but to do this." To that chant I fall asleep, forced back on the reality that I must work with what I have and whatever else I can get in time.

And I will learn in the coming fall 2006, after this DMAC summer, when I invite students in an advanced creative nonfiction class to compose digital essays, most will begin with images and sound, few with words, arriving in my classroom with the very instinct I lack. Thus, I begin my multimedia text making a very alphabetic move, I take an essay I have been working on, "On Senior Moments," to transfer into audiovisual mode. A lot of movies are, after all, as the phrase states,

"based on" books. My essay recounts a series of misadventures I shared with my parents one day in 2004 when they asked me to come with them, following in my own car, to meet a financial advisor they are thinking of seeking retirement advice from. The essay draft is twenty pages long and the series of incidents it's based on took around 90 minutes. I realize after a few hours of plotting that no direct translation from paper into audio-visual is plausible both for reasons of time and materials. My artifacts, as they are, won't work; I would need actors and actresses, an underground monthly parking garage, a back entrance into a high security building in post 9/11 mode, an angry young lawyer with red hair, a rude receptionist, a flustered security guard, and much, much more. So where is a connection between my materials and the essay? Finding it takes me longer than I think it should. The answer will seem pretty obvious in retrospect, but at the time, I struggle with my old ways until I finally toddle to what feels like an epiphany: *based on*, as in 'based on" a book, or even a short story, is the operative concept here. The connection lies in the concept of *based on* as *essence of.* What is the essence of the essay, its heart and goals? The essence of *Romeo and Juliet* lies at the heart of thousands of stories, poems, dramas, movies. This recognition of where I need to look for a connection is slowed, no doubt, by my inexperience with, perhaps inability with, thinking in pictures. Temple Grandin writes, "I think in pictures. Words are like a second language to me. I translate both spoken and written words into full-color movies, complete with sound, which run like a VCR tape in my head" (3). I don't. I imagine images, yes, and sometimes one even presents itself as a thought, but I quickly shift into words with narrative line and inner-ear sound, and making meaning from words depends on particular rules and logic that are less elastic, less plastic, than multimodal forms.

Diving into beginnership is not, in this instance easy for me.

I go into day four of DMAC with next-to-no sleep.

Cynthia Selfe gave us a lecture day one about how ingrained alphabetic thinking can be for many of us. I heard her clearly. I believed and believe I understood instantly what she was telling us. But breaking out of a lifetime default is its own, hard lesson. I have arrived at DMAC extremely bound to alphabetic texts and "notational texts" such as we use for music. I've been bound to the alphabetic and notational my entire life; my parents started reading to all of us when we were pre-verbal. I learned to read music at age 3. I began to read and write English around age four, pretty much simultaneously, suddenly intuiting the meaning of spaces between words of a book I had memorized when I needed words to make a sentence I wanted to write. Reading silently and aloud was part of my life into early teens because my family shared chapter books. I grew up in a household full of books and *National Geographic* magazines. While we did have a television by the time I was five, there were only three stations and two were fuzzy, one barely interpretable. My television highlights for the week began with *Captain Kangaroo* while waiting for it to be time to go to kindergarten, and a little later added *Walt Disney* and *Lassie*. Eventually, Saturday mornings were sometimes *Fury*, *My Friend Flicka*, and *Sky King*. My point with these specifics is that at most, television rarely consumed more that five hours of any week. Always greedy for stories, reading and writing alphabetic and notational texts took up far more of my time and even now I cannot say that I am a skilled watcher of television; thus my move to multimodal writing found me lacking the kind of sophistication most younger writers today cannot help but have.

But the moment I think *essence of* I am on my way because it frees me to break open that twenty-page essay and recast it multi-modally. I still begin by writing an alphabetic text that will become a voiceover, a perfectly legitimate but not the only place to begin, but I am able to pare my essence down to eight minutes of words (whittling away, thinking "No one needs to know this" or "No one needs to know that") that spoken with visuals will tell the essential story.

None of what I say here is news to anyone who has worked in film or theatre, except perhaps that in both contexts different folks have responsibility for managing different elements and often someone else is responsible for synchronizing them into a final production. But aside from the ever-present Cindy Selfe, Scott Lloyd Dewitt, and the graduate students, as I write, I am alone with my work, imagining end products, managing artifacts, and in the end, blending all into a humble digital essay. I know it has become current to say that writers don't really write alone, but the fact is, writers spend a lot of time by themselves with their materials. In a top floor corner room with a view in OSU's Jones Graduate Tower, physically alone, with a borrowed (and much coveted) Edirol R-1 digital recorder, I compose the audio doing take after take, again late into the night.

"Layers" and "layering" are an issue for me as I learn to write multi-modally—layering as in, say, building a sandwich, a Dagwood. When one makes such sandwiches by putting one item on top of another in a calculated series of steps, one must, before any layering, envision the simultaneity of the whole. Each layer must have just the right amount and must work with other layers for the desired taste, which may take several tries. Likewise for the digital essay, I work in a series of steps which are, in the end, dependent on each other simultaneously for making meaning. Revision is far more complicated than in an alphabetic text because of the constant matching and re-matching of layers. Complicating further is the issue of time.

As a presenter at 4Cs and other conferences, I know that the business of writing to fit a timeframe is not new. But selecting content when writing a paper or talk for a conference presentation has always been constrained by how much I feel I have and want to say and how fast I can read coherently.

A twenty-minute presentation in Richmond, Virginia, read with a subtle Southern drawl is about 5-7 pages. In Philadelphia reading time, I can read 10-12 pages in that time. And there are always handouts which can allow me to say more than I can actually present in that 20 minutes. But in digital media writing time, the challenges of time differ, particularly if there is no externally set time window. The don't-lose-the-audience challenge is, in part, a matter of time, but time is complicated by, and complicates, other elements of writing as well. The more I whittle away at the much too long original 30-minute dialogue track I record, the more the track concerns me stylistically both in terms of audience and in terms of how I need to tell the stories that anchor my essay. The more I whittle and the more skeletal my narrative becomes, the grimmer the overall content becomes. I usually write nonfiction about serious experiences, but in my alphabetic essays, even those with gravest topics, I always manage to evolve a balanced weaving of dark and light. By the time I cut the dialogue to ten minutes, what I have is deadly sad. My working title changes from "On Senior Moments" to "Keeping Folks Alive"—tragic, so much so that I spend most of night five up going back and forth between artifacts and dialogue to see how I can salvage the piece so it is true to my intentions and voice. I believe that voice does not need to change, perhaps should not change, as we move from alphabetic to digital writing.

And then an epiphany, a miracle, perhaps another of the many light bulbs that explode these two weeks. *Stop trying to digitally write any part of "On Senior Moments" except for the last paragraph.* Then another flash. *Stop trying to write an essay as you have perceived it through words on paper.*

I am always telling my fellow writers that essays are organic and we need to trust that at some point in the business of writing, we'll find our essays. And my dialogue shifts shape in a small but significant way. Instead of starting the voiceover layer with "I moved down to Richmond, Virginia,

in 1989, and not too long after, my parents join me, living on the first floor of the house and me on the second," I begin, "How did I end up living with my parents? Well, I took a job in Richmond, Virginia, in 1989 and they, well, my mother was retiring and my dad was retired and they were at loose ends—Mom was retiring and Dad was retired. They didn't like where they were living and the rent was going up. We'd always gotten along well, even when I was young, better than a lot of parents and teenagers." Pause. "My sister Kathy was the hellion." I totally break away from the text of the first dialogue I've written and have been attempting to speak into the coveted recorder. The original, written dialogue was well written, but sounded stilted when spoken. The revised dialogue is more natural to spoken discourse; I'm talking to *you*.

As I make this shift in point of view, I see pretty much which stills (photographs) I can use. I find the light to balance the dark, a photo of my sister Kathy in her kiwi green, 1960s bean bag chair, her arms crossed, huge headphones covering her ears against the older sister advice I was no doubt dishing out. In the photo, she takes her version of a rhetorical stance of defiance, but as the picture moves back from the screen (the rather invasive Ken Burns Effect in Apple), it becomes clear that she is unable to keep from grinning. Yet there is that touch of hellion about her (Figure 1).

Trust in the process. I recognize that the video will have five sections, each signaled by my repeating a question presumably asked by someone just out of earshot, a move that grounds the narrative interactively and perhaps the audience as well. The dialogue track gives the audience questions that might be of interest to them, and then answers the questions with spoken words and visuals that create a text that I perceive as far more three-dimensional than an alphabetic essay, a text that has no clear urgency of order until the final scene with its final story and reflection. Of the original essay, only the last paragraph survives translation into a digital text. And yet, there is

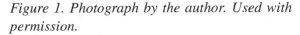

Figure 1. Photograph by the author. Used with permission.

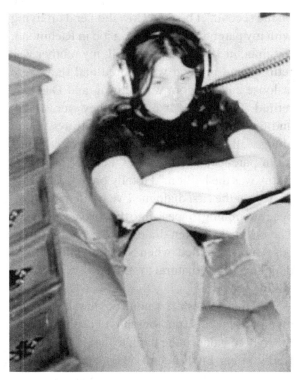

much of the original essay's meaning and style that carry over.

So what do I take away from this multi-modal writing experience?

For one thing, to make a move from words on paper, a domain I feel know very well how to control, I must let go of how I go about alphabetic writing and let what I am learning and my instincts lead the way to more epiphanies, thus more learning and a sharpening of instincts. At the same time, the principles that inform a successful alphabetic text apply to multimodal writing.

COMING HOME

My pedagogical goal for going to multimodal boot camp was to incorporate a digital writing element into my advanced nonfiction workshop. With a

good number of weeks left before fall semester starts, I make moves to use the time to hone the ideas and knowledge of software I've brought home with me—Audacity, iMovie, Photoshop, Flash, Dreamweaver, all with sequences of steps that take time to become natural. But I have learned on a Mac, and I come home to a PC department in which the occasional request for a Mac computer makes the grapevine big time. Making the transition from Mac to PC may have been rudimentary for some, but I cannot figure out how to make the move on my own. I tap a neighbor who teaches in our School of the Arts, one of the Mac sites around campus, and ask for help with Flash, software I'd had only a day with at boot camp. She meets with me, runs me through the kinds of things she can do with Flash, but helpful though it is to see possibilities, I am left, when she departs with her Mac laptop, pretty much where I was before she came, appreciative of the possibilities, no oars in my boat. So I make the perhaps more logical move to find out what's available for PCs and find that while there is software in the hands of various people, and while I can take classes with various knowledgeable technology folks, getting my hands on software so I can take my own tedious time learning to manipulate it means purchasing what I think I need that does not have some freeware counterpart. And this is where the system and I fail each other. I don't know quite what I want to do. For me writing is always an organic process. But the first question asked in any training sessions is "What do you want to do?" (the first question anyone I talk to asks me). I am still in the process of learning to see differently and I simply need access and time to explore.

The question, "What do you want to do?" is, on the surface, a logical one, but it fails to represent the whole of the challenge of writing multimodal texts, perhaps because it assumes an end product up front. In a sense it institutionalizes the process of writing in a way that reminds me of the devolution of Lincoln Logs from those I grew up with to how they are packaged today. There is always the possibility that the templates for the logs I built with once existed and had been misplaced, and that several batches of logs had been dumped together, rather like storing the pieces of several jigsaw puzzles in one box, but I don't think so. I don't believe that my parents had the option to purchase the Shady Pine Cabin or Horseshoe Station kits in the late 40s, early 40s, though I've heard that the original Lincoln Logs came with instructions for building Uncle Tom's Cabin. But by the time I inherited them from my older sister, there was just a large box full of logs and roof slats, enough accrued to build quite a spread, stack a very tall tower, or fence in the space beneath the dining room table. Perhaps I simply am a person with untidy inclinations and an inability to know what I want to end up with before I am done, but I found that question stopped me in my tracks.

Fall semester starts and I find myself in a computer lab with 15 willing students. We start our major two projects, a memoir and a personal essay, and when both are well underway, through several drafts and workshops, I asked them to take one of the projects and recast it as a 3-5 minute digital essay. I talk about layering visuals and sound some. I talk about my thoughts on *based on* and *essence of*. To my surprise, they aren't surprised. Only a few need help and find it easily either from classmates or someone they know outside class. The digital essays are complete before the final drafts of the projects they relate to. In fact, over the three classes when students share their multimodal essays, I learn that most feel that the multimodal project has helped them see their alphabetic drafts more fully and deeply, an insightful point I will return to shortly. And though a few of the multimodal essays are clunky, as was my own first stab at this genre, most demonstrate how profoundly acculturated to multimodal thinking these students, most juniors and seniors of traditional age, already are. The best analogy I can come up with for my own role so far as the multimodal writing this fall is rather like Robert Preston's Harold Hill in *The Music Man* (1962): "Think

Minuet in G," except that I never masquerade as a wiz for my students. At the outset, I shared my essay from DMAC; happily, they raised the ante and we all learned concretely the value of seeing discrete genres better by looking through the lens of one at another; that is, looking at alphabetic writing through a multimodal lens and multimodal through alphabetic, students improved their efforts in both genres.

This was not a new lesson for me, just a new version. In the late 70s I was privileged to take a class with a writer at Penn State who had us write a short story to start, then take that story and recast it as a poem, then as a dramatic scene.

Another not-so new lesson I learned from this enterprise is this: while I often felt like I was flying solo during the two weeks at DMAC, I was and I wasn't. There was always someone there to help when I got stuck with the software or concepts, a community. In that fall 2006 nonfiction workshop, students fell naturally into a community of writers pooling skills, abilities, strategies. When I got home from DMAC, however, there was no community for me. There had been such a community some years earlier, but it started at a point when I was working to finishing a book and meet a deadline. Starting something new with a host of commitments did not seem an option. Perhaps I should have made it one for I know the Epiphany Project[2], 1999-2000, did much to foster faculty knowledge and build the kind of multimodal community older and/or non-digital learners like me need to learn to swim in this new digital age.

CONCLUSION

But that was then and it is now 2013. While I have never created myself as the writer of multimodal essays I imagined in 2006, multimodal writing has become a constant presence in my work with students. While I have never had further opportunity to learn to manipulate relevant software or equipment, I have found that what I learned at DMAC, what I have learned from reading and working with students since, and what I know as a writer and rhetorician has contributed to my growth as a good mentor for those working with multimodal texts. That I would evolve to this point was no doubt inevitable; the 21st century brings with it what Wan Ng calls "digital natives" to our writing classes, and the human tendency to fall in love with what is new makes multimodal literacy a rather attractive, if not downright sexy, enterprise. As I write towards my conclusion here, I am driven to stop and search for this quote:

"There are going to be times," says Kesey, "when we can't wait for somebody. Now, you're either on the bus or off the bus. If you're on the bus, and you get left behind, then you'll find it again. If you're off the bus in the first place — then it won't make a damn." And nobody had to spell it out for them. Everything was becoming allegorical, understood by the group mind, and especially this: "You're either on the bus . . . or off the bus." (Wolfe, Electric Kool-Aid Acid Test, p. 83)

There's a mindset to this sort of thinking that can inspire what I've come to see as a dangerous but compelling fear endemic to our fast-evolving technological passion, the fear that we are in danger of being—or have been—left behind: the fear that what we know is not what we *should* know. Thinking about this, thinking like this, brings me to the two points, two cautionary points, I want to make about my experience of and since DMAC. The first caution comes out of my fall 2006 multimodal experience with my students. They came to me with the tools they needed to create their multimodal essays, but they did not come to me more sophisticated about alphabetic texts, and in fact, as I said above, the major theme of our three-day discussion of their multimodal essays was that working to digitally express the essence of their alphabetic essays pushed them deeper into their writing of their twenty-some page personal essays. In other words, the multimodal

essays proved to be a strategy for getting more successfully to the larger goals of the workshop: writing polished, reflective essayistic narratives that take a lot of critical, introspective effort and a lot of thought about using language in classic writerly ways. I am all for providing students with opportunities to work on their communicative abilities in non-alphabetic genres, but I worry that the pressure we might feel to make sure we are on that multimodal bus has some serious risks.

I recently reviewed a curriculum for a new version of a sophomore writing course, originally designed in the mid 90s to teach the craft of researched writing. As the lead designer of the original course, my metaphor for it was "the John McPhee course" because he's a quintessential researcher who masters what he researches and then relates his findings with full authority or, ownership of, the material, perhaps the toughest goal to achieve in a course on researched writing. When the McPhee course originated, it was implemented at the sophomore level and a second-semester first-year course was dropped from the books, thus making sure students had a course in which they did substantial writing during both of their first years. In the early 21st century, the creation of a new general education portal replaced the first-year writing course with a two-sequence set of first-year inquiry courses, a national trend in response to John N. Gardner's exemplary work on the First-Year Experience (now the Institute for Excellence[3]). Not all schools implemented first-year inquiry courses by replacing a writing course, but my school did; thus the sophomore writing course, the sole remaining course in which the subject was writing, began to take on more work. Originally, students in the McPhee course spent the semester writing one 18-20 page, researched essay. The length of that essay has decreased to 10 pages, and the most recent manifestation of the course devotes 8 weeks to the researched essay which counts as 25% of the final grave. The initial weeks of the course are devoted to critical reading and argumentation, the last two to creating a multimodal version of the 10-page researched essay. Instructors teaching the course tell me that their students can do this final multimodal project in a weekend.

My concern here is that the sole general education course that is focused on the subject of writing is trying to do so much that it might not succeed in giving students the tools they need to do the alphabetic writing expected of them in courses during their junior and senior years. Indeed, from the perspective of having taught writing at many levels for thirty-seven years, I am seeing what are for me upsetting weaknesses in the writing of my upper-class undergraduates as well as in my graduate students—and I am not talking about missing apostrophes and sentence boundary issues and such, thought they abound too. I am talking about lack of vocabulary, about not understanding the meaning, for example, of common prepositions, about not being able to craft complicated sentences, a weakness that suggests something about their abilities explicating and communicating complicated ideas. I am concerned, and I say that as someone who was never a fuddy duddy stickler about changes to standard dialect. I'm concerned about my students' abilities to communicate reflectively and deeply and articulately. We need as educators to learn to do our work in ways that richly incorporate new literacies, but we need to be careful not to do so at the expense of foundational traditional literacies.

A second point I come to as I close has to do with Kesey's bus in several senses. When I finished at DMAC and came home, I couldn't find the bus. It had been there in 1999 and left. I had not gotten on it at the time, and I couldn't find it to get access when I needed it. However, had I found that bus, I am not sure how accessible it would have been. Technological explorations have, in my experience to date, largely been sporadic, often sudden, because they rely on entrepreneurial sorts of funding which is often last minute, and they have seemed to pop up in isolated cells, often without the kind of fanfare necessary to attract a

large interest group. If we are going to use technology constructively and advance smoothly, we need a more thorough and accessible technological infrastructures than has, in my experience, come into existence. We need a stable digital community which is not exclusive, a concern addressed in "Building Digital Communities," an online source from the Institute of Museums and Libraries and the Technology and Social Change Group of the University of Washington's Information School, opens with this statement:

Digital inclusion is the ability of individuals and groups to access and use information and communication technologies. Digital inclusion encompasses not only access to the Internet but also the availability of hardware and software; relevant content and services; and training for the digital literacy skills required for effective use of information and communication technologies. The cost of digital exclusion is great. Without access, full participation in nearly every aspect of American society — from economic success and educational achievement, to positive health outcomes and civic engagement — is compromised.

I reread what I have written here and note that I keep saying that what I am saying is not new, that I keep learning the same lessons over again, albeit from different and new to me angles, which is always valuable, but this recognition points to a central issue for me. In *The Seven Basic Plots* (2006), Christopher Booker begins by pointing out something Aristotle observed in his *Poetics*: there are a limited number of stories we can tell, a limited number of plots. At the heart of most stories is the quest. For any quest to chance success, it is perhaps best not to start with end-product questions like the one I faced when I sought access to software after DMAC. We should start more broadly, more conceptually, perhaps with questions about what kind of stories we want to be telling about our adventures in creating digital communities. There is an African proverb that I like: "If you want to go fast, go alone. If you want to go far, go together." Perhaps we need to conceptualize a digital infrastructure that is not telling the a hero story about the quest for the cutting edge, a very attractive story for those of us in an institutional context that places much value of originality and cutting edge thinking. And I suspect my institution has recognized this need. This fall, 2013, I have been invited to participate in a newly established learning community of faculty from across the disciplines who will be exploring multimodal writing techniques for our own purposes and our uses in the classroom.

REFERENCES

Arnheim, R. (2004). *Visual thinking*. Berkeley, CA: University of California Press.

Booker, C. (2006). *The seven basic plots: Why we tell stories*. New York: Continuum Books.

Building Digital Communities, The Institute of Museum and Library Services, together with the University of Washington and the International City/County Management Association. (2012). Retrieved from http://www.imls.gov/about/building_digital_communities.aspx

Grandin, T. (2006). *Thinking in pictures*. New York: Vintage Books.

McNair, W. (1993). *My brother running and other poems*. Boston, MA: David R. Godine Press.

Ng, W. (2012). Can we teach digital natives digital literacy? *Computers & Education*, *59*, 1065–1078. doi:10.1016/j.compedu.2012.04.016

KEY TERMS AND DEFINITIONS

Alphabetic Mode: R refers to a way of thinking and proceeding to produce a text, starting with the written word.

Alphabetic Texts: Refers to the more traditional approach to writing, that which uses a screen or surface, such as paper, and writing technology such as pen or keyboard.

Digital Communities: Can be defined as those whose geography is completely virtual such as chat rooms, list-serves, instant message boards, service and professional Websites with interactive abilities, virtual worlds, blogs, virtual classrooms. "Digital communities" as used in "Going Digital" is speaking specifically of those involved, often in a specific geographical location, working together to expand members' knowledge about the uses of digital applications for expanding members' applications of those application in their research, writing, and teaching.

Digital Writing: Refers to e-writing, such as email, texting, blogging, and so forth. My use of the term in "Going Digital" is speaking specifically about multimodal writing.

DMAC: Is The Ohio State University Digital Media and Composition Institute that runs each summer under the leadership of Scott Loyd DeWitt.

Layering: Describes the superimposing of different modes of writing so that they work ensemble to create meaning. Real time becomes an issue in this genre of writing that it is not when writing alphabetic texts.

Multimodal Writing: Refers to writing that works with the layering of different communicative modes: sound (music, taped sounds, voice), visuals (such as photographs, artwork, video), and traditional alphabetic texts.

ENDNOTES

1 Information about the Digital Media Project: http://dmp.osu.edu/dmac/
2 Information about the Epiphany Project: http://www.has.vcu.edu/epiphany/
3 Information about John N. Gardener's Institute for Excellence: http://www.jngi.org/

Chapter 7
Moving Mountains:
Distributed Leadership and Cyberformance

Karen Keifer-Boyd[1]
The Pennsylvania State University, USA

Mary Elizabeth Meier
Mercyhurst University, USA

Wanda B. Knight
The Pennsylvania State University, USA

Ryan Patton
Virginia Commonwealth University, USA

Aaron Knochel
State University of New York at New Paltz, USA

Ryan Shin
University of Arizona, USA

Christine Liao
University of North Carolina Wilmington, USA

Robert W. Sweeny
Indiana University of Pennsylvania, USA

ABSTRACT

Moving Mountains is a collaborative venture by eight art educators who explore the notion of distributed leadership to transcend boundaries of proximity, ideation, and artistic production. Their distributed leadership, enacted through both human and non-human performers, involved sharing knowledge and skills to create a cyberformance and machinima. They completed these projects from conceptualization to artistic production without a designated leader and without hierarchical constraints. In this chapter, the authors view distributed leadership in Moving Mountains collaborations through actor-network theory, crowdsourcing, and transformative potential. Moving Mountains collaborators continue to create video art, written work, curriculum, and virtual world performances, through distributed leadership, in order to challenge oppression and transgress borders.

DOI: 10.4018/978-1-4666-5150-0.ch007

INTRODUCTION: (PER)FORMING DISTRIBUTED LEADERSHIP

Eight art educators performed *Moving Mountains,* a live cyberformance at *121212 UpStage Festival of Cyberformance*. Through cyberformance, we examined the challenges and barriers we have each encountered in our respective local, academic, social, and political domains.

Cyberformance is a term combining the words cyber and performance coined by artist Helen Varley Jamieson (2008). She states that "[i]t came out of the need to find a word that avoided the polarisation of virtual and real, and the need for a new term (rather than "online performance or virtual theatre") for a new genre" (Jamieson, n.d.). In other words, cyberformance focuses on the mixed-reality nature of performance made possible through digital communication networks. It is not a simulation, recording, or reproduction of a physical performance but a new kind of intentional art form that utilizes the characteristics of the Internet and digital media technologies to explore ideas in real time. Cyberformance can employ many different Internet technologies simultaneously and involve various forms of media such as text, video, images, animation, sound, and voice.

Following a successful performance in 2012 of *Moving Mountains* at *121212 UpStage Festival of Cyberformance,* we decided to share the project with different and diverse audiences. An ideal media for this purpose was machinima (digital film recorded in a virtual world). Like many film productions, the machinima production of our performance was very labor intensive. *Moving Mountains* machinima created in 2013 required us to perform the roles of concept developer, actor, scriptwriter, stage manager, set designer, cinematographer, soundtrack composer, and video editor. Using virtual worlds and social media, we realized we have collective strengths that we do not have individually. In order to achieve our larger vision of *Moving Mountains,* metaphorically speaking, we found that a distributed leadership model works best.

We represent different racial, ethnic and cultural backgrounds, including United States citizens with African and European ancestry; and international residents with Asian ancestry. Our distributed model of leadership is based on the interactions with, between, and amongst each of us as leaders.

In practice, our leadership roles evolve in relationship to the needs of the *Moving Mountains* projects. Our boundaries shift into performing multiple leadership roles such as initiator, opinion and information seeker, opinion and information giver, harmonizer, summarizer, synthesizer, actor, technician, and decision-maker. Leadership roles depend upon the context, the immediate project needs, time availability, and each other's capabilities. Our leadership model provides the creative space for dialogue and emergent roles that reflect not only the inherent diverse identities within our group but reflect the diversity in knowledge, skills, and abilities each leader brings to our collaborative endeavors.

COLLABORATION AND DISTRIBUTIVE LEADERSHIP

The process of eight art educators collaborating was quite complex. Part of the challenge of developing our collaborative media projects was coordinating meeting times for eight people from seven different universities and two different time zones. Additionally, we had varying technological and performance experience and expertise. Nevertheless, part of the opportunity was the diversity in our ways of thinking, personal experiences, and backgrounds that informed the structure and content of the efforts. We contributed to conversations both synchronously and asynchronously. Additionally, we conducted much of the preparation for the performance and film at a distance, through email, and computer applications including *Skype, Google Hangout, Google Docs, Livestream, Upstage*, and *Second Life* (see Figure 1).

We explored the notion of distributed leadership as a form of collaboration to push the boundaries of proximity, ideation, and production processes. Though distributed leadership is a form of collaboration, not all collaborations use a distributed leadership model. Collaborations bring together the skills of several people, often with fixed roles and jobs.

The impact of distributed leadership has much to do with the amount of time and input each contributes to the group or the project. However, leadership can be distributed in forming smaller breakout groups or nodes of activity in which ideation and decision-making toward the larger vision is respected rather than micromanaged or dismissed. Moreover, fluid reconfiguring of working groups cross-fertilizes ideas and furthers communication among the larger group.

In our distributed leadership model, ideas are emergent. We enact distributed leadership in ways that connect ideas, skills, motivations, and visions for our shared collaborative projects, including a live performance, a film, this chapter, and an interactive performance. In joining forces as a distributed leadership team to create a cyberformance about moving mountains and building bridges, we hoped that our model of leadership would empower others to imagine without perceived limits. Several members of our collaborative leadership team have used virtual world platforms for research and teaching.[2] These members provided guidance and support to those of us who were less familiar with the virtual worlds. One member, in particular, provided significant technical leadership on how to navigate and perform in a virtual world and on how to build or find objects to attach to actors' avatar bodies. During rehearsals for the live performance, those not in the immediate action could see and, from the filming avatar's camera, view the broadcasted live streaming Website, make suggestions of camera angle and actor movement through written chat or voice directions in the virtual world. Group critiques were important to determine whether additional filming was needed or where the script required revision.

Sharing skills and knowledge is an important part of learning and leading in virtual worlds and in online communities. Websites like instructables. com, craftster.org, and lifehacker.com allow people to share their maker knowledge with others, while virtual worlds like *VIEW* and the video game *World of Warcraft* encourages its members to help new members navigate the space. These forms of sharing initiate communities of collaboration, implicitly defining the nature of these communities, vital for their existence.

Figure 1. Authors collaborating through Google Hangout

This sharing of knowledge and skills as well as the forming of communities of collaboration highlight the distributed leadership we modeled throughout the cyberformance and machinima. It is evident that our projects did not follow a typical movie-making procedure as seen in Hollywood or commercial theatres. We realized that we had completed these projects with no director or hierarchical power distribution from the beginning stage of conceptualization to the following stages of script writing, performance, and self-reflective critique. At various stages, we faced logistic, strategic, and technical challenges that required creative solutions and brainstorming.

At different stages of the collaboration, we explored narratives of social justice, engaged pedagogical possibilities, examined how leadership can be shared between networks of human and non-human participants, and utilized virtual space for performance art and digital video production. By examining the possibilities of how technologies might support distributed leadership, in both virtual and physical spaces, we sought to understand the nuances of distributed leadership in our Moving Mountains projects. Even though there were risks taken as a critical part of our work, enacting the collaborative projects through a distributed leadership model was accomplished with networked relations that were formed in the virtual spaces where we met.

ACTOR-NETWORK THEORY: SPACES, OBJECTS, AND ACTANTS

The notion of moving a mountain by walking through it to make connections and build bridges is possible because of the technology woven into the virtual world performance. This complex interaction between technology and the performance of distributed leadership can be better understood

through actor-network theory (ANT), which is an approach to study relationships between nodes of influence among technological, natural, and social systems. ANT aids in the study of systems where the separation of human and non-human elements is difficult to see, offering a lens to discern how these performed networks enact transformation, empowerment, and reciprocal exchange. ANT sociologists consider non-human actors, or *actants,*[3] to be *symmetrical*, or equally important to the human elements in a network. Symmetrical human and non-human relationships form entities "held in balance with their interactions" (Fenwick & Edwards, 2012, p. xii). These interactions are framed as network formations. ANT focuses on tracing the transformations of both human and non-human actors, in which each element is viewed as a performing network (Fenwick & Edwards, 2012; Latour, 2005; Rowan & Bigum, 2012; Tatnall, 2010). In the formation of networks, ANT provides fluidity to the understanding of social interactions that include non-human contributions, creating a horizontal plane of analysis that avoids personification of objects, and instead investigates the proliferation of human-object collaborations. In the case of the *Moving Mountains* collaboration, human-technological interactions built networks of humans and non-humans, creating openings to (re)act and contribute to ideation and production processes.

Within the human-technological networks of *Moving Mountains*, agency is transformed when (re)conceived with clusters of *actants*. As demonstrated in the *Moving Mountains* cyberformance, agency frames how human action becomes exponentially multiplied, unbound by the limitations of sociological structures of "emancipation politics" (Latour, 2005, p. 52). As Tara Fenwick and Richard Edwards (2012) stated,

ANT does not conceptualize agency as an individuated source of empowerment rooted in conscious intentions that mobilize action. Instead, ANT focuses on the circulating forces that get things done through a network of elements acting upon one another. (p. xvi)

Agency becomes the *action* of relational effects between *actants* that gather network formations. ANT sociologists call these relational effects *translation* (Brown & Capdevila, 1999; Callon, 1986; Latour, 2005), which make associations central to understanding any social situation. Therefore, agency is distributed through the relational effects of translation of actants that are within, between, and among networks of human and non-human actors.

The actor-networks in our cyberformance unfold emancipatory narratives of people and avatars in the *action* of joining forces to move mountains. In the first scene of the *Moving Mountains* cyberformance, three avatars performed monologues about the difficulties and struggles they encounter in academia and everyday life. As a part of each monologue, the performers wore objects, virtual props attached to their virtual bodies (see Figure 2). These objects (e.g., signs, passports, chains, labels, books) are symbolic markers that link the virtual space to real-life space in which financial, cultural, racial, physical stereotypes, and burdens experienced are everyday struggles of those collaborating in *Moving Mountains*. Visually, these attached objects serve as physical impediments to the avatars' movements and are symbolic of impediments toward achieving social justice. The objects are also physical metaphors for how these and other impediments accumulate.

The *Moving Mountains* cyberformance began with actants describing their identities, and how (through their experiences) their identities were mired in stereotypes, obstacles, and systemic social oppression.

Avatar 1: I have always heard that the United States is a land of opportunity. As a woman of African heritage, born in the US, I wonder what lies ahead, when I cross these borders. Will things be better? I guess I won't know until I move the mountain, so to speak.

Avatar 2: I am Asian. I have a big dream. I want to go to America and attend a good college and find a decent job. I would like to raise my children with the opportunity for a better education. But I am not sure how I can go to America, the land of opportunity. I want to move a mountain.

Figure 2. Virtual objects worn on avatars symbolize stereotypes, obstacles, and oppression

Avatar 3: I want to study to be a teacher of art and science and all sorts of things to change the world. There are so many domains of knowledge that I can use to move mountains. I think I can move this mountain!

[Each goes into the virtual mountain hopeful and returns disappointed.]

Avatar 1: It is difficult to live in a society that devalues people because of their skin color, their gender, and their socio-economic class. Crossing borders, I experienced the negative effects of being a poor, Black woman, not only daily but simultaneously. I thought that I would be treated equally and be respected as I respect others. Perhaps I was too naïve. Look at me! Barriers are everywhere! And what frustrates me even more is that I don't know how to transcend these and other structures of oppression.

Avatar 2: Just look at this stuff. I am very disappointed. I wanted to get a good education and find work in America, but I wasn't allowed to enter this country. They asked me to show a VISA and passport that I couldn't get. To get an education in America, I have to prove that I have enough money in my bank account to obtain a VISA. They said that I could immigrate to America, if I have a lot of money to invest in this country. However, the problem is that I don't have enough money in my bank account. I feel stuck and rejected.

Avatar 3: My story is no better than yours. I believe that I can research educational phenomena and seek social justice by studying concepts and issues crossing boundaries of discipline. When I tried, I hit a brick wall. However, I will have to learn basic concepts of many subjects, which will take me five years. And, to explore other disciplinary concepts and theories, this will take another five years. Most importantly, I will have no job with my training. Nobody will hire me in the workplace. There is no way to go through these obstacles without burdens.

The objects in the *Moving Mountains* cyberformance also act: the attaching of symbolic objects of oppression to the performing avatars, and being able to walk through a mountain was possible because of the virtual world space.

TRANSFORMATIONS THROUGH VIRTUAL WORLD(S)

Moving Mountains cyberformance resulted in two kinds of transformation: one is the symbolic transformation we experienced as enacted in the story shared with the audience, and the other is the transformation of our perspectives and further understanding of the possibilities of virtual world(s) and virtual communities in education and beyond. Through our narrative and enacted performance, we recorded our own transformation of real world issues such as stereotypes and mistreatment related to skin color, ethnicity, location, as well as the deeply fractured divisions of academic disciplines. We made symbolic transformation by building bridges, creating connections, and moving mountains, educating others and ourselves about making changes, citing the positive grassroots examples of the Empty Bowls project and the Harry Potter Alliance as having an impact on social justice (see Figure 3).

Avatar 1: Wait! I recognize that, I know Harry Potter, but what does that have to do with social justice?

Avatar 4: Just as Dumbledore's Army awakens the world to Voldemort's return, it also works for equal rights of house elves and werewolves, and empowers its members, The Harry Potter Alliance works with partner NGOs in alerting the world to the dangers of global warming, poverty, and genocide. The Alliance also works with partners for equal rights regardless of race, gender, and sexuality. Further the Harry Potter Alliance encourages members to hone the magic of their creativity in endeavoring to make the world a better place.

Figure 3. Snapshot of bridges of possibilities from the Moving Mountains live cyberformance

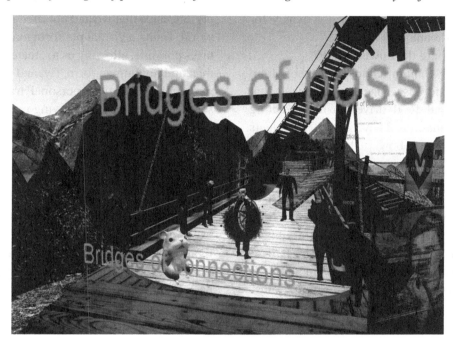

Avatar 1: But they are not real. Dumbledore is not real. Harry Potter is only a character.

Avatar 3: But the people who bring Harry Potter to life are real. They are an army of fans, activists, nerdfighters, teenagers, wizards and muggles dedicated to fighting for social justice with the greatest weapon we have—love. And The Harry Potter Alliance all started with one person.

Avatar 4: One person?

Avatar 1: How could all of this start with one person?

Avatar 3: It started with one person and an army of fans. Andrew Slack started The Harry Potter Alliance based around the Harry Potter fandom designed to raise funds towards charitable causes through campaigns and events related to the series. Their mission is to educate and mobilize young people (across the world) toward issues of literacy, equality, and human rights.

Avatar 1: The possibilities of joining an alliance working toward social justice is not like my first experience (crossing borders) when I went alone. We are here together. But, how do we share our burdens? They are so different.

Avatar 4: Our struggles bind us and so do our joys, our humanity. People can be amazing together, stronger than even imaginable.

Avatar 3: By bringing together fans of Harry Potter to harness the power of popular culture toward making our world a better place, the Harry Potter Alliance goal is to make civic engagement exciting by channeling the entertainment-saturated facets of our culture toward mobilization for deep and lasting social change.

Avatar 4: That is certainly an example of border crossing: from fiction to reality, from entertainment to civic action, from one to many. This reminds me of another group who started small and grew into a bigger movement—the Empty Bowls project.[4] Have you ever been to an Empty Bowls event?

Avatar 3: No, I haven't.

Avatar 4: Empty Bowls is an event to raise awareness about hunger and to raise money for local food banks.

Avatar 3: Why are the bowls empty?

Avatar 4: In 1990, high school art teachers John Hartom and Lisa Blackburn realized that their annual food drive wasn't attracting enough donations. They asked their students to make ceramic bowls to be used at a school luncheon. Every guest chose a bowl, ate a simple meal, and made a generous donation to their local food bank. Everyone kept their bowl as a reminder of all the empty bowls in their own community and throughout the world.

Avatar 3: What a great idea. Did the Empty Bowls project spread to other high school programs?

Avatar 4: Yes, Empty Bowls has become an international grassroots project to raise funds for local food banks.

Avatar 5: Wow, it is amazing how two art teachers started a project that has had worldwide impact in reducing hunger. I am going to look into this.

This excerpt from the *Moving Mountain* script provided an example to students in one of our collaborators' physical classroom, where students worked in teams to script a conversation from the study of social movements through reading articles. Students also created objects as metaphors for envisioning change. The recording of conversations layered onto images and objects can create powerful artworks that are both accessible and engaging forms of communication.

The second transformation we experienced was more fundamental in that the virtual world-based cyberformance involved us in a new digital media discourse that put strong educational possibilities and values on virtual realities. Most of us did not have extensive performance experiences in real life, not being formally trained in theatrical practices like script writing, stage direction, and acting. The opportunity for participating in a cy-berformance festival challenged us with creating a performance that we had not tried in the physical world. Using a virtual platform made impossible tasks possible, allowing us to create avatars in human and nonhuman form, fly, and move through mountains. Our own personal transformations serve as a metaphor of moving mountains.

MOVING ON: FUTURE RESEARCH DIRECTIONS

Moving Mountains advances through further exploration of augmentalist trajectories by investigating permutations of distributed leadership through cyberformance as a continuum of online and offline experience. Sociologist Sherry Turkle (2011) posits the way we use online connectivity today undermines deeper relationships in real life, but our challenge and risk in the *Moving Mountains* cyberformance is understanding dialogic spaces that facilitate equality and transformation in the real, tangible world. As bell hooks says, freedom is "always and intimately linked to the issue of transforming space" (1995, p. 147). She suggests that we think critically about the spaces that we inhabit, and in discussion with others gain "a concrete acknowledgement of [our] reality" (p. 146). Cyberformance as an artistic method of inhabiting spaces online and offline may present opportunities for modeling distributed leadership that is transformational and invested in creating deeper connection. In the following, we discuss current applications of distributed leadership manifesting in crowdsourced applications and how these can lead us to future research.

Crowdsourcing in other forms of digital media like games, software development, and scientific research provide opportunities for distributed leadership. Crowdsourcing uses a distributed problem-solving structure with a dispersed community of contributors. As Daren C. Brabham (2008) states, crowdsourcing is "a model capable of aggregating talent, leveraging ingenuity while reducing the costs and time formerly needed to solve problems ... [and] is enabled only through the technology of the Web, which is a creative mode of user interactivity" (p. 87). Players of the digital game *Foldit* (2008) are making scientific discoveries, where solving the game's protein folding puzzles is leading to solutions for real world disease (Marshall, 2012). In the digital game *Eyewire* (2012), players are helping scientists understand how vision works by tracing neurons in the eye, a task computers are not well suited to do (Plackett, 2013). Other kinds of games like *EVOKE* (2010) and competitions like the XPRIZE are attempts to open up fields of research to the general public by motivating individuals to help solve technological and social challenges (Gates, 2011; Voice of America, 2010). We see these examples of crowdsourcing as powerful articulations of distributed leadership that may have significant impact on social justice praxis, because of the careful balance of relational agency that can expand the networks of contributors. This balance requires renegotiation, improvisation, and redirection of the gathered actants, as we experienced in the *Moving Mountains* activities. We continue to develop an acute understanding of the emergent qualities of distributed leadership that would be important to future research.

As another form of distributed leadership, citizen-led crowdsourcing has enabled the public to report potholes via cellphones (Ovide, 2012), create a digital historical archive for neighborhoods that no longer exist through personal photographs and documents (Grant, 2013), and expand city services by developing smartphone apps from city data (NYC Digital, 2012). We see these citizen-led initiatives that cultivate change as powerful models for social justice and cyberformance when utilizing a distributed leadership model, putting into action ways that mobile technologies can be implemented through data augmented reality. Virtual space becomes a realization of space; a translation of what is possible, creating real world transformation and cyberformance. We believe

these kinds of digital tools will become more available in education, particularly for mobile devices that augment reality and empower individuals in their communities. Projects like ARIS (Gagnon, 2011), Aurasma (Autonomy, 2010), OpenDataKit (Borriello et al., 2010), and MobileActive (Verclas, 2005), show how developing research and scholarship for mobile devices will allow for distributed leadership in site-specific ways.

So how do we engage arts practice with civic engagement and forms of distributed leadership? Art making practices that use feminist and socially engaged methodologies (Helguera, 2011; Lacy, Roth, & Mey, 2010) offer artists models of making work that allows for distributed leadership to be part of the art making process. The *Fundred Dollar Bill Project* (2007-ongoing) started by Mel Chin is an excellent example of an arts-based initiative to engage civic discourse, utilizing distributed leadership by involving legions of participants in a national dialogue about lead contamination provoked by the creative practice of the Fundred project. We believe that *Moving Mountains* has the potential to grow in directions of civically engaged crowdsourcing that can evolve the emergent qualities of our distributed leadership network by expanding a network's capacity to transform spaces for equality. In the cyberformance of *Moving Mountains*, we make reference to just such important civically engaged crowdsourcing movements such as the Empty Bowls project and the Harry Potter Alliance, and now our task is to move on, to engage *Moving Mountains* in offline/online space with careful attention to understanding how distributed leadership networks function and where they break down.

Moving Mountains collaborators continue in 2014 to explore distributed leadership strategies that challenge oppression and transgress obstacles through mobilizing for large-scale actions. At the National Art Education Association conference, with audience participation, we will enact an interactive mixed-reality performance as a form of new media art education.

CONCLUSION: WHAT WE LEARNED

Moving Mountains was a terrific risk because it teetered on many edges of disaster: loss of connection, loss of control, loss of time, navigating between virtual and real spaces, and the frightening dissonance of voices swirling in a cacophony of collaboration. In earnest, we asked "Who could be this strong, strong enough to move a mountain?" (*Moving Mountains* script). However, we continued to support each other, through online and offline interactions such as emails, video chats, and virtual world platforms. The distribution of leadership was constantly renegotiated.

Our *Moving Mountains* cyberformance set in motion multiple projects simultaneously through our distributed leadership model, allowing our collaboration to create open spaces for communication and production using the many skills sets of different group members. As artists and educators, we engaged with a range of visual media production technologies: creation of virtual objects, performance within a virtual world, machinima recording, video post-production, audio production, and a range of real time communication spaces such as *Skype, Google Hangouts*, and *Google Docs* to enact our distributed leadership network, paying careful attention to the social effects of translation and sharing expertise. This kind of activity of sharing and supporting each other with creative skills, knowledge, and expertise is also found in maker culture, an extension of the DIY movement, gaining popularity through hackerspaces, creative and online communities, and events like the Maker Faire (The Economist, 2011). Collaborative writing (as seen in this chapter) is one expression of how distributed leadership can produce a physical outcome.

Our distributed leadership, enacted through a relational agency of both human and non-human actants, was an exploration of social justice advocacy and practice through the cyberformance and its educational impact. However, the conundrum of moving our social justice advocacy and practice to a more hybrid online/offline cyberformance propels important reconsiderations for what social justice looks like, and the qualities of distributed leadership that engender equality and freedom through digital tools and real world application. *Moving Mountains* is not just metaphor. It is action and risk taking, that is driven by our compulsion that the rewards of dialogic space, collaboration, and making meaning outweigh sedentary practice or hierarchical structures.

REFERENCES

Autonomy. (2010). *Aurasma*. Retrieved from http://www.aurasma.com/

Borriello, G., Breit, N., Brunette, W., Chaudhri, R., Dell, N., & Sundt, M. (2010). *Open data kit*. Retrieved from http://mobileactive.org/

Brabham, D. C. (2008). Crowdsourcing as a model for problem solving: An introduction and cases. *Convergence: The International Journal of Research into New Media Technologies*, *14*(1), 75–90. doi:10.1177/1354856507084420

Brown, S. D., & Capdevila, R. (1999). Perpetuum mobile: Substance, force, and the sociology of translation. In J. Law, & J. Hassard (Eds.), *Actor network theory and after* (pp. 26–50). Malden, MA: Blackwell Publishing.

Callon, M. (1986). Some elements of a sociology of translation domestication of the scallops and the fishermen of St. Brieux Bay. In J. Law (Ed.), *Power action and belief: A sociology of knowledge* (pp. 197–220). London: Routledge & Kegan Paul.

Economist. (2011, December 3). More than just digital quilting. *The Economist*. Retrieved from http://www.economist.com/node/21540392/

Fenwick, T., & Edwards, R. (Eds.). (2012). *Researching education through actor-network theory*. Malden, MA: Wiley-Blackwell. doi:10.1002/9781118275825

Gagnon, D. (2011). ARIS. Retrieved from http://arisgames.org/

Gates, B. (2011, November). *A report by Bill Gates to G20 leaders*. Retrieved from http://www.gatesfoundation.org/What-We-Do/Global-Policy/G20-Report

Grant, S. (2013, March 19). *A citizen-led crowdsourcing roadmap for the CI-BER big data project*. Retrieved from http://www.hastac.org/blogs/slgrant/2013/03/19/citizen-led-crowd-sourcing-roadmap-ci-ber-%E2%80%9Cbig-data%E2%80%9D-project

Helguera, P. (2011). *Education for socially engaged art: A materials and techniques handbook*. New York, NY: Jorge Pinto Books.

Hooks, B. (1995). *Art on my mind: Visual politics*. New York, NY: New Press.

Jamieson, H. V. (2008). *Adventures in cyberformance experiments at the interface of theatre and the internet*. (Unpublished master's thesis). Queensland University of Technology.

Jamieson, H. V. (n.d.). *Cyberformance*. Retrieved from http://creative-catalyst.com/cyberformance/

Lacy, S., Roth, M., & Mey, K. (2010). *Leaving art: Writings on performance, politics, and publics, 1974-2007*. Durham, NC: Duke University Press. doi:10.1215/9780822391227

Latour, B. (2005). *Reassembling the social: An introduction to actor-network theory*. Oxford, UK: Oxford University Press.

Marshall, J. (2012, January 22). Online gamers achieve first crowd-sourced redesign of protein. *Scientific American*. Retrieved from http://www.scientificamerican.com/article.cfm?id=victory-for-crowdsourced-biomolecule2&page=2

NYC Digital. (2012). *Digital RoadMap: The city of New York*. Retrieved from http://www.nyc.gov/html/digital/html/roadmap/roadmap.shtml

Ovide, S. (2012, June 12). Tapping big data to fill potholes. *The Wall Street Journal*. Retrieved from http://online.wsj.com/article/SB10001424052702303444204577460552615646874.html

Plackett, B. (2013, March 27). Citizen scientist: Eyewire's call to game. *The Connectivist*. Retrieved from http://www.theconnectivist.com/2013/03/citizen-scientist-eyewires-call-to-game/

Rowan, L., & Bigum, C. (Eds.). (2012). *Transformative approaches to new technologies and student diversity*. New York, NY: Springer. doi:10.1007/978-94-007-2642-0

Tatnall, A. (2010). *Actor-network theory and technology innovation: Advancements and new concepts*. Hershey, PA: IGI Global. doi:10.4018/978-1-60960-197-3

Turkle, S. (2011). *Alone together: Why we expect more from technology and less from each other*. New York, NY: Basic Books.

Verclas, K. (2005). *MobileActive*. Retrieved from http://mobileactive.org/

Voice of America. (2010, March 9). *World Bank online game invites youth to solve global problems*. [Video file]. Retrieved from http://www.voanews.com/content/world-bank-computer-game-invites-youth-to-be-creative--87240387/113855.html

ADDITIONAL READING

Anderson, T. (2010). *Art education for social justice*. Reston, VA: National Art Education Association.

Au, W. J. (2008). *The making of Second Life: Notes from the new world*. New York, NY: HarperCollins.

Bastos, F., & Zimmerman, E. (Eds.). (2014). Connecting creativity research and practice in art education: Foundations, pedagogies, and contemporary issues. Reston, VA: The National Art Education Association.

Bomer, R. (1995). *Time for meaning: Crafting literate lives in middle and high school*. Portsmouth, NH: Heinemann. Retrieved from http://catalog.hathitrust.org/Record/003056696

Bowles, N., & Daniel-Ramond, N. (2013). *Staging social justice: Collaborating to create activist theatre*. Carbondale, IL: Southern Illinois University Press.

Castronova, E. (2007). *Exodus to virtual world: How online fun is changing reality*. New York, NY: Palgrave Macmillan.

Church, C. R. (2010). Bridging: Feminist pedagogy and art education. *Visual Arts Research*, *36*(1), 68–72. doi:10.1353/var.2010.0004

Davies, T. (2002). Taking risks as a feature of creativity in the teaching and learning of design and technology. In G. Owen-Jackson (Ed.), *Aspects of teaching secondary design and technology: Perspectives on practice* (pp. 118–129). New York, NY: Routledge.

Dixon, S. (2007). *Digital performance: A history of new media in theater, dance, performance art, and installation*. Cambridge, MA: MIT Press.

Fem Bot Collective. *Feminism, new media, science, & technology*. Retrieved from http://fembotcollective.org/

FemTechNet listserv at http://fembotcollective.org/femtechnet/

Johnson, P., & Pettit, D. (2012). *Machinima: The art and practice of virtual filmmaking*. Jefferson, NC: McFarland.

Knobel, M., & Lankshear, C. (Eds.). (2010). *DIY media: Creating, sharing and learning with new technologies*. New York, NY: Peter Lang.

Latour, B. (2005). *Reassembling the social: An introduction to actor-network-theory*. Oxford, UK: Oxford University Press.

Livingstone, S., & Helsper, E. (2007). Taking risks when communicating on the Internet: The role of offline social-psychological factors in young people's vulnerability to online risks. *Information Communication and Society*, *10*(5), 619–643. doi:10.3402/rlt.v16i3.10899

Local Autonomy Networks. Retrieved from http://autonets.org/home

Lowood, H., & Nitsche, M. (Eds.). (2011). *The machinima reader*. Cambridge, MA: MIT Press. doi:10.7551/mitpress/9780262015332.001.0001

Middleton, A. J., & Mather, R. (2008). Machinima interventions: Innovative approaches to immersive virtual world curriculum integration. *Research in Learning Technology*, *16*(3), 207–220. doi:10.3402/rlt.v16i3.10899

Naidus, B. (2009). *Arts for change: Teaching outside the frame*. New York, NY: New Village Press.

Papagiannouli, C. (2011). Cyberformance and the Cyberstage. *International Journal of the Arts in Society*, *4*(6), 273–282.

Pearce, C. (2011). *Community of play*. Cambridge, MA: MIT Press.

Pepper, M. (2011). Virtual guerrillas and a world of extras: Shooting machinima in Second Life. In H. Urbanski (Ed.), *Writing and the digital generation, essays on new media rhetoric* (pp. 174–185). Jefferson, NC: McFarland & Company.

Quinn, T. M., Ploof, J., & Hochtritt, L. J. (2012). *Art and social justice education: Culture as commons.* New York, NY: Routledge.

Sensoy, Ö., & DiAngelo, R. (2012). *Is everyone really equal? An introduction to key concepts in social justice education.* New York, NY: Teachers College Press.

Sipe, J. W., & Frick, D. M. (2012). *Seven pillars of servant leadership: Practicing the wisdom of leading by serving.* Mahwah, NJ: Paulist Press.

Spillane, J. P. (2006). *Distributed leadership.* San Francisco, CA: Jossey-Bass.

Thompson, C. (2005, August 7). The xbox auteurs. *The New York Times.* Retrieved from http://www.nytimes.com/2005/08/07/magazine/07MACHINI.html

Timperley, H. S. (2005). Distributed leadership: Developing theory from practice. *Journal of Curriculum Studies*, *37*(4), 395–420. doi:10.1080/00220270500038545

KEY TERMS AND DEFINITIONS

Actor-Network Theory: Actor-network theory (ANT) is an approach to understanding the relationships between nodes of influence among technological, natural, and social systems.

Cyberformance: Live performance on the Internet coordinated by people in real time using different media such as text, video, images, avatars, Webcam, sound, voice, and animation.

Distributed Leadership: Distributed leadership practice is not only shared leadership, in which individuals take on different responsibilities, but more importantly, it focuses on generating leadership through the collaborations and the interactions between individuals and the situation/problem/environment.

Machinima: Filmmaking using existing games or virtual world engines. Machinima is a form of art-making that involves constructions of cultural narratives.

Social Justice Education: Social justice education teaches people to identify various forms of social injustice; where it is, how it happens, what makes the situation(s) unjust, and who is advantaged and/or who is disadvantaged.

Virtual World: An online community continually manifesting as a computer-based simulated environment where users can interact with one another and virtual objects.

ENDNOTES

[1] We list the authors alphabetically in this book chapter. Each contributed to writing this article. We used video conferencing at various stages to conceptualize and critique the work in progress, and to devise action plans for next steps. Meetings began with an open discussion and ended with a summary of next steps, visibly composed by all in a shared document.

[2] Although we met, performed, and filmed in *Second Life* (SL), there are many other virtual spaces that can be used for collaboration and creating cyberformance. Because of the limitation of SL for educators, many educators have moved onto the OpenSim platform, using it as an alternative to Second Life. OpenSim functions as a virtual world identical to Second Life, but can be set up

by educators who can employ their own rules of access and behavior. An example of educational OpenSim includes *VIEW*, a stand alone OpenSim for educators. A list of other OpenSim from educational institutions can be found here:_http://opensim-edu.org/blog/. Other technologies for cyberformance include *UpStage* (http://upstage.org.nz/) and

3   *Water Wheel* (http://water-wheel.net/). Both of these platforms are Web browser-based.

Actant, a term borrowed from social theory, refers to both humans and non-humans that enter into associations with one another through networks (Brown & Capdevila, 1999; Latour, 2005).

4   For more information about *Empty Bowls* see http://www.emptybowls.net/

Chapter 8
Faculty Users on Facebook:
What We Can Learn from Women Academics–Mothers' Rhetorical Methods for Visual Self-Presentation Online

Sarah Spangler
Old Dominion University, USA

ABSTRACT

Within the rhetorical spaces of the physical institution and the online realm of Facebook, faculty must negotiate community norms and expectations when self-presenting to their audiences. Given the pervasiveness of Facebook and the commonplace intersection of personal and professional audiences on this site, faculty users need to carefully consider how they construct their online identities, particularly in terms of their visual self-presentation through the profile picture. This chapter presents data from a survey that explores the rhetorical approaches of one group of Facebook users, women academics who are also mothers. Participant responses reveal that a majority of these users demonstrate audience awareness and a deliberate rhetorical process when visually self-presenting on Facebook. The insight garnered from this survey can assist faculty Facebook users, both men and women, in thinking more critically about how they navigate the rhetorical landscape of this site when visually self-presenting to their own audiences.

DOI: 10.4018/978-1-4666-5150-0.ch008

INTRODUCTION

With its wide ranging rhetorical contexts, Facebook no longer functions simply as an Internet playground where users can freely experiment with their identities without considering the potential ripple effect of their rhetorical choices. In 1995, Turkle discussed the user tendency "to take things at interface value" and claimed "we are moving toward a culture of simulation in which people are increasingly comfortable with substituting representations of reality for the real" (p. 23). Her more recent work (Turkle, 2011) builds on the theory that people's online lives are representational and simulated, asserting that "real life provides little space for consequence-free identity play" unlike the online realms of social networking sites and gaming forums (p. 193). Arguably, however, there is no *real* self versus a *digital* self, and the idea that our online and offline selves are separate has been contested (Baym, 2010; Consalvo & Paasonen, 2002). Baym (2002) asserts that the notion of the online and offline constituting "separate realms does not hold up to scrutiny" and that the ways in which users communicate and connect with one another online "can only be understood as deeply embedded in and influenced by the daily realities of embodied life (Baym, 2010, p. 152). She acknowledges that certain online forums may facilitate fantastical or fictitious self-presentation without directly affecting users' selves offline, but that "on close examination, even there the lines bleed" and "false identities…are exceptions, not the norm" (Baym, 2010, p. 152). This is not to say users do not construct versions of themselves online (and offline), which reflect different performances of self based on how they perceive various online rhetorical spaces and situations. But, although these constructions/performances may be different, they do not necessarily exist *separately* from one another or from users' offline identities. As such, the rhetorical and performative approaches to curating one's online identity(ies) potentially present far-reaching effects that constitute one's offline persona, as it is questionable the extent to which we can separate or conflate our digital selves from or with a more "real" self existing in the more "real" spaces of our physical lives. In a networked culture where identity collapses between the digital and the physical and boundaries between public and private are increasingly blurred, faculty and administrators must make critical and professionally influential choices when constructing their online identities, especially on pervasive social networking sites such as Facebook where their personal lives potentially intersect with and impact their academic/professional selves (and vice versa).

To this effect, the overarching aim of this chapter is to examine the extent to which the digital personas of women academics who are mothers intersect with, act upon, and reflect the identities they project in the physical space of the institution. While Facebook allows for multimodal (i.e., linguistic, visual, and/or aural modes of communication) self-presentation,[1] of particular interest is the visual rhetoric of women academics who construct an identity on Facebook by self-presenting (or not) through mother-child images and what informs their rhetorical decisions about how they merge their personal and professional lives in this digital space. How do women academics who are mothers define their purposes for using Facebook? Who are their audiences, and how do they consider these audiences when choosing how to visually self-present in this space? Do they negotiate institutional perceptions of motherhood and scholarly identity when visually self-presenting on Facebook? What can faculty users, men and women alike, learn from the rhetorical strategies of these users? This chapter attempts to shed light on these questions by considering the responses of women academics-mothers who participated in a study designed to understand their rhetorical methods for visual self-presentation on Facebook; the degree to which institutional expectations and attitudes about motherhood influence their online rhetorical choices when visually self-presenting;

and whether these users have adopted identifiable rhetorical strategies for adapting their visual self-presentation to multiple audiences. Developing a stronger understanding of these faculty users' multimodal rhetorical processes on Facebook by directly consulting the users themselves benefits both men and women faculty who actively and consciously manage their "visual impression[s]" (Siibak, 2009, p. 2) on Facebook and who are mindful of their own deliberate and rhetorically-informed action when curating their online identities through images. Although a sample of 42 participants does not generate a body of data generalizable across all Facebook users who are both mothers and academics, the data does provide several worthwhile points of insight that can potentially assist faculty users—be they women or men, single or married, parents or not—who are concerned about how they visually self-present in this digital space.

BACKGROUND

Identity Construction on Social Networking Sites

Although users typically construct[2] their Facebook identities through multiple rhetorical modes (e.g., visual, linguistic, aural), recent research has emphasized the profile picture "as a primary identity marker" (Strano, 2008, p. 1) and "one of the most telling pieces of self-disclosure or image construction" (Hum et al., 2011, p. 1828). Strano (2008) describes it "as the most pointed attempt of photographic self-presentation on the Facebook profile. In essence, this image 'stands in' for the user's body in this virtual environment" (p. 2). Arola (2010) notes that "the profile picture will most likely be the first place the eyes go" and that "the Facebook template encourages an understanding of ourselves and each other through the image we choose of ourselves" (p. 8). Even when users visually self-present through an object

or picture other than an image of themselves, they still make a rhetorical move, as that object/picture also functions as a "stand-in" for the user. No matter what *kind* of image is there, the profile picture plays a prominent role in defining the user's identity regardless of whether or not she plays or experiments with, pushes against, or "conforms" to conventional ways of performing and self-presenting in this space. Indeed, the selection and management of users' profile images have been noted as deliberate and performative (Manago, Graham, Greenfield, & Salimkhan, 2008; Siibak, 2009). Hum et al. (2011) argue that because the Facebook profile picture "offers an important first attempt to construct one's online identity, it is logical to assume that a significant amount of deliberate and conscious thought is put into offering this first important clue" (p. 1832). Manago et al. (2008) assert that MySpace "users are not necessarily presenting themselves through one-on-one interactions, but rather displaying the self as if on a stage to a mass audience observing a performance" (p. 450). These observations suggest the powerful role of the visual in composing a user's online identity, particularly the profile picture and, now, perhaps, the Facebook cover photo as well. And, if these images are, indeed, "the first place the eyes will go," then users, especially faculty and other professionals, might carefully consider how the images they select for their profile pictures and cover photos project a first impression on their audiences.

Within the physical space of the institution, faculty construct and project a professional identity for a face-to-face audience(s) typically defined by the professional environment of their departments and universities. Whether interacting with colleagues, administration, or students, faculty can likely gauge how these audiences will respond to their performances and, if necessary, adjust those performances accordingly. However, if the institutional expectations that contextualize faculty's face-to-face audience are strictly defined, faculty may have limited options for determining which audiences they will engage or how they will visually construct themselves for these audiences. Facebook appears to offer faculty users more rhetorical control over how they visually self-present in this space as compared to what they may experience offline when managing their identities in the physical space of the institution. Manago et al. (2008) note that "the nearly infinite number of ways to display oneself to others through the profile may give users expanded opportunities to realize aspects of selves limited in their offline lives" (p. 447). Within the rhetorical context of Facebook, faculty users seemingly have more control over who comprises their audiences in that they can choose whom they "friend" and then manage those "friends" in various groups. Presumably, faculty can present a more relaxed and personal side and visually communicate through images of themselves and family and friends and pets that might not necessarily be appropriate in the halls of the university.

Yet, when faculty users' rhetorical purposes for using Facebook straddle the personal and the professional, these "choices" may be somewhat limited. Although faculty can manage different audiences in groups, the rhetorical context of Facebook inherently pushes faculty, and all users, toward accumulating "friends" whether those friends be family members, high school friends, professional colleagues, students, etc. The norms that have emerged within this digital context tend to pressure users to accept friendship requests from people they might not have chosen to initiate friendships with online or offline. Turkle (2011) observes that "when media are always there, waiting to be wanted, people lose a sense of choosing to communicate" (p. 163), and she also notes the tenuous nature of many online connections forged on a "network [that] prepares us for the 'relationships with less'" (p. 154). What are faculty members to do, for example, when they are friended by a professional colleague, perhaps a supervisor or administrator, with whom they have little more than an acquaintanceship? Regardless

of how the faculty user chooses to manage her academic and non-academic audiences on Facebook through the groups feature or other privacy settings, all audiences will see how the faculty member visually self-presents through the profile picture and cover photo. Thus, when rhetorically strategizing how to visually self-present through the profile image—that first visual encounter between rhetor and audience—faculty users have multiple audiences to consider which complicates and, perhaps, restricts their options for composing themselves in an environment that otherwise presents as a space for self-expression and playful identity experimenting.

Given the commonplace intersection between professional and personal on Facebook, "it is a mistake to naively assume that new media bestow the power to communicate freely, without constraints" (Nelson, Hull, & Roche-Smith, 2008, p. 437). This assertion holds especially true for faculty users who engage personal and academic/professional audiences on Facebook. Van House (2011) argues that due to the design of many social networking sites, "agency is complex and contestable" (p. 426). The templated nature of these sites directs users to self-present in categorized ways as well as directs and predetermines audiences' interpretations and responses, constructs that reflect the network's influence on users' interactions and identity composing practices. Nelson, Hull, & Roche-Smith (2008) argue that when composing multimodally in digital spaces "extrinsic forces like time, space, and power—Kantian in scope—also bear upon agency and authorial choices, conscious and deliberate though those choices may be" (p. 437). In this sense, the rhetorical contexts of the physical space of the institution and the digital realm of Facebook might be described in terms of powerful forces that impact, constrain, inform, and/or dictate the rhetorical choices of faculty users composing themselves in these spaces.

An "invisible social layer of affordances for and constraints on meaning making" complicates users' multimodal self-presentation in new media texts and results in "meaning making at the *intersection* of the social and the textual" (Nelson, Hull, & Roche-Smith, 2008, p. 421). Users' practices and the conventions of the social groups constituting their audiences as well as the site itself determine the social norms contextualizing the habits, practices, activities, and performances of and interactions between users as well as what is of interest to one's audiences (Van House, 2011, p. 426). The social norms and expectations that define a faculty user's often mixed and disparate Facebook audiences complicate the rhetorical process of visually constructing oneself because the user must negotiate multiple and competing social values and expectations when determining how to appropriately self-present in ways that meet those various social expectations. In the physical space of the institution, most faculty understand the social norms that define their institutional and/or departmental contexts (e.g., conservative vs. liberal climate; suits vs. jeans when teaching). On Facebook, these same norms and expectations may heavily determine what are socially acceptable practices for visual self-presentation, for example, avoiding party pictures or politically charged or crudely humorous profile images or cover photos. An awareness and understanding of the group norms that form the social layers of Facebook might be seen as affordances in that faculty are able to make critically informed decisions about how they compose themselves online; however, these same affordances might also be viewed as constraints when faculty users feel beholden to the default norms of powerful and influential institutions represented by their professional audiences.

In either rhetorical context, the physical space of the institution or the digital realm of Facebook, faculty can, of course, choose the extent to which they visually self-present in ways that conform to or push against institutional norms, and an individual's position and/or rank in the institution may affect these choices. However, women academics who are mothers may have additional rhetorical considerations when visually self-presenting on Facebook in light of institutional perceptions of motherhood that have influenced the ways women have sometimes chosen to construct their identities within the physical space of the academy. This said, although all faculty need to think critically about the rhetorical choices they face when curating their identities online, women academics who are mothers should consider whether or not posting pregnancy or other maternal images as their profile pictures places them in professionally compromising positions in the context of the social norms of their particular academic and professional audiences.

Institutional Perceptions of Motherhood

Depending on the culture of a particular institutional setting, women academics who are mothers may or may not feel "supported" and are still sometimes "the exception in their department or school, working with faculty who either do not have children or whose children are grown or cared for by wives" (Philipsen & Bostic, 2008, p. 86). Historically, the academy has fostered an environment inhospitable, inflexible, and unsupportive of motherhood and has perpetuated perceptions of pregnancy and motherhood that have traditionally discouraged, tacitly or otherwise, the visibility of motherhood in the academy. In this way, the academy certainly functions as an extrinsic force of space and power that potentially limits or hinders women academics' agency in constructing an overlapping identity of mother and scholar that is visible. These institutional constraints may prompt women academics to carefully consider the effects of their rhetorical choices when constructing their identities as professionals and mothers.

Stockdell-Giesler and Ingalls (2007) assert that institutions assume mothers will be too distracted to be academically and professionally productive and that the highly visual and "superpresent" existence of a pregnant woman's body adds to an institutional perception that pregnancy is "a threat" to a woman's ability to meet strictly defined expectations for performance. Cucciarre, Morris, Nickoson, Owens, and Sheridan (2011) suggest that institutions have tacitly discouraged women from having children while on tenure track by neglecting to discuss institutional support and benefits available for faculty forming a family and by penalizing women during evaluations for tenure because of gaps in their CVs "due to pregnancy and bearing/rearing a child" (p. 57). Connelly and Ghodsee (2011) advise that men are not the only ones inclined to view pregnancy and motherhood as impediments to meeting the rigors of academia. Women faculty, especially of the previous generation, "were often forced to make a choice between family and career…and they paid a high price for their success if they decided not to have children when they really wanted them. Given the sacrifices most of them had to make, they may be even more critical [than] senior male colleagues " (Connelly & Ghodsee, 2011, p. 39).

Consequently, many women academics who have chosen to have children while in graduate school or on tenure track have faced challenges in defining their identities as mothers and scholars (Curriarre et al., 2011; Marquez, 2011; Philipsen & Bostic, 2008; Stockdell-Giesler & Ingalls, 2011) within the physical space of the institution, and many have felt pressured or have been advised to downplay their identities as mothers in the workplace while striving to achieve a narrowly defined image of "success" (Curriarre et al., 2011; Marquez, 2011; Stockdell-Giesler & Ingalls, 2011). To enter the male dominated realm of university teaching, researching, and publishing, women have often had to adopt men's ways of being successful. Another way of describing this phenomenon is in terms of *identity*—to achieve gender equality in the academy, women academics have been expected to carve out androcentric identities that have traditionally been valued in the academy and have been connected with images of scholarly success. The expectations for women academics to project an androcentric identity in the academy to be successful coupled with institutional misconceptions about motherhood resulting in poor work performance constrain the agency of women academics to compose multidimensional identities that visibly and productively intersect.

Such institutional perceptions of motherhood and narrow definitions of success have a far-reaching negative impact when women who *want* to have children while in graduate school or on the tenure track choose *not* to because they fear being penalized for this choice. If women academics deliberately postpone having children or downplay the visibility of their maternal identities for fear of being regarded as less professionally capable, they have, arguably, engaged in a physical, multimodal rhetorical process. This process, one that emphasizes the visual mode, reflects a desire and attempt to control the degree to which their identities as mothers, or desire to become mothers, are *visible* to their audiences. If a woman's professional objective, for example, is to earn tenure and she anticipates that her professional audience regards motherhood as an impediment or "handicap" (Kittelstrom, 2011) to this process, she may make the rhetorical move to visually diminish her identity as mother to this particular audience with the intention of controlling her audiences' perceptions of her in this particular space.

Women Academics- Mothers' Visual Self-Presentation on Facebook

Given the active personal and professional online presences many women academics have established, these rhetorical challenges extend beyond the brick and mortar structure of the academy, as women academics who are mothers must think about the overarching effects of their rhetorical decisions when self-presenting in digital spaces, especially via images and, more specifically, through mother-child images. That women's ways of visually constructing and presenting themselves, offline and online, are often scrutinized, women academics may have even more of an impetus than their male colleagues to be (hyper)vigilant about how they visually self-present. Recently, the common rhetorical practice of self-presenting on social networking sites through mother-child images has been characterized as an "ominous self-effacement" (Roiphe, 2012). Roiphe (2012) compares the digital "trend" with physically encountering "brilliant and accomplished" women who, after becoming mothers, expend all their intellectual "rigour and analytical depth and verve" on discussing little else besides their children. Roiphe's critique of this trend points to how women academics have grappled with defining identities separate from the "traditional" roles of being a mother and wife. However, her observations somewhat echo the perceptions about pregnancy and motherhood that have discouraged women academics from making motherhood visible, prompting them to mask or keep silent about their identities as mothers for fear of being perceived as weak and distracted from their academic work. If, within social networking sites like Facebook, women academics perceive and navigate institutionally defined perceptions regarding the visibility of motherhood in the academy, then it is possible that these women visually self-present according to a set of institutional (social) norms and practices that "bear upon [their] agency and authorial choices" when self-presenting in the physical space of the academy (Nelson, Hull, & Roche-Smith, 2008, p. 437).

METHODOLOGY

Study Design

The purpose of this study has been to discover the kinds of rhetorical choices women academics who are mothers make when visually self-presenting on Facebook. Initially the study was designed based, in part, on the hypothesis that institutional perceptions of motherhood influence women's rhetorical decisions for visual self-presentation. However, participants were not asked questions directly related to motherhood and the academy or how being a mother and an academic does or does not influence how participants consider their audiences. The questions were, instead, designed to allow for responses that were not heavily guided by the researcher's personal theoretical speculations. Participants were, however, provided with a general description of the project that describes the goal of analyzing users' rhetorical processes of visually self-presenting through mother-child images. As a result, many participants independently contextualized their responses within the stated goals of the project despite the generalness and openness of the survey instrument itself. On the whole, women participants responded in ways that point toward wide-ranging rhetorical motivations and methods regarding audience and context awareness as well as how women respond to the cultural and professional milieu(s) of the institution.

Research Questions

1. What do these users see as the purpose(s) of their Facebook accounts?

2. Who do they see as their primary audience (or even secondary audiences), and, when deciding how to visually self-present on Facebook, do they take into account potential audience response to or interpretation of their profile picture?

3. Do women academics who are mothers think about their present or future employers (who might see their pictures on Facebook) when making these decisions? And, to what extent might their rank and status influence their rhetorical decisions?

4. Do these users revise their visual self-presentation when on the market or up for tenure/promotion or in conjunction with other important scholarly milestones?

5. To what degree do women academics attempt to align their online identities on social networking spaces with the identities they construct in the physical space of the academy?

Procedure and Participants

The instrument for this study consists of a 26-item, anonymous survey that includes multiple choice, short answer, visual coding, open-ended, and Likert-type questions. The survey was disseminated via various listservs, word of mouth, department and college administrators, and Facebook snowball sampling. The study and instrument are IRB exempt, and a total of 42 qualified respondents participated in the survey. The survey was designed to collect data specifically from women academics (broadly defined as faculty, administrators, and graduate students) in higher education, specifically two-year colleges and above, who are also mothers and Facebook users. The following tables breakdown the rank/status of participants (Table 1) as well as the institution types (Table 2) and departments (Table 3) to which participants belong.

Data Analysis

For the purposes of this chapter, only select results have been included for analysis and discussion. The following four qualitative items have been included, and identifiable thematic trends and key words across participant responses to Question 9 are provided in Table 7:

- **Question 9:** What is your method for choosing/designing your profile picture?
- **Question 19:** Please briefly explain why you are comfortable or why you are concerned with the way the above audiences

Table 1. Respondents by rank/position/status

Rank/Status	Number of Participants
Professor	4[a]
Associate Professor	4[b]
Assistant Professor	9[c]
Instructor	2[d]
Adjunct Instructor	7
Faculty/Full-time Staff	5[e]
Graduate Student/Ph.D. Candidate/TAs	10
Other	1[f]

Note. [a]One participant also identified as a "Dean." [b]One participant also identified as "Chair;" [c]One participant also identified as "Director;" one participant also identified as a "librarian." [d]One participant also identified as "WAC Coordinator;" the other clarifies she is "tenured." [e]One participant identifies as "faculty" and "instructor" but has only been included in this category. [f]One participant identified as "IRB Research Coordinator."

Table 2. Respondents by institution type

Institution Type	Number of Participants
Community college	13[a]
Four-Year Institutions	
Four-year	4
Four-year private/for profit	3
Four-year public	1
Four-year research	3
Four-year teaching	4
Research Institutions (1 & 2)	16

Note. [a]Two participants noted that they worked in both community colleges as well as four-year institutions, which accounts for the additional two institutions above the base of 42.

[see Figure 1 for categories] respond to/interpret the way you visually self-present on Facebook.

- **Question 20:** How might your institutional rank/status influence the choices you make when visually self-presenting on Facebook?

Table 3. Respondents by department or college type[a]

Department Type	Number of Participants
Department	
Art & Design	1
Art History	1
Behavioral Science	1
Biology	1
Communication & Theater Arts	1
Developmental Ed	1
English	23[b]
Epidemiology	1
Humanities	1
Languages	1
Languages and Linguistics	1
Library & Information Science	1
Literature	1
Sociology & Anthropology	1
University Library	1
Urban Studies and Public Administration	1
College	
English Language Institute	1
Professional Studies	1
Veterinary Medicine	1

Note. [a]One participant did not respond to this question. [b]The number of participants from English departments likely results from the researcher's position within the English department and College of Arts and Letters at Old Dominion University where the survey was first distributed. [c]This participant identified her department and/or college as "Languages, Math and Science."

- **Question 21:** What strategies have you adopted to present yourself to multiple audiences? And, how do specific events influence these strategies? For example, have you ever revised or modified your visual self-presentation on Facebook while on the market or up for tenure/promotion or in conjunction with other important scholarly milestones? What did you do? And, why (why not) did you make the revisions or modifications?

Participant Coded Data and Quantitative Data

One of the main goals of this survey was to collect data about how women academics who are mothers visually self-present on Facebook, specifically through profile pictures and cover pictures. Participants were asked to logon to Facebook, count the number of pictures posted to their profile picture and cover photo albums,[3] and then code their images according to nine categories provided in the survey (see Table 4). The quantitative data addressed in this chapter relate mostly to questions designed to measure how "comfortable" or "concerned" users are with how their various audiences interpret or respond to their profile pictures. Question 5 of the survey asks participants to identify their target audiences for Facebook by checking off all applicable categories and naming other audience categories not listed (see Figure 1). Questions 12-17 of the survey ask participants to choose from a Likert-type scale to indicate how comfortable or concerned they are with the responses from and interpretations of their Facebook audiences they have identified in question five (see Table 5). Question 18 asks participants to choose from a Likert-type scale to indicate how comfortable or concerned they are with how present or future employers respond to or interpret their profile pictures (see Figure 2). Finally, in question 22, participants are asked to consider the degree to which their online identities on Facebook align with their offline identities in the physical space of the academy (see Table 6).

Discussion of Quantitative Data

In general, the responses to the above quantitative questions suggest that most participants are not overly concerned with how their audiences might interpret or respond to their profile pictures. A majority of participants (90.5%) report that their academic friends and non-academic friends equally constitute their primary Facebook audiences, with extended family (71.4%)

Table 4. How participants visually self-present according to self-coding and prescribed categories

Primary Focus of Profile Picture	% (No.) of Participants
User only	93% (39)
User and child(ren) together	76% (32)
User's child(ren) only	45% (19)
User & partner together	57% (24)
User, partner, & children together	43% (18)
User's partner & children together	14% (6)
User with friends and/or family	67% (28)
Other person, object, and/or place	81% (34)
Other	71% (3)

and academic acquaintances (69%) reported as the next two primary audiences, respectively. Interestingly, participants indicate that they are nearly as "comfortable" with how their academic friends might respond to or interpret their profile pictures as they are with their non-academic audiences, and the variance between participants who reported feeling "very comfortable" with these same audiences' responses is only slight (29% report being very comfortable with their

academic audience's response; 35% report being very comfortable with their non-academic audiences). Comparatively, only a little more than 7% of participants reported feeling concerned about these audiences' responses to or interpretations of their profile pictures. The majority of participants (63.4%) said they are comfortable or very comfortable with the way present or future employers might respond to their visual self-presentation on Facebook while only 12.2% report feelings of concern. The results suggest that participants are confident when visually self-presenting and do not view their visual self-presentation as problematic for their academic audiences, administrators (i.e., present/future employers) included. Significantly, not only are most users comfortable with the way they visually self-present on Facebook when considering their academic audiences, 71.5% of women academics assert that their online identities on Facebook are extremely or very aligned with their offline identities in the institution.

The findings also demonstrate that women academics who are mothers not only visually self-present with profile pictures where the primary focus is just themselves (93%), but they also compose themselves visually through mother-child images (76%) as well as images where the primary focus is their children (45%). Here, it is

Figure 1. Participants' audiences on Facebook

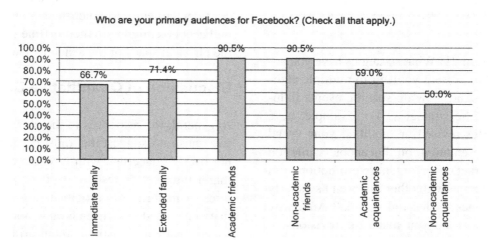

Table 5. Participants' degree of comfort or concern regarding audiences' responses to/interpretations of participants' profile pictures

Audience (Question=Q) Level of Comfort/Concern	% (No.) of Participants
Q12. How do you feel about your IMMEDIATE family's response to or interpretation of your profile pictures, cover photos, or other photos you post?[a]	
Very comfortable	58.5% (24)
Comfortable	34.1% (14)
Neutral	7.3% (3)
Concerned	0
Very concerned	0
Q13. How do you feel about your EXTENDED family's response to or interpretation of your profile pictures, cover photos, or other photos you post?[a]	
Very comfortable	48.8% (20)
Comfortable	34.1% (14)
Neutral	17.1% (7)
Concerned	0
Very concerned	0
Q14. How do you feel about your ACADEMIC/PROFESSIONAL friends' responses to or interpretations of your profile pictures, cover photos, or other photos you post?[a]	
Very comfortable	29.3% (12)
Comfortable	41.5% (17)
Neutral	22.0% (9)
Concerned	7.3% (3)
Very concerned	0
Q15. How do you feel about your NON-ACADEMIC friends' responses to or interpretations of your profile pictures, cover photos, or other photos you post?[b]	
Very comfortable	35.0% (14)
Comfortable	42.5% (17)
Neutral	15.0% (6)
Concerned	7.5% (3)
Very concerned	0
Q16. How do you feel about your ACADEMIC ACQUAINTANCES' responses to or interpretations of your profile pictures, cover photos, or other photos you post?[a]	
Very comfortable	29.3%(12)
Comfortable	36.6% (15)
Neutral	29.3% (12)
Concerned	4.9% (2)
Very concerned	0
Q17. How do you feel about your NON-ACADEMIC ACQUAINTANCES' responses to or interpretations of your profile pictures, cover photos, or other photos you post?b	
Very comfortable	30.0% (12)
Comfortable	32.5% (13)
Neutral	27.5% (11)
Concerned	10.0% (4)
Very concerned	0

Note. [a]One participant did not respond to this question. [b]Two participants did not respond to this question. [a]One participant of the 42 skipped this question.

Figure 2. How participants feel about their employer's reaction to their images[a]

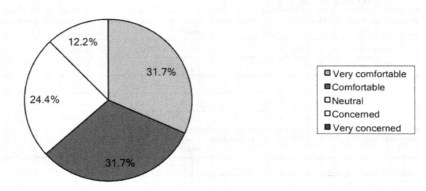

How do you feel about your present/future employer's response to or interpretation of your profile pictures, cover photos, or other photos you post?

Table 6. Degree to which participants' online and offline identities are aligned

Degree of Alignment	% (No.) of Participants
Extremely aligned	28.6% (12)
Very aligned	42.9% (18)
Moderately aligned	16.7% (7)
Slightly aligned	9.5% (4)
Not at all aligned	2.4% (1)

worth emphasizing the percentage of participants who are visually self-presenting with mother-child images in an online rhetorical context they report to be largely defined by an academic or institutional presence. That so many participants use mother-child images or images of their children only for their profile pictures is significant in relation to the fact that a majority of participants who also report strong alignment between their online and offline (institutional) identities. These findings suggest that some women academics deliberately construct a maternal identity in both the digital realm of Facebook as well as the offline world of the academy, an important observation in light of research documenting the historically inhospitable culture of the academy as it relates to motherhood.

Such results seem to suggest that some women academics do not feel obligated to conform to institutional constraints regarding motherhood while constructing their identities on Facebook or within the rhetorical context of the physical institution itself. The deliberate rhetorical intention revealed here may corroborate Manago et al.'s (2008) claim that "when users display images that do have veracity in the offline world, the online display strengthens the reality of the event and its relationship to the individual" (p. 451). In other words, by deliberately choosing to use maternal images to visually self-present online, these women academics are illuminating a role, a reality, that, in part, defines their offline selves. Given the fact that these users have audiences largely comprised of academic friends and acquaintances, consciously curating an online identity that is visually constructed through maternal images might be read as a bold rhetorical move that makes motherhood visible in an online space clearly influenced by the social norms of the institution. It might also be argued that the deliberate choice of women academics to visually self-present *as mothers* on Facebook, a place where the professional and personal intersect, challenges long-held institutional perceptions about motherhood being a "handicap."

Table 7. Thematic trends across responses to open-ended items #9, 19-21 which provide insight into participants' rhetorical methods for visually self-representing through their profile pictures

Thematic Category	Key Terms	Example Responses
Q9. What is your method for choosing/designing your profile picture?		
Aesthetics/looks	beauty, look good, pretty, photogenic, flattering, cute	A picture that is flattering… I have to like the way I look in it!
Authentic/representative/up-to-date	"authentic self," recent, representative, new, me, recognizable	Something that is representative of "me" and my life.
Professional	neutrality, professional, current, "shows me"	My profile photo is one that is a current, professional photo of me (usually just my head).
Feelings/beliefs/interests	"feeling strongly," life, happening, event, seasonal	It depends what's going on in my life.
Motherhood	children, kids, child	I usually choose close-ups of the kids or the kids and me for profile pics.

Qualitative Data

Although the quantitative data suggest that most participants are comfortable with the way they visually self-present on Facebook for their academic audiences, the question of *why* they feel this way is raised. Also important is the fact that 7.3% of participants report feeling concerned and 22% report feeling neutral about how their academic audiences will respond to or interpret their visual self-presentation raises the question as to why some women academics feel concerned when others do not. The qualitative data from this survey shed light on these questions by providing insight into participants' rhetorical methods for visually self-presenting on Facebook. Question 9 asks participants to describe their method(s) for choosing/designing their profile/cover picture in order to yield explanatory data regarding questions 6 and 7, which ask participants to self-code/categorize their profile and cover photos. The following table presents trends across participants' responses to question 9; key words are included as well as select representative responses from participants' explanations to further anchor thematic categories.

In follow-up to questions 12-18, which ask participants to rate their level of comfort or concern regarding how various audiences respond to or interpret their profile/cover pictures, question 19 asks participants to consider *why* they are either comfortable or concerned. Question 20 asks users to consider whether or not and to what degree their institutional rank/status influences how they choose to visually self-present on Facebook through their profile and cover photos. Finally, question 21 asks participants to describe the strategies they have used to visually present themselves to multiple audiences and to discuss instances where they may have modified their visual self-presentation in correlation with a specific event, for example, being on the market or up for promotion. The following paragraphs present a broad overview of the diversity of participants' responses.

Question 19: Please briefly explain why you are comfortable or why you are concerned with the way the above audiences respond to/interpret the way you visually self-present on Facebook.

One participant expresses concern about how her academic/professional audiences might construe pictures depicting her children: "Some of the pictures are of my family, and I don't want future employers thinking that I am not serious about work because of those images." Another participant echoes this concern, stating, "I don't want to present myself as less serious, [and] I know that women perceived as on the mommy track might be." However, eight participants defend the rhetorical move to visually self-present with mother-child photos. Collectively, these responses describe participants as women who "work hard" and do not believe that pictures of their children undermine them professionally and who have broadcast the importance of their children, family, and parenting philosophies (e.g., one participant mentions breastfeeding her child at an academic conference). The majority of additional responses to the question of comfort or concern reflect participants' conscious rhetorical decisions to avoid posting profile pictures that are, for example, "questionable," "scandalous," "controversial," or "reactionary." One participant asserts, "I am 'comfortable' with most of my choices because I do explicitly consider all those audiences as I post."

Question 20: How might your institutional rank/status influence the choices you make when visually self-presenting on Facebook?

Forty-six percent (18) of participants indicated that their institutional rank/status might influence the choices they make when visually self-presenting on Facebook. The level of influence varies greatly across responses. For example, several participants qualify their responses with words such as "somewhat," "might," and "suppose," suggesting only moderate influence. Other participants' responses indicate that their institutional rank/status plays a more influential role in how they visually self-present in this space. For example, one participant recognizes her "wide audience" and reports not wanting to "deal with the backlash" of using visuals that "better represent [her] sense of humor…or political beliefs." One respondent states, "I am tenured, so it makes a big difference!," suggesting she has more freedom in posting than someone without tenure. A few

respondents indicate that being on the job market or tenure track would influence how they might visually self-present during these events. One participant shares, "Because the job market is on my mind, I am very conscious of how I self-present. Perhaps when my professional status is more secure, I can be more open about my early life." An interesting trend across several responses is that participants envisioned themselves in higher ranking positions, especially administrative ones, and described what they would do if they were, for example, a dean or provost: "If I was a college administrator, I might seek to have a more professional (head shot) pic."

Finally, participants who report their rank/status does not influence the way they visually self-present on Facebook include a wide range of explanations. One participant has made it a practice to always post a professional picture regardless of her rank, and another participant reports "feeling comfortable in [her] job" but taking "rhetorical responsibility" for posting pictures that are not "questionable." Similarly, one participant considers her "public persona and reputation" and takes the same approach to personal and professional self-presentation online and offline. Limiting the use of Facebook to personal use and avoiding professional relations are strategies one participant employs. Another describes her colleagues as "welcoming" and "diverse with lots of moms, dads." For one participant, her tenured position and 20+ years at her college make for a less worrisome situation regarding how she visually self-presents; however, this participant qualifies her response by asserting that "if she were not tenured, and at a high pressure research university," she might not use Facebook period, and if she did, she might restrict it to academic purposes and avoid "blending" the personal and professional aspects of her life. Interestingly, this response underscores that of another participant who contemplates cancelling her Facebook because "privacy is harder to control than I thought."

Question 21: What strategies have you adopted to present yourself to multiple audiences? And, how do specific events influence these strategies? For example, have you ever revised or modified your visual self-presentation on Facebook while on the market or up for tenure/promotion or in conjunction with other important scholarly milestones? What did you do? And, why (why not) did you make the revisions or modifications?

In response to this question, a majority of participants explain that because they choose profile pictures cautiously and responsibly in the first place, avoiding "questionable" or "controversial" photos, for example, that they do not need to modify their profile images in connection with professional events or milestones; however, seven participants confirmed otherwise. Two participants report changing their profile images while on the job market, one to emphasize her recent graduation and one to *de*emphasize pictures of her child, though the latter did not delete pictures of her child entirely. One participant explains changes she made to her profile when she applied to graduate school: "I untagged any pictures that had my son in them and made most of my pictures private. I wanted to make sure that being a parent was something I hid at the time because I feel many don't think grad school and parenting a young child go together. I wanted to give myself the best chance." Two participants note changes to their profile pictures that correspond with professional events, such as a book publication or an upcoming "presentation, conference, or workshop." One respondent who maintains two Facebook accounts—one for her personal audiences and one for her student audience—explains how she makes a weekly post on her student profile to engage them in the place where "they reside" but is careful not to post anything extensively personal on either page given Facebook's history of frequently changing the way viewers/audiences gain access to posts. Finally, one user

reports that before accepting a friend request from her employer, she took care to make sure that her pictures did not contain "negative imagery."

Discussion of Qualitative Data

Responses to question 9, which asks participants to describe their method(s) for designing/choosing a Facebook profile picture, shed light on the rhetorical choices some women academics make when considering how to visually construct themselves on Facebook. Five major thematic categories emerged from this data set. The first category of responses suggests that participants choose pictures based on aesthetics, meaning they are concerned with how they look in the pictures. Participants reported that they choose images that are flattering and that cast them in a photogenic light, which seems to correspond with Manago et al. (2008) who report the perception "that women work harder on profiles to impress others, especially in terms of physical beauty" (p. 453). Images are also chosen based on how "authentic" they are, meaning some participants choose images they feel accurately represent their physical characteristics in recognizable ways as well as authentically reflect their lives. Several participants say their methods for choosing images reflect their attempt to self-present in professional ways; interestingly, three participants report that they maintain more than one Facebook profile, one of which is dedicated to constructing a professional persona apart from the more personal profile maintained for family and friends. A small number of respondents say they visually self-present in ways that reflect their feelings, beliefs, and/or interests. They might, for example, use images that reflect a current or seasonal life event or images that represent a particular belief or cause, such as the red equal sign symbolizing gay marriage equality that many users have adopted as a rhetorical move of solidarity. A fifth thematic category to emerge is the use of mother-child images to visually self-present. Significantly, one participant makes a connection between self-representativeness and motherhood when she says she chooses "something that is representative of 'me' and my life. It may be a picture of me, a favorite piece of art, or me with my children/partner." In contrast, one participant emphasizes her method for choosing/designing her profile picture is driven by the fact that it is a space specifically for her: "Again, as it is MY Facebook page, both photos are of me (close up)."

When asked why they feel comfortable or concerned with the way audiences might respond to or interpret their profile pictures, a majority of participants explain that they consciously choose to avoid posting pictures that are questionable or controversial/reactionary. Although participants are not prompted to explain *why* they avoid this, one might reasonably assume a rhetorical connection between purpose, text, and audience since 90% of participants report earlier in the survey that their Facebook audiences are in part comprised of academic friends. In other words, users make deliberate decisions concerning the text, an image in this case, they will use when considering how their audiences will respond. This speculation also helps unpack why a majority of participants feel comfortable or very comfortable concerning the way their academic audiences have responded: they have consciously chosen to visually self-present in ways that do not place their image at uncertain risk with their audiences. To some extent, this suggests that participants recognize and have voluntarily conformed, to varying degrees, to the norms defined by the social groups that constitute their Facebook audiences. Correspondingly, a majority of participants who feel comfortable or very comfortable visually self-presenting to their academic (and other) audiences through mother-child images imply that they have, through face-to-face interactions, made known the importance of their children and family and have also proven themselves professionally and that the former

does not undermine the latter. One participant emphasizes, "I work very hard, and I'm good at what I do. No one could possibly say that being a mom has compromised my work performance. I dare them to. Being a mom helps me learn to be a better teacher and administrator."

Relatedly, different institutional settings as well as women's institutional rank and status seem to have some influence on the degree to which women feel empowered or limited when constructing their identities visually via their Facebook profile pictures. Some, but not all, women academics who do not technically "hold rank," such as doctoral students, PhD candidates, and non-tenured faculty, are concerned with how their academic audiences might respond to or interpret their visual self-presentation, particularly as this relates to women who have self-presented with images that depict them in motherhood roles. That women are voicing this concern and that some participants report making the deliberate choice to visually self-present *without* their child(ren) indicates that some women academics, prior to establishing institutionally defined success, are aware of the privileging of the male scholar as well as an institutional perception that motherhood is an academic handicap. This hyperawareness about their visual self-presentation on Facebook may reflect a concern for how visual texts potentially "fix representations of identity in potent and sometimes narrow and unwanted ways" (Nelson, Hull, & Roche-Smith, 2008, p. 435). In other words, these participants demonstrate the rhetorical awareness that audiences may develop ideas about users' identities based on an interaction with a particular visual artifact at a fixed point in time, which may, in turn, establish an impression for the audience that does not necessarily reflect the authorial intention of the user. In this case, participants are concerned about "narrow and unwanted" impressions related to their visual self-presentation as mothers.

Discussion of Cross-Analyzed Data

An initial hypothesis informing this study was that institutional rank/status would impact how comfortable or concerned women academics are with their visual self-presentation on Facebook, specifically that women with less rank, such as graduate students and women who have not yet achieved tenure, would be more concerned. However, in cross-analyzing how participants describe their rank/status with their reported levels of comfort and concern about audience response to their profile pictures, eight participants who report some degree of concern derive from several groups of respondents including professors, assistant professors, adjunct faculty, and graduate students. Also, participants report a range of reasons regarding why they are concerned, reasons that extend beyond concerns about motherhood. One associate professor reports concern that present and/or future employers might perceive her as less serious if she posts mother-child images as her profile picture. This same participant shares that she deemphasized pictures of her child when on the job market. However, another participant, an assistant professor with two children, does not directly refer to mother-child images when describing her concern but instead emphasizes her professionalism, stating that she attempts to visually self-present "in a way that is consistent with my values and my personal and professional reputation."

Concerning present/future employer responses, one graduate assistant explains, "I worry about showing family or other interests so much that it seems like I'm not dedicated to my professional life as much." Contrastingly, another graduate student reports feeling neutral about responses from academic friends, acquaintances, and present/future employers but reports being concerned about *non-academic* friends and acquaintances. She specifically refers to having had her child while in graduate school and that her "academic achievements have not been affected by [her] new role [as a mother]" and, therefore, does not refrain from posting mother-child images. An adjunct instructor responds similarly in that she is concerned about the responses of non-academic friends and acquaintances, but that she is very comfortable with how her academic friends and acquaintances as well as present/future employers might interpret or respond to her profile picture. This participant says she attempts to "remain very neutral in [her] postings and public life in the social media" and that she has "always been aware of what is visible." Still, another participant, an adjunct faculty, responds that she has neutral feelings about the perceptions of all her audiences with the exception of present/future employers. She adds, "I suppose I don't want to have my kids out there as 'me' because it's not the only thing I am. I post pictures of them occasionally, but never as my profile picture."

Because this chapter both addresses the borders between faculty users' online and offline identities as well as the degree to which women academics visually self-present as mothers in the online space of Facebook, another necessary point of cross analysis exists between how this group of users rates the degree of alignment between their online and offline identities and the extent to which they use mother-child images when visually self-presenting through the profile picture. To examine this, information about how participants ranked the alignment of their online identities on Facebook and their offline identities in the physical space of the institution was cross-analyzed with the ages and number of their children as well as the number of profile pictures the participants coded as images where the primary focus is the user only, the user with her child(ren), and the user's child(ren) only. Women who ranked their online and offline identities as "extremely" or "very" aligned have children ranging in number from one to four, with a majority of women having either one or two children. Users in these categories also present wide-ranging practices regarding the raw number of profile pictures, which points towards users' low or high activity regarding how often they modify their profile pictures. Also, the degree to which these users construct a visual self-presentation through mother-child images differs significantly. Only four women who report an extremely or very aligned online and offline identity also report *not* using mother-child images. The remaining participants visually self-present through images of themselves as well as through images of themselves with their children and over half (17/27) report visually self-presenting through images where the primary focus is on their child(ren) only.

Six participants report a moderately aligned online and offline identity; four participants report a slightly aligned online and offline identity; and one participant reports that her online and offline identities are not at all aligned. Of these 11 participants, only five use mother-child images to visually self-present through the profile image, and even fewer (2) report posting profile pictures that feature their children only. Additionally, two participants report that they do not ever use pictures of themselves or of other people to visually self-present (one participant uses a field of flowers instead). The open-ended comments of women who choose not to use mother-child images to self-present, again, vary greatly. One woman explains that not using many images of herself and children represents an attempt to protect her privacy. Another woman says simply that when she set up her profile she had a dog and no children and, therefore, used a picture of herself and her dog and has not changed it since. A couple of participants explain that since they use Facebook at least partly for professional reasons, they choose shots of themselves. One woman asserts that she feels "strongly" about using pictures that feature only her because she "is not [her] children." Relatedly, one woman from the "very aligned" category who reports using mother-child images as her profile picture explains that she deliberately

avoids posting pictures of her children *only* for her profile and cover photos, stating "[because] my kids are not 'me.'"

CONCLUSION

Many faculty inhabit heavily digitized professional and personal lives and, therefore, find themselves managing their professional personas not only within the brick and mortar environment of the academy, but also within the digital environment of social networking spaces like Facebook. From a rhetorical standpoint, both of these spaces embody contexts faculty must consciously navigate when making deliberate decisions concerning how they will visually present themselves to various audiences when fulfilling wide-ranging purposes. The physical space of the institution, indeed, presents itself as a rhetorical context in which faculty's audiences are comprised of students, other faculty, and professional colleagues and acquaintances. The selves they present in this context reflect a conscious anticipation of how their audiences will interpret and respond to them and the rhetorical methods they employ to control or persuade how their audiences perceive them. One's ability to successfully navigate institutional expectations when constructing an academic persona may directly or implicitly impact professional endeavors like earning tenure. For faculty who maintain a profile page on Facebook, many of the same rhetorical and performative situations played out in their offline lives are also played out in their online lives. Of users' digitally constructed selves, Van House (2011) argues:

These constructed self-representations are part of a complex interplay among the offline self, with its complexity, contingency, and dynamism; one's (often multiple) online representation(s); the subject's aspirations; his or her assumptions about others' expectations; social comparisons; actual and desired group membership and social connections; gender roles and other normative influences; historical and cultural situatedness; and feedback from viewers; as well as (our primary interest here) the intended and emergent design and practices of a site. (p. 426)

Facebook presents as a rhetorical context that faculty users must navigate much like the physical rhetorical context of the institution; thus, both spaces, by virtue of being forums for social encounters and individual self-presentation, require faculty to consciously think about how they will visually self-present to their audiences. However, Facebook is a particularly sticky rhetorical context. Facebook's popularity and the site norm that users present themselves in seemingly authentic ways (i.e., pseudonyms are not generally tolerated and Facebook attempts to enforce the use of real names) require faculty users to address multiple and sometimes disparate audiences, which potentially complicates how faculty construct themselves in this space.

On the whole, the women academics who participated in this study demonstrate audience awareness and deliberate rhetorical strategies for managing their identities and visual impressions on Facebook. Importantly, women academics' comfort with visually self-presenting as mothers suggests that many are confident in defining themselves as mothers and professionals in both the digital realm of Facebook and the physical space of the academy. This further suggests that some women academics may feel less beholden to institutional perceptions of motherhood and, instead, are choosing to make their roles as mothers visible by posting Facebook profile pictures that highlight their maternal roles, pictures that are visible to a Facebook audience in part comprised of academic friends, acquaintances, and employers. However, the data cannot reasonably be viewed as generalizable and should not be misconstrued as an indication that institutional perceptions of

motherhood have changed altogether, though it does seem reasonable to conclude these women's responses point toward a perceptional shift of some degree.

The insight gained from this study underscores the complexity of Facebook as a rhetorical context and reveals the diversity of users' rhetorical approaches to defining themselves in this space and visually constructing themselves in ways they find acceptable and advantageous both personally and professionally. The data suggest that Facebook potentially constitutes a rhetorical space in which faculty users can successfully anticipate and navigate the expectations of different audiences as defined by the offline and online norms of the communities that contextualize those audiences. Many of the participants in this study demonstrate an active approach to managing their visual impressions, particularly their profile pictures, through deliberately and thoughtfully selecting images, avoiding questionable or excessively controversial images, and organizing their Facebook audiences through the group option while still managing to visually self-present in ways that they feel accurately reflect who they are. When constructing their own online identities on Facebook and elsewhere, faculty users can benefit from considering the rhetorical methods of visual self-presentation described in this chapter by keeping in mind the prominence of the Facebook profile picture and emulating the audience awareness and savvy decision-making processes that these women academics who are mothers display when visually composing themselves in this space.

FUTURE RESEARCH OBJECTIVES

The results of this study provide insight into how women academics who are mothers negotiate the expectations of multiple Facebook audiences when determining how they will visually self-present themselves. Future studies might include more pointed questions regarding how women academics who are mothers feel about their own practices of visually self-presenting through mother-child images and whether they feel pressured to conform to any particular institutional perceptions about motherhood. Relatedly, future research might further examine how various institutional settings with differing publication and promotion expectations/requirements influence women academics' rhetorical decisions for self-presentation online. Another approach to understanding this subject more thoroughly would be to investigate why some women academics who are mothers deliberately avoid visually self-presenting through mother-child images. Additionally, because women academics do not constitute a "monolithic group" but, instead, "differ in income, marital status, sexual orientation, domestic involvement, points in their career when they had their children, and more" (Philipsen & Bostic, 2008, p. 86), follow-up research should focus on other female academic populations. Women teaching and researching in an international setting constitute an important female academic population whose rhetorical strategies for online self-presentation should be examined. Also, women in the STEM fields should be surveyed to examine how women academics from disciplines outside the humanities self-present online and whether they experience similar or different institutional pressures as represented in the responses of this initial, mostly humanities-based pool of participants.

REFERENCES

Arola, K. L. (2010). The design of web 2.0: The rise of the template, the fall of design. *Computers and Composition*, *27*(1), 4–14. doi:10.1016/j.compcom.2009.11.004

Baym, N. (2010). *Personal connections in the digital age*. Cambridge, UK: Polity Press.

Connelly, R., & Ghodsee, K. (2011). *Professor mommy: Finding work-family balance in academia*. Lanham, MD: Rowman & Littlefield.

Consalvo, M., & Paasonen, S. (Eds.). (2002). *Women & everyday uses of the internet: Agency & identity*. New York, NY: Peter Lang Publishing.

Cucciarre, C., Morris, D. E., Nickoson, L., Owens, K., & Sheridan, M. P. (2011). Mothers' ways of making it--Or making do? Making (over) academic lives in rhetoric and composition with children. *Composition Studies*, *39*(1), 41–61.

DePew, K. E., & Miller-Cochran, S. (n.d.). Social networking in a second language: Engaging multiple literate practices through identity composition. In M. Cox, J. Jordan, C. Ortmeier-Hooper, & G. Schwartz (Eds.), *Inventing identities in second language writing* (pp. 273–295). Urbana, IL: NCTE.

Hum, N. J., Chamberlin, P. E., Hambright, B. L., Portwood, A. C., Schat, A. C., & Bevan, J. L. (2011). A picture is worth a thousand words: A content analysis of Facebook profile photographs. *Computers in Human Behavior*, *27*, 1828–1833. doi:10.1016/j.chb.2011.04.003

Kittelstrom, A. (2010). The academic-motherhood handicap. *The Chronicle of Higher Education*. Retrieved from http://chronicle.com/article/The-Academic-Motherhood/64073

Manago, A. M., Graham, M. B., Greenfield, P. M., & Salimkhan, G. (2008). Self-presentation and gender on MySpace. *Journal of Applied Developmental Psychology*, *29*(6), 446–458. doi:10.1016/j.appdev.2008.07.001

Marquez, L. (2011). Narrating our lives: Retelling mothering and professional work in composition studies. *Composition Studies*, *39*(1), 73–85.

Nelson, M. E., Hull, G. A., & Roche-Smith, J. (2008). Challenges of multimedia self-presentation. *Written Communication*, 25(4), 415–440. doi:10.1177/0741088308322552

Philipsen, M. I., & Bostic, T. (2008). *Challenges of the faculty career for women*. San Francisco, CA: Jossey-Bass.

Roiphe, K. (2012, August). Disappearing mothers. *Financial Times Magazine*. Retrieved from http://www.ft.com/intl/cms/s/2/0bf95f3c-f234-11e1-bba3-00144feabdc0.html#axzz26UO8WkoC

Siibak, A. (2009). Constructing the self through the photo selection: Visual impression management on social networking websites. *Cyberpsychology*, 3(1), 1–9.

Stockdell-Giesler, A., & Ingalls, R. (2007). Faculty mothers. *Academe*, 93(4).

Strano, M. M. (2008). User descriptions and interpretations of self-presentation through Facebook profile images. *Cyberpsychology*, 2(2), 1–11.

Turkle, S. (1995). Taking things at interface value. In S. Turkle (Ed.), *Life on the screen* (pp. 102–124). New York, NY: Touchstone.

Turkle, S. (2011). *Alone together: Why we expect more from technology and less from each other*. New York, NY: Basic Books.

Van House, N. A. (2011). Feminist HCI meets Facebook: Performativity and social networking sites. *Interacting with Computers*, 23, 422–429. doi:10.1016/j.intcom.2011.03.003

ADDITIONAL READING

Ballif, M., Davis, D., & Mountford, R. (2008). *Women's ways of making it in rhetoric and composition*. New York, NY: Routledge.

Bullingham, L., & Vasconcelos, A. C. (2013). 'The presentation of self in the online world': Goffman and the study of online identities. *Journal of Information Science*, 39(1), 101–112. doi:10.1177/0165551512470051

Danberg, R. (2011). On (not) making it in rhetoric and composition. *Composition Studies*, 39(1), 63–72.

DePew, K. (2011). Social media at academia's periphery: Studying multilingual developmental writers' Facebook composing strategies. *Reading Matrix: An International Online Journal*, 11(1), 54–75.

Ellison, N., Heino, R., & Gibbs, J. (2006). Managing impressions online: Self-presentation processes in the online dating environment. *Journal of Computer-Mediated Communication*, 11(2), 415–441. doi:10.1111/j.1083-6101.2006.00020.x

Goffman, E. (1959). *The presentation of self in everyday life*. New York, NY: Macmillan.

Goldsborough, R. (2009). Looking good on social networking sites. *Teacher Librarian*, 36(3), 62.

Haferkamp, N., Eimler, S. C., Papadakis, A., & Kruck, J. (2012). Men are from Mars, women are from Venus? Examining gender differences in self-presentation on social networking sites. *Cyberpsychology. Behavior & Social Networking*, 15(2), 91–98. doi:10.1089/cyber.2011.0151

Hall, P. P., West, J., & McIntyre, E. (2012). Female self-sexualization in MySpace.com personal profile photographs. *Sexuality & Culture*, 16(1), 1–16. doi:10.1007/s12119-011-9095-0

Hawisher, G. E. (2000). Constructing our identities through online images. *Journal of Adolescent & Adult Literacy*, 43(6), 544.

Hawisher, G. E., & Sullivan, P. A. (1999). Fleeting images: Women visually writing the web. In G. E. Hawisher & C. L. Selfe (Eds.), P*assions, pedagogies, and 21st century technologies* (268-291). Logan, Utah: Utah State University Press.

Hogan, B. (2010). The presentation of self in the age of social media: Distinguishing performances and exhibitions online. *Bulletin of Science, Technology & Society*, *30*(6), 377–386. doi:10.1177/0270467610385893

Kawash, S. (2011). New directions in motherhood studies. *Signs: Journal Of Women In Culture & Society*, *36*(4), 969–1003. doi:10.1086/658637

Lasén, A. (2009). Digital photography and picture sharing: Redefining the public/private divide. *Knowledge, Technology & Policy*, *22*(3), 205. doi:10.1007/s12130-009-9086-8

Mason, M. A., & Goulden, M. (2004). Do babies matter (part II)? *Academe*, *90*(6), 10–15. doi:10.2307/40252699

Mason, M.A., Goulden, M., & Frasch, K. (2009). Why graduate students reject the fast track. *Academe, 95*(1), 11-16. *Academic Search Complete.* Web. 22 Nov. 2011.

McAndrew, F., & Jeong, H. (2012). Who does what on Facebook? Age, sex, and relationship status as predictors of Facebook use. *Computers in Human Behavior*, *28*(6), 2359–2365. doi:10.1016/j.chb.2012.07.007

Mills, M. (2008). Intersections between work and family: When a playpen can be office furniture. *Women's. Studies in Communications*, *31*(2), 213–217.

O'Laughlin, E. M., & Bischoff, L. G. (2005). Balancing parenthood and academia: Work/family stress as influenced by gender and tenure status. *Journal of Family Issues*, *26*(1), 79–106. doi:10.1177/0192513X04265942

Philipsen, M. I., & Bostic, T. (2010). *Helping faculty find work-life balance: The path toward family-friendly institutions*. San Francisco, California: Jossey-Bass.

Steinfield, C., Ellison, N. B., & Lampe, C. (2008). Social capital, self-esteem, and use of online social network sites: A longitudinal analysis. *Journal of Applied Developmental Psychology*, *29*, 434–445. doi:10.1016/j.appdev.2008.07.002

Van Der Heide, B., D'Angelo, J. D., & Schumaker, E. M. (2012). The effects of verbal versus photographic self-presentation on impression formation in Facebook. *The Journal of Communication*, *62*(1), 98–116. doi:10.1111/j.1460-2466.2011.01617.x

Van Dijck, J. (2008). Digital photography: Communication, identity, memory. *Visual Communication*, *7*, 57–76. doi:10.1177/1470357207084865

Wolf-Wendel, L., & Ward, K. (2006). Academic life and motherhood: Variations by institutional type. *Higher Education*, *52*(3), 487–521. doi:10.1007/s10734-005-0364-4

Wolf-Wendel, L., & Ward, K. (2012). *Academic motherhood: How faculty manage work and family*. New Brunswick, New Jersey: Rutgers.

Wolf-Wendel, L., Ward, K., & Twombly, S. B. (2007). Faculty life at community colleges: The perspective of women with children. *Community College Review*, *34*(4), 255–281. doi:10.1177/0091552107300282

Zhao, S., Grasmuch, S., & Martin, J. (2008). Identity construction on Facebook: Digital empowerment in anchored relationships. *Computers in Human Behavior*, *24*, 1816–1836. doi:10.1016/j.chb.2008.02.012

KEY TERMS AND DEFINITIONS

Affordances: Refers to applications or features of a program that facilitate a particular action, usually viewed as beneficial, helpful, or advantageous.

Cover Photo: A feature on Facebook that allows users to post a banner image across the top of their profile pages. This image is viewable to all of a user's friends.

Institutional Perceptions/Constraints/Realities: Refers to ideas, views, expectations, and norms that are defined by and engrained in the institutional setting, specifically that of the academy.

Multimodal: Refers to multiple means (or modes) of composing and meaning making, for example, linguistic (e.g., written text), visual (e.g., images, photos, drawings, etc.) and/or aural (e.g., audio files) modes or any combination of these modes used together.

Profile Picture: The image Facebook users choose to represent them visually; along with the cover photo, it is one of the first visuals audiences encounter. This image is viewable to all of a user's friends.

Social Media: Web-based applications/sites whose main purpose is to facilitate social interaction and communication between friends or followers.

Visual Self-Presentation: The deliberate and thoughtful use of images (not limited to photos) to compose or construct aspects of one's identity either online or offline.

Visual Rhetoric: The means of persuasion via visual elements (e.g., images, photographs, charts and graphs, drawings, etc.).

Women Academics-Mothers: Women who hold an academic position of some sort (e.g., graduate student, faculty, administrator) and who are also mothers.

ENDNOTES

[1] Several articles on users' presentation and performance of self use Erving Goffman's *The Presentation of Self in Everyday Life* to frame the discussion.

[2] Throughout this chapter, identity *construction* and *composition* are used interchangeably with the acknowledgement that some scholars prefer one term to the other. For example, DePew and Miller-Cochran (2010) prefer the phrase "*identity composition*, as opposed to the often used *identity construction*, because [they] perceive that materials that are 'constructed' tend to be monolithic and evoke a more Cartesian understanding of identity" and that "materials that are 'composed' [are] more rhetorical and subject to kairotic revisions" (p. 292).

[3] In this chapter, I have limited my discussion to a primary focus on participants' responses and comments pertaining to profile pictures and *not* cover photos.

Section 4
Social Values and Ethics in Online Gaming

Chapter 9
Friends and Rivals:
Loyalty, Ethics, and Leadership in BioWare's "Dragon Age II"

Kristin M. S. Bezio
University of Richmond, USA

ABSTRACT

This chapter explores how through both narrative and gameplay mechanics, BioWare's 2011 digital role-playing game Dragon Age II seeks to help players redefine their understanding of ethics in terms of human emotion and interaction. These interaction-based ethics are the product of our desire to situate ourselves within a social community rather than on an abstract continuum of universal "right" and "wrong." The ambiguity contained within the friendship-rivalry system factionalizes Hawke and his/her companions, forcing the player, as the group's leader, to ally with one of the two sides in the game's overarching conflict. This coercive mechanic produces awareness in the player of the way in which interpersonal relationships form our responses in ethical situations, and causes the player to question whether their decisions are the product of "pure" ethics, or the consequence of deliberate or unconscious submission to the ethical mores of others.

DOI: 10.4018/978-1-4666-5150-0.ch009

INTRODUCTION

Traditional forms of gaming and play have long served to unite communities, as Mikhail Bakhtin (1984) has noted, by "liberat[ing] them from the usual laws and conventions" in order to unite them across conventional social and hierarchical borders through the space of the carnivalesque (p. 235). Gamespace – the physical and psychological realm of play – has always been an alternate, "virtual" reality constructed by the temporary liberations and limitations of gameplay. Games, McKenzie Wark (2007) explains, "are not representations of this world. They are more like allegories of a world made over as gamespace. They encode the abstract principles upon which decisions about realness of this or that world are now decided" (para. 020).[1] As allegorical space, gamespace "is at once manifestly 'there', some *place* where performances can be *seen*, and then again diaphanously 'here', an imaginative *space* suffused with the potential of the virtual, where some other/ Other *scene* might appear" (Bealer, 2012, p. 31). Within these "virtual" spaces, players are able to (re)negotiate their identities in relative terms, positioning themselves as allies or antagonists within the game.

Modern digital games create electronically generated virtual spaces into which players are thrust as active creative agents complicit in both play and the creation of a unique, player-controlled narrative experience. Such games, suggests Mary Flanagan (2009), "not only provide outlets for entertainment but also function as means for creative expression, as instruments for conceptual thinking, or as tools to help examine or work through social issues" (p. 1). As virtual simulations, videogames are often criticized, Ian Bogost (2008) notes, as being inaccurate or unrealistic, and therefore unable to transmit didactic or reflective content; in short, videogames are dismissed as nothing more than "low-reflection, high-gloss entertainment" (p. 117). As simulations, they are often rejected as

being unable to translate meaning from virtual to real space: "Simulation denial acknowledges that sims are subjective, and concludes that they are therefore useless, untrustworthy, or even dangerous tools" (Bogost, 2008, p. 107). However, videogames have the capacity not only for self-reflection, but for the production of simulated communities designed to direct the player's self-examination toward their potential as an ethical social subject (Sicart, 2009, p. 5).

I argue that the narrative and gameplay of many single-player campaign games – and here I will specifically examine digital role playing games (DRPGs) – participate in the construction of a virtual social gamespace despite being ostensibly solitary play-experiences.[2] Single-player DRPGs, although only played by one player at a time, are populous gamespaces: a DRPG's "gamescape…is a social space, marked by the spatial practices of both playable and non-playable characters whose comings and goings are lived and mapped within it" (Bealer, 2012, p. 41). Because the gamespaces of DRPGs are populated by these non-player characters (NPCs), the player-character – as avatar for the player – must interact with them in order to accomplish gameplay tasks. Therefore, despite the solitary mode of play, many DRPGs nevertheless attempt to simulate community dynamics through the inclusion of NPCs who function throughout the campaign as the player's digital community.

In BioWare's 2011 *Dragon Age II*, we find a particularly interesting experiment in virtual social dynamics that encourages the player to consider the complex interplay of ethics and leadership within community. In the process of playing *Dragon Age II*, the player constructs relationships between Hawke – the player-character – and a set of non-player "companion" characters (NPCCs) as a necessary part of gameplay. This process of determining the player-character's persona through relational interactivity is a unique component of BioWare's NPCC mechanics. BioWare's use of player-NPCC relationships as a core component of *Dragon Age II*'s ludic construction encourages cooperative play, self-evaluation, and ethical reflection in the comparative safety of a single-player environment (Crawford, 1982, p. 12). The social, ethical, and leadership challenges in *Dragon Age II* rely specifically on the conflict between the ideological paradigms of the NPCCs and the player-character, Hawke.

In *Dragon Age II*, Hawke is not only responsible for choosing which NPCCs will accompany him on each specific quest, but which will even be included in the general "party," or group of potential companions.[3] Each of these NPCCs, like "real people," has a particular ethos that governs his or her actions and attitude throughout the game. What makes these NPCCs particularly interesting to a study of virtual community is that each evaluates Hawke's actions and dialogue choices on individual evaluative continua that range from "friend" to "rival." This friendship-rivalry mechanic is unique to BioWare's *Dragon Age* series (*Dragon Age: Origins* [2009], *Dragon Age: Awakening* [2010], and *Dragon Age II*, as of 2013). The mechanic's significance to this volume is that its presence indicates BioWare's interest in community interaction over individualistic behavior or beliefs.

DRPG GAMES AND ALLEGORICAL GAMESPACE

Although a game's story is important to a complete understanding of its critical function – and this is particularly true of DRPGs in general, and BioWare DRPGs in specific – it is necessary to understand game narrative as something more than conventional, literary narrative. Games, particularly videogames, possess both procedural or algorithmic functions – game mechanics – and literary narrative or story, and it is important to consider both (Bogost, 2008, p. 53). The genre of traditional, linear narrative is fundamentally

altered in games by the presence of a player, rather than a reader or audience (Wark, 2007, para. 030; Cassidy, 2011, p. 293). Sicart (2009) explains that

the complete understanding of games and their capabilities is only possible when described as experiences. Those experiences have a formal, material sense that conditions the possible ways the users perform those experiences. In game research terms, games have an ergodic nature. (p. 30)

Ergodics, or the need for deliberate effort, separate games from literature, cinema, television, and other spectator-based forms of popular culture. Gameplay ergodics are autotelic, as Chad Carlson (2011) explains: "Game players, in the deepest sense of those terms, are looking for and engaging artificial problems *as an end in itself*" (p. 78). In essence, players are participants rather than audience, experiencing rather than watching the process of gameplay.

The experiential nature of videogame play is a partial consequence of identification with the player's avatar, termed the "player-character," since it is not simply a virtual "skin," but a specific persona associated with the game's narrative (Call, Whitlock, & Voorhees, 2012, p. 17). The player-character in DRPGs thus becomes a hybrid entity: part avatar for the player, part independent character (Bealer, 2012, p. 31). The most prominent – and important – consequence of this hybridity is that neither the developer nor the player has absolute control over the player's narrative or gameplay experience (McDowell, 2012, p. 185). This, in turn, produces a game's unique "ludonarrative," the construction of both story events and gameplay events specific to one particular play-through of a game (Juul, 2001, para. 15; Cassidy, 2011, p. 295). Slavoj Žižek (1999) remarks that "There are two standard uses of cyberspace narrative: the linear, single-path maze adventure" – whose ludonarratives are necessarily similar although not identical from player to player – "and the 'postmodern' hypertext undetermined form of rhizome fiction" (para. 6). This "rhizome fiction" forms the core experience of many DRPG ludonarratives. In the case of a DRPG like *Dragon Age II*, which has not only optional quests, but choices of NPCCs, conversation trees, player-character class and gender options, and "tech" and "skill" trees, the experience of one player might differ vastly from that of another.[4]

What is particularly interesting is that this variance is a significant part of DRPGs' popularity because it opens a significant space for exploration and experimentation. As Žižek (1999) explains,

the very lack of the final point of closure serves as a kind of denial which protects us from confronting the trauma of our finitude, of the fact that there our story has to end at some point — there is no ultimate irreversible point, since, in this multiple universe, there are always other paths to explore, alternate realities into which one can take refuge when one seems to reach a deadlock. (para. 6)

When we consider the impact of a game, we must examine the various components of its potential ludonarratives: both story and mechanics (Sicart, 2009, p. 24; Henton, 2012, p. 68). In the case of *Dragon Age II*, mechanics are especially important in evaluating the game's virtual sociality, as these mechanics are what enable the game to create and encourage exploration of questions of ethics, leadership, and community.

VIRTUAL COMMUNITIES AND LEADERSHIP IN *DRAGON AGE II*

Playing Hawke: Constructing Player-Character Identity

I want to begin my exploration of *Dragon Age II* as the player would begin the game: with the player-character, Hawke. As in other BioWare

DRPG titles, *Dragon Age II* allows for a significant level of player customization, "a ludic convention which engages the player in building a reflection of some facet of self" (Whitlock, 2012, p. 137). Katie Whitlock (2012) assumes that players will recreate "some facet of the self" in their Hawke, and it is likely that many players do seek to emulate themselves in some capacity in the process of character creation (Roberts & Parks, 1999, pp. 525-526; Yee, 2008; Consalvo & Harper, 2009, p. 98), but players can also take the opportunity to deliberately create a Hawke who is substantially different from their self-conception.

The first choice the player must make is straightforward: gender and class. The player is presented with a screen that contains six figures: male warrior, female warrior, male mage, female mage, male rogue, female rogue. All six have the same "default" appearance (gender markers such as silhouette and facial hair aside), although the player will be presented with the opportunity to customize his or her Hawke's appearance in greater detail: skin tone, hair color and style, age, eye color and shape, facial feature size and shape, and facial tattoos. "They are," Karen Zook (2012) remarks, "both implicitly and explicitly, encouraged to experiment with identity as they create and direct player-characters" (p. 224). The player's choice of class and gender do not appreciably alter the subsequent ludonarrative, although there are minor differences in dialogue and some differences in gameplay based on class.[5]

This freedom to "experiment" with the player-character also extends into the overall gameplay experience of *Dragon Age II* (and other BioWare games). While *Dragon Age II* is broken into three Acts, within each Act, the player has the freedom to construct the game's ludonarrative in almost any way he or she wishes. Players may even deliberately choose to ignore or refuse any quest not marked "Main Plot" in their Journal.[6] Zook (2012) describes this as "not a directed play experience; players may choose the order in which they progress through the world and what choices they make while they do so" (p.

221). The abundance of choice is a larger part of *Dragon Age II*'s emphasis on player agency and control over the ludonarrative on both story and gameplay levels.

Ultimately, the purpose of all this freedom is to enable the player to make explicit comparisons between Hawke's choices and his or her own. The hybrid avatar of the player-character allows the player the ability to test ethical and social hypotheses within the safety of solitary virtual gamespace. There are in-game consequences for Hawke's actions, certainly, but the player need not be concerned about real-world repercussions, enabling experimentation with both action and conversation that might be stressful (or even inappropriate) in a non-single-player or real-world situation. It is worth noting that the gameworld consequences of Hawke's actions and conversations are not always immediately (or fully) apparent to the player. The complexity of the cause-and-effect algorithms within *Dragon Age II* (and other DRPGs) often means that the player – as in real life – has to make significant decisions with incomplete information.[7] Roger Travis (2012) explains that

the player at every moment shapes his or her performance with reference to a ludic system that renders the performance meaningful in relation to the entire system of the game, which is at the same time an overdetermined version of the player's world that productively mystifies him or her about the meaning of his or her choices, both in the game and in 'real' culture. (p. 246)

This translation from gameworld to real-world lies at the core of *Dragon Age II* as a critical ethical game; the game's intent is to provoke critical reflection on the part of the player about his or her real-world actions and relationships in the process of gameplay, ultimately guiding the player toward social tolerance through the use of its friendship-rivalry mechanic.

Social Judgment: The Friendship-Rivalry Mechanic

The most important gameplay element for our purposes is *Dragon Age II*'s friendship-rivalry mechanic: a system of evaluative continua by which Hawke's actions are judged. The mechanic of an evaluative continuum is common to BioWare games; however, unlike other BioWare titles, each of which employs a universal evaluative continuum, the *Dragon Age* games contain a multifaceted system in which each companion character evaluates the player-character. Travis (2012) describes the friendship-rivalry mechanic in *Dragon Age: Origins*, the basis for the system used in *Dragon Age II*:

In DAO, the sliders appear not on the PC's own character-screen but on the party-character's individual screen, and represent the character's approval or disapproval of the actions of the PC. These scales can be affected either by dialogue choices, as in KOTOR [Knights of the Old Republic] and Mass Effect, or by the giving of certain gifts to be found throughout the narrative geography of the game. The PC's position on these sliders determines whether dialogue options with the party-characters are open to them; these dialogue options, in turn, open others, including, for example, options that themselves lead to themes (that is, quests) that the player would otherwise have no opportunity to perform. (p. 244)

In *Dragon Age II*, this system evaluates Hawke's relationship to his companions based on a continuum that runs between "Friendship" and "Rivalry" and is individual to each companion, influenced by actions, conversation choices, companion-specific quests, and gifts. These continua are specific to each NPCC, and often contradict those of other NPCCs, requiring the player-qua-Hawke to make gameplay decisions that have the potential to cause conflicting – and sometimes severe – consequences.

Dragon Age II's friendship-rivalry mechanic removes the player's sense of moral absolutes; there is no easily ascertainable "right" or "wrong" answer in most of the situations Hawke encounters, only answers that gain "approval" or "disapproval" (friendship or rivalry) from the NPCCs. Mechanically, the player can use the "Character" menu to examine an NPCC's friendship-rivalry status. The continuum ranges from blue to red, with wings as the graphic for friendship and a spear-tip and laurel wreath for rivalry. The ethical implication of this mechanic is to produce awareness in the player of the way in which interpersonal relationships form and inform our responses in ethical situations, and to cause the player to question whether their decisions are the product of the player's natural ethical inclination, or of ethics changed by in-game motivations, such as the desire to placate or antagonize an NPCC. In so doing, *Dragon Age II* interrogates our understanding of ethics, redefining them in terms of human emotion and interaction, the product of our desire to situate ourselves within a social community rather than on an abstract continuum of universal "right" and "wrong."

Within *Dragon Age II*, the player has a variety of persuasion tactics he or she can use in order to secure the friendship or rivalry of the NPCCs. Conversation choices are one of the most obvious methods, and are marked with "attitudes" on the conversation dial: a blue olive branch for diplomacy; a pink drama mask for humor; red crossed swords, a fist, or a gavel (judgment) for aggression; a blue halo and wings for idealism; a pink gem for "charm;" a pink heart for "flirt" ("romance"); gold coins for "mercenary;" uncolored arrows for neutral; uncolored question mark to ask for further information; uncolored crossed fingers to lie; a green profile to defer to one of the NPCCs; or, rarely, a star, which indicates a "special choice" which differs depending on game events, Hawke's general attitude, or based on class or present NPCCs (Dragon Age Wiki, 2013). Although these attitudes assist the player

in projecting the emotion they wish to convey, the game's conversation dials are often deliberately difficult to interpret.

A hallmark of a BioWare conversation dial is that the words that appear on the screen are not the words that the player-character actually speaks; this disparity occasionally produces frustration, as the way the player interprets the label and what the player-character says sometimes seem quite disparate. For instance, in "Repentance," the conversation dial reads "The demon is dead," but Hawke says, "Everyone's dead. Your mother, too" (BioWare, 2011), in what one forum-poster describes as "the most ****-ish voice I've ever heard" (nranola, 2011).[8] However, this difference forces the player – especially a conscientious player attempting to manage the friendship-rivalry statuses of the NPCCs present for the conversation – to think about which choice he or she is going to make: in effect, to think before speaking, a valuable social lesson that becomes habit as the player progresses through the game (and which hopefully translates to the real-world).

Actions are the primary way in which the player can earn approval or disapproval from the NPCCs. NPCCs not in the party do not express opinions about the choices Hawke makes, so party selection is one of the means by which Hawke can manage friendship-rivalry continua. For each quest, Hawke is able to take three NPCCs in the active party, and is able to change the composition of the party frequently. While the player controls Hawke by default, he or she can switch avatars and play as any of the active NPCCs, enabling the player to give "commands" to each NPCC in turn. Inappropriately managing NPCCs – refusing to perform companion-specific quests or causing direct conflict by choosing the "wrong" NPCC for a quest – can result in the "loss" of those NPCCs to exile, departure, or even death, making their skills and equipment (and the quests they might offer) unavailable to the player for the rest of the game.[9]

Through party selection, the player is able to control the friendship-rivalry continua for the entire party, but must sometimes sacrifice the breadth of the party's skill-sets in order to do so. The player must therefore decide how he or she wishes to privilege the gameplay process: to balance NPCC skills for optimum combat success, to maximize friendship or rivalry among members of the party, or to adhere to a single ideology.

What is perhaps most interesting about the friendship-rivalry system with regard to Hawke's virtual community of NPCCs is its focus on the extreme ends of the spectrum. If the friendship-rivalry scale has reached the far end on either side, the companion's status ceases to fluctuate and remains at friend or rival for the remainder of the game, regardless of the choices the player makes. The ethical consequence for the player is that he or she must choose where to place Hawke's loyalties – if at all. The player's decision to be loyal to any of Hawke's companions is an ethical one in the realm of gameplay; by cultivating a "full friendship" or "full rivalry" with the NPCCs, the player is able to alter the gameplay consequences of certain missions and even eliminate companions from the party altogether. The game even rewards the player with achievements for maximizing each: twenty-five points for the "Friend" achievement, twenty-five for "Rival."[10]

Loyalty, therefore, appears specifically in two contexts: first, in Hawke's decisions to support his companions by being loyal to their ideals; second, because by maximizing friendship or rivalry, Hawke can guarantee the loyalty of his companions to him.[11] The reward is largely one of emotional investment and additional narrative; Hawke does receive companion "benefits" to statistics (5% damage or defense increase, for example) from some of his companions who have maximum friendship or rivalry, but even 50% progress toward either friendship or rivalry will unlock a specialization tree of abilities for the companion (Dragon Age Wiki, 2013). A high enough friendship-rivalry status

also unlocks a "romance" option for Hawke and one of the companions (or one at a time, at least, although the twenty-five point achievement for "Romance" may only be completed for one character per playthrough). All NPCCs benefit statistically from maximizing one side of the friendship-rivalry spectrum, but these boosts are not necessary to the successful completion of the game. While conversations will indicate a companion's approval or disapproval, the companion will remain loyal or disloyal to Hawke once the endpoint on the trajectory has been reached. This produces the effect of the player being able to compromise his or her position on an issue until the companion in question reaches full friend or rival status, and then being able to choose more "naturally" or to accommodate another NPCC to the same end.

Family, Friends, Rivals, and Companions: Hawke's Companions and Their Beliefs

It is important to understand that while the friendship-rivalry mechanic is individualized to each NPCC, many of the actions and choices with which Hawke is presented – and which impact each NPCC's friendship-rivalry "slider" – address the extremely polarized "social problems" of the gameworld. This context is crucial to Hawke's interactions with the NPCCs, as each has his or her own opinion on the "social issues" in Kirkwall (the city in which the game is set). The most prominent of them is the opposition between the mages and the Templars (the military branch of the game's religious order, controlled by the Chantry), complicated by the tension between the citizens of Kirkwall and the Qunari people occupying a compound within its bounds. These two conflicts permeate every quest and are significant to nearly every NPCC (and most NPCs) in the game.

The mage-Templar dichotomy is presented in the first playable sequence of the game following the introduction.[12] As the Hawke family attempts to escape the darkspawn (demonic, unthinking ghoulish creatures) overrunning Ferelden (their homeland), the player is introduced to the parameters of this conflict within the family itself. Hawke's younger twin siblings – Bethany and Carver – each represent one side: Bethany is an "apostate" (a mage unconfined by the Circle) and Carver a warrior sympathetic to the Templars. The player's companion party at this point consists of Hawke's family: Hawke, Bethany, Carver, and their mother, Leandra. Both Bethany and Carver are automatically included as NPCCs, while Leandra "follows" the trio of siblings as an NPC with whom the player-character interacts conversationally. Leandra immediately tells her children, "We have to stay together," and Hawke agrees, saying that "Wherever we go, what's important is that we don't separate" (BioWare, 2011). This goal of family unity immediately establishes for the player the importance of the companion system in narrative terms.

The key to understanding the role of the friendship-rivalry mechanic within the game-world's virtual community lies in the personality and background of each NPCC. As an apostate mage, Bethany – who at the beginning is predisposed toward friendship – approves of speech and actions that support freedom for mages and the unrestricted use of magic. Carver – predisposed toward rivalry – is biased toward the Templars and approves of aggression and the restriction of magic. As the player immediately discovers, two such opposing NPCCs disagree about most of Hawke's actions – there is no way to satisfy both. Before the party leaves Ferelden, however, the game narratively resolves the major sources of ideological conflict in the family; the game switches from playable to a cut-scene (a cinematic sequence over which the player has no control), in which one of the twins is attacked and killed. Which sibling dies depends on Hawke's class: if Hawke is a mage, Carver survives; if Hawke is a rogue or warrior,

Bethany lives. Mechanically, this is for balance: one of the two survivors will always be a mage (either Hawke or Bethany). However, it is also narratively important for Hawke and his sibling to be ideologically divided so that when Hawke must make his final choice to side with either the mages or the Templars he must consider his sibling as either enemy or ally.[13]

Compounding the family conflict is the addition other NPCCs. Aveline Vallen, whom the Hawke family saves from the darkspawn, balances Bethany and Carver: she is law-abiding and favors the Templars, but is practical and empathetic, preferring justice and fairness even when it requires bending the rules, as her first statement demonstrates. Merrill is a mage and an elf of Dalish (the wood-elf clan) heritage with a profound distaste (ironically) for what she views as unnecessary violence, and she approves of freedom for mages and equality for elves (who are severely oppressed and impoverished in Kirkwall, ostracized by the city and forced to live in the Alienage, which is tantamount to a ghetto). A strong foil to Merrill, Anders is a former Grey Warden and apostate mage who approves of choices that grant freedom to mages (but not blood mages), and disapproves of Templars. Anders's diametric opposition is Fenris, a Tevinter elf and former slave to a powerful and abusive Magister (mage). An unessential NPCC, Fenris disapproves of apostates and blood magic, and including him in a party with Merrill, Bethany, and/or Anders will produce hostile background conversations between the NPCCs. Isabela, a pirate rogue, approves of humor, freedom, and choice; if taken on a mission with Fenris, the elf will ask her about her opinion on mages, saying "So I hear you think mages should be free," to which she replies, "everyone should be free...It's about having choices" (BioWare, 2011). Contrary to Isabela's licentious freedom is Sebastian Vael, a rogue-class Chantry Brother whose devotion to dogma and asceticism place him in opposition to most of the other NPCCs. Sebastian approves of adherence to religious belief, restricting magic, and justice, and disapproves of excessive violence, freeing mages, or participating in excess.

I have postponed discussing Varric Tethras, another rogue, because of the distinctive nature of his character and role in the game's narrative. Varric is the first NPCC to be recruited in Kirkwall during the official "start" to Act One, and is the only NPCC whom Hawke cannot lose at or before the game's conclusion. The player first meets Varric in a cinematic cut-scene even before being able to customize or control Hawke. The entire game is actually Varric's story; the game begins with the dwarf being interrogated about Hawke by the Chantry Seeker Cassandra Pendegast. Varric's story – embodied in a book whose illustrations serve as transitional animations between Acts, narrated by Varric's voice – is actually comprised of the game's ludonarrative. As such, Varric is Hawke's "chronicler," and he, too, may be either friend or rival: humor and cleverness earn his approval, as these "sell" well to his audience, although he disapproves of violence and cruelty (Head_Fish, 2011; Dragon Age Wiki, 2013). As the central "voice" of the game, Varric's ethos – which privileges wit and fun – is the closest we can come to understanding the "ideals" of the game itself, although neither one is ultimately prepared to judge the player for most of his or her ideological choices. It is through Varric that we frequently see the game's critical intentionality, since it is ultimately his version of Hawke's story that the player participates in constructing.

Other than intercessions at the game's beginning and end, and at the start and end of each Act, Varric's role is primarily as just another NPCC.[14] However, the moments in which the player is narratively returned to the frame remind us that for all the ludic control of gameplay, the player is still constrained by the options created by the development team; complete player agency is always only an illusion, as there can be no true freedom within the confines of a game. Given that one of the primary components of play is freedom – as play is inherently autotelic, rather

than coerced – the fact that the game deliberately calls attention to the limitations on that freedom is critically interesting. The fact that this reminder of player limitation comes specifically from one of the NPCCs comments on the nature of social interactions as limiting factors on individual behaviors outside of the gamespace.

The rules of society place similar limitations on our behavior in real-world interactions, acting differently within different "virtual" spaces. I say "virtual" because the space itself does not proscribe these limitations on behavior; people have the capacity to act in whatever way they wish. However, the functionality of a space, such as a playing field or a workplace, alters the "virtual" rules about behavior in that space, reforming the mechanics of social interaction within its boundaries. The gamespace DRPGs is more restrictive than such real-world "virtual" spaces because it is procedural and algorithmic; it is literally impossible for a player to break the "rules" in the virtual gamespace of a videogame. Yet the absoluteness of the limitations frees the player to experiment more fully within the boundaries of the game's rules; there is no fear – as there is in real life – of transgressing a rule because such transgressions are impossible.

While certain games – like BioWare's *Knights of the Old Republic* or *Mass Effect* series, Lion-Head Studios' *Fable* series or Irrational's *Bioshock* – offer ostensibly moral decisions with which players are free to experiment, the mechanics themselves guide the player to a "right" side. In *Knights of the Old Republic*, the player chooses the "dark side" or "light side" of the Force, terms which have clear ethical valences both within the game and imported from the outside *Star Wars* franchise fiction. Similarly, in *Fable* the choices presented to players are clearly positive or negative, as an early conversation in *Fable III* presents the choice to "shake hands" or "belch." In *Mass Effect*, the terms "Paragon" and "Renegade" have similar, although less moralistic, resonance. Irrational's *Bioshock* seems to present ethical freedom in the decision to "Harvest" or "Rescue" the Little Sisters (girls possessed by parasitic sea slugs that make their eyes glow), but the game's mechanics actually guide the player significantly toward the "Rescue" option by making the Little Sisters profoundly sympathetic and, in fact, by providing better rewards and additional powers to players who make the "right" decision. Sicart suggests that such mechanical manipulation of players is itself unethical because it inhibits a player's ability for self-reflection, altering their decisions based on self-interested gameplay choices (Sicart, 2009, pp. 160-161). In *Dragon Age II*, however, everything that Hawke does is "allowed," including making choices that the player might consider unethical or inappropriate. Within the gamespace, such actions are permitted and even encouraged as a mechanic of ethical reflection. In games like this, the player is granted the freedom to explore immorality as a means of encouraging critical thought about such actions and their consequences without fear of judgment or reprisal (Sicart, 2009, p. 44), at least outside of the in-game judgment of the NPCs and NPCCs.[15]

Unquestioning Loyalty: Maximizing the Friendship-Rivalry Mechanic

The focus on loyalty as a product of the friendship-rivalry mechanic reveals that loyalty is a fundamental ethical principle in the game's design. Johan Huizinga (1955) argues that loyalty is a critical component to the social aspect of games and play as a whole:

Among the human virtues – or had we better say "qualities"? – there is one that seems to have sprung direct from the aristocratic and agnostic warrior-life of archaic times: loyalty. Loyalty is the surrender of the self to a person, cause or idea without arguing the reasons for this surrender or doubting the lasting nature of it….It would not be too far-fetched to derive this "virtue" – so beneficial in its pure form and so demoniacal a

ferment when perverted – straight from the play-sphere. (p. 104)

The fact that loyalty lies at the core of the friendship-rivalry mechanic in *Dragon Age II* reinforces the game's overall focus on virtual community; loyalty is a communal virtue, and *Dragon Age II*'s insistence on its significance reveals the game's attempt to integrate elements of community into a single-player experience.

Without overtly impressing this virtue on the player – Hawke does not *have* earn loyalty in order for the player to complete the game – the game nevertheless allows for and rewards loyalty on the part of the player with reciprocal loyalty from the companions, even if they are asked to compromise their personal ethics in order to do so. Securing the loyalty of an NPCC to Hawke, regardless of future conflicts with that NPCC's ideology, teaches the player to privilege social interaction over ideological conflict – or at least to recognize when he or she is unwilling to compromise ideology in order to maintain a relationship. But the game does not simply want Hawke to focus on a single NPCC as a "best friend" or "ultimate rival;" the game contains an achievement entitled "Great Minds Think Alike," which rewards the player with fifty points for maximizing the friendship-rivalry track for *four* NPCCs.[16] Given the distribution of opinions among Hawke's party (which can contain a maximum of seven NPCCs), this achievement requires that Hawke be willing to compromise ideology for loyalty. With three mages (Bethany, Merrill, Anders), three Templar-sympathizers (Fenris, Carver, Aveline), and two lawless rogues (Varric, Isabela), it is difficult for Hawke to successfully secure the loyalty of four without making very specific strategic decisions about which NPCCs accompany him on certain missions.[17] This task becomes easier since full rivalry can also secure loyalty, although a failure to maximize the friendship-rivalry slider quickly enough for some NPCCs will result in their departure.

Throughout the game, Hawke must choose between NPCCs and ideology: whether he is willing to compromise his own ideological preferences to satisfy theirs, or whether he is willing to risk losing them later in the game. Ideological pressures can also cause Hawke to reject an NPCC outright – a refusal to help Anders in "Dissent" or "Justice" can exclude Anders from the party. Similarly, if Hawke chooses to support slavery or turns Fenris over to his former master in "Alone," Fenris will leave Hawke's companions. At the end of Act Two, insufficient friendship or rivalry will cause Isabela to leave the party with the relic, an act which further complicates Hawke's battle with the Qunari leader. And in the final battle at the conclusion of Act Three, several NPCCs will leave if their friendship-rivalry status is not high enough, and they will not assist Hawke in combat. This is perhaps the most interesting mechanical element of the game concerning leadership; if Hawke is an effective leader, he will be able to secure the loyalty even of those who oppose his ideological positioning, a much more difficult task than maintaining the loyalty of someone with whom he agrees.

The game's emphasis on the importance of cultivating high friendship-rivalry quotients indicates the primacy of loyalty and sociality to the game's central premise. It is ultimately unimportant whether Hawke sides with the Templars or the mages, as both will turn against him, but it is crucial thematically, narratively, and mechanically that Hawke has secured the loyalty of the NPCCs so that he receives their "moral" and gameplay support in the final combat. The ultimate consequence of this emphasis is the *de*emphasis on ideology; it is more important for Hawke to be a member of a community (of NPCCs) than it is for him to have a clear ethos based on religious, social, political, or class ideology.

Pride and Prejudice: Intolerance, Diplomacy, and Irreconcilable Differences

As has already been stated, the vast majority of the quests – especially those marked "Main Plot" – in *Dragon Age II* are related to one of the two major socio-religious conflicts in the city of Kirkwall: either the mage-Templar dichotomy, or the occupation of the Qunari.[18] Conflicting beliefs form the crux of both, with the Chantry standing at the center of each. The purpose of the game's concentration on social and religious Otherness aligns with its attempts to inculcate the player with an attitude of tolerance as a part of its virtual social system. Not only does the game's party system function as a microscopic virtual society which Hawke – as its leader – must manage, but by situating that small-scale community within a larger, realistically problematic society (Kirkwall), the game places the social dynamics of the party within an heterogeneous virtual social context even more reflective of external, real-world conflict. Produced in the years leading up to 2011 (the average development time for a game of *Dragon Age II*'s scale runs three to five years), the focus of *Dragon Age II* on religious and class intolerance in the at-large society of Kirkwall can hardly be surprising.

Yet if Hawke himself displays tolerance and a willingness to embrace equality, he is more likely to secure the loyalty of several of his companions, namely Merrill, Fenris, Isabela, and Varric.[19] Likewise, if he shows respect to the Qunari leader, the Arishok, during "Blackpowder Promise" and "Blackpowder Courtesy" (missions in Acts One and Two, respectively), the Arishok respects him in return, despite their cultural and religious differences.

Yet even a diplomatic Hawke is unable to adequately defuse the situation with the Qunari, and whether or not the Arishok respects Hawke, the tensions between the Qunari and the city come to a head in "Demands of the Qun." When the Arishok discovers that the Tome of Koslun has been withheld from him, no amount of diplomacy can succeed, and the Qunari attack the city, killing civilians and executing the Viscount. But the game makes it clear that it is not simply the failure of the Viscount to hand over the relic that has occasioned Qunari violence against Kirkwall; in "Blackpowder Courtesy," the Arishok wants to know how the Viscount can allow the "selfishness" in the city "to continue," asks Hawke how he can "bear to stay in this chaos," and refers to the city as a "pustule" (BioWare, 2011). The Arishok's disdain for the cultural intolerance of Kirkwall and his disgust at the treatment of his people (Ashaad in "Unbidden Rescue," the emissaries in "Offered and Lost," and the patrol in "Missing Patrol") all contribute to his decision to destroy the city.[20]

Although the severity of the Qunari conflict ravages the city, it is a subset of the larger problem in Kirkwall with the oppressive oversight of the Templars as the military branch of the Chantry. As with Mother Patrice's intolerance for the Qunari, Knight Commander Meredith – whose name is invoked repeatedly as the source of Templar oppression – has little patience for apostasy or mages in general, seeing them as a constant source of threat to her city and her power. Quests throughout the remainder of the game reiterate both sides of the conflict, each asking Hawke to make the choice to confine or free mages, to kill or release mages, to denounce mages or Templars, or to condone or condemn repression on both sides. For the most part, Hawke is able (should the player so choose) to negotiate a middle line in which mages are kept confined but not oppressed, as in "Act of Mercy," where Hawke can turn a group of apostate mages over to the Templar Thrask, who promises to protect them, rather than kill Thrask to free the mages or allow another Templar to kill them. Similarly, in the opening of Act Three, Hawke is asked to mediate in a public

confrontation between Meredith, Knight Commander of the Templars, and Orsino, the First Enchanter of the Circle. Ultimately, however, the game forces Hawke to choose between them, although neither choice is "good" in a moral or social sense, and regardless of his choice, the eventual outcome is virtually the same.

The Champion: Hawke's Relational Leadership

The similitude of the game's conclusion regardless of Hawke's decision to side with Templars or mages is perhaps the clearest indication that the game itself is uninterested in promoting a single ideology. The final test of Hawke's abilities as a leader comes not in his decision, but in his ability to convince the NPCCs to follow him to whichever side he takes. This focus on sociality over ideology has been hinted at repeatedly throughout the game, both narratively and mechanically, and comes to fruition in the final conflict at the conclusion of Act Three. But before we examine this scene in detail, it is important to recognize how the game focuses the player's attention on Hawke as not simply a member of both a small community and a larger society, but as an exemplary leader for both.

Relative to the small community of NPCCs, Hawke's leadership is obvious in terms of game mechanics. The player begins by controlling Hawke-as-player-character, but once the game presents the player with NPCCs, he or she has the ability to control whichever of them happen to be in the active party at any given time. Similarly, the player is responsible for managing the role-playing statistical aspects of each NPCC – their attributes, abilities, equipment, and tactics. As such, Hawke, as the player's character-avatar, is the obvious leader of the NPCC party. Narratively, the game reinforces this in Hawke's characterization: Hawke is the elder sibling, is described as the better warrior (regardless of whether the player's abilities match this description), and is the character to whom NPCs and NPCCs alike come for assistance. Yet the game does not simply presume that the player-character will be an effective leader, either of his NPCC community or within Kirkwall society.

The friendship-rivalry mechanic in general, and the maximization element in specific, functions to reinforce the need for Hawke to make decisions that are leadership-oriented rather than exclusively self-serving. Altruistic decisions, particularly in companion-specific quests, lead to increases in friendship for NPCCs, and partial friendship ensures greater loyalty than partial rivalry. Maximized friendship or rivalry will secure loyalty, but managing the party to the degree necessary to do this for all NPCCs also requires that the player accommodate the beliefs and wishes of the NPCCs (either positively or negatively). Higher friendship-rivalry quotients also produce additional companion quests in Acts Two and Three, most obviously, the "Questioning Belief" quests that appear for each NPCC when their friendship-rivalry status reaches a certain percentage in either direction. In addition, the inclusion of gift-quests and other companion-specific quests encourage Hawke to interact with the NPCC community as a relational leader.

Relational leadership is based upon an understanding that the leader (if he or she is to be effective) makes leadership decisions, both goal- and behavior-oriented, based on his or her relationships with followers (Yukl, 2013, pp. 55-57). In *Dragon Age II*, the player-character is encouraged to be a responsive relational leader; the actions of the NPCCs are designed to reinforce Hawke's positive leadership decisions by offering themselves as companions and assisting Hawke in the completion of tasks. The positively-skewed nature of the friendship-rivalry mechanic in favor of friendship reinforces this understanding of effective relational leadership, as friendship-oriented NPCCs are more likely to continue granting Hawke approval and are more likely to remain in the party even when confronting a situation opposed to their ideological predisposition.[21] The more responsive Hawke is to

the NPCCs' requests and beliefs by fulfilling their companion-quests and managing the party so that they accompany him on quests that will further the friendship-rivalry track the player has chosen for them, the more benefits the player-character receives from them in combat bonuses, additional quests for experience points, and combat support in the final combat of the game.

In addition to leading his NPCC community, Hawke has the opportunity to act in a leadership capacity in the larger virtual society of Kirkwall. Following the events that conclude Act Two in which the Viscount is killed, Hawke is named Champion of Kirkwall. In the third act's introduction, Varric says that Hawke isn't just a hero, he's "the most important person in the city. Except for Knight Commander Meredith, of course" (BioWare, 2011). As Champion, Hawke occupies a position of political authority, although he is unable to mitigate the conflict between Meredith and Orsino, as the first scene in Act Three demonstrates, without interference from Elthina. Although Hawke can publically take sides, he doesn't have the official power necessary to enforce his will. If Hawke sides with the Templars at the end of the game, he can become Viscount (only in the narrative describing the game's aftermath, and only temporarily, according to Varric's account), but this official leadership position is clearly not meant to be the focus or goal of the game, given that it appears as an aside, if at all.

Instead, the central purpose of the game's final quest, "The Last Straw," is the insufficiency of ideology and the importance of human relationships in the face of institutional failure. Throughout this quest, and the game as a whole, references to intolerance are generally condemned. Meredith's intolerance here thus indicates to the player that her stance is not completely supportable within the game's framework, even though the player may choose to do so. At the end of the quest, Anders detonates an explosive compound which destroys the Chantry, killing Elthina and bringing the conflict between mages and Templars to a head. It is at this point that the game forces Hawke to make a decision between the two ideological poles. Because the game's fiction eliminates the voice of its spokeswoman of the divine by killing Elthina at the precise moment when Hawke must make his choice, there is neither a fictionalized nor designed voice of morality when the player most wants to rely upon having one. If Hawke attempts to avoid the issue, saying, "I don't want to get involved in this," Meredith replies, "You are already involved. You are the Champion of Kirkwall" (BioWare, 2011), placing the responsibility for making a decision with Hawke's role as a sociopolitical figure of leadership. It is at this point that the player *must* make a choice: mages or Templars, one extreme, or the other.

Such extremism, the game reveals, is profoundly destructive, and acts as a self-fulfilling prophecy; in the face of Anders's actions, his insistence that "There can be no peace" (BioWare, 2011) is correct, but only because he has guaranteed violence with his actions. In destroying the Chantry, Anders commits an act of terrorism that players can clearly identify as such; what is interesting is that the game chose to deliberately allow the player-qua-Hawke to cultivate friendship and sympathy with him – and, even after he destroys the Chantry, allows the player to continue to perpetuate that friendship. Having already made the choice to side with the mages or Templars, the player must decide Anders's fate. If Hawke spares Anders, Sebastian leaves the party. If he kills Anders, Anders (obviously) ceases to be an NPCC.

As with so many of Hawke's other quests, his party is polarized, but unlike with earlier quests, all of the NPCCs are present and have an opinion about which side Hawke takes in the conflict. Merrill and Bethany are pro-mage (as, obviously, is Anders); Fenris, Carver, Sebastian, and Aveline are pro-Templar. Isabela and Varric, unsurprisingly, don't like either option, although Isabela seems to slightly prefer the mages, and Varric slightly favors the Templars.

At this point, an insufficient friendship or rivalry quotient among Hawke's followers will result in their departure: if not loyal to Hawke, Merrill and Anders will join the mages; Fenris and Aveline will join the Templars; Sebastian (if Anders is killed), Isabela (if she returned at the end of Act Two), and Varric will side with Hawke regardless. Hawke's sibling will eventually rejoin his side, no matter the level of friendship-rivalry.[22] With a high enough friendship-rivalry status for all party members, it is possible for Hawke to retain all but one – either Anders or Sebastian will leave the party following Hawke's decision to spare or execute Anders.

During this quest the player comes to recognize the importance of cultivating loyalty; in the battles with Meredith and Orsino, the companion NPCs (those not in Hawke's immediate party) assist in combat, making the fights easier for Hawke to win. It is, of course, still possible for the player-character to defeat his enemies without the assistance of other party members, but in rewarding interpersonal loyalty the game demonstrates the value of social relationships, both within and beyond ideological similitude. Once Hawke makes his choice – mages or Templars – he is allied with that faction for the remainder of the game. This is one of the many opportunities the game presents for replayability as experimentation, as the player may choose to save and replay the final quest with both factions to test which is "better" or aligns more closely with his or her personal ethics.

A Templar-allied Hawke (Templar-Hawke, from this point on) addresses his party, saying, "We didn't want this. The mages, they're our brothers and sisters. It's sad, but still necessary. Kirkwall needs us to set this right. We need order, or we lose ourselves. It's the only choice we have" (BioWare, 2011), echoing Meredith's earlier statement that "It breaks my heart...but we must be vigilant." A mage-allied Hawke (Mage-Hawke) says to those gathered in the Gallows: "We're cornered, and the Templars know it. But this is bigger than their hate, their fear. They've come to take your lives, and we're saying no. We didn't want this, but sometimes you just have to stand" (BioWare, 2011). The tenor of both addresses further reveals the game's bias toward the mages and toward the oppressed in general. Hawke's appeal against hate and fear is more compelling than the insistence that the execution of all the mages is "necessary." Given that either Hawke's living sibling (Bethany) or Hawke himself will be a mage, the Templars' claim of necessary magical genocide rings even more hollow.[23]

Following the next combat, Mage-Hawke witnesses Orsino turn to blood magic in despair, saying that "Why don't they just drown us as in-fants? Why do they give us the illusion of hope?....I see now that there is no other way. Meredith expects blood magic, then I will give it to her" (BioWare, 2011). Templar-Hawke witnesses a similar transformation later in the quest, during which Orsino says, "The irony of it is that until this moment, I have never used blood magic" (BioWare, 2011), but now Meredith has driven him to it. In both, the game presents yet another self-fulfilling prophecy; because Meredith treats all mages as corrupt, they have internalized her oppression and bigotry and become what she has accused them of being, perpetuating the cycle of blood magic – just as oppression and bigotry in real-world societies can perpetuate cycles of crime and poverty among oppressed classes and minority groups, particularly in poor neighborhoods and inner cities.[24]

Once Orsino is dead, Hawke and his party find their way to the Gallows Courtyard, where Meredith is waiting. She informs Templar-Hawke that she will tell "the people you died battling the mages. A righteous cause," and says to a Mage-Hawke that "You'll pay for what you've done here. I'll be rewarded for what I've done, in this world and the next. I have done nothing but perform my duty. What happens to you now is your own doing" (BioWare, 2011). In either case, Hawke is betrayed by the faction he chose to

support, and must combat the faction he chose to oppose, leaving it clear that ideological purity or piety cannot salvage a corrupt institution. For Templar-Hawke, Meredith's betrayal is more condemnable than Orsino's was to Mage-Hawke; in the latter, Orsino is driven to desperation by oppression, while Meredith is provoked into treachery by ambition and – Hawke soon learns – the corrupting influence of a lyrium idol found in the Deep Roads at the end of Act One.

Upon declaring her intent to kill Hawke, Meredith reveals the influence of the corrupt lyrium by drawing her corrupt-lyrium sword (which glows red, as opposed to "pure" lyrium, which is a blue-white). She is opposed by her own Captain Cullen and by Carver (if he is present), regardless of whether Hawke has allied with the mages or Templars. Depending on the player's decisions throughout the game, Hawke can be assisted by up to eight NPCCs and NPCs in this final combat (in order of priority): the three NPCCs Hawke has chosen to accompany him; Cullen; Bethany/Carver (if not an NPCC); the remaining party members not currently active; and other ally-NPCs.[25] This is a case where loyalty among Hawke's NPCCs and playing altruistically by assisting NPCs (gaining their appreciation) is rewarded by providing Hawke with support. At this point, the gameplay ends, and the player cedes control back to Varric as the game's nar-rative voice.

Regardless of Hawke's decision, Varric ex-plains that Circles across Thedas rebel against the Chantry, overthrowing the Templars and in-stigating wide-spread war. The Seeker interrupts Varric to remark that Meredith was to blame for the conflict in Kirkwall, to which Varric replies, "Or that damned idol. Or Anders. Take your pick" (BioWare, 2011). Varric's seeming apathy to lay-ing blame is interesting; certainly, he insists that the fault is not (entirely) Hawke's, but he is also not interested in locating a source of blame, because the origin of the conflict is no longer important – ending it is. He asks how his story is going to help the Seeker's cause, remarking that "You've already lost all the Circles. In fact, haven't the Templars rebelled as well? I thought you decided to abandon the Chantry to hunt the mages" (BioWare, 2011). When she says that "Not all of us desire war, Varric….The Champion could stop this madness before it's too late. He may be the only one who can," Varric becomes more sympathetic to her, but says simply, "In that case, I wish I could help you" (BioWare, 2011). In essence, the game refuses to present the player with a solution – the city of Kirkwall was all but destroyed by the conflict between mages and Templars, a war that has spread throughout the gameworld, fueled by social intolerance and exclusion rather than community.

This conclusion shows us that Hawke's decision concerning the mages and the Templars is not the point of the game's ethos. Our best option as players of *Dragon Age II*, or, the game seems to imply, as ethical subjects, is to cultivate a community of loyalty based on mutual beliefs, but also on a willingness to compromise for the sake of friendship. In many ways, the friendship-rivalry mechanic is highly progressive in its implications; a game with a single universal continuum of good and evil implies a static objective moral code imposed upon the gameworld by the designer-deity. In the gameworld of *Dragon Age*, there is an overarching deity called the Maker, but there is no design mechanic imposing an overall moral evaluative system.[26] Instead, the ethics of *Dragon Age* are human ethics, the kinds of ethics that the player – in the real-world – encounters on a daily basis. It creates the opportunity for the player to consider his or her own ethics as the product of human interactions, the result of the innate human desire to build and maintain a community, and the drive to construct our own ethical identities based on the evaluations of and relationships with both our friends and our rivals.

An Uncertain Conclusion: The Problematic Ending of *Dragon Age II*

So what are we to make of the uncertain conclusion of the game's narrative with the Seeker and Sister Nightingale discussing the absence of both Hawke and the Warden (from *Dragon Age: Origins* and *Awakening*) in conjunction with the Chantry's "plan" (BioWare, 2011) – and the promise of *Dragon Age III: Inquisition* in 2014 (Darrah, 2013)? How do we reconcile the dissolution of Hawke's companions, who all left his side "for one reason or another" (BioWare, 2011), except for his romantic interest (if any), with the game's ethos of loyalty and sociality? One answer would be for game design purposes: the developer wants the freedom to be able to create new NPCCs – or to bring back popular ones in *Dragon Age III* without being restricted by the fiction of the earlier game(s). Furthermore, narratively speaking, Varric cannot accompany Hawke if he is to be interrogated by Seeker Pendegast (especially not if he is to tell her the truth when he says he does not know Hawke's whereabouts). But these are simplistic answers that do not do justice to the game's complexity.

Rather, I would argue that *Dragon Age II* removes Hawke from his companions because of the inherently fluid nature of communities. The real-world communities with which we surround ourselves are not static and fluctuate according to the choices and events that surround us. So, too, does the virtual community in *Dragon Age II*. Even within the game itself the community changes: one sibling dies early in the game, Leandra is murdered, the Hawke family fortunes change, the other sibling either dies or leaves the household (to join the Templars, the Circle, or the Wardens), and Hawke adds or loses companions based on his choices. That the community would shift yet again after the tumultuous events of Act Three should not be surprising.

But, ultimately, the community shifts because it has served its purpose within the symbolic framework of *Dragon Age II*. The player has succeeded – or failed – as a relational leader within the NPCC community and discovered that there is no place for such cooperation within a society structured around extremism and intolerance. For, in the end, although Hawke has defeated the Arishok, Orsino, and Meredith, the atmosphere of oppression and radical reactivism that characterizes the society of Kirkwall is toxic and non-sustainable, and Hawke has no part in it. Hawke's role as mediator and Champion – and the desirability of tolerance and moderation that accompanies that role – is underscored by Seeker Pendegast's insistence that "The Champion could stop this madness before it's too late." Hawke has hopefully succeeded at fostering a community of NPCCs, but the larger society of the game is (as of yet) unprepared to relinquish the false sense of security which intolerance and extremism provides. This leaves the player unsettled at the game's ending; even though they have "won," completed the game and defeated the "final boss," they have still lost the city to the greed and chaos that the Arishok condemned in Act Two. But this ending, as the game's frame-narrative reveals, is also a beginning to something larger and yet-to-be-determined, leaving the player curious about their – and Hawke's – role in an ideal society.

FROM CONSOLE TO COMMUNITY: TRANSLATING THE LESSONS OF *DRAGON AGE II*

Stepping once more outside of virtual gamespace, *Dragon Age II*'s conclusion is meant to encourage the player to engage in critical self-reflection, to become, as Sicart (2009) suggests, an ethical subject:

players build their ethical subjectivity – their capacity to ethically interpret the content and experience of a game – only by being players, by virtue of experience. Playing, then, develops

players' ethics through the development of their player repertoires and their virtues, alone and as a part of a player community. (p. 66)

Although the content of the game in narrative terms is vital to this process, particularly in a story-heavy DRPG like *Dragon Age II*, the mechanics of the game are just as significant. The management of NPCCs' friendship-rivalry status through action and conversation choice, in particular, serves as "training" for the player in terms of consideration of social consequences in real-world situations. This is not to say that a player should expect to find him- or herself in the same situations in which Hawke is placed in the gameworld; there are no actual dragons to slay outside of digital and fantasy realms, although there may be figurative ones. However, players of DRPGs do find themselves in social situations – online and offline – in which the other participants do not agree ideologically, and it is in everyone's best interest to compromise or balance ideology with cooperation, a situational parallel to Hawke's interactions with NPCCs.

The simple fact that games *can* teach or model social interaction does not inherently answer why we should use them to do so. First, as mentioned before, virtual space and virtual communities (as opposed to virtual space with real communities, such as *World of Warcraft* or *Second Life*) permit experimentation with ethics without concern for consequences that reverberate outside gameplay (Crawford, 1982, p. 12; Sicart, 2009, p. 44). In addition, Jane McGonigal (2011) suggests that "Although we think of computer games as virtual experience, they do give us *real agency*: the opportunity to do something that feels concrete because it produces measurable results, and the power to act directly on the virtual world" (p. 60). The recognition that although our actions as players have virtual consequences, the fact that those consequences are *safe* encourages experimentation and consideration without fear; players have (limited) control over their actions and the consequences, but those consequences cause no real harm, and players even have the ability to "replay" all or part of a game in order to alter their actions in order to achieve more favorable outcomes: to learn through experimentation.

Games are also important as didactic tools because the autotelic nature of gameplay increases the likelihood of absorption due to the intensity of the interactive experience. In short, what makes digital games – whether single- or multi-player – effective as agents for self-reflection is the simple fact that they are "fun" (Castronova, 2007, p. 15). Because the player experiences enjoyment in the process of play, the player is more likely to accept (rather than resist) the game's didactic mission because

when game players complain about why their games are enjoyable or not, they talk about justice, they talk about equity, they talk about growth, they talk about efficiency. And the underlying objective in the real world for our policies is the improvement of human well-being. Successful game designs improve well-being. (Castronova, 2007, p. 17)

So when the player has finished *Dragon Age II*, when Hawke has left behind the oppressive walls of the Gallows, what is the player-as-ethical-subject meant to take away from the game? All too often our considerations of ethics presume the existence of moral absolutes, ideological conceptions of how "things should be" that preclude us from understanding the way "things should be" for others, an inherent tendency to reject both their beliefs and the others themselves. The multiplicity of *Dragon Age II*'s NPCCs is designed (in multiple senses) to counteract this instinctive herd behavior. Hawke's companions hail from different races, genders, religious creeds, sexual orientations, and ethical systems. It is the player's job, through Hawke, to take these disparate elements

and make of them a coherent virtual community, to mediate and moderate between them in order to find the common elements that make them all worthy of respect. In doing so, *Dragon Age II* rejects the cultural primacy of ideology, supplanting it with the importance of human relationships and social tolerance within both real-world and online communities.[27]

While not everyone in Hawke's world is human, his companions are all reflections of humanity's positives and negatives, virtues and vices, prejudice and tolerance. Through its complex narrative and socially-oriented friendship-rivalry mechanic, *Dragon Age II* attempts to ensure that the player-as-ethical-subject finds his or her own potential for leadership and loyalty, and, if the game is successful, comes to recognize the role of and necessity for human relationships in the development of the self as an ethical and social being.

REFERENCES

Bakhtin, M. (1984). *Rabelais and his world* (H. Iswolsky, Trans.). Bloomington, IN: Indiana University Press.

Bealer, A. H. (2012). Eco-performance in the digital RPG gamescape. In *Dungeons, dragons, and digital denizens: The digital role-playing game* (Vol. 1, pp. 27–47). New York: The Continuum International Publishing Group.

BioWare. (2009). *Dragon age: Origins*. DRPG, Electronic Arts.

BioWare. (2010). *Dragon age: Awakening*. DRPG, Electronic Arts.

BioWare. (2011). *Dragon age II*. DRPG, Electronic Arts.

Bogost, I. (2008). *Unit operations: An approach to videogame criticism*. Cambridge, MA: MIT Press.

Call, J., Whitlock, K., & Voorhees, G. (2012). From dungeons to digital denizens. In *Dungeons, dragons, and digital denizens: The digital role-playing game* (Vol. 1, pp. 11–24). New York: The Continuum International Publishing Group.

Carlson, C. (2011). The playing field: Attitudes, activities, and the conflation of play and games. *Journal of the Philosophy of Sport, 38*(1), 74–87. doi:10.1080/00948705.2011.9714550

Cassidy, S. B. (2011). The videogame as narrative. *Quarterly Review of Film and Video, 28*(4), 292–306. doi:10.1080/10509200902820266

Castronova, E. (2007). *Exodus to the virtual world: How online fun is changing reality*. New York: Palgrave Macmillan.

Consalvo, M., & Harper, T. (2009). The sexi(e)st of all: Avatars, gender, and online games. In N. Panteli (Ed.), *Virtual social networks: Mediated, massive and multiplayer sites* (pp. 98–113). New York: Palgrave Macmillan.

Crawford, C. (1982). *The art of computer game design*. Vancouver, WA: Washington State University. Retrieved from http://www.google.com/url?sa=t&rct=j&q=&esrc=s&source=web&cd=3&ved=0CDoQFjAC&url=http%3A%2F%2Fwww-rohan.sdsu.edu%2F~stewart%2Fcs583%2FACGD_ArtComputerGameDesign_ChrisCrawford_1982.pdf&ei=oAWUUebBOOnD4AOH9YCYBA&usg=AFQjCNEsgNzqFHKmE6Ca_l7c8jgHxBtF9w&sig2=MdrYFyAFB8gDIAye5nKfzA&bvm=bv.46471029,d.dmg

Darrah, M. (2013). An open letter from Mark Darrah, executive producer. *Dragon Age III: Inquisition*. Retrieved from http://dragonage.bioware.com/inquisition/

Day, D. V., & Antonakis, J. (2012). Leadership: Past, present, and future. In D. V. Day, & J. Antonakis (Eds.), *The nature of leadership* (pp. 3–25). Los Angeles, CA: Sage.

Dragon Age, I. I. (2013). *Dragon age wiki*. Retrieved from http://dragonage.wikia.com/wiki/Dragon_Age_Wiki

Flanagan, M. (2009). *Critical play: Radical game design*. Cambridge: MIT Press.

Gaider, D. (2011). *To the op... dragon age II official campaign quests and story (SPOILERS)*. Retrieved from http://social.bioware.com/forum/1/topic/304/index/6661775&lf=8

Head_Fish. (2011). Dragon age 2 companion guide. *Bone Fish Gamer*. Retrieved from http://www.bonefishgamer.com/2011/06/dragon-age-2-companion-guide/

Henton, A. (2012). Game and narrative in dragon age: Origins: Playing the archive in digital rpgs. In *Dungeons, dragons, and digital denizens: The digital role-playing game* (Vol. 1, pp. 66–87). New York: The Continuum International Publishing Group.

Huizinga, J. (1955). *Homo ludens: A study of the play-element in culture*. Beacon Press.

Juul, J. (2001). Games telling stories? A brief note on games and narratives. *Game Studies, 1*(1).

Malanek999. (2011). *The worst was when I. dialogue wheel mishaps*. Retrieved from http://social.bioware.com/forum/1/topic/304/index/6757005/1

McDowell, Z. (2012). Postcards from the other side: Interactive revelation in post-apocalyptic rpgs. In *Dungeons, dragons, and digital denizens: The digital role-playing game* (Vol. 1, pp. 174–193). New York: The Continuum International Publishing Group.

McGonigal, J. (2011). *Reality is broken: why games make us better and how they can change the world*. New York: The Penguin Press.

nranola. (2011). *Oh boy, the dialogue wheel: Dialogue wheel mishaps*. Retrieved from http://social.bioware.com/forum/1/topic/304/index/6757005/2

Roberts, L., & Parks, M. R. (1999). The social geography of gender-switching in virtual environments on the internet. *Information Communication and Society*, 2, 521–540. doi:10.1080/136911899359538

Sicart, M. (2009). *The ethics of computer games*. Cambridge, MA: MIT Press. doi:10.7551/mitpress/9780262012652.001.0001

Travis, R. (2012). Epic style: Re-compositional performance in the bioware digital RPG. In *Dungeons, dragons, and digital denizens: The digital role-playing game* (Vol. 1, pp. 235–255). New York: The Continuum International Publishing Group.

Wark, M. (2007). *Gamer theory*. Cambridge, MA: Harvard University Press.

Whitlock, K. (2012). Traumatic origins: Memory, crisis, and identity in digital RPGs. In *Dungeons, dragons, and digital denizens: The digital role-playing game* (Vol. 1, pp. 135–152). New York: The Continuum International Publishing Group.

Yee, N. (2008). *Characters and main character*. The Daedalus Project. Retrieved from http://www.nickyee.com/daedalus/archives/001634.php

Yukl, G. (2013). *Leadership in organizations* (8th ed.). Boston: Pearson.

Zizek, S. (1999). *The cyberspace real*. Retrieved from http://www.egs.edu/faculty/slavoj-zizek/articles/the-cyberspace-real/

Zook, K. (2012). In the blood of dragon age: Origins: Metaphor and identity in digital RPGs. In *Dungeons, dragons, and digital denizens: The digital role-playing game* (Vol. 1, pp. 219–234). New York: The Continuum International Publishing Group.

ADDITIONAL READING

Adams, E. W. (2006). Will computer games ever be a legitimate art form? *Journal of Media Practice*, 7(1), 67–77. doi:10.1386/jmpr.7.1.67/1

Bayliss, P. (2007). Beings in the game-world: Characters, avatars, and players. IE '07 Proceedings of the 4th Australasian Conference on Interactive Entertainment.

BioWare. (2007). *Mass effect*. DRPG, Electronic Arts.

BioWare. (2010). *Mass effect 2*. DRPG, Electronic Arts.

BioWare. (2012). *Mass effect 3*. DRPG, Electronic Arts.

Bogost, I. (2010). *Persuasive games: the expressive power of videogames*. The MIT Press.

Brooker, W. (2009). Camera-eye, cg-eye: Videogames and the cinematic. *Cinema Journal*, 48(3), 122–128. doi:10.1353/cj.0.0126

Ciulla, J. (2012). Ethics and effectiveness: The nature of good leadership. In J. Antonakis, & D. V. Day (Eds.), *The nature of leadership* (2nd ed., pp. 508–540). Los Angeles: Sage.

Galloway, A. (2006). *Gaming: Essays on algorithmic culture*. Minneapolis: University of Minnesota Press.

Iacovides, I., Aczel, J., Scanlon, E., & Woods, W. (2013). Making sense of game-play: How can we examine learning and involvement? *Transactions of the digital games research association*, 1(1). Retrieved from http://todigra.org/index.php/todigra/article/view/6

Jones, S. E. (2008). *The meaning of video games: Gaming and textual strategies*. New York: Routledge.

Juul, J. (2005). *Half-real: Video games between real rules and fictional worlds*. Cambridge: MIT Press.

King, G., & Krzywinska, T. (2006). Tomb raiders & space invaders: Videogame forms & contexts. New York: I.B. Taurus. King, L. (Ed.). Game on: The history and culture of video games. London: Laurence King Publishing.

Lowood, H. (2008). Impotence and agency: Computer games as a post-9/11 battlefield. In A. Jahn-Sudmann (Ed.), *Computer games as a sociocultural phenomenon: Games without frontiers, war without tears* (pp. 140–149). New York: Palgrave Macmillan.

Luce, R. D., & Raiffa, H. (1989). *Games and decisions: Introduction and critical survey*. New York: Dover.

Mäyrä, F. (2008). *An introduction to game studies: Games in culture*. Los Angeles: Sage.

Miller, T. (2006). Gaming for beginners. *Games and Culture*, *1*(1), 5–12. doi:10.1177/1555412005281403

Murray, J. (1997). *Hamlet on the holodeck: The future of narrative in cyberspace*. Cambridge: MIT Press.

Newman, J. (2002). The Myth of the ergodic videogame: Some thoughts on player-character relationships in videogames. *Game Studies, 2*(1).

Przybylski, A. K., Weinstein, N., Murayama, K., Lynch, M. F., & Ryan, R. M. (2012). the ideal self at play: The appeal of video games that let you be all you can be. *Psychological Science*, *23*(1), 69–76. doi:10.1177/0956797611418676 PMID:22173739

Przybylski, A. K., Weinstein, N., Ryan, R. M., & Rigby, C. S. (2009). Having to versus wanting to play, Background and consequences of harmonious versus obsessive engagement in video games. *Cyberpsychology & Behavior*, *12*(5), 485–492. doi:10.1089/cpb.2009.0083 PMID:19772442

Said, E. (1978). *Orientalism*. New York: Routledge & Kegan Paul.

Sutton-Smith, B. (2001). *The ambiguity of play* (2nd ed.). Cambridge: Harvard University Press.

Von Benthem, J., Pacuit, E., & Roy, O. (2011). Toward a theory of play: A logical perspective on games and interaction. *Games*, *2*, 52–86. doi:10.3390/g2010052

Voorhees, G., Call, J., & Whitlock, K. (Eds.). (2012). Guns, grenades, and grunts: First-person shooter games (Vol. Volume 2). New York: Continuum.

Wolf, M. J. P., & Perron, B. (Eds.). (2003). *The video game theory reader*. New York: Routledge.

KEY TERMS AND DEFINITIONS

Achievement: An award tied into gameplay by a developer which gives the player points on an out-of-game system visible to other players on the Xbox Live network available on the Xbox 360 gaming console.

Autotelic: When something, like play, is done for its own sake.

Digital Role-Playing Game: A videogame whose central focus is the "playing" of a player-character, including the management of that player-character's characteristics, abilities, equipment, and statistics.

Ergodic: Requiring effort.

Ludonarrative: The linear narrative of both story and gameplay produced in a single play-through of a videogame.

Non-Player Character: A programmed character within a digital game who responds to the player-character and to the events in the digital world.

Non-Player Companion Character: A programmed non-player character placed into a party with the player-character whose statistics and actions are controllable by the player.

Party: The group of player and non-player characters used to accomplish quests in a digital role-playing game.

Player-Character: The character played by the player in a videogame.

ENDNOTES

[1] Wark's (2007) text, *Gamer Theory*, uses an unconventional format in which paragraphs are indicated by bracketed numbers, rather than using traditional page numbers, even though it is available in print format.

[2] DRPGs, in this context, are distinct from Massively Multiplayer Online Role Playing Games (MMORPGs) primarily because there is no online gameplay component. Where MMOs may offer the possibility of single-player gameplay, the player is still within a virtual space that contains other players, which is not the case in a single-player DRPG. Certainly, there are single-player DRPG games with online community components – like the multiplayer "modes" of titles like *Mass Effect 3* or *Gears of War 3* or, more popularly, *Call of Duty: Modern Warfare*. However, these have a more overt and obvious tie to their fan communities, since the games themselves are communal experiences. But even single-player games – like *Dragon Age II* or *Skyrim* – foster communal identification and discussion of unique experiences within those gameworlds.

[3] Although Hawke's gender can be either male or female (player-chosen), because the "default" Hawke is male, I will use the male pronoun for simplicity.

[4] Some NPCCs are "required" in order to progress through the game, while others need not be "recruited" into the party at all. Conversation trees appear in gameplay and provide the player with optional responses to questions from NPCs and NPCCs. These conversation choices impact Hawke's relationships with the NPCCs, both directly and indirectly (through their reaction to a choice Hawke makes). The skill and "tech" trees allow the player to customize the abilities and combat actions of Hawke and the NPCCs. The player cannot "fully upgrade" any character, and must choose "tracks" for both Hawke and the NPCCs. For example, the player might choose to make Hawke a "Force Mage," which opens up several possible skills for "purchase" with experience points (earned by playing the game and defeating enemies).

[5] Gender distinction appears to be limited to conversational remarks from NPCs and NPCCs. The only appreciable differences produced by gender choice are changes to Hawke's possible "romance" options. Different NPCCs are "interested" in player-characters of each gender – and some in player-characters of both genders.

[6] The list of available and completed quests is found under Journal in the gameplay menu. Within each Act the player has control over the order in which he or she takes on quests. Some quests are unlocked

(made available) by the completion of others, but once a quest appears, the player has the choice when (or if) to complete it. Some quests – labeled "Main Plot"– are not optional, but it is up to the player whether he or she wishes to play the others.

7   Unless, of course, the player uses a guide or walk-through. However, while this might clarify causal relationships within the game, it simply changes the nature of the decision the player has to make, as there are rarely obviously "right" answers in BioWare games. For instance, knowing the consequences of siding with the mages over the Templars at the end of *Dragon Age II* does not clarify for the player which choice is the "right" one (and, in fact, has convinced me that there is no "right" choice).

8   The fact that there is an entire forum thread on BioWare's *Dragon Age II* page entitled "Dialogue Wheel Mishaps" illustrates the complexity of this problem. Perhaps the funniest post comes from Malanek999 (2011), who writes that "The worst was when I accidentally told Isabella to **** herself out to that mage at the hanged man. Not what I intended. Felt terrible about that," when he or she chose the "defer to companion" option from the dial.

9   The "loss" of NPCCs appears in other games, such as BioWare's *Mass Effect* series and *Knights of the Old Republic*, and Bethesda's *Fallout* and *Elder Scrolls* games.

10   On the Xbox 360 system, achievement points are awarded to players for completing games, quests, and other skill-based gameplay feats. These points appear in conjunction with the player's online avatar outside of the games, and are an indication of the player's skill level and commitment to playing through games. Many players take pride in their level of XP (experience points) within the Xbox Live community, and actively pursue achievements in order to raise this score.

11   In BioWare's *Mass Effect 2*, the player-character can engage in "loyalty missions" which "guarantee" the loyalty of that companion character to Shepard (the player-character). In *Dragon Age II*, however, there are no "loyalty missions," only recruitment missions (when Hawke first meets the NPCCs). Loyalty can only be guaranteed by maximizing either friendship or rivalry, whereas in *Mass Effect 2* there is no friendship-rivalry mechanic, only a single mission which, if successfully completed, "locks" the loyalty of that NPCC.

12   Players of *Dragon Age: Origins* would already be familiar with this conflict from the earlier game.

13   It is possible for Hawke to cause the death of his second sibling during the quest "The Deep Roads," which eliminates this potential "problem."

14   "A Story Being Told" and "Friendly Concern" in Act Two discuss Varric's role as a storyteller, and in "Family Matter," during which he briefly takes on the role of player-character for a combat sequence.

15   It is perhaps worth noting that players might dislike a decision they have made or desire to backtrack to change an earlier decision, and thus "lose" gameplay by going back to an earlier save (*Dragon Age II* permits players to save at any point other than mid-conversation or mid-combat). In this sense, players can lose time as the result of an action they regret within the game, but there are no external legal or social ramifications for gameplay decisions.

16   The game does reward individual maximization, as indicated earlier, but it privileges multiple maximizations by adding this additional achievement. This means that in accomplishing the "Great Minds Think Alike" achievement, the player will have received a minimum of seventy-five points (as they will have to have already accomplished either "Friend" or "Rival," and possibly both), and perhaps one hundred. To put this in perspective, the achievement for completing the game twice ("Epic") is also worth fifty points.

17   Sebastian, if his DLC has been acquired, sympathizes with the Templars, as well. It is also important to remember that Hawke's party will not have both Bethany and Carver, which further complicates Hawke's ability to secure loyalty from four party members.

18   The Qunari are in Kirkwall, the Arishok explains at the end of "Blackpowder Courtesy" in Act Two, because someone has stolen the Tome of Koslun, a sacred relic, from them.

19   If "tolerance" includes equality for mages, this will also strengthen his friendship with Bethany and Anders, but is likely to increase rivalry with Sebastian, Carver, and Fenris.

20   Grudging respect between Hawke and the Arishok can, however, mitigate the level of violence in the final conflict of Act Two, as Hawke will be able to negotiate for a resolution through hand-to-hand combat.

21   This theory of leadership is described as LMX, or "leader-member-exchange," theory in which the leader-follower relationship is "based on trust and mutual respect, whereas low-quality relations between a leader and his or her followers (i.e., the 'out group') are based on the fulfillment of contractual obligations" (Day and Antonakis, 2012, p. 9).

22   In order to return Bethany/Carver to NPCC status (instead of NPC), Hawke needs to choose the side that sibling is on (mages for Bethany, if she is in the Circle, Templars for Carver, if he is a Templar). A Warden sibling will rejoin the party as a potential NPCC irrespective of Hawke's choice, should he accept the offer of help.

23   The only way that a living Hawke mage is not present is if Bethany died in the Deep Roads – otherwise, she will rejoin the party as a Warden mage or will be part of the Circle, or Hawke himself will be a mage.

24   The fact that the mages are confined to a former prison further highlights the game's awareness of this allegory, as the Western prison system is a significant contributor to the cycle of poverty and crime in many urban centers.

25   The other possible NPCs are Donnic Hendyr (Aveline's husband, if "The Long Road" was completed), Zevran Arainai (if spared in "A Murder of Crows"), and Nathaniel Howe (if "Finding Nathaniel" was completed). The prioritization order of these NPCs means that if Hawke's entire party is loyal to him, the "party" assisting in the final battle will consist of Bethany/Carver, Sebastian/Anders, Cullen, Aveline, Fenris, Merrill, Varric, and Isabela. If any one of them has been "lost," he or she will be replaced by Donnic (if Aveline is in the party), Zevran (if either Varric or Isabela is in the party), and/or Nathaniel. If all of Hawke's NPCCs who can leave or die are absent and Hawke has not completed any optional quests, the party will consist only of Cullen and Varric. If Hawke has completed the necessary quests but lost the loyalty of his NPCCs, the party will contain Cullen, Varric, Zevran (provided Varric is "active"), and Nathaniel (Dragon Age Wiki, 2013).

26   Although the world of *Dragon Age II* is structured around a religious framework – including the name of the city, "Churchwall" – the game's mechanics suggest an interpretation of the *Dragon Age* series that argues against institutional intolerance (religious or otherwise) as dangerous to social harmony.

27   Tolerance, in particular, has become a touchstone for many BioWare developers. David Gaider, a writer and designer for BioWare who has worked on both *Dragon Age* titles, has garnered Internet infamy for an open letter written to a poster on the BioWare Forums which has since become known as the "Letter to a Straight Male Gamer." In it, Gaider says the following: The romances in the game are not for 'the straight male gamer'. They're for everyone. We have a lot of fans, many of whom are neither straight nor male, and they deserve no less attention…[and] have just as much right to play the kind of game they wish as anyone else. The "rights" of anyone with regards to a game are murky at best, but anyone who takes that stance must apply it equally to both the minority as well as the majority. The majority has no inherent "right" to get more options than anyone else. (Gaider, 2011)

Chapter 10
Supporting Visibility and Resilience in Play:
Gender–Supportive Online Gaming Communities as a Model of Identity and Confidence Building in Play and Learning

Gabriela T. Richard
University of Pennsylvania, USA

ABSTRACT

Scholars have highlighted the learning opportunities afforded by online gaming communities of practice, which include providing authentic and meaningful contexts for engaging in and learning 21st century skills and digital literacies. However, lesser attention has been paid to how these environments can be inequitable in including and supporting members across gender. This chapter highlights the importance of gender supportive online gaming communities and their role in increasing the visibility of and resiliency necessary for equitable online play and learning. The history of a gender-supportive community and its structures are explored. The chapter further provides recommendations for educators, based on the social structures of this gender-supportive community and related research on educational climates and equitable learning.

DOI: 10.4018/978-1-4666-5150-0.ch010

INTRODUCTION

Several scholars have begun to explore the relevance of online communities and fan sites to education, often calling them "affinity spaces" (Gee, 2004); in these informal learning communities, individuals have the opportunity to engage in 21st century skills and apply their knowledge and learning in contexts that are meaningful to them and where they can have an authentic audience for their skills (Gee, 2007; Squire, 2011). Online gaming communities, often popularly termed "clans" or "guilds" offer a glimpse into this informal learning process, by providing spaces where players can knowledge-share, build relationships, and impart their skills and expertise in meaningful ways that provide value to other individuals. Such assistance includes helping other players better their gaming abilities by sharing strategies, helping others learn technical skills relevant to live-streaming their game play, and designing image-based avatars and forum signatures in Photoshop.

Affinity spaces, such as the ones formed among these gamers or the toy collectors noted in Author Four's chapter, are akin to communities of practice (Lave & Wenger, 1991) in that they highlight learning and application in context:

The concept of community underlying the notion of legitimate peripheral participation, and hence of 'knowledge' and its 'location' in the lived-in world, is both crucial and subtle... A community of practice is a set of relations among persons, activity and world, over time and in relation with other tangential and overlapping communities of practice... participation in the cultural practice in which any knowledge exists is an epistemological principle of learning. The social structure of this practice, its power relations and its conditions for legitimacy define possibilities for learning (i.e., for legitimate peripheral participation). (Lave & Wenger, 2002, p. 115)

Both the pioneering work of Lave and Wenger (1991, 2002) and Gee (2004) point to the importance of community and cultural practice in the learning context, and propose that power relations can have an impact on learning, identity and participation. In her study of the "digital identity divide," Goode (2010) argued that "technology identity" is shaped considerably by socio-cultural context and in communities of practice (Lave & Wenger, 1991); in other words, individuals' sense of ability, performance and engagement with computers, technology, and digital literacy are often shaped by access, and early experiences with technology that are often grounded in socio-cultural experiences and economic realities, which, in turn, create "opportunities and obstacles" (p. 509). Thus, an individual who may not have been afforded the ability to use a computer at a younger age like her colleagues, or wasn't equally socially supported by being in a family or community of tech-savvy users, would be less likely to develop the same kinds of efficacy and identity with technology than an individual for whom both early access and social support was readily available.

In addition to providing authentic contexts for learning, some communities also provide spaces for supportive play. While equity has often arisen as a potential crisis for engagement and learning in affinity spaces (Gee, 2007; Duncan & Hayes, 2012), little has been explored when it comes to understanding how inequity shapes play, and how communities can seek to support inclusive practices around play and learning. In gaming spaces, these inequities have traditionally been seen as operating along gender lines, though more contemporary research points to racial and ethnic inequities that similarly impact play (e.g., Gray, 2012; Nakamura, 2009; Richard, 2012b; Richard, 2013a; Richard, 2013b; Shaw, 2012).

This chapter will specifically explore how players are using a gender-supportive community as an authentic context for informal learning around games and 21st century skills, as well as how this learning would be relevant, more broadly, for education. The chapter will further provide a historical framework for the formation of the community, its relationship to the greater game culture, which has often been unsupportive and openly hostile to females, as well as its changing state from a community of resistance to one of resilience and support. While the community was initially formed to be supportive for females, it has evolved to include male participation, and emerging research (Richard & Hoadley, 2013) is showing that its supportive structure benefits players across gender. The chapter will also highlight research (Richard, 2014 that shows the community can support identity and efficacy in play. Specifically, the chapter will focus on how the community provides structure for supportive play across gender, as well as how the community deals with conflict and hostility from the greater gaming culture. Further, the chapter will touch on case studies that highlight diverging views on dealing with this conflict within the community. The chapter will end with a discussion on implications for supporting effective and inclusive technology mediated learning.

BACKGROUND

Decades of research sought to understand why gender differences existed in gaming (e.g., Bryce & Rutter, 2002; Bryce & Rutter, 2003; Carr, 2005; Cassell & Jenkins, 1998; Dickey, 2006; Greenfield, 1994; Hartmann & Klimmt, 2006; Hayes, 2008; Jensen & de Castell, 2011; Laurel, 2008; Kafai, 1996; Kafai, 1998; Kafai, Heeter, Denner, & Sun, 2008; Kiesler, Sproull, & Eccles, 1985; Schott & Horrell, 2000; Taylor, 2003; Taylor, 2008; Subrahmanyam & Greenfield, 1994; Yee, 2008), with some research assuming sex or gender differences at onset, and others pointing out that context is important in shaping the kinds of relationships individuals have with gaming and technology, which often operates through gendered assumptions (for more information, see Richard, 2012a).

Some research in this area pointed to socio-cultural context as impacting play disproportionately for females. This line of research found that games were often designed by heterosexual White and Asian males (Fron, Fullerton, Morie, & Pearce, 2007) and came with social assumptions and cultural practices that favored males as developing agency in gaming (e.g., Cassell & Jenkins, 1998; Kiesler, Sproull, & Eccles, 1985); conversely, females were often encouraged to take on supportive roles to males, who were often encouraged to dominate play spaces and demonstrate their gaming skills (Bryce & Rutter, 2003). This research has often demonstrated that gaming is an early gateway to developing confidence and skills in computers, science and technology, and that unequal access can undermine females in the development of these skills (e.g., Hayes, 2008; Kiesler, Sproull, & Eccles, 1985); however, equity in encouragement and play can diminish gender differences (e.g., Jensen & de Castell, 2011). Some researchers, most notably Kafai (1996), sought to encourage equity through the development of game design skills.

Digital games have been seen as potentially powerful tools for learning (e.g., Gee, 2004; Gee, 2007; Squire, 2003; Squire, 2005). Specifically, scholars feel that digital games can provide rich contexts for visualization, problem-solving, creativity and deconstructing systematic and interrelated constructs. In particular, learners can become situated in contexts where they must solve problems, and apply their creativity, reasoning and logic to do so. Scholars contend that 21st century skills require learners to adapt to an increasingly changing world, which requires flexibility, creativity and problem-solving (e.g., Jenkins, 2006; Gee, 2007; Shute, 2007; Squire, 2011; Thomas & Brown, 2011). As games become more social, scholars have postulated that they can provide rich contexts for collaboration and learning with others (e.g., Gee, 2007; Squire, 2011). In particular, the research on communities or "affinity spaces" built around play shows that these spaces offer the promise of collaborative play and distributed learning, as well as the pitfalls of the new digital divide (Gee, 2007). Not all communities are supportive or inclusive (Gee & Hayes, 2012), and exclusivity can limit one's development of technology identities and competencies.

Research is finding that technology literacy, identification with technology, along with skills, performance and perceptions of performance are shaped by experiences. In other words, and as Author 13 also explores for both the Zapatista and Occupy Wall Street movements, the new digital divide is a complex mix of access, experience and resulting efficacy, which is often grounded in social experiences as well as economic inequalities. Goode (2010) found that individuals' experiences were shaped by inequities in access, which often structured their learning experiences and technology identities in contexts where technology proficiency and digital literacy were assumed, such as higher education. The inability to have an early sense of efficacy and knowledge, or access to those fluent with it and willing to teach those skills, formally or informally, tended to create continued disenfranchisement, which limited learning opportunities and career choices.

Some scholars have argued that certain spaces, which include gaming and its social spaces, have become places where young, typically White and typically heterosexual males, can dominance bond (Kimmel, 2008) and perform masculinity (Jenkins, 1998), and that the presence of females and others who don't share similar experiences threaten the ability for males to engage in these practices (Kimmel, 2008). Kimmel (2008) asserts that these spaces have become increasingly claimed for masculine identity development and bonding as the greater culture becomes more inclusive. In other words, exclusionary practices in online gaming culture could be due in part to threatening what is seen as masculine spaces for expression and bonding.

Research has shown that females and ethnic minorities are more likely to be underrepresented as primary or secondary characters in games, and, when they are visible, they tend to be highly stereotyped, or, in the case of females, highly sexualized (e.g., Miller & Summers, 2007; Williams, Martins, Consalvo & Ivory, 2009). Research has shown that these marginalizing representations have negative effects on how ethnic minority and female players view themselves, as well as how others view them (see, for example, Behm-Morawitz & Mastro, 2009; Dill & Burgess, 2012; Lee & Park, 2011). More concretely, females and ethnic minorities are less likely to feel that they belong in gaming spaces or are equally capable of playing certain kinds of games depending on representation. Furthermore, stereotypes can have the unfortunate effect of making others less likely to appraise them as equally capable as well.

Emerging research on harassment in game culture demonstrates that females and ethnic minorities are more likely to be harassed (e.g., Gray, 2012; Kuznekoff & Rose, 2013; Nakamura, 2009; Richard, 2012b; Richard, 2013a; Richard, 2013b; Shaw, 2012). As a recent controlled experiment highlighted, a female voice is three times more likely to receive negative harassment in online gaming than a male voice, stating the same phrases, in a popular online multiplayer game (Kuznekoff & Rose, 2013). Researchers argue that this is often a gate-keeping practice to maintain the social hierarchy, which heavily favors White males, and discourages others from playing or participating equally in online play spaces (Gray, 2012; Richard, 2013b). In her detailed analysis of gender and ethnic harassment in online gaming, Richard (2013b) found that marginalized groups were often harassed based on the most salient descriptors of deviance from the assumed White, male, heterosexual majority: females were most likely to be harassed for their gender, unless they had significant ethnic identifiers (through voice chat or through their avatars), and ethnic minority males were most likely to be harassed for their race or ethnicity (typically through linguistic profiling).

These practices of exclusion and marginalization weaken the ability for marginalized groups to learn from, form identities around, and engage in cultural practices in online gaming. Emerging research is finding evidence that supportive communities can provide a model for promoting confidence for marginalized players while also increasing their visibility and resilience (Richard & Hoadley, 2013); specifically, this research is finding that a gender-supportive community can increase players' sense of ability and performance in gaming, which is particularly useful to understand in order to design equitable learning environments built around play. In their study, Richard and Hoadley (2013) found that male and female gamers that played in *PMS Clan*, the largest and most renowned female-oriented online gaming community in North America, had equal identification with gaming, and relatively equal self-concept with gaming (self-concept, or perceived ability, was higher for males than females, but not statistically significantly different in the female supportive community). Conversely, gamers in other clans scored statistically significantly lower and had wider gender disparities in gaming identification and self-concept. In other words, their study found that structures that promoted equity in play could reduce gender disparities in identification and perceived ability in gaming.

SUPPORTING EQUITY IN PLAY AND LEARNING

While scholars such as Taylor (2006) and Sunden and Sveningsson (2012) have discussed the complexity of female play and practices in online gaming communities, little is known about how structures designed specifically around female support and inclusion can promote fairness in play and learning. Extending upon the quantita-

tive findings of Richard and Hoadley (2013), this chapter will explore how *PMS Clan* structures an environment that promotes (and demonstrates measurable support for) equity in online game play and its resulting identities and confidence in gaming.

Playing with "Power" to Playing with Resiliency

PMS Clan can trace its history back to the late-1990s, when the emergence of all-female clans was documented academically. At the time, the acronym of PMS stood for "Psychotic Man Slayerz" (PMS, 2012), and reflected the provocative flavor of empowerment and the resistance of "all fixed [gender] identities" (Cassell & Jenkins, 1998, p. 33) typically ascribed to women by the "Game Grrls" movement. These all-female gaming clans and teams that played against males in a space perceived of as for males, gave female gamers a "chance to 'play with power,' to compete aggressively with men and to refuse to accept traditional limitations on female accomplishments" (Cassell & Jenkins, 1998, p. 34). This often meant playing "hardcore" first-person shooters, in highly competitive team deathmatches against other players online and in person at tournaments; these game types were often the most male-dominated, prompting the need or desire for all-female groups. Cassell and Jenkins (1998) propose that the female clans of the time offered females the chance to express female empowerment through participation in traditionally male spaces, which allowed them the opportunity to reject rigid gender identities.

PMS Clan is now known as Pandora's Mighty Soldiers (PMS, 2012), and explicitly promotes the mission "to provide a fun, competitive, and positive environment to female gamers while promoting respect for women in matches and tournaments" (PMS, 2011a). PMS Clan details a formal debut in 2002, with the launch of *Xbox Live* (PMS, 2012). Males have been able to join its linked "brother" clan, H2O, since 2004, when they initially had to be sponsored by a current PMS member (PMS, 2011b), though they have been able to join independently since 2008. While males and females can join PMS|H2O independently, most divisions are strictly divided by sex, such that females play with other females, and males with males during official practices.

PMS Clan has expanded on the kinds of games it supports. Joining the clan, whether male or female, is a process that takes several weeks of participation in officially sponsored clan practices, for whatever game on whatever platform (console or PC) supported by the clan during which time recruits are evaluated for adherence to clan policies. In order to join the clan, and remain active, gamers must join a division that features a game that allows for online matches and tournaments. As a result, the clan is often focused on competitive game types that offer some form of team-oriented play. These game types span from Massively Multiplayer Online Role Playing Games, to racing games and shooters. There has even been some support for "casual" games, which often allow for cooperative play through creativity and exploration, as opposed to overt competition, like *Minecraft*. In order to remain an active member, one must play at least four hours a week in sanctioned practices with clan members, on a team, often against teams of non-members in public matches. Members will also play together to learn strategies and skills through private matches, and more competitive players can join small teams where they can compete in online and in-person tournaments.

There are strict codes of conduct for recruits and members regarding gaming lingo (i.e., the use of the word "rape," which is often used in online gaming to demonstrate besting an opponent and asserting dominance is strictly forbidden), professionalism in matches (members are expected refrain from negative "smack" talk and to always say "good game" during public matches and online play, even if they won't receive it in return), appropriateness in dress and online images (i.e.,

no full or partial nudity, sexually suggestive imagery, or drug use), and respect for others in and outside of the clan (i.e., intolerance for harassment or "griefing," a term for deliberate abuse or unsportsmanlike behavior).

Specifically, however, the mission of the clan, and its structural practices all reinforce breaking down barriers when it comes to perceptions of gendered participation in gaming, while promoting a safer and more inclusive space for play. As embodied through *PMS Clan*'s message to potential female members:

You may be a new Member, just attending orientation or a long standing Member, with years of experience behind you, but you are both here for the same reason - you believe in breaking down the long-standing stereotypes of gamers, specifically in regards to female gamers. You believe in creating and supporting a safe-haven for all gamers to play and discuss video games and video game culture (PMS, 2012).

Similarly, potential male members are asked to participate in reshaping the gaming space to be more inclusive, along lines that extend beyond gender:

One of the most important things in being a true H2O is being respectful gamer. What we can do in random rooms is ask people to treat those that are in there with respect. This is paramount to our success as a clan. What we can do together is help create a better gaming environment for us all, not just women gamers, but ourselves and children. This is part of what being a H2O is all about. H2O's are bound by their code to be respectful, loyal, honest, dedicated and reliable. They are able to do what is right no matter the pressures placed on them in any environment. We're all here to play video games, and play the games as H2Os. It encompasses all the above, but it's also something more. We support PMS as gamers and friends, play with our clan mates, and actively create a positive friendly environment for every gamer out there. And as gamers we're competitive, we encourage those who wish to take their gaming to the next level, just as we encourage those who support the community and choose to play on a recreational level (PMS, 2012).

Through the messages sent specifically to females and males, we see how the clan attempts to create an environment of inclusive play, in which females and males are asked to promote "safe," "positive," "respectful" play that extends beyond the clan to shape the general gaming community.

While the goal is to promote safe, supportive and respectful play, normative social experiences in the online gaming environment often ran counter to this, and female gamers, in particular, were subjected to marginalizing practices including harassment. In this sense, clan structures of playing with members of the same gender (and, perceived experiences) through structures that explicitly reinforced respectful and inclusive practices, offered members the ability to develop resiliency in the face of adversity. In the community, rules and practices mandated positivity in social interactions, and muting other players who may be hostile or harassing. While this didn't change the other players' ability to harass you through game or environmental actions (i.e., targeting you in game, or sending you messages during a game), it did promote coping and resiliency tactics in the face of adversity; in other words, you may not be able to change (at least immediately) how others are treating you online, but you have the ability to limit their effectiveness on your play and participation. By playing with other females who countered stereotypes about female abilities to play games as well as males, in groups in which you felt empowered to do so and receive support in return, *PMS Clan* promotes an environment for equitable play, while also providing coping strategies in the face of adversity.

Differential Support to Play and Engage in Online Gaming

Differential support in the online gaming social space, and in its affinity groups is often presented in the form of gender harassment. Racial and ethnic harassment was largely not discussed in the clan or on public forums, conceivably because the mission of the clan was around gender support (though there are strict policies around respect that include intolerance for racist and homophobic behavior). Female gamers in *PMS Clan* often recounted how harassment in the greater gaming culture outside of the clan shaped their play, often in negative ways. When playing with gamers outside of the clan, either within the presence of other clan members or otherwise, female gamers often recounted being subjected to harassment and marginalizing practices. As one PMS member stated in a public forum, "all I know is whenever I am on now I never talk before a match mostly to… not get totally overwhelmed with the whole team looking for me." Another PMS member, who is a mother in her 30s, detailed one of her earliest experiences playing online, discussing how it debilitated her from playing online for several months:

The first thing I ever heard the first time I played online was "Go back to the kitchen and make a sandwich [bitch]." It took me months before I ventured online again!!! I have gotten used to it sadly.

As one 18-year-old PMS clan member recounted:

My own personal experiences with online gaming started when I was about twelve, I played on Xbox Live and I played a MMO named Runescape. On both of these, I experienced many harsh comments and being so young I never knew why, mind you, these are two completely different platforms, with Xbox Live being on the Xbox 360 and Runescape being on the computer. I remember trying to play when I was younger, and every time I spoke on the microphone I would almost instantaneously start being harassed, hearing things like "oh my god, are you a girl?" and "you're not a girl, you're just a little boy who sounds like a girl." Or even worse, I'd get males who would send me photos of their private parts, or ask for photos of mine.

Many PMS Clan members had stories around harassment, which they tended to vent about in online forums. Some female gamers recount first being mistaken for male, reinforcing the tendency for males to assume a male-dominated space. When this happens, it typically is through profile or avatar stalking (or the process of reading through bios or looking up player information during the game for information you can use against another player), that one will realize that the player is female. As one member expressed on a public forum post:

The first thing I get is, "Shut up, little boy"... I typically don't say anything about it and just continue talking to my boyfriend, but eventually someone will get it or read my bio and say, "Wait, you're a girl? Are you ugly? Are you fat? You're a slut [...] etc. It's starting to get obnoxious. I rarely ever run into just decent guys who either don't say anything about it or say, "Hey, you're pretty good."

For female gamers, harassment was more likely to happen with more females present, as opposed to being one of the few females playing with a larger group of males. For PMS Clan members, this often meant that playing in a group mostly made up of H2Os could provide a safe space. As one PMS member relayed in a public forum, "usually if I am in a party full of H2Os and I am the only PMS I don't hear anything, but when there are 3 or more PMS together that's when you usually run into it." However, this also served to reinforce that

a large presence of females appeared to be more threatening to non-H2O males in the game space.

Harassment can take on many forms, and female gamers are often harassed verbally, but can also receive negative messages. As exemplified through one member's post, this can often lead to frustration, and alienation, as females isolate themselves from negative online communication:

*...seriously......when I say...."The sniper is in the bottom corner in the bushes under the Tower." How does that warrant a barrage of-"Get back in the kitchen *insert any degrading word for a female here* e.g., [Whore], [Slut], [Bitch] & even C---." I can only Mute so many people and it's soooo frustrating that it's almost getting to the point that the [mic] stays off most of the time... I get messages sent to me to. I'll add a couple of people as friends-(often friends of friends) we'll play together as a group well for a while, then one day, it'll just be me and one of them on the mike and then it turns feral and nasty...I am just sick of it.*

In order to avoid negativity, female gamers often engaged in avoidance strategies when not in the clan. One female gamer on a public PMS Clan forum explains, "If I am gaming on my own, I usually play some music and keep my mic off... or I go into a party chat with my friends," while another posts, "I never play matchmaking on my own on my main tag, I'm always on my 2nd....which you can't tell if I'm a girl or guy." In these examples, female gamers discuss how their play has been marginalized by harassment. Instead of disinvesting in gaming completely, they have chosen to disinvest in social interaction in the greater gaming social context. However, online competitive gaming is highly dependent on social interaction: choosing to mute yourself online means that you are limiting your abilities as a team player, and often can mean, depending on the game, that your fellow players may not find you to be a valuable contribution to the team. In game types that require a high amount of team coordination and strategizing for success (such as tactical game modes, like Search & Destroy in *Call of Duty*, or cooperative, team-based first-person-shooter games, like *Left 4 Dead*), limiting one's ability to contribute to collaborative play is often seen as undesirable, and can get one booted from play. More importantly, disinvesting in social interaction, particularly in communities of practice where learning and applying skills in authentic context is shaped by opportunities to engage and learn with others, means that technology identity and domain literacy becomes limited. Gender-supportive communities can help to fill this rift by offering supportive and inclusive environments with similar learning opportunities. These communities have evolved from structures of resistance to structures of resilience and support.

Supporting Visibility in Online Play

Amber Dalton, former leader (she stepped down in 2012) and clan co-founder, stressed the importance and multidimensionality of learning in her opening welcome letter in the handbook:

This is not just a game when each of you are gaining skills in teamwork, leadership, and commitment. It is not just a game when we are learning valuable skill-sets such as time management, conflict resolution, and importance of community. It is not just a game when you can build lifetime friends—and for some of us—second families... (PMS, 2012)

While this was a clan focused on bettering informal skills, the structure of the clan, and the requirements to remain active, all helped to reinforce how seriously each member was required to take their play. Many who remained invested in the clan often went on to increasing leadership roles, which required further supporting the mission and bettering our management and coordination skills in the process. In addition to playing more competitively, members often took on the central role

of representing and changing standards regarding female play, participation and contribution in gaming as a whole. As Amber Dalton further states:

You are each helping to change a mentality in this industry, and are helping to pave the way for the next generation of women gamers, women developers, women company owners...so have passion for your own daughters of the future and support all the members who help make this possible. (PMS, 2012)

As further evidenced by the high visibility of the clan, and its various connections to the industry (several current and former members have gone on to work in the industry in various ways, including development), *PMS Clan* was often the first platform for females serious about getting into the industry, and central to launching several careers. In this sense, it continued to increase the presence of role models who had high visibility, whether it be on the showroom floor, in the corporate offices, or in gaming tournaments. *PMS Clan* continues to increase the visibility of females in the gaming space, and also produces role models at various levels that helped to defy the stereotypes of gender in gaming, and, theoretically, increase female efficacy in the space.

A central part of clan activities was playing together in ways that improved our skills, and encouraged us to compete and represent the clan and its mission competitively. The clan was structured around practices to improve play; for example, most practices involved learning maps and advanced skills in the game, while also incorporating public matches to further apply those skills in "real world" settings (a rather constructivist enterprise). While not all practice captains were adequately skilled to meet that objective (often there was more of a demand for practice captains than available ones with the right skill sets and capacities to teach), the expectation was that learning involved playing with highly skilled other players, in a supportive environment, such that skills would improve over time. In my own observations, on average, I saw that to be true: having been in the clan for close to four years, I saw recruits come in time and time again with little confidence and measurable skills, and wind up being some of the strongest players, who, later on went on to lead divisions (and, in some cases, transition to industry jobs).

Tensions in Co-Ed Play in an Uneven Playing Field

With the exception of three divisions, most of PMS|H2O was strictly divided by gender since allowing H2Os to freely join through the linked "brother" clan. One of the earliest threads on the complexity of co-ed divisions and teams was from 2008, written by a former PMS member and division leader, which sums it up as follows:

The [Ghost Recon 2] division was the very first division that was allowed to go co-ed due to the fact we couldn't keep 8 active girls after [Rainbow 6 Vegas 2] came out. That was all fine and dandy, and we made a lot of great friends that I still have to this day. However, I saw several issues with this. After we went co-ed, the need to rebuild our division and actively recruit PMS girls went away. We had enough players, and we were ALWAYS constantly only playing with each other, and not trying to branch out and build our division. We also started running into issues trying to balance out leadership within the division.

The thread was mostly responded to with support from other highly ranked PMSs and H2Os, who felt that the two clans needed to keep their distinctions, while continuing to support the mission of supporting female gamers. However, one highly ranked former H2O member and division leader responded with concern over the strict separation of the sexes:

H2O was founded to be brothers and supporters of PMS. We are supposed to be a family. This is just separating people and making everyone afraid of being disciplined over having fun with friends....with family. I don't wanna see people leave or get kicked, or lose interest. This is how separation starts and it has started.

However, as much as PMS wanted to support H2O and encourage PMS and H2O members to play together, they also felt the need to keep their identity and original mission alive. As a high ranking PMS operations manager pointed out:

The core of the issue is that the line between both clans is starting to blur. It's vital for PMS to retain our uniqueness ... and our individuality.... More important than getting sponsors is the idea that PMS helps nourish in all women: the idea that we can do it on our own. We may never be #1 in a coed competition, but the fact that we're trying and that we're doing it together says so much more.

As another longtime PMS member stressed:

We are a team Made of Women who should be working on improving each other, not allowing separation based on who's better than who. Especially if we have to resort to picking up the H2Os to improve [our] teams.

While the clan has always encouraged PMS and H2O members to play together, it is often done outside of sanctioned practices that members must attend to maintain active membership. As I noted in my own experiences playing in a co-ed division, the focus on the best players often, unintentionally, relegates improving female play in an uneven playing field as secondary, and reinforces the power structures already at play in the greater gaming space. Since female play is often not as socially supported in gaming spaces, females can often be at a greater disadvantage when it comes to skills and confidence, and female-supportive spaces are still few and far between. Research has found, for example, that females are at significant disadvantage when it comes to having confidence in their gaming abilities, compared to males (see, Richard & Hoadley, 2013); however, being in supportive spaces where they have equal chances to play and train puts them reduces this discrepancy (e.g., Jensen & de Castell, 2011; Richard & Hoadley, 2013). When divisions were co-ed, there was less of a focus on building up and supporting female play, as opposed to the division's play as a whole, which typically meant that male play ended up at the forefront. The tension between how best females could be supported and nurtured in their play, and the male role in that process was never fully resolved in the clan, which remains divided by sex for sanctioned division practices to this day (while there are a few co-ed divisions, the vast majority are separated by sex, though players across gender can play together outside of practices and form small competitive teams together).

One reason for this tension can be, in part, explained by the gendered nature of the greater socio-cultural hierarchy, which often has to be renegotiated in subcultures. As Cassell and Jenkins (1998) note, when girls play in boys' spaces or with what is conceived of as boys' games, it doesn't change the association of the game with masculinity; females who play in male spaces are still considered an anomaly. As similarly found in the punk women's movement in the 1990s, female roles were often relegated to rejecting feminine values and adopting all male dress and behavior, or taking on highly gender stereotyped and supportive roles as a girlfriend, wife or sex object (Leblanc, 1999). In this way, "power" remained central to male experience and values. In these male-dominated play spaces, females are often orienting their experiences around male experience, which can relegate feminine experience as one that is only significant in relation to male experience; this could be seen, for example, in the increased likelihood for female gamers to be harassed when in large groups of females, as opposed to being the lone female amongst a larger group of male gamers. Having female-oriented spaces is one way of focusing on female experience and female abilities, in the hopes of identity and confidence building that isn't solely juxtaposed to male experience.

Solutions and Recommendations

Equitable confidence, identity and skill development in fields that are typically male dominated offer increased challenges for educators because co-ed practices can reinforce gender dynamics, assumptions and power structures that reinforce the gender imbalances in the first place. While, ideally, promoting equity should also mean promoting inclusiveness across gender, ethnicity, sexuality, class, and other social structures, in practice, this is often more complicated. Research, for example, has shown that same sex schools can help to lower access to negative gender stereotypes for females in pursuing male-dominated subjects and fields in part because of the mission to support students equally along gender lines, and in part because of the prevalence of female role models who defy the stereotype (Picho & Stephens, 2012). However, I, by no means, am proposing that promoting equity means promoting separatism; as research also shows, learning climates and school environments that promote equity in the pursuit of fields, across gender, can lessen the gender gap (Legewie & DiPrete, 2011). In this way, it's important to think about how we promote and support gaming, computers, and technology in learning contexts and education.

Research shows that gaming identification, skills and literacy are highly connected to pursuit and efficacy in science, engineering, math and technology (STEM) fields (Kiesler, Sproull, & Eccles, 1985; Cassell & Jenkins, 1998). Research further shows that lowered access to technology in different areas, can lead to a greater digital divide where lack of skills and efficacy, can lead to lack of support in higher education around those technologies, which further exacerbates divides in digital literacy, technology identification, and experience (Good, 2010). In gaming spaces, the divide is often along gender lines, with females traditionally less likely to see themselves as efficacious in gaming, and its related skills, like spatial skills (e.g., Feng, Spence, & Pratt, 2007), without intervention. Research shows that females in male-oriented domains, particularly ones where they are stereotyped to underachieve, can undergo identity interference, which hinders their ability to develop strong domain identification (e.g., Pronin, Steele, & Ross, 2004; Settles, Jellison, & Pratt-Hyatt, 2009). In other words, not only are females less likely to see themselves as capable in gaming, due to socio-cultural incongruence with their gender identities, but they are also less likely to develop related skill and career identifications.

While understanding that promoting inclusiveness and equity in formal educational contexts can be difficult, school environments should make efforts to promote gaming and technology access equally across gender. Gaming has been shown to not only be a gateway to STEM fields but also to certain skills needed to be successful in them. Gaming as both a platform for learning about complex systems (from organisms to historical decision-making) and as a tool in which learners can design and develop with, has the potential to increase 21st century skills valuable to a workforce that needs to be flexible to ever-changing demands. Supportive environments for female play, show measurable significance in leveling the playing field across gender for both identification and confidence in gaming. Professors, instructors and teachers can think through practices that are differentially supportive around gender and ethnic inclusiveness in learning activities. Increasing role models in various ways can help to support inclusive practices. While it may not be feasible to change who teaches at various levels, from elementary school to higher education and even the workplace, access to role models can be provided in other ways, such as through outreach programs

that connect learners to females or underrepresented minorities who have succeeded in fields where they are typically outnumbered.

Areas where we often do have control as educators involves regulating classroom behavior and expectations. In many ways, these expectations should be translated to other learning contexts we have control over, which include promoting understanding around gender imbalanced expectations in online social environments. Educating students about these inequities is one step. If we have control over online social spaces connected to our learning, we should promote equitable practices in those spaces as well.

FUTURE RESEARCH DIRECTIONS

Areas related to this research would center on how students are measured and assessed in their learning with games and related technologies. Some of my current research focuses on the role of stereotype threat vulnerability (the inclination for negatively stereotyped groups to underachieve in an area) in game culture and its potential effects on learning from games (see, Richard & Hoadley, 2013; Richard, 2014). Stereotype threat research has demonstrated time and time again that bias in learning environments and expectations negatively affects the performance of groups stereotyped to underachieve in a particular domain, such as math (Steele & Aronson, 1995; Steele, 1997); groups most likely to be affected by stereotype threat have been females and ethnic minorities in math, science, technology, and related domains. My research has shown support for stereotype threat vulnerability happening in online gaming, and that gender-supportive communities can reduce that vulnerability. However, future research would need to explicitly measure whether stereotype threat actively affects the performance of females and minorities when playing certain games, or when learning from educational games. More would need to be understood about the concrete link between gendered expectations and experiences with games, and measurable performance outcomes in learning contexts.

CONCLUSION

For the most part, social spaces around online gaming have often been thought of as not integrated with formal learning or legitimately tied to greater cultural practice. However, as the literature on affinity spaces and communities of practice show, these informal and interest-driven spaces often create opportunities for learning not currently contained in formal education; for example, individuals can design and make artifacts in the context of a real audience for whom to authentically apply what they have learned and to learn with. If these communities of practice are colored by differential access and expectations, we will continue to disenfranchise certain learners from engaging in these skills, competencies and discourses. An important role of educators is to think through how we represent equity in learning, and promote practices that shape the discourses around learning and experience in online game play and related communities of practice.

ACKNOWLEDGMENT

This work was partially funded by the National Science Foundation (grant #SES-1028637, awarded in 2010) and the American Association of University Women. Opinions expressed within are those of the author and not necessarily those of the funders.

REFERENCES

Behm-Morawitz, E., & Mastro, D. (2009). The effects of the sexualization of female video game characters on gender stereotyping and female self-concept. *Sex Roles*, *61*(11-12), 808–823. doi:10.1007/s11199-009-9683-8

Bryce, J., & Rutter, J. (2002, June). *Killing like a girl: Gendered gaming and girl gamers' visibility*. Paper presented at the Computer Games and Digital Culture Conferences. Tampere, Finland.

Bryce, J., & Rutter, J. (2003). Gender dynamics and the social and spatial organization of computer gaming. *Leisure Studies*, *22*, 1–15. doi:10.1080/02614360306571

Carr, D. (2005). Contexts, gaming pleasures, and gendered preferences. *Simulation & Gaming*, *36*(4), 464–482. doi:10.1177/1046878105282160

Cassell, J., & Jenkins, H. (1998). Chess for girls? Feminism and computer games. In J. Cassell, & H. Jenkins (Eds.), *From Barbie to Mortal Kombat: Gender and computer games* (pp. 2–45). London: MIT Press.

Dickey, M. D. (2006). Girl gamers: The controversy of girl games and the relevance of female-oriented game design for instructional design. *British Journal of Educational Technology*, *37*(5), 785–793. doi:10.1111/j.1467-8535.2006.00561.x

Dill, K. E., & Burgess, M. C. (2012). Influence of Black masculinity game exemplars on social judgments. *Simulation & Gaming*. Retrieved December 19, 2012, from http://sag.sagepub.com/content/early/2012/07/24/1046878112449958.abstract?rss=1

Duncan, S. C., & Hayes, E. R. (2012). Expanding the affinity space: An introduction. In E. R. Hayes, & S. C. Duncan (Eds.), *Learning in video game affinity spaces*. New York, NY: Peter Lang.

Feng, J., Spence, I., & Pratt, J. (2007). Playing an action video game reduces gender differences in spatial cognition. *Psychological Science*, *18*(10), 850–855. doi:10.1111/j.1467-9280.2007.01990.x PMID:17894600

Fron, J., Fullerton, T., Morie, J. F., & Pearce, C. (2007). The hegemony of play. In *Proceedings of DiGRA (Digital Games Research Association) 2007: Situated Play*. DiGRA.

Gee, J. P. (2004). *Situated language and learning: A critique of traditional schooling*. London: Routledge.

Gee, J. P. (2007). *Good video games + good learning: Collected essays on video games, learning, and literacy*. New York, NY: Peter Lang.

Goode, J. (2010). The digital identity divide: How technology knowledge impacts college students. *New Media & Society*, *12*(3), 497–513. doi:10.1177/1461444809343560

Gray, K. L. (2012). Intersecting oppressions and online communities: Examining the experiences of women of color in Xbox live. *Information Communication and Society*, *15*(3), 411–428. doi:10.1080/1369118X.2011.642401

Greenfield, P. M. (1994). Video games as cultural artifacts. *Journal of Applied Developmental Psychology*, *15*(1), 3–12. doi:10.1016/0193-3973(94)90003-5

Hartmann, T., & Klimmt, C. (2006). Gender and computer games: Exploring females' dislikes. *Journal of Computer-Mediated Communication*, *11*(4), 910–931. doi:10.1111/j.1083-6101.2006.00301.x

Jenkins, H. (1998). Complete freedom of movement: Video games as gendered play spaces. In J. Cassell, & H. Jenkins (Eds.), *From Barbie to Mortal Kombat: Gender and computer games* (pp. 262–297). London: MIT Press.

Jenkins, H. (2006). *Confronting the challenges of participatory culture: Media education for the 21st century*. White paper for the MacArthur Foundation. Retrieved on December 4, 2011, from www.digitallearning.macfound.org

Jensen, J., & de Castell, S. (2011). Girls@Play: An ethnographic study of gender and digital gameplay. *Feminist Media Studies*, *11*(2), 167–179. doi:10.1080/14680777.2010.521625

Kafai, Y. B. (1996). Gender differences in children's constructions of video games. In P. Greenfield, & R. Cocking (Eds.), *Interacting with video* (pp. 39–66). Norwood, NJ: Ablex.

Kafai, Y. B. (1998). Video game designs by girls and boys: Variability and consistency of gender differences. In J. Cassell, & H. Jenkins (Eds.), *From Barbie to Mortal Kombat: Gender and computer games* (pp. 90–114). London: MIT Press.

Kafai, Y. B., Heeter, C., Denner, J., & Sun, J. Y. (2008). Pink, purple, casual, or mainstream games: Moving beyond the gender divide. In Y. B. Kafai, C. Heeter, J. Denner, & J. Y. Sun (Eds.), *Beyond Barbie and Mortal Kombat: Perspectives on gender and gaming*. Cambridge, MA: MIT Press.

Kiesler, S., Sproull, L., & Eccles, J. S. (1985). Pool halls, chips, and war games: Women in the culture of computing. *Psychology of Women Quarterly*, *9*(4), 451–462. doi:10.1111/j.1471-6402.1985.tb00895.x

Kimmel, M. (2008). *Guyland: The perilous world where boys become men*. New York, NY: Harper Collins.

Kuznekoff, J. H., & Rose, L. M. (2013). Communication in multiplayer gaming: Examining player responses to gender cues. *New Media & Society*, *15*(4), 541–556. doi:10.1177/1461444812458271

Lave, J., & Wenger, E. (1991). *Situated learning: Legitimate peripheral participation*. Cambridge, UK: Cambridge University Press. doi:10.1017/CBO9780511815355

Lave, J., & Wenger, E. (2002). Legitimate peripheral participation in communities of practice. In M. R. Lea, & K. Nicholl (Eds.), *Distributed learning, social and cultural approaches to practice*. London: Routledge.

Lebanc, L. (1999). *Pretty in punk: Girls' gender resistance in a boys' subculture*. New Brunswick, NJ: Rutgers University Press.

Lee, J. E. R., & Park, S. G. (2011). Whose second life is this? How avatar-based racial cues shape ethno-racial minorities' perception of virtual worlds. *Cyberpsychology, Behavior, and Social Networking*, *14*(11), 637–642. doi:10.1089/cyber.2010.0501 PMID:21486164

Legewie, J., & DiPrete, T. A. (2011). *High school environments, stem orientations, and the gender gap in science and engineering degrees*. Unpublished Working Paper. Retrieved from http://papers.ssrn.com/sol3/papers.cfm?abstract_id=2008733

Matthew, E. (2012, September 6). *Sexism in video games: There is sexism in gaming*. Retrieved from: http://blog.pricecharting.com/2012/09/emilyami-sexism-in-video-games-study.html

Miller, M. K., & Summers, A. (2007). Gender differences in video game characters' roles, appearances, and attire as portrayed in video game magazines. *Sex Roles*, *57*(9-10), 733–742. doi:10.1007/s11199-007-9307-0

Nakamura, L. (2009). Don't hate the player, hate the game: The racialization of labor in World of Warcraft. *Critical Studies in Media Communication*, *26*(2), 128–144. doi:10.1080/15295030902860252

Pandora's Mighty Soliders (PMS). (2011a). *Homepage*. Retrieved on December 1, 2011 from http://www.pmsclan.com/index.html

Pandora's Mighty Soliders (PMS). (2011b). *About us*. Retrieved on December 1, 2011 from http://www.pmsclan.com/page.php?page=About%20Us

Pandora's Mighty Soliders (PMS). (2012). *Handbook*. Retrieved on January 25, 2012 from http://www.pmsclan.com/forum/showthread.php?t=30905

Pronin, E., Steele, C. M., & Ross, L. (2004). Identity bifurcation in response to stereotype threat: Women and mathematics. *Journal of Experimental Social Psychology*, *40*(2), 152–168. doi:10.1016/S0022-1031(03)00088-X

Richard, G. T. (2012a). Gender and game play: Research and future directions. In B. Bigl, & S. Stoppe (Eds.), *Playing with virtuality, theories and methods of computer game studies*. Frankfurt, Germany: Peter Lang.

Richard, G. T. (2012b). *On the periphery of video game culture: Understanding urban Latino gamers' experiences*. Paper presented at Meaningful Play 2012. East Lansing, MI.

Richard, G. T. (2014). *Understanding gender, context and game culture for the development of equitable digital games as learning environments*. (Doctoral Dissertation). New York University, New York, NY.

Richard, G. T. (2013a). Designing games that foster equity and inclusion: Encouraging equitable social experiences across gender and ethnicity in online games. In G. Christou, E. L. Law, D. Geerts, L. E. Nacke, & P. Zaphiris (Eds.), *Proceedings of the CHI'2013 Workshop: Designing and Evaluating Sociability in Online Video Games*. ACM Press.

Richard, G. T. (2013b). The interplay between gender and ethnic harassment in game culture and its implications for play and learning. In *Proceedings of DiGRA (Digital Games Research Association) 2013: Defragging Game Studies*. DiGRA.

Richard, G. T., & Hoadley, C. M. (2013). Investigating a supportive online gaming community as a means of reducing stereotype threat vulnerability across gender. In *Proceedings of Games, Learning & Society 2013*. ETC Press

Schott, G., & Horrell, K. (2000). Girl gamers and their relationship with gaming culture. *Convergence*, *6*(4), 36–53. doi:10.1177/135485650000600404

Settles, I. H., Jellison, W. A., & Pratt-Hyatt, J. S. (2009). Identification with multiple social groups: The moderating role of identity change over time among women-scientists. *Journal of Research in Personality*, *43*(5), 856–867. doi:10.1016/j.jrp.2009.04.005

Shaw, A. (2012). Do you identify as a gamer? Gender, race, sexuality, and gamer identity. *New Media & Society*, *14*(1), 28–44. doi:10.1177/1461444811410394

Shute, V. J. (2007). Tensions, trends, tools and technologies: Time for an educational sea change. In C. A. Dwyer (Ed.), *The future of assessment: Shaping teaching and learning* (pp. 139–187). New York: Lawrence Earlbaum / Taylor & Francis.

Squire, K. (2003). Video games in education. *International Journal of Intelligent Simulations and Gaming*, *2*(1), 49–62.

Squire, K. (2005). Changing the game: What happens when video games enter the classroom. *Innovate: Journal of Online Education, 1* (6).

Squire, K. (2011). *Video games and learning: Teaching and participatory culture in the digital age*. New York: Teachers College Press.

Steele, C. M. (1997). A threat in the air: how stereotypes shape intellectual identity and performance. *The American Psychologist*, *52*, 613–629. doi:10.1037/0003-066X.52.6.613 PMID:9174398

Steele, C. M., & Aronson, J. (1995). Stereotype threat and the intellectual test performance of African Americans. *Journal of Personality and Social Psychology*, *69*(5), 797–811. doi:10.1037/0022-3514.69.5.797 PMID:7473032

Subrahmanyam, K., & Greenfield, P. M. (1994). Effect of video game practice on spatial skills in girls and boys. *Journal of Applied Developmental Psychology*, *15*, 13–32. doi:10.1016/0193-3973(94)90004-3

Sunden, J., & Sveningsson, M. (2012). *Gender and sexuality in online game cultures*. New York, NY: Routledge.

Taylor, T. L. (2003). Multiple pleasures: Women and online gaming. *Convergence*, *9*(1), 21–46. doi:10.1177/135485650300900103

Taylor, T. L. (2006). *Play between worlds: Exploring online game culture*. Cambridge, MA: MIT Press.

Taylor, T. L. (2008). Becoming a player: Networks, structure and imagined futures. In Y. B. Kafai, C. Heeter, J. Denner, & J. Y. Sun (Eds.), *Beyond Barbie and Mortal Kombat: Perspectives on gender and gaming* (pp. 51–66). Cambridge, MA: MIT Press.

Thomas, D., & Brown, J. S. (2011). *A new culture of learning: Cultivating the imagination for a world of constant change*. Lexington, KY: CreateSpace.

Williams, D., Martins, N., Consalvo, M., & Ivory, J. D. (2009). The virtual census: Representations of gender, race and age in video games. *New Media & Society*, *11*(5), 815–834. doi:10.1177/1461444809105354

Yee, N. (2008). Maps of digital desires: Exploring the topography of gender and play in online games. In Y. B. Kafai, C. Heeter, J. Denner, & J. Y. Sun (Eds.), *Beyond Barbie and Mortal Kombat: Perspectives on gender and gaming* (pp. 83–96). Cambridge, MA: MIT Press.

KEY TERMS AND DEFINITIONS

Affinity Spaces: Communities, fan sites and social spaces formed around shared interest activities, most notably game-based ones.

Casual: Casual is a term often used to denote games that are more accessible due to less complex game mechanics. Casual games are often not as competitive or complex as hardcore games. "Casual" gaming has often been scrutinized as implying female interest in less difficult gaming tasks.

Clan: An organized group of players who typically play a certain game or game type. Clans and guilds are very similar, though guilds are more often associated with MMORPGs and clans with FPSs. Some clans can span many games and game types, whereas others may only be formed for the purpose of competing with a single game. Clans can also be formed based on interest groups or group identities, such as female gamers or LGBT gamers. The lifespan of a clan varies based on its reputation, whether it was formed for a specific game, its accessibility to new membership, the dedication of its members, and other factors.

Deathmatch: Deathmatch is a game type often contained in first-person-shooters where players win by gaining the most kills (in free-for-all type matches) or players win by being on the team with the most kills (in team-based deathmatches).

First-Person-Shooters (FPS): A digital game type often associated with shooting enemies from the first-person perspective. These game types have often been considered military themed (even though some feature fantasy themes) and highly masculine-oriented. Players often play online against other players, either alone or on a team, in matches where one team must best another, often through the most kills.

Griefing: Griefing is the act of abusing, harassing, team-killing or otherwise intentionally agitating other players. Sometimes, it is used to explicitly gain an advantage.

Guild: Guilds and clans are both organized groups of players who regularly play certain games or game types together. Guilds are more notable in MMORPGs (whereas clans are more notable in FPSs, and, increasingly, other game types).

Hardcore: Hardcore is a term often used to denote individuals who are highly invested in gaming and game culture to the extent that they often play to master games, and are highly aware of and play many popular titles. Hardcore is also used to denote games with a high amount of complexity and skill requirements, often gained by being familiar with a certain genre or game type. Games that are often more competitive have often been implied as more hardcore than others.

Massively Multiplayer Online Role Playing Games (MMORPGs): Digital game types that feature role playing with fantasy-based characters and themes. Players often play with other players who take on different characters with different strengths and attributes that will benefit a team structure in order to successfully complete quests.

Stereotype Threat: Often negatively impacts the performance of groups stereotyped to underachieve in an area when they are in a situation where the negative stereotype is activated. Research tends to show that females and ethnic minorities are most vulnerable to stereotype threat. Stereotype threat vulnerability measures how susceptible one is to threat based on individual characteristics, such as how much one identifies with a negatively stereotyped group.

Section 5
Building and Sustaining Communities Online

Chapter 11
Internet Past Tense:
Trolls, Sock–Puppets, and Good Joes in the Sandbox Newsgroup

Joe Essid
University of Richmond, USA

ABSTRACT

From the time of privately hosted computer bulletin boards to the rise of social networking, USENET hosted a broad array of newsgroups that hobbyists enjoyed. At The Sandbox group for collectors of 1:6 scale GI Joe toys, members developed a set of conventions governing an online community without moderation, countered trolls, and established reputations for fairness among members using pseudonyms. In time, however, these conventions began to weaken as the hobby waned in popularity. Eventually, The Sandbox at USENET came to an end as a vital community, and a diaspora to Facebook and privately hosted, moderated forums followed. This chapter studies how the USENET community worked socially, how its language evolved, and its fate when what the author calls "the Old Internet" gave way to today's array of social-networking and multimedia applications.

INTRODUCTION

Point a Web browser to the Sandbox < http://groups.google.com/group/alt.toys.gi-joe > to get a sense of the sort of unmoderated newsgroup that flourished between the development of ARPANET in the late 1960s and the gradual demise of such

DOI: 10.4018/978-1-4666-5150-0.ch011

venues in today's era of Social Media (Markoff, 2006). Be wary, as the first message when I last checked was off-topic, and, frankly, disgusting even by pornographic standards.

Such was what I've come to call "the Old Internet." That Sandbox is a ghost town today, its chaotic energy having flowed to moderated groups, one part of Facebook, another a private forum called "The Trenches." Yet in its newsgroup heyday, Sandbox participants discussed GI Joe, other toys, and often wildly OT (off-topic) issues. Something like this would pop up on the screen:

Wally World has reduced prices on the latest wave of 40th. Got a repro medic helmet from Cots for the fig and also pre-ordered one of the second-wave 40th AM sets. While I was at it, I ordered KFG hands; can't stand that stupid nosepicker --can't hold any gear. Oh, yeah, I'm going to send my extra coffin boxes to Sherman who karma bombed me with some parts.

This article will look at what generated that energy, where it went, and how participants accrued influence and became leaders without ever, with a few exceptions, having met each other in the flesh. Participants in the discussion, whether leaders, lurkers, or losers, often employed arcane code and social conventions to follow an unending stream of conversation. One goal of this chapter will be to archive and present that ephemeral sociolect of a small group of enthusiasts.

BACKGROUND: OLD TOYS, OLD INTERNET

Like other surviving parts of the Old Internet, USENET's The Sandbox newsgroup is a fossil of sorts. First, it always attracted a fossilized crowd: collectors of old toys, in particular, Hasbro's GI Joes of the 1960s and 70s. We—and the author is one of that group—are not a demographic on the rise. Later incarnations of Hasbro's action figure from the Reagan Era (think Cobra Commander) have their own online groups, and this chapter will focus on those collectors who formed a community around the original GI Joe, several re-issues of that toy by Hasbro, or similar military-or-adventure themed toys by other firms.

Academics are not immune to the American mania for collecting things. One professor I know owns and races British sports cars, some

have incredible wine cellars, and many are ardent bibliophiles. Though I am owned by two antique vehicles ('68 Chevy C-10 pickup and '70 El Camino), my passion for many years was old toys, specifically the 12" tall GI Joe action figures made in the 1960s and 70s. The Sandbox served, after the revival of interest in older GI Joe collectibles in the mid 90s, as the best meeting place online for hobbyists.

That sense of shared community has been true since the earliest days of networked computing. The history is complex, even though the Internet as we know it today seems like an inevitable progression from primitive technologies to a gradual networking of more advanced systems. In reality, its development actually proceeded in fits and starts. (Markoff, 2005) notes that despite pioneering work in networked communications by Douglas Englebart and several other pioneers affiliated with Stanford or MIT starting in about 1960, later the history of computing took another path:

When personal computing finally blossomed in Silicon Valley in the mid-seventies, it do so largely without the history and research that had gone before it. As a consequence, the personal-computer industry would be deformed for years, creating a world of isolated desktop boxes, in contrast to the communities of shared information that had been pioneered in the sixties and early seventies. (Markoff, 2005, p. 179)

This "deformed" history contributed to the ad-hoc system of bulletin-boards locally hosted, international networks such as Bitnet, and dial-up access to university systems by the late 1980s. America Online entered the market as a walled garden for cautious users before it was annexed by the larger Internet. What we may forget, in the New Internet's mix of popular social applications, is how Markoff's "communities of shared information" evolved in the Old Internet's mélange of often-competing systems and protocols. In many cases, such as the Sandbox discussed here, information was not all that got shared. In fact, the Sandbox came to be a non-academic "community of practice" as participants educated each other about the collecting, history, and lucrative sale of old toys (Lave & Wenger, 1991). Lore, even collaborative photo-stories featuring old GI Joes, flourished, some of them quite sophisticated in their story lines and creative use of photography and digital video (Figure 1). Often the results poke fun at the suspension of disbelief that accompanies childhood play or the sheer silliness of some of the toys we once thought so cool; consider the likely IQ of any secret agent who'd need to have "Bullet Proof Vest" stenciled across the appropriate item in his inventory.

As with the other communities that flourished on the Old Internet, a shared sense of lore led to group-specific language evolving in The Sandbox over several years, often by happenstance. An appendix to this chapter provides a glossary of terminology unique to the Sandbox's collectors.

These ways of communicating lacked any formal terms of service such as Facebook mandates, albeit to the ignorance of many who simply click through that lengthy document.

As a surviving .alt newsgroup, The Sandbox may be impossible to access from certain Internet Service Providers who block access to .alt groups or USENET itself out of fear of child pornography or pirated intellectual property. In the mid 1990s, however, long before blogs and social media appeared on the scene, USENET's largely unregulated collection of forums allowed users to post messages without creating an account, setting up a Web site, subscribing officially, or having messaged approved by a moderator. Part of the thrill for a writing teacher was discovering, in a forum dedicated to toys, an analogue to the 1970s version of a writing classroom without teachers where "everyone reads everyone else's writing. Everyone tries to give each writer a sense of how his words were experienced (Elbow, 1973, p. 77). This sort of a supportive, if anarchic, community

Figure 1. Panel from photo-story "Escape from the Gulag" by the author. Used with permission.

reaches consensus using a set of self-created and unwritten rhetorical and stylistic rules to protect the integrity of how members talk, trade, resolve conflicts, and fend off malicious outsiders.

As I interviewed several Sandbox members for this article, I began to see how fully we live in a cybernetic future that, only twenty years ago, would have amazed us. After a period of openness and a frontier ethos of rugged individualism, today's Internet seems contracted, safer, and, in a word, less interesting. This closure and the rise of telecom and software giants follows earlier era in telecommunications, a phenomenon Wu (2011) names "The Cycle." Academics did not predict this amalgamation of user experience into monopoly-controlled interactions, from the gated communities of Blackboard's courseware to the social cliques of Facebook.

In fact, anthologies of articles from the 1990s are heavily weighed either toward visions of empowerment for writing teachers and their students or cautionary tales about educators whose enthusiasm for technology led to pedagogical mistakes (Hawisher & Selfe, 1991). At the time, it was a bit cloying to me. I tend to distrust "wonder of it all" rhetoric about technology; these too often veer into utopian narratives about changing the entire world. Instead, I have heeded those who lambasted the shallowness of online discourse and the difficulty of getting student writers to a sophisticated level of engagement. Moran (1995), writing at the time when USENET-style anarchy online provided the model for how writers interacted, fumed about how his students used Daedalus, a software suite for writing classes, not to build a supportive community but to engage in ad-hominem attacks or merely spew lots of text without any sustained dialectic. Dery (1993) explored the idea of a "flame war," claiming that "on-line group psychology is shaped by the medium itself" (p. 564). That was a reasonable and McLuhanesque claim, reflecting both the power of community and the limits of technology. The era's line-editing programs and dial-in Bulletin-Board systems often worked poorly for seamless and nuanced communication.

Unlike early critics of technology in the classroom, I want colleagues and students to see what has, over more than a decade's span, worked *well*. Today, the concerns of the 1990s appear less vexing, or at least vexing in a different way, in the more regulated spaces provided by Twitter and Facebook. As our students use these and other services, becoming ever more savvy about authoring and sharing material completely outside the classroom, faculty face tough choices about how to teach in a "writing" classroom for these digital natives (Yancey, 2004, pp. 308-311).

Given the scope and pace of the changes before us, we might turn our attention again to how the rhetorical and stylistic aspects of the ubiquitous, usually transparent medium developed. In my classes, we often study one remarkable feature of Internet use: the emergence of long-lasting online forums, especially the vitality of those self-governed without moderators. The communities are very different from the circles of friends and family that dominate social media. My experience with Facebook has shown that the social circle mostly encompasses those people known in person. The Sandbox, much like some of the virtual-world community Boellstorff (2008) explored in Second Life, featured a circle of acquaintances who rarely met in the flesh until an event such as the annual "Joelanta" convention began.

ABOUT THE SANDBOX AS A COMMUNITY

Becoming a Good Joe: Karma Happens

Participating in the USENET Sandbox discussions not only helped expand my collection and learn facts about toys, it also put me in touch with an instant community that includes elders, merchants, jesters and keepers of lore. As I spent more time with the group, however, it seemed remarkable for its ability to withstand flame-wars between insiders or provocations from outsiders.

Most online groups with specialized interests employ jargon specific to their setting or subject. Behind this code, archived by several of us "Boxers" in an online glossary, lies something much more interesting for those studying style and teaching writing. In an odd way, the Sandbox realized some of the fondest dreams from the early days of networked writing classrooms. All of the Boxers here are given pseudonyms different from the screen-names employed in their responses to the author, unless the Boxer posted something to a public forum.

Ethos in any hobbyist community involves demonstrating knowledge and providing advice. What set the USENET Sandbox apart from other hobbyist forums may be "karma." When I joined the Sandbox, my respondent (and life-long friend and fellow collector) Midnight Angel advised that if I wanted to be taken seriously there, I should start giving my extra pieces of GI Joe equipment to the first person to reply to an offer, and in return I'd get karma back. My respondent Sherman claimed that this makes the Sandbox "second to no other forum. Imagine some 180 guys and girls sending freebies to each other just because!"

Members of both the USENET forum and the Facebook group that followed its decline take such free trades, and the belief that "karma happens," very seriously. It is a grave breach of decorum to promise a free item and not send it. One gets labeled a "Good Joe," often eliciting posts with the subject "Good Joe Report" for a trade or sale. As respondent Astronaut noted, " It takes a lot to lose your 'Good Joe' status, but it can happen. If so, it happens through the consensus of a number of established members."

Members enjoyed building up the lore of the Sandbox and the sense of permanence of our "place" online. Susan Storm, a member for a decade, felt that the Box "has a history and a legacy. It's a true community." Midnight Angel used a similar metaphor, "a place Joeheads could gather and talk about anything, even beyond collecting, including politics." Astronaut reflected that "There's a corner-pub feel to the place that I enjoy." Real pubs can play a part, too. Boxers occasionally meet in person, as Soho did when he gave me and my wife an insider's tour of traditional London public houses, not long after I interviewed him for this study of The Sandbox.

Boxers used a number of stratagems and ways of writing to maintain this atmosphere. For instance, many of us wrote at length, and with nostalgia or at least collector's glee, about karma received whenever we attain a "Holy Grail" item long sought in our collecting. In my case, my being a Good Joe was interpreted by the group as leading to good karma: a non-collector selling me, at a very cheap price, the lost childhood treasure of a rare GI Joe Astronaut rocket-pack. This led to a nostalgia-laden post in which I recounted how my father, whose death was still a recent and painful memory for me, had hidden the toy beneath the Christmas tree in 1971.

Many early members of the Sandbox had, by the mid 2000s, left hobby or no longer took time to post regularly. But a few remained, despite a daunting volume of messages. Sherman, a member for nine years at the time of his interview in 2006, stayed with it because:

We stick up for each other, we openly apologize to each other, and when the chips are down we care for our own. Births, deaths and illnesses we have been through it. . . . I have yet to see this in other groups and forums.

Susan Storm seconded this, noting "People don't just bring Joe talk to the Box but also share their personal triumphs and tragedies." While this sharing, as well as our "karmic" altruism, sound at face value like the characteristics of what Howard (1997) calls a "sentimental community" (p. 72), the Sandbox also passes two of Howard's conditions for working as an "individualistic community" online (Howard, 1997, p. 118). First, members have a joint interest and second, they are willing to make sacrifices for each other, something Howard (1997) terms a "reciprocity mechanism." As Freefall noted, regulars qualify disagreements with "language such as 'you are a good friend but....' I think what enables this is an underlying sense of social capital or mutual trust that prevents conflict from becoming toxic."

At both the original USENET site and what gradually replaced it, Boxers often send best wishes to others with ailing family members or other difficulties. Freefall recalled "One of my most poignant memories will be crying after reading another Boxer's poem to his son (also a Joe collector) who passed away." This type of emotional engagement happens more often than one might suspect, based on my knowledge of the beekeeping and antique-car hobbies. Such sentiments seem unusually strong, however, in the Sandbox, a group that interacts mostly online. Given the author's personal experiences as a collector and data gathered in interviews of the Sandbox members, it may have to do with the object of the forum: GI Joe. Nearly all of the Boxers formed strong bonds with this line of toys as children, and that leads them to powerful nostalgia that overpowers feelings of monetary value. Compared to the classic-car hobbyists the author has met while repairing and driving classics, it has been uncommon at the Sandbox to talk about money. In fact, worrying too much about the costs of things seems to lead to negative responses. When I recently posted about declining values for a reissued GI Joe item, several Boxers responded to the effect GI Joe is a toy we love, not an investment.

Boxing a Troll's Ears: Leaders Arise

Not all karma was good at the USENET Sandbox. When asked about what happens when serious disagreements flare up between members, respondents gave different impressions of how well the community reacts. Radiohead claimed that in his experience "Usually, it's a train wreck" and Midnight Angel saw "Open war, but usually a good outcome," whereas Sherman, who sometimes sparred with Radiohead over politics, believed "Most of the permanent cadre/members will apologize or take it to email while newbies will whine about how it is not Joe-related, while those same conflicting members will tell them how to filter us out." Susan Storm believed Radiohead's "train wreck" to be a rarity, adding "I've never seen the Box all gang up on a someone who didn't absolutely deserve it and I wouldn't call someone like that a 'serious member.'"

Soho summed up the typical cues that a thread is about to erupt into a flame-war. Claims appear "often prefaced with statements such as 'As a member of the law enforcement community.. .,' 'As a Republican...' or 'As a Christian....' " "These confrontations usually escalate until a trusted party intervenes to chide the others.

Normally, the worst difficulties occur when a troll decides to post to the list. Like their mythical namesakes, trolls online come out of the shadows to attack others. They post outrageous ideas, personal attacks, and adopt contrarian positions. After an initial salvo, some trolls hope to disrupt conversation and have other members of a newsgroup fight while the instigator pulls back and watches the fun.

In moderated forums this is rare, claimed Sherman. "Moderators may not like the fact that you are putting down a particular collector, company, and member and have little toleration for human interaction and criticism." Of course, moderators can quickly ban a troll, as I have done in lists I managed. This is a two-edged sword, because in my experience as blogger and forum-member, a list that is too heavily moderated usually loses members. Several Sandbox respondents, however, describe the USENET forum of the 1990s and early 2000s as both "lively" and "self-policing." The newer destinations for Sandbox members, after the rise of social media, do not follow the unwritten rules of the Old Internet; self-policing gave way to moderation by a single person.

Despite living up to the corner-pub metaphor, with welcoming regulars sharing stories at the bar, the USENET Box was never immune to troll-attacks. Watching how Boxers responded to threats reveals a diversity of stylistic techniques. Some, by filtering out conflict, employing humor or sarcasm, or even revealing the identity of a malcontent, established a voice apparent in every post.

I'll call a famous troll of the late 1990s "The Hiker," because he acquired multiple free e-mail accounts from an outdoor-sports publication. He attacked others, often employing a "sock puppet": pretending to be another person while using the troll's voice and rhetorical strategies. This tactic is not as serious as what Dibbell (1993) describes; unlike the wizards and gods who can control Multiple-User-Dungeon, Object-Oriented (MOO) coding, no troll can post using the identity of another Usenet user. So Usenet trolls must attack in writing under their own pseudonyms and use various tricks to get forum members to fight with the troll or each other. Often The Hiker took neo-fascist positions about toy collecting, as in this post made under the identity "Jabario," who asked "if anyone knows if anyone ever produced a good Mussolini figure. Such a great world leader needs to be immortalized in 1/6 scale!!"

Most of the Boxers interviewed for this article initially reacted with sarcasm, including the author and Midnight Angel, Soho, and Freefall. A typical reply was sent by this last Boxer, who wrote, "I had one and he came with a nice lamp post from which he could be hanged. I kept the lamp post." After a series of replies about various morbid accessories that might accompany the Mussolini action figure, such as removable bruises or a coffin, The Hiker shot back with his provocation:

You fools know nothing of history. Few historians or Italians during that era reaaly [sic] have anything bad to say about Mussolini. I asked a

legitimate question since far worse individuals have been immortalized in 1/6 scale.

This ad-hominem shift changed the tone of the thread of messages. Soho, a Londoner whose nation endured the Blitz and other terrors of the fascist war machine, was the first to take the troll's bait:

I think us fools know our history well enough:

(a) Mussolini was indeed a fascist

(b) He ended his days hanging from a lamp post

(c) No great loss

Now, please feel free to correct us . . .

Soho's critique, of course, merely valorized the troll's stance and got the rest of us to chime in to support a trusted insider. The replies escalated after The Hiker fed our collective hatred of fascism:

>>(c) No great loss <<

That's debatable. Was JFK a loss? A whoring liar from a bootlegger family. Lincoln? Instigated the war of northern aggression and suspended liberties to those in the US. These leaders were far more despotic than Il Duce. Yet there are action figures of lincoln [sic] and others.

Things got rather interesting from here. The tirade escalated, until The Hiker played the standard neo-Nazi rhetorical trump card: denying the Holocaust. His use of pathos worked: I replied with a mostly unprintable diatribe that began, "Aha! I was fishing for exactly that reply. You are a Nazi sympathizer worthy of death, as are all Nazi scum."

Before things could get even worse, a Boxer who had not participated in the Mussolini discussion chided me and Midnight Angel, whose father fought in WW II, for getting too far from the subject of our list and reminded us that we'd fallen prey to a troll. So I apologized to the list, saying I would never reply to The Hiker again, and all of us simmered down as "Jabario" went back under his bridge. This situation matches perfectly a mechanism described by Soho for flame-wars, where "eventually someone (possibly) known to both parties will step in as peace maker and remind them of the absurdity of 40 year-old men playing with dolls!"

Most self-aware and articulate Boxers never keep this far from their thoughts. In response just quoted, Soho employs the wry sense of humor typical of Sandbox regulars. Soho knowingly breaks a rule in the expected "form of address" for a communications medium (Barnes, S., 2000, p. 172). In the Sandbox, an insider would never, except in jest, call a GI Joe a "doll," yet a new-comer might use the locution out of ignorance or malice. Trolls love to bait us, for instance, by calling us "bald, fat nerds who play with dolls." Well, I'm not fat. . .

Several survey respondents felt that trolls' humorless provocations and responses lead members to leave the Sandbox or "lurk," wary that a troll might target them. Other Boxers took a more active approach, noting The Hiker's style and peculiar use of pathos, as well as his consistent ideological position as a fascist sympathizer. Such knowledge can be useful; The Hiker soon reappeared as his sock-puppet "Big Jim," and when others recognized a unique combination of misspelling and sarcasm, he shot back, "You guys seem quick to pounce on people who simply want to be part of this online community. The jabrol [sic] person has his/her name speeled [sic] differently than the person you accuse me of being. . . .Thanks again for the warm welcome." Yet not long after this, Big Jim posted a diatribe criticizing African-American survivors of Katrina who had stayed in New Orleans during the storm. These messages were cross-posted to Usenet forums about mountain-biking and Subaru cars; this tactic clogged our list with angry replies from people

having no interest in old toys but who, in rage, hit "reply all."

The off-topic cross-postings accelerated until some regular members considered leaving the list completely. A few other regulars decided to point out that one malicious person was behind all the trouble. They added that it would be up to the community to deal with him. A long-time Boxer prepared a side-by-side analysis of The Hiker's posts; it would be meritorious work in a composition classroom:

1) Single paragraph. Yes, sure, the post is short, so that by itself is no indication, but the format looks very similar.

2) Two spaces before the first word in each post.

3) Two spaces after the periods before the next word. I don't know too many people who do that. (In the first post, the ". W" only has one space, so the sample may not be valid. However, thereafter, two spaces. And in other posts, this also applies.)

4) Compare "dont" and "wouldnt," each missing the apostrophe. On its own, this wouldn't be too damning, but put together with the formatting similarities, the address similarities and the spacing, [it is] pretty convincing to me.

As revealing as a 19th Century telegraphers' "fist," that the astute could use to identify a particular operator, The Hiker's stylistic tic and signature errors revealed the typist behind the sock puppet. Grammatical lapses and missing-word errors often occur in posts by regulars, who then apologize for mistakes made in haste. For a troll, however, such mistakes provide insiders with yet another way to marginalize an offender by calling into question his intelligence. In a recent exchange, a Boxer said of what is likely The Hiker's latest sock-puppet, "I can't resist: Isn't it grand when someone using 'your' for 'you're' and 'bobby prize' for 'booby prize' calls others morons?"

The troll's power as rhetor weakened considerably when everyone was laughing at his writing, but ironically such commentary "fed the troll" and kept his messages current in the queue of topics. Hickey (2014) discusses the consequences of troll-feeding at the political blog Firedoglake, and the ways in which that online community, using tactics rather different from those at The Sandbox, avoided such provocations through united action. Facing with this sort of unified response, the Hiker, or his sock puppets, lay low for a time. He or another troll who had been watching the list then switched tactics to attack the GI Joe Club, an organization that produces exclusive figures and holds an annual convention. While the Club is not universally popular, those who dislike it do not join and rarely criticize it online. Alternately, trolls repeatedly attacked the officers of the Club, accusing them of theft, then posted the home addresses of members outraged enough by the accusations to reply. That could be dangerous to a person who owns collectible toys worth many thousands of dollars.

Astronaut explained that some Boxers go to great lengths to "engage in old-fashioned detective work to track down and identify persistent troublemakers. I can think of a couple of occasions where that's been effective, at least in chasing someone out of the Sandbox." On occasion, ISP tracing by technically savvy Boxers has figuratively pulled a sock-puppet from a troll's hand to show that one person was behind dozens of attacks. Sherman did this to the Hiker, and he got the troll's free e-mail accounts stopped because the Hiker had violated the policies under which the accounts were given. The Hiker finally dropped his masks with a pathetic, and finally, powerless boast:

You think you've won little man? You can't stop me. I RULE this and every other group I post to. Every time I post, people respond. You can call me names threaten etc. but you cant stop me. I'm here to stay.

Did it even matter if the Hiker stayed? Would anyone be listening? An easier, and more popular stratagem in these situations appears to be using a "killfile" to screen out any messages from a troll or his sock-puppets. Astronaut did this so well that when he read his messages it "was like watching a whole room full of people boxing with ghosts."

This does not work for all newsreaders and it can filter out useful threads with the bad ones. A few regulars tried a different approach: replying to the troll's thread (but not content) and changing the subject lines and content to on-topic issues, in an attempt to bury the troll's subject until it vanished from the queue. This tactic has not been popular with Boxers at USENET, because it makes the list-archives harder to follow.

To this day, I have kept my promise to the list and never replied to any of The Hiker's posts, even seemingly serious queries that often devolve into racist tirades. My favored approach has been to post to legitimate topics and continue these discussions with enough frequency to marginalize the troll. No individual can sabotage dozens of threaded topics at once, and the volume of the list itself soon tends to push the troll's rants lower in the queue until they vanish, unread, into the archives.

Besides, as one poster put it, when serious members reply to a troll at all:

it's as if he's not in MY killfile, because you copy all of what he said in YOUR post. Just put him in the killfile and ignore him. Otherwise his messages still percolate throughout the group. But yes. It's delicious when a real idiot calls a non-idiot one.

Trolls do not employ terms like "delicious" and "percolate." Instead, they follow Dery's (1993) stereotype of flaming by "fish-banging punctuation, emphatic capitals, and the kill-'em-all-and let-God-sort-'em-out rhetoric patented by Hunter S. Thompson" (p. 563). Well, almost. Thompson, for all his under-the-influence gonzo energy, could spell.

Few of the Boxers could have imagined that in just a few years, the antics of a writer like The Hiker would seem quaint, precisely because such antics would become difficult, if not impossible, on The New Internet.

The Sandbox Scatters

Several points lead me to wonder if, as we age with our old toys, the Box will still exist to celebrate GI Joe's 50th anniversary in 2014.

As a vital Usenet group, it will not.

First of all, even before Facebook and other social media arrived, the Boxers were aging. In the Sandbox's heyday of the mid-to-late 1990s, collectors who went to Sears or Woolco in the 1960s for GI Joe had reached their 30s. By that point, many had families and encouraged play with dad's old toys; still, the number of young hobbyists was not large. Moreover, the next generation to have played with GI Joe experienced Hasbro's toy differently, as a small plastic soldier with many weapons and vehicles, plus ready-made enemies in the form of Cobra. These younger collectors generally did not remember, let alone covet, the uniform sets of GI Joe's first military era or his

packaged exploits—retrieving a stolen Buddha made of solid gold, trapping alive a rare white tiger, capping a blazing oil well—of the more peaceful 1970s Adventure Team. More ominously for the toy industry, a phenomenon called "age compression" means that contemporary children spend fewer years playing with toys and more with mobile computing applications and gaming consoles (Barnes, 2001). GI Joe today means a movie franchise with related toys and, naturally, a first-person shooter video game.

At the same time as their children put down toys and picked up small screens, most adult collectors' incomes rose, so much so that many had extensive "Joe Rooms" dedicated to displaying hundreds of GI Joes in climate-controlled dioramas or, as in the author's study, a bookshelf of ready-for-action GI Joes, equipped or for any potential danger. In the end, even in their peak-earning years few collectors could build an entire museum, so Boxers' collecting slowed or stopped. Some reported that they hoard thousands of GI Joes in boxes stacked ceiling high: that way madness lies and, thankfully for the hobby, such collectors are not typical (Figure 2).

Figure 2. From the author's study, a shelf of GI Joe action marine and sailors

That said, Boxers do not like to contemplate the long-term fates of their meticulously organized GI Joe collections and from conversations online, the author gets the sense that of late, "less is more" for collectors. This became evident when in 2004 Hasbro introduced carefully made reproductions of the entire 1964 GI Joe line (at least 40 items by the author's count). Most collectors were so fatigued, out of space, or convinced by a sane spouse to only purchase a portion of these toys. A spokesman at Cotwold, a company selling vintage and reproduction 1/6 scale toys, recently noted in a phone conversation that he had "a semi truck" full of classic GI Joes coming in for sale, all from the estate of a deceased collector.

Closer to home, Soho and Midnight Angel have passed away since being interviewed for this article. Prices for vintage GI Joes fell heavily during the years following the end of the Housing Bubble of 2008. While this slump enabled some to complete their collections, the overall downturn signals the aging of the Sandbox's membership. Because toys of all sorts tend to be collected by those who played with them as children, toys provide an ephemeral instrument for investors. The author's personal experience, buying and reselling a few collections as well as a few classic cars, supports this commonly held belief about collectibles. Prices for many 1940s-50s cars and other older collectibles have likewise declined since 2008 and seem, to this collector, unlikely to rebound greatly.

As the Sandbox's Joes grayed, along with enthusiasts for other traditional hobbies such as model trains (Pristin, 2003), the Internet changed around them. Howard Rheingold (2001) notes how for the Old Internet, "norms of cooperation, information-sharing, netiquette [were] taught to newbies by the first generations of users. The celebrated 'anarchy' of the early days was possible only because of the near-universal adherence to largely unwritten rules." As fewer serious hobbyists bothered with USENET, the unmoderated format meant that old strategies for containing trolls failed. Threads continually went off-topic and none could tell the real identity of some purported Boxers. Earlier, that feature cut both ways; it facilitated the deeds of trolls and sock-puppets, but it protected collectors, if would-be burglars read the threads of discussion. Later, without as many Good Joes around, the USENET Sandbox became a ghost-town, and surviving on-topic threads were drowned in a tsunami of hard-core pornography, financial scams, and similar. The Old Internet was dead. As long-time Boxer "Mr. Scott" noted in a public posting in early 2013, "I check in every couple months. I've been over at The Trenches. Most everyone is there now. Its sad to see how the box has taken a turn. Hopefully one day it will be back again." That hope seems forlorn. Only four old-time members, including Mr. Scott, replied to a poster's "roll call." In the 90s or early 2000s, roll calls brought scores of replies. The Box's decline may well simply mirror the decline in the use of USENET, though as noted, the hobby itself has declined since the turn of the century.

In March of 2013, a Boxer posted "I know plenty of Joes that can handle this mission. Its not that difficult." That reference to Talking GI Joe's famous saying "I've got a tough assignment for you. Do you think you can handle it?" fell on deaf ears. Another Boxer advised the poster to join the Facebook Sandbox group.

By that point, the population had moved in two directions, to Facebook and a privately hosted forum, The Trenches. Both are tightly moderated and trolls such as The Hiker find themselves banned quickly. At the same time, Facebook lends itself to distraction, rather than a focus on Joe. It offers status updates for non-Boxer friends, links to other content, games to play. Unlike the USENET group, it is not a destination but rather a shop in a city of destinations. This author has found himself posting less there than in the old group, and very seldom at The Trenches, even though both forums permit easy sharing of photos, a feature the USENET group lacked.

The Facebook group posts information about Boxers using their real-life identities, and it is moderated by a long-time Boxer from the old group. The Trenches, also moderated, permits pseudonyms for its more than 1,100 members and includes hundreds of threads for different interests. It is also a thicket as impenetrable as any that imperiled The GI Joe Adventure Team. This may overwhelm newcomers, though a high-level thread asks new users to post an autobiography, and many users include their real names. At the much smaller Facebook group, navigating the single thread of conversation is simple business, much like the old Box. Yet it has far fewer members, about 200 as of August, 2013. An irony of the new Box is that I have recently asked for assistance locating a toy-buyer in my region for the 1000+ pieces in the collection of Midnight Angel, who died in 2012. As with the Old Sandbox, advice and condolences for me and the estate's executor were plentiful. Within a day, I had a toy-buyer from a trusted firm asking for more information and photos.

Other Boxers wanted to purchase some of the toys not for their value, but for the connection to a lost friend. In acts of karma, I also began again to give some of Midnight Angel's and my own collection away. It was a touching moment and it re-ignited my own interest in collecting. While my personal collection is gradually shrinking in size, my desire to remain active in the hobby grows again. On the Facebook Sandbox, I find myself helping those new to the hobby identify vintage items they have acquired and commenting kindly on their photographs. I've berated a few off-topic trolls and helped the moderator flag and delete their posts, something not possible with the Old Internet. Then, on the day this article went to the publisher, in a final act of karma on Midnight Angel's behalf I sent a reproduction GI Joe tank commander to Sherman. He had befriended Midnight Angel during his final illnesses.

I got a message at Facebook saying "You are a true Joe." The Sandbox and its small-town sense of community live on, on the New Internet, even as members age.

CONCLUSION

It is difficult to predict anything regarding the future of computing, but barring some fundamental interruption to the Internet, one trend should continue that both encourages older people to collect toys even as it discourages actual children from playing with them: the robust use of the Internet for entertainment and socializing. For hobbyists it has been a boon. If one needs to know, say, which GI Joe sets included the tragically comic "Bullet Proof Vest" then the answer is only a Google search away.

There is a downside to such ubiquitous computing. Nearly all of us, faculty and students alike, probably spend more time online than the theorists in computers and composition could have predicted in the 1990s. One canny prediction from that era remains Hawisher's and Selfe's (1993); we live in what they label as "prefigurative" times, when elders can no longer predict the shape or scope of technological change for the young. Inexpensive, high-speed connections in the home and fast wireless will only broaden the transformation underway. Entire businesses, from photo-finishing, music or video stores, book shops, to newspapers, have faced difficult times if not outright extinction. Toys are no longer those of the 1960s, even as the Internet provides the chance for community we collectors could never have envisioned half a century ago.

That mixed reality of decline and opportunity remains bittersweet for Boxers. Had it not been for the Sandbox, the hobby would not be the same. Values for old toys may never have soared without renewed interest by grown-up Boomer and Xer children. Some of us became opportunists. I do admit to a sin of sins when the market for old toys reached its peak: selling a number of valuable GI Joes in 1996 to make a down-payment on a house, an investment that, from that point in time, steadily accrued value despite the correction in home prices after 2008. At that point, along with the housing market, the values of most collectibles declined and this encouraged some companies to abandon the market for 1:6 scale military figures. Selling toys was not the only method for making money from them, however; Radiohead, Astronaut, and I write professionally, and we all have published pieces about toys. For nearly all Boxers, however, GI Joe remains less a source of income than a fairly expensive hobby. Many of us are professionals leading lives full of family and career responsibilities.

I sense--but cannot prove--that we toy collectors don't seem to have the confidence in the future that one finds in the old-car or record-collecting sets, where vinyl LPs and many vehicles such as 1960s muscle-cars have cross-generational appeal. Toy collectors, in my experience, want the same toys they had as children. It seems that only a handful of younger hobbyists join us to collect the traditional 12" tall Joes, and we collectors wish for more parents like Freefall, who plays with his children, "passing along the tradition of GI Joe because he meant something to me as a kid and to this day reflects a more unstructured form of play that I believe we have lost." His observation nicely squares with observations of how Millennials' childhood has changed, radically, not merely through the arrival of hand-held computing but also from the structuring of time by parents and the grooming for higher education from even the earliest years of childhood (Howe & Strauss, 2001).

That sense of a childhood altered, if not lost, may be an unspoken reason for the vitality of the Sandbox community. Many of us are in the 1970s demographic called "Generation Jones" whose salient emotion, sandwiched between affluent Boomers and cynical Xers, is a type of unsatis-

fied longing for what is lost (TJG, 2012). We have gathered like the neighborhood kids we once were, Jonesing for GI Joe, dragging footlockers of toys to the park in a time when children were permitted more unsupervised play. We bicker and make up, then band together when a bully appears. In time, as our virtual park became nearly empty, populated mostly by unwelcome strangers offering candy, the overgrown kids moved on. USENET, a relic of the free-for-all early years of the Internet, is probably doomed, a fate Astronaut claims "people have been predicting. . . since at least 1980." Now the numbers bear out the end of the Sandbox there, at least. As Otnes (2012) reports, the number of posts to the USENET Sandbox in June of 2012 were exactly 2, the same number as its first month, October 1995. That compares to a peak of more than 9,000 posts in a few months of late 1998 and early 1999:

Some fans likened the original Sandbox to the "Wild West;" a wide open, unregulated community with limited capabilities and no oversight. Today's more carefully moderated forums have more features and capabilities it's true, but they can also feel like a "gated community" at times, requiring passwords, moderator approval and other restrictions. Indeed, the raw honesty of the old, uncensored Sandbox posts may soon become a thing of the past. (Otnes, 2012)

For a fearless online adventurer with spare time, and perhaps a toy budget, the USENET Sandbox's two diaspora communities remains active, with hundreds of Good Joes happily playing online.

ADVENTURE TEAM IS NEEDED: FUTURE RESEARCH DIRECTIONS

As Rheingold (2001) notes, the Internet of the 1990s is long gone. With mass adoption of the technology, a casualty has been the mores that typified the era before Web browsing and social media emerged as dominant experiences for users. The Sandbox survived, in its multiple forms, but what of other once popular, even trend-setting, online communities? The Well, based in the Bay Area and broadly considered one of the Web's most influential early communities and was "the place where Howard Rheingold first coined the term 'virtual community'," (Well, 2013) was looking for a financial savior as recently as 2012, after owner Salon.com laid off the staff and put The Well up for sale. The community, which had once hosted writers like Bruce Sterling, Cory Doctorow, William Gibson, and Neal Stephenson, was having trouble (Au, 2012).

While The Well went on to survive, with $100+ for annual memberships and under new staff, but its near demise should suggest to researchers to study similar surviving communities while they can, gathering the sociolects of the group, charting their history, leadership, conflicts, and peculiarities. In this anthology, Hickey's essay does precisely that for Firedoglake, before that community underwent a seismic shift during the run-up to the 2008 US Presidential election.

Such historiography is critical as Old Internet cedes to its offspring. We may consider a homogenous Internet an impossibility, but again consider the "Cycle" that Wu (2011) charts for every single earlier telecommunications medium. After a period of openness and experimentation, once-revolutionary technologies of radio, telephony, television, and cable TV all became ossified under the control of a single company or a small circle of competitors. With the rise of Apple's, Google's, and Microsoft's ecosystems Wu's Cycle seems bound to occur again, with the amalgamation of much user-generated content onto sites like Facebook. That said, the sorting is far from over, and there's considerable academic value in studying the history of the anarchic time that preceded today's more uniform Internet, while the pioneers who built it and participated are still living.

As for the toys? Researchers may need to spend more time studying changing habits of play while they can. Traditional children's toys face a peril even the GI Joe Adventure Team could not easily overcome.

REFERENCES

AdvTeamMadman. (2013). *The sandbox glossary: A rosetta stone for joe-heads*. Retrieved from http://www.beegeeks.com/atmadman/joeglossary.html

Au, W. J. (2012, July 2). *Will the well survive?* [Web log post]. Retrieved from http://nwn.blogs.com/nwn/2012/07/will-the-well-survive-members-pledge-to-buy-from-salon.html

Barnes, J. (2001, February 10). Where did you go, Raggedy Ann? Toys in the age of electronics. *The New York Times*. Retrieved from http://www.nytimes.com

Barnes, S. (2000). Developing a concept of self in cyberspace communities. In S. B. Gibson, & O. O. Oviedo (Eds.), *The emerging cyberculture* (pp. 169–201). Cresskill, NJ: Hampton Press.

Boellstorff, T. (2008). *Coming of age in Second Life*. Princeton, NJ: Princeton University Press.

Dery, M. (1993). Flame wars. *The South Atlantic Quarterly*, *92*(4), 559–568.

Dibbell, J. (1993, December 21). A rape in cyberspace. *Village Voice*, pp. 36-42.

Elbow, P. (1977). *Writing without teachers*. Oxford, UK: Oxford University Press.

Hawisher, G., & Selfe, C. L. (Eds.). (1991). *Evolving perspectives on computers and composition studies: Questions for the 1990s*. Urbana, IL: National Council of Teachers of English.

Hawisher, G., & Selfe, C. L. (1993). Tradition and change in computer-supported writing environments: A call for action. In P. Kahaney (Ed.), *Theoretical and critical perspectives on teacher change* (pp. 155–186). Norwood, NJ: Ablex.

Hickey, D. J. (2014). Firedogs at the lake: Ties that bind until they don't. In D. J. Hickey, & J. Essid (Eds.), *Identity and leadership in virtual communities: Establishing credibility and influence*. Hershey, PA: IGI Global.

Howard, T. (1997). *A rhetoric of electronic communities*. Greenwich, CT: Ablex.

Howe, N., & Strauss, W. (2000). *Millennials rising: The next great generation*. New York, NY: Vintage.

Lave, J., & Wenger, E. (1991). *Situated learning: Legitimate peripheral participation*. Cambridge, UK: Cambridge University Press. doi:10.1017/CBO9780511815355

Markoff, J. (2005). *What the dormouse said: How the sixties counterculture shaped the personal computer industry*. New York, NY: Penguin.

Moran, C. (1995). We write, but do we read? *Computers and Composition, 8*(3), 51–61.

Mr. Scott. (2013, February 28). *Roll call for old time...* [Online newsgroup post]. Retrieved from http://groups.google.com/group/alt.toys.gi-joe

Otnes, M. (2012, July 26). *The sandbox is dead: Long live the sandbox! The Joe report*. [Web log post]. Retrieved from http://patchesofpride.wordpress.com/2012/06/26/the-sandbox-is-dead-long-live-the-sandbox/

Pristin, T. (2003, January 15). Graying, and playing with trains. *The New York Times*. Retrieved from http://www.nytimes.com/2003/01/15/nyregion/graying-playing-with-trains-2-midtown-hobby-shops-struggle-customers-dwindle.html

Rheingold, H. (2001). Look who's talking. *Wired, 7*(1).

TJG. (2012). *Generation jones*. Retrieved from http://www.generationjones.com/

Well. (n.d.). *About the well*. Retrieved from http://www.well.com/aboutwell.html

Wu, T. (2010). *The master switch*. New York, NY: Knopf.

Yancey, K. B. (2004). Made not only in words: Composition in a new key. *College Composition and Communication, 56*(2), 297–328. doi:10.2307/4140651

KEY TERMS AND DEFINITIONS

Flame: To engage in discussion that personally attacks others or tries to provoke hostility.

Flame War: The eruption of conflict online that is neither temperate nor reasoned.

Newsgroup: online forum, often but not always moderated, with a focal point such as a common interest that unites participants.

Sock Puppet: An alternate identity that a member of an online community will assume to espouse his or her views, often after the person in question has been banned or ostrasized by others in the group.

Troll: Individual who attempts to derail the normal flow of conversation online by posting deliberately outrageous messages or replies to others, often in the form of ad-hominem attacks.

APPENDIX: A SANDBOX GLOSSARY

This partial glossary preserves neologisms that capture the humor and creativity of Sandbox members. Simple abbreviations such as "AM" for Palitoy's Action Man (GI Joe's first cousin from the United Kingdom) are left out. Since all online communities of typists use such abbreviations, arising from expedience rather than creativity, listing them serves little purpose.

What follows may at first glance seem of scant academic value, yet over time such ephemera vanish and merit archiving. One wonders if the special language of Thomas Edison's youth, when we was a "telegraph boy" for the railway, has been preserved? Or a century later, when Palo Alto's computing circle called the Homebrew Computer Club, gathered in the 1970s, did anyone pause to record how they spoke?

Communities in constant contact bend language to suit their purposes. What starts as mere jargon and shorthand soon morphs into a type of sociolect. Communities of nerds of all sorts—*Star Trek* fans, old-car hobbyists, and similar—use language of the sort here to distinguish insider from outsider. In the Box, however, outsiders who showed respect for the community were soon initiated, in much the may Rheingold (2001) notes. Here is the "best of the Box," linguistically.

Action Hands: A replacement hand for vintage GI Joes produced by Cotswold Collectables. Designed as a replacement for the vintage Kung-Fu Grip hand (which often rotted and shed fingers) its appearance is somewhat different, and is usually not favored by collectors.

Babs: Barbie, or items from the line of Barbie dolls and accessories produced by Mattel.

Babyfeet, Babyfoot: Either early vintage GI Joes with smaller feet or a modern GI Joe variation having such feet.

'Bash, Bash: see Kitbash.

Blockhead: A 1990s-era GI Joe in 1/6 scale with a pronounced crewcut, wide-set eyes, and lantern jaw. The figure has an almost comically square head.

Box, The: The Sandbox newsgroup. Participants are often called Boxers or Sandboxers.

Club, The: Today's GI Joe collector's club.

Coffin Box: The tall, narrow cardboard boxes that held individual GI Joes in 1960s store displays. Also used for reproductions of these boxes.

Cots: Cotswold Collectibles, producer of reproduction GI Joe accessories, replacement parts, and their own line of figures known as The Elite Brigade. Cots played a significant role in keeping interest in 12" GI Joes alive during the drought between when Hasbro stopped making them in the 70s and their return to retail shelves in the 90s.

Crumbler: An older figure with plastic beginning to degenerate after exposure to UV light and the outgassing of plasticizers. Often the extremities of these Joes crack and crumble.

Custom: Usually items crafted individually by hand or in very short runs for display or sale. Can also be used for mass-produced items that have been extensively modified by hand.

DOB: Defenders of Bulletman, the often-maligned superhero figure produced by Hasbro as part of the Adventure Team. The group enjoys defending an underdog toy that is less collectible than much of the GI Joe line and does not fit well into the themes established by Hasbro's GI Joe line of the 1970s.

Ethnic: A toy industry term used to refer to a doll or action figure having non-white features or coloring, especially where this is offered as a variation in an otherwise identical figure or set. African American, Native American, Latino and Asian figures are all considered "ethnic." Usage might be, "I already had a 'Danger of the Depths' set with a white Joe, and so I was glad to find a stock-boy opening a case of ethnic figures."

Flipper Hands: A GI Joe hand variation featuring long, flattened hands.

Fuzzhead: A figure having "life-like" flocked hair, such as the GI Joe Adventure Team figures from the 70s.

Exclusive: A product or variation of a product sold only through particular retailers, clubs, conventions, Web-sites, or chains. Not available for general distribution.

Good Joe: A hobbyist of good character. One who has recently done you a favor or kindness, often earning a "Good Joe Report" on the Box.

Joe: Either our favorite toy, of any era, or a Joe-collector (also known as a *Joe-head*).

Karma: A metaphysical concept among Joe-heads. Karma is a gift to another collector. Collectors believe that "what goes around, comes around" and good deeds of that sort are repaid, often randomly. The verb is usually phrasal, to *karma bomb* someone is to spread karma around.

Kit Bash: A customized figure created by collectors from parts of various sets.

Knock-Off: A vintage-era piece of equipment closely resembling Hasbro's line but made by another company. Many knock-offs are good copies of the GI Joe line while others are terrible.

Lobster Claw: A GI Joe hand variation featuring large hands in a claw-like pose.

Mascara (or Eyeliner) Joe: Early-issue GI Joes with extra painting around the eyelids.

Nosepicker: The right hand of the many early and all 40th anniversary GI Joes, with fingers curled but thumb and forefinger extended. You'll know why we call them nosepickers the minute you see them (Figure 3).

Peg Warmer: See Shelf Warmer.

Photo-Story: A story or cartoon strip illustrated with photographs of action-figures, most often presented on a Web-page or blog.

PH: Painted-hair Joes, the original 1960s military line of Hasbro figures and the 1969 "Adventures of GI Joe" line. Refers to "pinhead" as well, after the tendency of some older Joes to develop a "pointed" head as the plastic ages.

Pink Aisle: The fashion-doll section of the toy department, or any item that might be found in that section. As in, "I couldn't find a panel van for GI Joe, so repainted a camper from the pink aisle."

Pinhead: See "PH."

Sigma Sux: GI Joe Sigma Six. A derisive term for this line of 8" Hasbro action figures which replaced 12" (and other) GI Joes on retail shelves in the first decade of the 21st century.

Shelf Dive: A fall, with comic or tragic results, in which Joes or other figures tumble off display cases all by themselves.

Shelf Warmer: A figure that stays on store shelves unsold, often because it is overpriced or unpopular.

Figure 3. Detail of nosepicker hand from author's GI Joe collection

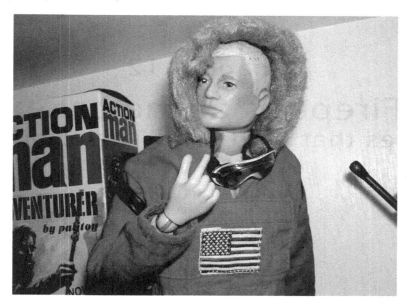

Spot in the Sand: One's place (usually respected) in the Sandbox. As in, "We'll keep your spot in the sand warm until you return from duty in Iraq."

Stress Crack: A particular kind of crack often found in vintage GI Joes, cause by stress where pins and posts are forced into the plastic limb.

Talker: Any Joe with a voice box.

Target Duke: A limited issue 1/6 figure that appeared in Target stores in 1991.

Vintage: Some debate exists over whether AT items from the 70s are truly "vintage." In general usage, however, "vintage" refers to any of the original series of Joes produced by Hasbro in the 1960s and 70s. Radiohead notes Vintage could mean "any toy more than five years old. Technically. . . the term is mostly useless."

WM, Wally's, Wally World: Wal-Mart.

Chapter 12
Firepups at the Lake:
Ties that Bind Until They Don't

Dona J. Hickey
University of Richmond, USA

ABSTRACT

This chapter examines how a social community was created and developed on a left-leaning political blog, Firedoglake; in particular, it explores how readers, as commenters, engaged each other, establishing credibility, or rhetorically speaking, acquiring and enhancing their ethos and attaining the status of a respected member of the blog's community. All excerpted threads include pseudonyms or screen names of users and all material from the designated blogs is, of course, in the public domain. In part 2, the chapter describes how the character of the blog itself, Firedoglake, changed over time as it grew to include an increasing number of front-page posters, became generally identified as hypercritical of the Obama administration, and became an umbrella site for smaller blogs under its banner. The discussion in both parts explores identity creation and the question of community in computer-mediated communication.

INTRODUCTION

My general purpose in this chapter is to explore the creation and development of social community within a blog expressly designed for political discourse. In selecting Firedoglake as the representative example, I examine how a blog

DOI: 10.4018/978-1-4666-5150-0.ch012

transforms itself over a period of five years based on its design, the interests and biases of its owner and host, and the readership that gathers there to form a community fostered not only by the site's owner, but by the readers themselves. Part 1 examines the ways readers develop ethos within the community and what ties form to bind interests and social connections. Part 2 examines how those same ties may fray, and for some otherwise regular participants, break. This section raises questions about the nature of computer-mediated community and identity in virtual spaces compared to that in our physical and face-to-face social lives. Let me begin by describing the history of the blog as it existed in the early years of its popularity.

Firedoglake (FDL), one word that combines the three pleasures of sitting by the fire with dogs at a lake, is a left-leaning political blog founded by Jane Hamsher, author and film producer. She and Christy Hardin Smith, former attorney, brought the blog into prominence during the Valerie Plame case (described below) when their reporting and analysis generated increasing numbers of readers and commenters, many of whom became regular visitors to the "Lake." These regulars formed a community based on their mutual political interests, first, but also a social community based on other life interests. Over time, as the community of commenters grew, Jane and Christy invited guests (some of them original commenters) to post "front pages," the main posts on the site to which people respond. The comments' section grew, of course, some posts eliciting more than 200 comments. Still, the addition of more "front pages" by guest posters helped reduce what had become extremely long threads, too long for most regular readers to scan before adding a comment of their own. Earlier in the life of FDL, readers were accustomed to following the whole post and the comments before wading into the water. After five years of observation, I can say that practice was, at least in the early years of my reading, expected and rewarded by readers.

As with all communities, real and virtual, people moved on, moved in, or moved back for occasional visits. Some became acquaintances or friends outside the blog. Some were inspired to create their own blogs, some to become more politically active, and many found at the lake not only a place to engage in conversation about national and local issues, but also about their personal lives as the political and the personal merged.

At the time I stepped off the shore to wade in the lake, my interest was political; I was fascinated by the Plame case and was following the story and analysis, beginning with the appointment of Patrick Fitzgerald to convene a grand jury investigation into who in the George W. Bush administration may have leaked the identity of CIA agent, Valerie Plame. While no one was indicted for a crime in connection with the leak, Scooter Libby, Chief of Staff of Vice President Dick Cheney was indicted on one count of obstruction of justice, one count of perjury, and three counts of making false statements to the grand jury and federal investigators on October 28, 2005. The federal trial, United States v. Libby began in January 2007 and ended in March 2007 with Libby's conviction on four of five counts listed above. (For the timeline on this investigation, please see the Washington Post summary at http://www.washingtonpost.com/wpdyn/content/custom/2007/03/06/CU2007030600916.html) As I closely followed Libby's case and the legal and political analysis at FDL, I also began following the community development at the blog, specifically, the rhetorical construction of the virtual community. The conversation there was not confined to the Plame case, but varied topically, as I previously noted, across national, local, and personal lines of interest, and it varied widely as the blog grew in popularity.

In analyzing the rhetorical construction, I relied on my own experience as a reader and occasional commenter, a rhetorician, and a literature professor. Having guided students who were learning how to engage their peers in asynchronous and synchronous conferencing as well as in class, person-to-person, I found useful the work being done by Albert Rouzie (2001) on serio-ludic play, by Neal Stephenson (2000) on the use of metaphor in maintaining virtual landscapes, and by Sherry Turkle (2011) on the attractions and complications of our relationship to computers; in particular, her explorations of identity creation and the complexity of community itself both on- and off-line. Their work, as well as that of a few others, has been incorporated into this chapter's exploration of community building and change.

PART 1: THE TIES THAT BIND (2005-07)

The first questions across my first two years of daily reading were: How do people become respected regulars in the comments section of posts, effectively creating a social community within a political blog? How do they acquire and enhance their ethos? While these questions have been addressed in numerous articles about listservs, blogs, and other on-line communities, it is valuable to address them again in a sustained exploration across time of particular community building and change at particular sites. At *Firedoglake,* as in *The Sandbox* discussed elsewhere in this collection (Essid, 2014), one sure way to acquire the status of a regular is to write substantive comments on the topic at hand, including links to relevant articles. When someone consistently moves the conversation forward with dependably solid points and supporting links to news or analytical articles, she or he acquires and gains ethos within the community. Once that status is attained, the commenter is defended and even given a pass on culpability if a conflict or misunderstanding ensues within a thread. Moreover, a reputation for substantive comments is exactly how some commenters became front-page posters over time. Nonetheless, not every welcomed newbie or familiar commenter acquires ethos or the status of a regular because she or he writes substantive comments or frequently offers supportive links from other news sources.

Some become regulars because of their ability to engage the personal, not the political, and acquire an identity as well as ethos, their on-line personalities emerging as comment after comment scrolls down the page. That emergence is possible, in part, because *Firedoglake* is a heavily moderated forum that excludes spam, trolls, and personal attacks directed at readers and posters. Certainly, there are heated disagreements at times, but In short, there's less interference in the field than in un-moderated, or only loosely moderated, blogs.

Inviting readers to step off the shore into the community of Firedoglake was accomplished in a number of ways: individual welcoming remarks from one regular commenter to a new one; an expression of appreciation for a helpful link or insight (both of which are illustrated in the excerpted thread below); and the creation of two popular weekly threads—the Saturday morning "Pull up a Chair" and the "Sunday Talking Heads," which highlighted the Sunday talk shows and was accompanied by a photo of a different bird each week, the photo itself eliciting comments. Another popular, occasional thread was, and currently, still is "Book Salon," which focuses on political books of interest to progressives and requires readers to stay on topic. The most casual, most discursive exchange of ideas and humor was predictably "Late Nite" and "Late, Late Nite" where off-topic is always on-topic.

Christy led the Saturday morning threads with the personal, as in this typical start: "Let's talk a bit this morning about building more ties that bind. I'm going to grab myself a muffin and a fresh cuppa coffee. Pull up a chair...." This is the "exhale," as Christy called it that followed a week of serious discussion, even if that discussion was occasionally lightened with humor. On Saturday morning threads, readers were invited to respond with talk of their lives, and the photo on Saturdays could be a cup of coffee, a favorite food, or a pretty landscape. It was not unusual for recipes to be shared, and in fact, Saturday morning threads were created, in part, to collect the recipes that showed up from time to time in other discussions. Favorite books and authors might also appear. Here is a snippet of one Saturday's exchange that begins with Christy's post, "Pull Up a Chair," on the morning of September 29, 2007:

September has seemed awfully long for a number of reasons. So, let's pause this morning for a little gratitude and a moment or two of exhale. Because, frankly, we have all earned it. What made you smile this week? Pull up a chair...

Jim C says: *I love Saturday mornings at the lake. This community gives me hope that my children may live in a better world. We have something precious here and I feel among family. Thanks Egregious for your welcome to all prospective firepups.*

Carmen says: *Crisp, white Cortland apples fresh from the farmer's market, fantastically shaped gourds, zinnias and sunflowers, gladiola. I love this time of year too. I'm grateful for Pull up a chair Saturdays, and all the great tips. My week was enriched by books recommended here: Eat, Pray, Love by Elizabeth Gilbert, Mountains beyond Mountains by Tracy Kidder and Notes from a Small Island by Bill Bryson, special thanks to those who recommended them.*

Later, Jim responds to her: *Carmen, I love Bill Bryson's works. Thanks for the tip passed along among the community. My best to you.*

The previous exchange illustrates the easiest way to get in the swim. Accept the invitation from the poster by offering a supporting point or illustration, and then a bit later, respond appreciatively to another commenter. A second way is to make a virtual splash as Suzanne does below, who then greets Mr. and Mrs. CTuttle with a hug (as indicated by enclosing their names with triple parentheses). The following takes place within the comments section of "Late Nite FDL: Unknown Soldiers" on the evening of August 22, 2007:

Suzanne enters the scene: *Boing reverse one and a half somersaults with three and a half twists, in the free position, no splash g'evening everyone (((mr and mrs ct)))*

CTuttle says in response to Suzanne: *Bon Soir, Ma Cheri!!! It's refreshing to see your graceful dive again!!! *g**

Later, Suzanne greets another familiar front-page poster and commenter, Trex: *you missed my dive, TRex, so I'm gonna do a do over boing reverse one and a half somersaults with three and a half twists, in the free position, no splash*

madmommy interjects: *After the heat today, I am looking forward to a nice cool dip in the lake. It sucks to be cutting the grass at 8 am and feeling as though you are knocking at the gates of Hell.*

althespook returns to Suzanne's dive: *The judges hold up their placards: 9.1 8.9 (Dayam Bulgarian!) 9.3 In the lead for the gold!*

Suzanne is a moderator who jumped into a thread now and again to urge courtesy, but who regularly announced her presence with a dive. Here is a good juncture to note the importance of maintaining the dominant metaphor of place. Maintaining the metaphor is a central concern for game designers and informs social media too. As Neal Stephenson says in *Snow Crash (2000)*,

You can't just materialize anywhere in the Metaverse, like Captain Kirk beaming down from on high. This would be confusing and irritating to the people around you. It would break the metaphor. Materializing out of nowhere (or vanishing back into Reality) is considered to be a private function best done in the confines of your own House (p. 36).

Regulars at *Firedoglake,* even if they engage in periodic references to life on the shore, don't break the dominant metaphor. They preserve the lake domain. As you can see in the previous exchange, Suzanne and CT greet each other, and she welcomes the arrival of TRex (a longtime regular who became a front-page poster, then left the lake for his own blog, a figurative tree house that elicited its own metaphorical sense of place, which commenters respectfully and playfully maintained). CT and others engage Suzanne by commenting on the dive. In another thread months later, the game continued between TRex and Suzanne. In the following exchange that takes place in the comments section of "Late Nite FDL: The Graduation Bell," November 27, 2007, she imagines standing on the prehistoric TRex's shoulders:

Suzanne says: *I'm working, on a dive from up here on the big guy's shoulder but these scales are amazingly comfy.*

Suzanne then performs the dive: **reverse two and a half somersaults with three and a half twists, in the free position, holding lit sparklers in each hand**

TRex responds: *Niiiiiiiice. Just climb back up once you've dried off. And bring me a popsicle from the freezer, would you?*

Suzanne answers: **snagging popcicle from freezer after drying off* dood, you gotta get an elevator - my fake knee can't do this up and down all nite.*

eCAHNomics compliments Suzanne: *I love the sparklers, but the dive is fantastic too. About 8 years ago the NY Pops performed Handel's Fireworks with fireworks accompaniment, for the first time since its original performance (or at least that's the myth they perpetrated). So my suggestion is that you start thinking about musical accompaniment for your dives. The imagination runs wild.*

The previous exchange is an interlude, a section of comments within a long thread. It illustrates the value of play within a virtual space, the recognition of regular visitors who are familiar with each other's virtual image and on-line personality, and a way into the conversation, whether by diving, observing, or altering the virtual space by enhancing the figures within it. The offering of food or drink (the popsicle, for example) was common during "Late Nite" or "Late, Late Nite" as another welcoming gesture and community builder, just as such an offering functions in our off-line lives. The value of play as goodwill cannot be underestimated, particularly in a discourse community that focuses on political conflict. *Serio-ludic* rhetoric, as coined and explored by Albert Rouzie (2001), is discourse in which the serious and playful can join purpose to mediate conflict and to provoke it. At *Firedoglake* and in other computer mediated communication, play with language and images demonstrates the rhetorical usefulness of combining the serious and playful, alternating, or in effect, mixing it up, either within a thread devoted to a serious issue or between threads where play can be a means of defusing a previous conflict in which tempers had flared.

For example, the following thread from the comments section of "Reviving Eugenics," August 22, 2007, illustrates conflict created by a troll (someone who enters the conversation to disrupt it) or by a commenter who's become peevish and in effect disrupts the conversation. Commenters, already engaged in responding to a new post, are alerted to trouble "downstairs" (blogging jargon that references a previous post where some are still engaged and have not departed to participate in the new post, "upstairs.") The metaphor, therefore, temporarily changes from water to land, from lake to shore:

wangdangdoodle says: *Ed, go to bed.*

LoudounLib says: *oh good lord...*

Fern responds to wangdangdoodle's command to Ed: *Uh huh. There is a point where tenacity ceases to be a virtue.*

Suzanne, speaking as a moderator, says to Ed: *Ed, you have been warned numerous times. Continued disregard will result in you not being permitted to comment - if that is what you are after, keep stepping o on my last nerve.*

madmommy says to wangdangdoodle: *Don't tell ed where we went. Things were getting a bit heated downstairs.*

Gnome de Plume says: *OK, you got me. Now I have to go downstairs and read what going on. Be back in a bit.*

althespook quotes, then greets a newcomer, Snarkassandra who's just come aboard: *Hiya everybody! Happy Wednesday. Hey Cassie. Watch out for a troll named "ed." He made a mess on the floor downstairs and wouldn't clean it up.*

Suzanne, the moderator, says: **gentle reminder* lets not flame other commenters - even trolls - we can certainly discuss the message and do so without attacking the messenger.*

wangdangdoodle quotes and responds to TRex, author of the current front page: "Guys, I'm running around like a crazy man here. I may not get to read most of your comments. I ended up spending way more time than I expected on this post and now I'm all behind here at work." 's OK Trex, we can entertain ourselves.:)

althespook quotes and responds to EvilDrPuma: *"Folks, I'm going to call it a night. Be excellent to each other." Night EDP. I'm afraid it was choppy with ugly winds in places at the lake tonight.*

And with althespook's goodnight, he returns to the dominant metaphor of the lake and its environs.

Two evenings later, within the comments section of "Late Nite FDL: What Could Possibly Go Wrong," August 24, 2007, the waters are again a little choppy, Suzanne comforts someone worried about counterfeit identity, someone offers to play a tune on the virtual jukebox through links to a favorite tune, and Suzanne dives back in to talk about moderating at the Lake. Beginning with the hypothetical question about someone using another's handle (screen name), someone has asked, "How would others know?" Another answers, "That's why the mods get the big bucks."

Suzanne says: *There's big bucks? No one told me (laughing) The Mod Squad is made up of a wonderful group of volunteers who donate their time to help keep the Lake the Lake.*

CTuttle, in response to TexBetsy who's quoted below, says: *"Good evening dear friends." Evening, Ma'am, the Lake a'roiling tonite, enter at your own risk...!!! *g**

Suzanne follows with a remark for Texbetsy: *I kept your spot at the lake placid for ya tex.*

Another arrival, burnspbesq, posts an invitation: *I've got a dollar in quarters and I'm headed over to the jukebox. Any requests?*

madmommy answers: *Something bouncy, mid-sixties, Motown.*

Suzanne returns to the issue of moderating threads: *Number of trolls - varies. Number of trolls that run away crying after dealing with moi: every friggin one of em - they didn't call me a bitch with a badge for nuttin. Modding at the Lake: priceless*

althespook says: *(a ghostly periscope emerges from the depths of the lake, scans the shoreline, and slips out of sight. A few moments later, Al Da Spook slithers ashore in his Ectoplasmic Wet Suit and hangs it on the live oak as he curls up by the campfire to toast marshmallows.) Evening all! (finally)*

wangdangdoodle returns the greeting: *Hi Alfred!!*

And so it goes metaphor-by-metaphor, virtual landscapes, virtual community, but real people are engaging each other in play and often in sympathy for each other. In the illustration below, the event described elicits not just sympathy for the commenter but for others who may share the commenter's feelings for a pet. In the following exchange on October 6, 2007 (the thread is no longer archived), LS responds to a question about her parakeet that recently died:

His "funeral" will be tomorrow with Mr. LS, who is on the road. We will plant him next to our "Rose of Sharon" tree, and place a stepping-stone that I made with beautiful tile on it over his resting place, so we can see it from our window. He was sooooo cute, and soooo funny..he loved music. In fact, his favorite music was the music that is played on Washingon Journal, as well as Janice [sic] Joplin and James Brown!! My husband is a lead guitar player, and Burt will be buried in his Fender T-shirt. He had absolute opinion about music. Since I found him, we deduced that he had lived with Spanish speaking people, because he went nuts about the language and music. Someone lost him, and we found him for a year and a half. He was a riot. He used to dive into a "Bustello" coffee can with coins and retrieve them and throw them out…when he wasn't doing music reviews, that is. A wonderful soul. I figure he's still here… where would he go? Maybe the Rainbow thing, I don't know. Who knows. I can't believe what a huge personality was in this creature with the brain the size of something smaller than a pea. Can't be what life is. It is something else.

Shortly after, Petrocelli responds: "You are one of the most intuitive people I know … that parakeet was blessed to have been in your presence!"

Then a few comments later, someone asks, "Any word on Christie's wiener dog?"

To which another responds, "See this morning's "Pull Up a Chair…" thread. But dog is doing OK after tooth surgery yesterday."

Over time, on a blog mostly devoted to political issues, there have been some excruciatingly sad exchanges about illness, death, legal troubles, and accidents in which people ask for sympathy from, you might say, virtual strangers, and yet, the responses are empathic and often helpful in practical advice from commenters who are in relevant professions—lawyers, doctors, psychologists, for example. Even in these cases, I've not noted anyone who gave advice without all the usual caveats regarding personal knowledge of a case. However, as I mentioned earlier, *Firedoglake* is a moderated blog, and therefore, readers are not subjected to openly hostile remarks or flaming. Even that being the case, I've often asked myself why people air their suffering or troubles to people most will never meet. And why, when the tenor is playful, would they choose to entertain virtual strangers instead of their real and near friends, acquaintances, and family? Explanations abound, and from my close reading of particular on-line communities, some people are housebound, some disabled, some lonely, or in a distant place, some

searching for like-minded others, and some love to write and reach a wider audience as most writers desire.

As much of the research on MOOs and MUDs shows, some people enjoy assuming a role or identity they don't, and perhaps can't, play in real life. They can be actors creating a new experience for themselves, playing a part in virtual space with fewer consequences than in their real lives. That experience, as a testing ground, may positively or negatively change their future behavior (off-and on-line) in ways that may be incalculable. The fiction they create on-line is also a way for writers to win applause, or at the least, free responses.

In the case of airing personal troubles or suffering on a blog, there are notable differences between conversations in literal rooms with friends or family and those that occur in cyberspace between strangers. The risks, in particular, are quite different. In *Alone Together* Sherry Turkle (2011) focuses on confessional sites in "True Confessions," but her point in this passage applies to any site where people talk about something deeply personal outside their usual boundaries and beyond their social bonds with trusted others in their lives:

Confessing to a friend might bring disapproval. But disapproval, while hard to take, can be part of an ongoing and sustaining relationship. It can mean that someone cares enough to consider your actions and talk to you about their feelings. And if a face-face confession meets criticism, we have some basis for evaluating its source. None of this happens in an online confession to strangers. One says one's piece, and the opinions of others come as a barrage of anonymous reactions. It's hard, say those who post, to pay attention only to the kind ones. (p. 231)

While regularly reading FDL, I did not find any intentionally unkind responses to those seeking sympathy or advice because, as previously explained, the blog is heavily moderated. However,

I bore witness to some expressions of emotional pain or confusion that made me wonder to what degree these public exchanges relieved or intensified a sense of helplessness in either the confessor or the responder. My focus, as I've said, was rhetorical. How do people gain ethos and credibility in a virtual community? And yet that very ethos and credibility can lead to misunderstanding about who we are when we are "alone together" in a virtual community of strangers. To what extent are people communicating truthfully? Turkle (2011) asks, "Am I watching a performance" (p. 240)? We can't know with the same level of perception that we acquire after spending extended time face-to-face and learning a person's history and interpersonal conflicts and challenges.

Social threads or off-topic commentary within a thread may permit, but do not invite, sustained confessional discourse of the kind Turkle (2011) describes in "True Confessions." Firedoglake and other blogs primarily devoted to national politics (and within that, cultural and social issues) do create space for building social community, such as recipes, pet rescue, music, books, movie, and open threads. Those threads are generally intended to defuse conflict and provide genial distraction from other political threads where disagreements can be intense, an objective I pointed out earlier in this chapter. When people are later engaged in argument, they may, because of the more playful and conflict-free conversations where they acquire a broader view of a particular screen personality, and be less inclined to fire off insults (*flame*) and derail a thread.

I want to return here to the idea of performance and why we might ask, as Turkle does, "Am I watching a performance?" Once commenters move away from supported opinion about events affecting our national discourse and toward social play or personal topics of interest, the notion of credibility, of truthfulness becomes more difficult to assess. Sometimes a commenter's status as a trusted regular at a blog has transference value when he or she enters a thread focused on a per-sonal or social topic. But the question remains to some extent. Blogs (originally called *Weblogs*) developed and grew in popularity from chat rooms and MUDs/MOOs (Herring, 2004) where writers need to create their identities and the space they inhabit through textual description.

The lack of visuals and sound sparks imaginative use of language. (We see that in some of the metaphorical play earlier in this chapter.) With the emergence of *Second Life*, identities are visual in that a writer has an avatar whose image and actions are virtual representations of the writer as he or she wishes that representation to be. T. Boellstroff (2008) says,

In most virtual worlds during the period of my research, certainly including Second Life, residents lavished time and money on their avatars. The goal was typically not just an attractive or unusual avatar, but multiple embodiments, often across gender, race, even species (for instance, a handsome man, a wolf, and a robot). (p. 129)

The incentive, therefore, for many, is to invent and reinvent themselves as they go from site to site or even within one.

Although not within the bounds of this chapter, it will be fascinating to observe how a community of avatars analogous to that of FDL and other sites, might operate, given that political candidates already build virtual headquarters and social spaces for their supporters in *Second Life*.

Whatever virtual worlds hold for political and personal discourse, blogs are likely to remain a popular medium for FDL's type of virtual community. Blogs are a place to author without publishers and without editors (apart from moderators in blogs where they exist), and in the best of blogs they require only that commenters respect their hosts as would be expected at any dinner party. The best posters and blog owners, as illustrated at *Firedoglake*, invite you to step off shore, wade into the conversation, and even if you can't dive, you can become a meaningful, welcome participant in an ever-changing flow. However, the ties that bind people to a virtual community can be strained in that every-changing flow just as in real life. In the previous section, I tried to demonstrate some of the ways community was built and maintained, and how people acquired standing in that community. I would like to move now from the "Ties that bind" to "Until they don't."

PART 2: UNTIL THEY DON'T (2007-08 AND THEREAFTER)

During the presidential primary season in which several candidates were competing for the nomination and election in 2008, FDL was a hive of information and opinion about whom to support and why. Supporters for one candidate or another tended to band together, and while disagreements were occasionally intense, people were joined in their desire for a Democratic win in November. The blog was bound by a common objective, and many people were actively working for one candidate or another. Then the primary candidates were down to two: Hillary Clinton and Barack Obama. Ties began to fray. When Jane Hamsher and a few other prominent voices known from earlier days of the Plame case were seen as clearly supporting Clinton and often disparaging Obama, some regular commenters began to disappear. No number of pet stories, gardening threads, late nite play, or music and recipe threads made a difference to those who felt they were diving into the lake at some risk. It seemed that the social community was only as inviting as the political climate that fostered it. Suffice it to say, the lake was choppy, the winds blew, and some boats headed for other ports.

After Barack Obama was elected in 2008, criticism of him grew at FDL while support for him solidified and grew at other designated Democratic blogs. Even though there was, and of course, still is, disagreement about policy, cabinet appointments, and presidential decision-making at other left-leaning sites, FDL became increasingly seen as hypercritical and reflexively anti-Obama by those hosting or frequenting more moderate Democratic blogs. What appeared to cement that opinion was FDL's founder, Jane Hamsher, appearing on Fox News to decry the Affordable Care Act (ACA or Obamacare) and engaging Grover Norquist (conservative libertarian) and members of the Tea Party in criticism of the President. Democratic moderates began referring to the FDL community as "firebaggers":

A term of derision used (usually on blogs) by supporters of U.S. President Barack Obama in arguments with people who criticize Obama and other Democrats from the political left. The term is a conflation of "Teabagger" the term of derision used to describe right wing Tea party activists and Firedoglake, a left-leaning political blogging community founded by Jane Hamsher. (http://www.urbandictionary.com/define. php?term=Firebagger)

Within the political blogging world, firebaggers and teabaggers, therefore, represent the extremes on either side of the left-to-right political spectrum.

From its rather humble beginnings during the Bush administration and its rise in popularity during the Plame investigation, FDL has developed into a large umbrella site with numerous authored posts hovering beneath its banner. It is, at this date, a different community: broad and narrow at the same time: broad, in the sense that FDL features several sub-blogs; and narrow in the sense that the comments are considerably fewer in number for any one poster than they were in 2005 when FDL featured only its co-founders and a bit later, several invited front-pagers. Given its new design and expansion, it's not surprising that relatively few posts garner the comments that the earlier smaller site did. Here is how FDL describes itself today:

Firedoglake.com (FDL) is a leading progressive news site, online community, and action organization consistently ranked as one of the most influential political Websites. FDL's work and contributors are frequently featured by CNN, MSNBC, FOX News, ABC, CBS, and countless print and online publications.

Our family of sites includes FDL News Desk, FDL Action, FDL Elections, Tbogg, La Figa, and The Dissenter. The FDL Book Salon is a weekly discussion with book authors on Saturdays and Sundays at 5pm EDT sponsored by the FDL Writers Foundation.

MyFDL is Firedoglake's community site, where anyone can sign up for a free account and start their own blog. Diaries or comments on MyFDL do not necessarily represent the views and opinions of, or the endorsement of, Firedoglake.

FDL is supported in part by the FDL Membership Association, a growing community of activists who shape the future of our work. Join Firedoglake's annual membership program today to support in-depth news analysis and hard-hitting activism. (http://firedoglake.com/about-firedoglake/)

As stated, FDL is a "community site," but that community has fundamentally changed. Currently, the staff and contributors comprise a long list with at least 10 (by my count) from the mid-2000's who were then commenters and later invited front-pagers, and among them, at least one invited moderator. Along with those familiar voices representing diverse social, educational, and professional backgrounds, are also familiar features such as book salon, late night, and movies. The fact remains, however, that many readers who frequented FDL during those early years, who were committed to the small community there and often made it their first stop of the day when traveling across blogs, found other sites more congenial to their political tastes. And yet,

while the perception of FDL as hypercritical of President Obama made its shores less welcoming for some, other readers and commenters dove in and found the water just fine. For those who left, there are multiple left-leaning political blogs where readers can also enjoy many of the same diversions from politics that FDL does: threads devoted to pet rescue, movies, music, books, gardening, recipes, etc.

In the case of community-building, some readers prefer a smaller space in which to share ideas, a place where the online identities of the common readership and posters become more quickly familiar, and where acquaintance with even the resident trolls makes it an easier environment to enter and to engage. At *Balloon* Juice, the host, John Cole, also includes a lexicon that introduces readers to many acronyms, inside jokes, and narratives known to front-page posters and longtime readers. It's a history of sorts, descriptive of the rhetorical environment, sometimes serious but mostly playful (http://www.balloon-juice.com). To my lights, however, the level of engagement at any blog, no matter how welcoming and helpful to new readers, should not be confused with that of person-to-person relationships. The understanding of, and commitment to, each other is decidedly different. Turkle (2011) offers a more nuanced view of online social connections:

Virtual places offer connection with uncertain claims to commitment. We don't count on cyberfriends to come by if we are ill, to celebrate our children's successes, or help us mourn the death of our parents. People know this, and yet the emotional charge on cyberspace is high. (p. 153)

In her note to this passage, Turkle (2011) admits that her statements

put me on a contested terrain of what constitutes support and shared celebration. I have interviewed people who say that flurries of virtual condolences and congratulations are sustaining; others say it just reminds them of how alone they are. And this in fact is my thesis: we are confused about when we are alone and when we are together. (p. 329)

To illustrate Turkle's points, let's view a recent set of exchanges at *Balloon Juice* after notification that a regular commenter, who had a high visibility over a period of years, had disappeared. Typically, he would announce his leave-taking and return. Because several commenters voiced their concern about his silent departure, the blog's host placed that concern at the top of another thread, and a long sequence of questions ensued. He was known only by his screen name, General Stuck, his real identity concealed. As comments and questions scrolled by, it became increasingly clear that we knew little to nothing about who he was off the screen. From that thread, Ted & Hellen respond to JPL:

Ted & Hellen says:

May 11, 2013 at 7:44 pm

@JPL: even though we are a community, when the comments stop, there is no way of telling what happened.

No. Actually, my child, Stuck's long absence and the total inability of anyone in this "community" to find out what happened to him or if he is ok, is a stark reminder that any online "community" is anything but. Few of us know who the others are IRL and the "connections" one feels are in the head and imagination only. http://www.balloon-juice.com/2013/05/11/gen-stuck-update/

And a month later, June 15th, another open thread includes the following from John Cole: "Speaking of, have we heard from General Stuck? He never responded to any of my emails." At comment #135, The Moar You Know writes:

To business: I fear the worst about Stuck. He was pretty involved here since before I found the place,

he wasn't the type to take time off from the place, and we know he was not in good health. I'm not one who will chase a guy down outside of the Internet – that's poor form and frequently when people vanish from the net it's because they don't want to be found, or are sick of somebody's shit – but I'd sure like to know what's happened to him regardless. Sure, he was a bit crazy and unreasonable sometimes, but then again, so am I. So are we all. http://www.balloon-juice.com/2013/06/15/blackhawks-v-bruins-open-thread/

And later, at comment #160 in the same thread, *dance around your bones* says

General Stuck was a fixture around here for so many years....he often said very insightful things and other times he got bit tedious. To have him just disappear is weird and, I suppose, in the nature of online 'relationships'. They can feel so intimate and yet ultimately so ephemeral.

Sigh – I hope he's ok, but I fear the worst.

The fears of *dance around your bones* were realized on July 13th in a thread hosted by John Cole who had confirmed the death through communication with Stuck's pastor who was found by a circuitous route of clues to Stuck's identity. There were 240 responses to "RIP, General Stuck." On the same date, Cole announced that his beloved cat, Tunch, considered the blog mascot and Cole's feline doppelganger by some readers, was killed by his sister's dog: "RIP, Tunch, the Best Cat Ever." In that post, Cole asked for donations to Miracle Animal Recue Center (MARC) in memory of his cat whose photos were sometimes used to head animal-rescue threads, but more often than not, to provide humor as well as relief from serious topics in the news. There were more than one thousand responses to this thread, and in response to the request for donation, 250 donations were made, totaling more than $7,750 with donations still arriving ("You Guys are the Best," July 14th).

A number of threads devoted to Tunch followed Cole's announcement of his loss, and those threads attracted hundreds of readers. On July 15th, *The Red Pen* says:

July 15, 2013 at 10:02 am

A kindhearted coworker spotted my wiping tears from my face this morning. I didn't read BJ all weekend because I couldn't bear to see the Trayvon discussions. He asked me what was wrong and I wanted to say:

I'm upset because a cat died. I don't really know the guy who owns the cat — in fact he's made some effort to keep his private life separate from the blog — and I never met the cat. Am I just experiencing self-pity projected onto conveniently amorphous entities, or am I experiencing some legitimate loss, having established some kind of tangible attachment to other sentient beings through a medium that exists only because of our mutual capacity for intentionality? Do I even have a right to feel such attachment to these entities without the consent implicit in traditional forms of social connection?

Instead I said, "I got bad news about the death of a friend." It seemed simpler.

These events and the responses to them put in sharp relief the question of community itself. What does it mean in an age of computer connectivity? We create identities that may or may not represent who we are in the physical spaces we inhabit, and our identities may shift from one site to another, whether it's the game world, Facebook (or other social Websites), or Second Life, for example. We wear many masks and interact differently with different people even person-to-person. Among our families, friends, neighbors, and professional relationships, our identities are multi-faceted. We conceal some parts of ourselves and reveal others, depending on the occasion, the audience, and the

subject. And we may not be fully aware, or aware at all, of what we are concealing and revealing as we wend our way across the Web represented by our avatars or by our physical selves in our complex social lives.

DIRECTIONS FOR FURTHER RESEARCH

It would be interesting to study further and compare the uses of dominant metaphors by ideological opposites as they affect not only political thought but also the invention and perception of individual identities as well as that of social communities on-line. One could expand upon George Lakoff's and Mark Johnson's studies on metaphors and how they structure our understanding of experience and our behavior. Beginning with the now classic *Metaphors We Live By* (1980) and beyond, one could apply Lakoff's later analyses of structural metaphor in political thought to on-line communities where the social community is affected by particular metaphors that serve as a priori truths or accepted assumptions. For example, The Tea Party began as a structural metaphor, one that evokes an older revolt against the power to tax by a distant and centralized authority and then maps that history onto current political conditions, shaping a generalized perception of those conditions. The slogan, "Don't tread on me" is one illustration of the inherently emotional and moral tone of political rhetoric.

CONCLUSION

What we can do, I believe, is learn some rhetorical strategies for engaging each other meaningfully in computer-mediated conversation on a topic of common interest: learning how to gain a hearing from participants and how to give a hearing to others. It's experience that can enrich our lives both on and off the screen. The play of identity on screen is not trivial if it increases our sense of who we are, alone or together and in our living rooms or in cyberspace. Expectations of meaningful communication and of self-knowledge rise and fall, but by the changing winds in our sails, we can be buffeted from shore to shore without learning anything about our relationship to computers and the multiple identities we create or meet online. Or we can steer and plot our course toward self-knowledge as we engage both worlds in healthy balance. A healthy balance between communities on- and off- line is what many of us must strive for as technology advances and further blurs our sense of what community is, and what we mean to each other when we meet face-to-face or avatar-to-avatar.

REFERENCES

Balloon Juice. (n.d.). Retrieved from http://www.balloon-juice.com/

Boellstroff, T. (2008). *Coming of age in Second Life*. Princeton, NJ: Princeton University Press.

Essid, J. (2014). Internet past tense: Trolls, sockpuppets, and good Joes in the sandbox newsgroup. In D. J. Hickey, & J. Essid (Eds.), *Identity and leadership in virtual communities: Establishing credibility and influence*. Hershey, PA: IGI Global.

Firedoglake. (n.d.). Retrieved from http://www.firedoglake.com

Herring, S. (2004). Slouching toward the ordinary: Current trends in computer-mediated communication. *New Media & Society*, *6*(1), 26–36. doi:10.1177/1461444804039906

Post, W. (2007). *Timeline: The criminal investigation*. Retrieved from http://www.washingtonpost.com/wpdyn/content/custom/2007/03/06/CU2007030600916.html

Rouzie, A. (2001). Conversation and carrying-on: play, conflict, and serio-ludic discourse in synchronous computer conferencing. *College Composition and Communication*, *53*(2), 251–299. doi:10.2307/359078

Stephenson, N. (2000). *Snow crash*. New York: Bantam Spectra.

Turkle, S. (2011). *Alone together*. New York: Basic Books.

Urban Dictionary. (n.d.). Retrieved from http://www.urbandictionary.com/

KEY TERMS AND DEFINITIONS

Firebaggers: A conflation of firedogs and teabaggers (derogatory name for members of the Tea Party, an extreme right-wing faction of the Republican Party). Firebaggers, coined in the political blogosphere, represents the extreme left. Together, both derogatory terms indicate the extremes in the left-to-right continuum.

MOOs: Multi-user, object-oriented domains.
MUDs: Multi-user domains.
Serio-Ludic Play: Mix of serious and playful discourse to provoke and mediate conflict.

Section 6
Digital Spaces that Influence Socio-Political Discourse

Chapter 13
Digital is Dead:
Techno–Seduction at the Colonial Difference, from Zapatismo to Occupy Wall Street

Santos Felipe Ramos
Independent Scholar, USA

ABSTRACT

This chapter draws from a 6-month participant-observation with an Occupy Wall Street group in Richmond, Virginia—Occupy Richmond—to deliver an ethnography of public discourse in postcolonial, queer, and multimedia contexts, as part of a critical analysis of imperialism in the digital age. The author develops techno-seduction as a term to deconstruct the lure of technological determinism that promotes static interpretations of democracy, participation, and the digital, in addition to considering how these interpretations impact intrapersonal and group identity formation. Finally, the chapter asks that we suspend our conception of the digital/non-digital dichotomy by thinking of the digital as dead, as a force that guides and influences our sociopolitical interactions, rather than as an isolated concept wholly separable from the non-digital.

INTRODUCTION

Gloria Anzaldúa's *Borderlands/La Frontera* was a seminal decolonial text that shifted the work of many scholars towards more truly interdisciplinary approaches aimed at addressing the evolution of colonialism. By blending poetry with autoethnography and historical analysis, Anzaldúa has shown that deconstructing the aesthetic writing standards of academic scholarship serves to challenge colonialism as much as does the content of writing itself. In a similar vein, this essay adopts an interdisciplinary approach in examining the function of digital technologies within recent

DOI: 10.4018/978-1-4666-5150-0.ch013

social movements, paying particular attention to the ways in which these movements construct a particular identity for *the digital*. The discussions that follow also assume that the colonial period never ended. "Colonial," then, does not refer to a clearly defined portion of history, but to the complex system of exploitation that has come to dominate economic, social, cultural, cognitive, spiritual, and even biological relations.

One of the primary ways we have constructed a collective understanding of *the digital* as a sphere of virtual existence is framed through the idea of the Digital Divide (DD), which separates human beings into digital and non-digital categories. It is essential that we treat the DD pragmatically by looking at the economic implications it exposes across a variety cultural contexts, but this essay first works to resituate our understanding of *the digital* by discussing the underlying assumptions at work within the construction of the DD (as an idea) itself. The focus of this chapter necessarily shifts, then, to examine the ways in which humanitarians, scholars, and activists come to adopt these questionable assumptions, and it presents an explication of how these assumptions have functioned within recent social movements—most specifically, among the Zapatista uprising in Mexico, as well as the Global Justice Movement (GJM) and Occupy Wall Street in the United States.

BACKGROUND

The concept of the DD was introduced in the late 20th century as a way of conceptualizing the separation between people with varying level of access to Information and Communication Technologies (ICTs)—usually based on their preexisting economic conditions—and the term was subsequently expanded to also take into consideration differences in race, gender, age, and literacy (Jackson, 2008; Norris, 2001; Pew, 2002; Ruecker, 2012). Despite these complications, much of the scholarship

addressing the DD falls short of utilizing a truly intersectional approach that would focus on the interdependency of various cultural, economic, and social dynamics at play within the DD. A "single-axis framework" typically scaffolds the work of scholars who address the DD—the tendency to treat race, gender, age, and literacy as mutually exclusive categories of experience and analysis. It is necessary for us "to examine how this tendency is perpetuated by a single-axis framework that is dominant in antidiscrimination law and that is also reflected in feminist theory and antiracist politics" (Crenshaw, 1989, p. 139). One pathway to constructing a more intersectional analysis is to decolonize the framework of digital technology that we have constructed through a lens of the DD.

Decolonizing digital technology does not presume a distinct opposition to the development or use of these technologies. Rather, such a decolonization effort challenges the assumption that bridging the DD is an adequate method for correcting vast economic inequality perpetuated by, and the cultural dominance of, White America. Borrowing from the work of contemporary decolonial scholars allows us to take developing terms and conceptual approaches—such as "coloniality" and "the colonial difference"—that are more commonly applied to social constructions of race, gender, age and literacy (Lugones, 2010; Mignolo, 2000; Quijano, 2000) and apply them to the emergence of *digital* as an identity category that also functions as a tactic of colonialism.

A single-axis framework is particularly prevalent within (the activism of, and scholarship concerning) recent social movements, perpetuated by the provocative nature of the infosphere that has led us to assume an inherent democratic quality about emergent digital technologies. Furthermore, it has become vital for us to reconsider standards we have set that determine what makes a technology "digital," and this essay looks to certain seemingly non-digital technologies within recent social movements to examine the ways in which they actually reify digital (or computational) technologies. Of particular interest is the people's microphone, which some scholars have examined as a postliterate device—a device situated within the electronic age, yet reminiscent of oral tradition (Garces, 2011; Ruby, 2012).

I ask that we suspend our conception of the *digital/non-digital* dichotomy by thinking of the digital as dead, as a force that guides and influences our sociopolitical interactions, rather than as a static structure separate from non-digital spaces. "Digital is dead" is not a literal statement as much as it is a method for reconsidering the relationship between individuals, social movements, the digital and death. Too often does the dominant Western approach to rationalism impose its empirical interpretation of death and the dead upon us, seducing us into superficial relationships with our dead that erase histories of resistance to colonial-capitalist conquest. We need only look to some of the ways in which certain other cultures relate to their dead in order to further expose this superficiality: "Here in the highlands of the Mexican Southeast, our dead ones are alive. Our dead ones who live in the mountains know many things. Their death talked to us and we listened" (qtd. in Mignolo, 2002, p. 253). Highlighted here is a unidirectional flow of knowledge between the indigenous Maya of southeastern Mexico, alive and dead. It suggests that the Maya do not simply interpret their dead, but that they are also engaged in a full dialogue, which includes an aspect *listening* to the dead. The dead are alive, and the alive must die in order to be reborn. This understanding disrupts the alive/dead dichotomy and treats the categories more as fluid descriptors than as static states of being, and it prepares us to reapproach some of our most basic assumptions about that which constitutes the digital realm or digital subjects.

THE COLONIALITY OF THE DIGITAL (DIVIDE)

"The Digital Divide" (DD) is a commonly used term to refer to the separation between civilized and uncivilized human beings in the electronic age. On one side of the DD, civilized humans have access to Information and Communication Technologies (ICTs). On the other side of the DD, uncivilized humans have comparatively less (or no) access to ICTs. In this context, there is also a distinction between civilized and uncivilized technologies. Speech and written language, for example, are not typically considered to be ICTs unless they are filtered through a more civilized technology—a computer, a cellphone, etc. Many humanitarians have tasked themselves with bridging the DD in order to civilize the uncivilized. From this perspective, those on the uncivilized side of the DD must be made to integrate ICTs into their communities if they are to adapt to the increasingly digitized world. They must digitize. They must become digital.

These are necessary criticisms to make of the DD, for it is imperative that we challenge colonial mentalities many of us have adopted amidst our widespread disposition to continue digitizing the entire world. This is not to dismiss the importance of charitable work that seeks build wider access to ICTs throughout marginalized communities. The concrete world we live in does not bend to appease academic theory, so access becomes concretized as a necessary tool for marginalized communities to survive while the spread of digitization is compounded into a global crisis. I do not reject the expansion of technologies outright. There is no inherent malice within these technologies, and the gap constructed by our conceptualization of the DD certainly points to some devastating effects of digital globalization that deserve our attention. Some scholars have complicated the issue by building *a multifaceted definition of the digital divide that considers not only type of access but the way individuals have developed technological literacy through self-sponsorship or sponsorship by another figure, such as a teacher, in a way that enables them to more effectively contribute to societal discourses (Ruecker, 2010, p. 241).*

Work of this nature serves an important purpose. Applying static, two-dimensional definitions of the DD is an oversimplification of a highly complex subject. ICTs are accessed in a variety of ways, and we bring a diversity of accesses and varying degrees of relevant experience and knowledge to them. It is important to understand the particular ways in which certain aspects of access to ICTs are being accepted or rejected by people across different cultural, economic, and social contexts, because for many people, accessing ICTs and developing appropriate technological literacies is a simply matter of survival. What I make suspect in this discussion is not the practical economics of the DD, but rather the underlying assumptions that drive our pursuit to bridge the DD, the assumption that further digitizing the world will lead to a more equal distribution of wealth and greater contributions to societal discourse. I will continue by arguing that, in certain ways, *digital* functions as an identity category of colonial-capitalism, and that the framework of the DD actually serves to increase economic and cultural exploitation, not to bridge it.

Gian Maria Greco and Luciano Floridi warn of the danger in conceptualizing the infosphere as an infinite space that expands without consequence. They suggest that the infosphere might actually be more comparable to the biosphere in that it is "a bounded environment, whose resources are exhaustible, that is, finite, not immediately renewable and not totally salient" (Greco, 2004, p. 74). While they draw conceptual connections between the biosphere and the inforsphere, Greco and Floridi do not address pragmatic implications for the biosphere when the infosphere is expanded,

so let us note that expansion of the infosphere is made possible only through continued exploitation of the biosphere; further expansion of the infosphere ultimately threatens the sustainability of our relationships with the biosphere.

Considering the relationship between these two spheres is essential, yet simultaneously questioning how this might also function as a reification of coloniality is also of great importance. The biosphere and the infosphere must not be seen as wholly separate ecologies—digital and non-digital—but as two spheres existing within the same network of life, communication, and environment. Without the resources given to us by the biosphere, the infosphere would not be possible, and an expansion of the infosphere certainly impacts the harmony of the biosphere. Greco and Floridi argue that we should be careful in bridging the DD because such an expansion of the infosphere might result in unforeseeable consequences (not to the biosphere, but to the infosphere itself). With this idea in mind, they come close to suggesting that we should withhold access from marginalized communities to ICTs—because an expansion of the infosphere might be destructive to the infosphere. Taken to the extreme, this mentality results in a sort of environmental reductionism whereby environmental issues are prioritized over other humanitarian issues. What we need is not a hierarchy of more prominent and less prominent issues, but a complex understanding of the interconnectedness and interdependency between humans and our multiple environments, the biosphere and the infosphere, the digital and the non-digital—an understanding that avoids these dichotomies by refusing to separate them into completely distinct categories.

Attempting to wholly separate the digital from the non-digital creates a complex Web of problems. This separation creates incentives for us to adopt a technological determinism that assumes digitizing the entire world is an essential step in combating economic inequality. Within this framework, it has been common for scholars to assume that the major humanitarian task of the electronic age should be to digitize—that is, rapidly impose Internet access and computational hardware upon—marginalized communities who have been slower in gaining access to ICTs, without much consideration of how these changes should be adapted differently into different contexts, based on the nuances of local economies and cultures. This adaptation could broadly be seen as a matter of access, but should also be localized and complicated enough to consider the varying types of access and the ways in which people use their access. Furthermore, discussions of access to ICTs are important in dealing with some of the practical implications of digital colonialism; however, in a structural sense, I see few unprecedented elements with the DD in comparison to socioeconomic and technological contexts historically prior to the DD.

Some aspects of digital colonialism are different from what we have previously called colonialism, imperialism, capitalism, or Empire.[1] However, these similarities are still recognizably "colonial" in a somewhat traditional understanding of the term, and I am not convinced that we have entered into an altogether unprecedented phase of struggle with the digital. While it has transformed, colonialism has not left us.

We need a much more complex understanding of the digital. We should treat the digital not only as an indication of technological development, or simply as a pathway into a particular conceptual sphere of existence (the infosphere), but also as a socially constructed category that manipulates interpersonal and intrapersonal negotiations of cultural identity. As an identity category, digital functions similarly to other socially constructed, colonial identity categories as well. Maria Lugones, for example, has addressed the coloniality of gender as a method of colonialism that dehumanizes people into normative gender categories. She extends Anibal Quijano's use of "coloniality" as a way

to name not just a classification of people in terms of the coloniality of power and gender, but also the process of active reduction of people, the dehumanization that fits them for the classification, the process of subjectification, the attempt to turn the colonized into less than human beings (Lugones, 2010, p. 745).

This is not a linear process by which people are first conditioned and next classified as a particular gender. Dehumanization occurs as categorization emerges, and the continuous interplay, interdependency, and transformation between/of dehumanization and categorization is what I am here calling "coloniality." Whereas gender normativity presents us with two specific boxes in which we can exist—male or female—digital provides a similar framework. The emergence of "digital" as an identity category simultaneously creates "non-digital" as an identity category, dehumanizing while simultaneously categorizing people as digital or non-digital. As with gender, these dual categories are not actually static. People can present as male, female, gender-nonconforming and more, regardless of their sex. And how people present and/or identify in terms of gender can change from day-to-day, even situation-by-situation.

If we think of *being digital* as broadly having access to ICTs, and as having met whatever standards we set for one to have achieved "technological literacy," the line between digital and non-digital also becomes blurry. There is the systemic categorization of people into specific categories, but there are also the varying degrees of differences between communities and individuals in relation to the digital as well. In attempting to bridge the DD, we essentially work to "civilize" marginalized communities—those on the other side of that bridge, the non-digital—who are dehumanized by the framework of the DD. For Lugones, the imposition of gender normativity indicates that *[t]he civilizing transformation justified the colonization of memory, and thus of people's senses of self, of intersubjective relation, of their relation to the spirit world, to land, to the very fabric of their conception of relation, identity, and social, ecological, and cosmological organization (Lugones, 2010, p. 745).*

Likewise, the civilizing transformation brought about by digitization justifies colonization by way of the DD. The digital permeates not only our methods of communication, but also the formation of our own communal and intrapersonal identities; it disrupts our most basic understandings about what it means to be human. Therefore, we must re-assess (in both concrete and abstract ways) our understanding of the digital and the human, of life and death.

Capitalism is antithetical to life. Digital is dead because it presents an advanced phase of capitalism, a life-denying sphere of non-existence wherein human beings and computers become fully integrated. Digital is also death: the process of dehumanizing human beings, the breaking down of humans to be fit for digitization, and the digitization (re-making) of human beings into the digital. The digital integrates itself into the human in order to proliferate, colonizing physical, cognitive, and spiritual aspects of the human in order to more fully prepare humans to project capitalism deeper into the future, into a more a globally homogenized consciousness with exponentially countless centers of power—the emergence of a globally networked society. The digital-human exists as an abrasively rounded-off approximation of itself. As French philosopher Jean Baudrillard wrote explained, "simulation is no longer that of a territory, a referential being or a substance. It is the generation by models of a real without origin or reality: a hyperreal" (1981). Understandings of what it means to be human have always been approximations, but digitization presents standardized approximations instead of a diversity of fluid and transforming approximations. The origin of the human is lost within the full integration of the human

with the digital, within the hyperreal. The imposition of these approximations, coupled with assumptions that privilege global digitization, is what I understand to be the coloniality of the digital (divide).

THE DIGITAL COLONIAL DIFFERENCE

If the coloniality of the digital (divide) is a conception of the ways in which colonization works within the electronic age toward the perpetuation of colonial-capitalism, then the digital colonial difference is a framework I propose to counteract these constructions. I have asked us to think of *the digital* as dead in order to sidestep the dichotomous framework manifesting as the DD, but again, this is not to suggest that the digital is inconsequential or non-existent. Quite the contrary, I find it appropriate to think of the digital as dead because of its posthuman qualities, its ability to work both within and outside of human control. The digital is consequential in a concrete sense, yet so much about what it is, what it does, and the impact it is capable of having upon cultures that adopt it without question, is still largely unknown to us. Accordingly, we must fashion new ways of thinking about the digital if we are to demystify its character.

I borrow "the colonial difference" from Walter Mignolo, who develops the term in *Local Histories/Global Designs* by describing it as "the space where coloniality of power is enacted" (2000, p. ix). Maria Lugones notes that Mingolo's use of the colonial difference necessarily evades static definition, and like her, my discussion does not attempt to lock down a static definition of Mignolo's term. Instead, my discussion is guided by the multidimensional and shifting usages Mignolo extracts from the idea of the colonial difference. I argue that the colonial difference is an effective space in which to deconstruct digital colonialism precisely because it is the space in which the coloniality of the digital (divide) is enacted.

Therefore, I propose that we look at the digitization of the world through a lens of the Digital Colonial Difference by considering the ways in which the coloniality of the digital (divide) is enacted—that is, the ways in which we come to submit ourselves to the assumption that the digital is an inherently liberating or democratizing force. In what follows, I will look to recent social movements in order to provide a comparative examination of how this technological determinist assumption influences political organization, societal discourse, and identity formation.

TECHNO-SEDUCTION AT THE DIGITAL COLONIAL DIFFERENCE

As a group that has been simultaneously dependent on indigenous Maya culture and the technologies of globalization, the Zapatistas are often credited for leading the world's first postmodern revolution. Emerging in 1994, they were able to utilize the Internet in gaining support from leftist sympathizers around the world, and global awareness of Zapatismo continues to be an obstacle for a hostile Mexican government that has otherwise been clear about its inclination to level the uprising completely (though it should also be noted that they still face frequent harassment and violence from both state and paramilitary forces). Some have labeled the Zapatistas as "cyber-guerillas," implying a greater reliance on ICTs than is probably accurate. As their spokesman (Subcomandante Marcos) has humorously explained, the ICTS they used in the early days of the rebellion to transmit communiqués from the mountains in southeastern Mexico were far from advanced:

a processor that was so fast that you could turn it on, go make coffee, come back, and you could still reheat the coffee, 7x7 times, before you could start to write...In the mountains to get it to work, we used a converter attached to a car battery. (qtd. in Esch, 2013)

But while the Zapatistas may have had limited access to highly sophisticated ICTs, word of their rebellion and philosophy have been able to spread across the world largely because it has been extracted and transmitted by outsiders: "Compas arrived who knew something about computers, and soon they started other Webpages, and we got to the way things are now, that is, with this damned server that doesn't work like it should" (qtd. in Esch, 2013).

The Zapatistas' existence as a "contradiction" within the electronic age has been a matter of survival. Their success has been the result of conscious choices about how (and when) to integrate emergent technologies into their organizational framework, an ability to deflect the technological seduction of globalization that functions somewhat like a preacher of advanced capitalism. This preacher promises us the world, seduces us with an abstract utopian vision of a globalized democracy that he says can only be realized through an adoption of the technology he intends to give us. He plays to our pathos and elicits an anti-critical, emo-spiritual commitment from us to technologies we think will deliver us from political marginalization. (Note the irony of "democracy" emerging from something extrinsic to the human subject.) He does not tell us, however, that they are designed to exponentially accelerate the speed of our world—the speed of our *selves*, even—and that in our struggle to keep pace with his technology we may be compromising our autonomy in clandestine ways. This is the new ecology: "an environment that increasingly dominates the space and times that individuals and societies live within...through streams of binary information that flow at an ever-accelerating rate through the Internet...through the networked totality that comprises the network society" (Hassan, 2009, p. 123).

Or the preacher tells us this acceleration is a good thing, that we move faster towards democracy because of it. So we project ourselves into the current of his technology. We let it carry us forward, forgetting where we come from, and assuming we control the course. We hope this technological current is the game-changer that will finally level the playing field between us and the corporatists. As well-intentioned people, we cling to the most easily identifiable manifestations of our new digital democracy—the tweets that saved the lives of many Iranian protesters, the YouTube videos that ignited the citizen occupation of Tahrir Square, the female bloggers who drew attention to the Serbian reprisals against Muslim citizens in Bosnia. Techo-seduction imbibes us with a thrill of social unrest that would have us believe it is safer to commit ourselves to this technological current than to organize outside of it.

To be sure, there are many positive examples of how digital technology can be harnessed to aid in the organization of dissent. But what does an increasing dependence upon these technologies do to the *infrastructure* of dissent? How often do we even see this question being raised? Over the past 500 years we have seen the colonization of lands, minds, and bodies to a horrifying extent, with virtually every resource in the world succumbing to the process of colonization in one way and/or another. So how do we justify the consolidation of our dissident infrastructures into the digital, as though this somehow makes them impervious to colonial-capitalist control? It would seem that such consolidation, despite any new and provocative transformations that emerge from it as a result, makes us infinitely more vulnerable to domination by homogenizing our tactical and strategic diversity. A cultivation of these diversities should be primary to the philosophy of dissent, if we are to sidestep digital homogenization and to challenge the acceleration of digitization under which "[s]ociety, in a word, becomes the loyal servant of the *technocosme* and of its techno-temporality" (Chesneaux, 2000, p. 408).

We might look to the Amish as an example of how to deflect techno-temporality, or the hasty integration of technology into our social, economic, and biological structures. The Amish have been able to retain much of their culture and remain relatively autonomous from mainstream society by developing sophisticated methods for assessing technologies *before* adopting them. If we made more of a conscious effort to develop our own methods of assessment, then spreading infrastructure across both digital and non-digital realms would be an attainable goal, and this would allow us to dismantle oppressive systems and build alternatives to replace them with. It is not pointed out often enough that, perhaps, the digital is not as dependable or sustainable as it is often made out to be, for if the infosphere is dependent upon the finite resources of the biosphere, we know that the infosphere itself is also finite. The sexiness of emergent technological development centralizes our livelihood while making us think it does the opposite. The global shift towards digitization is itself evidence of the vulnerability we adopt when we invest in this singular current of communicative organization.

This is *techno-seduction*—the absorption of resistance into empire, the grand illusion of participation and decentralization, and the shallow comfort of a masked impermanence. We allow ourselves to be seduced because seduction itself feels like participation. We see people willing to pull themselves away from their computer screens and occupy their local town square in demanding, more than anything, a role in deciding the trajectory of their own lives. It is exciting, inspiring, and misleading, for we often have little to *pro*-pose amidst our disposition to *op*-pose. Occupy Wall Street was right in attempting to function as its own demand, but it did not have a leg to stand on in delivering tangible alternatives to corporatist governments. What infrastructure did OWS have to fall back on when its encampments were wiped out? What purpose did it serve outside of its physical occupation of visible public space? The vast majority of OWS groups dissipated after they were no longer able to sustain visible occupations, and the absence of a systematic set of demands shows further that the Occupy moment—the tactic of occupation—preceded any real plan or strategy geared towards dismantling capitalism. To borrow once more from Baudrillard, "the territory no longer precedes the map, nor survives it. Henceforth, it is the map that precedes the territory" (1981).

So, of what use is the speediness of new technologies if they're only going to accelerate us into situations we are not equipped to handle? If our technology will henceforth precede our physical reality, or our own cognition? We are sold on a hollow efficiency that leaves little room (or time) to build organizational infrastructures that include but are not limited to the digital. It is important to side-step extreme technological determinism in any direction, yet we cannot deny that dissidents have had trouble keeping pace with the impact of these new technologies—on both conceptual and practical levels. In nearly all of the examples touched on here, technology can be seen as a deterrent from sustainable infrastructure. We pursue revolution in hopes of supplanting corrupt leaders, but more work needs to be done to simultaneously build alternative systems of organization. The rapidity that technology tends to impose upon us forces us into a cycle between corruption and revolution—"failed" and "successful." Corruption is replaced only with new forms of corruption, because our "revolutions" are not structural.

To be clear, this is not about rejecting technology outright. It is about reworking traditional interpretations of what constitutes *a technology*, remembering that it is not confined to the digital, and entertaining an understanding of technology as a self-organizing life form that is impacted by, but not wholly at the disposal of, human control. Furthermore, this chapter only begins to address one of many complex threads aimed at deflecting the colonial lure of what I call *techno-seduction*. I am indebted to the work of many post-colonial, queer, and post-humanist thinkers who have already begun to provoke further discussion on how to build a more critical analysis of imperialism in the digital age—Jose Muñoz, for example,

who sees "[q]ueerness's ecstatic and horizontal temporality" as "a path and a movement to a great openness to the world" (2009, p. 25). I am also indebted to the work of many activists who have already begun to mold these theories into everyday practice. I contend that it is vital for the struggle against colonial-capitalism to task itself with further deconstructing imperial temporality—a technology of colonial-capitalist time—and I shift my focus to processes of consensus because they are designed to do precisely this (though to varying degrees and with varying levels of success). The slow-moving nature of the Zapatista consensus model should be interpreted as an invaluable filtration system in making sober decisions about when it is best to integrate traditional and emergent technologies, as well as an example of how this process can be used to build more sustainable infrastructures of dissent. This filtration system was mimicked by OWS, but any lasting impact it may have had on the way we organize communities has been minimal. Occupiers were fully engaged in a conflict between their sluggish consensus model and their extreme dependence on media coverage. Moving forward, I will provide further historical background necessary to contextualizing later discussions more specifically focused on consensus processes themselves.

FROM ZAPATISMO TO OCCUPY: PROLIFERATIONS OF CONSENSUS AND NETWAR

In 1996, a study was published through RAND Arroyo Center's Strategy and Doctrine Program in response to the Zapatista uprising, *The Zapatista Social Netwar in Mexico*. The book attempts to build an understanding of the nature of conflict in the information age by developing the concept of *netwar*, which it defines as "an emerging mode of conflict (and crime) at societal levels, involving measures short of traditional war, in which the protagonists use network forms of organization and related doctrines, strategies, and technologies attuned to the information age" (Ronfeldt, 1998, p. 9). These "network forms of organization" refer to groups with decentralized organizational infrastructures that depend on digital technologies to spread information across their networks. It is not my intention to spend too much time disputing the specifics of this particular study. I read it as a *how-to guide* for governments to squash not only leftist rebellions, but any informal group of people attempting to organize in a way that might threaten the reputation of the state, even when these groups are adamantly non-violent. I present this scenario, rather, in order to contextualize a transnational conflict between interpretations of hierarchy and horizontalism, approaching the conflict through a framework of technological innovation and tradition. I further situate this struggle as one pitted against the seduction of technology by examining specific transliterate devices as they relate to the (de)centralization of power. A key vantage point in this exploration comes through an examination of the consensus process, which has gained much traction among left-leaning organizers over the past three decades, from Zapatismo to Occupy Wall Street (OWS).

Many comparisons have been drawn between the Zapatistas and OWS, primarily because both groups use consensus-based models of decision-making. Zapatismo has had a direct impact on Occupy in many ways, and while it is debatable as to whether or not Occupiers have been generally cognizant of this historical stream, there is a clear line that can be traced between the two. The Zapatistas were initially very intentional about inviting supporters from around the world into their communities, so organizers within the US Global Justice Movement (GJM) quickly came to be influenced by the conflict in Mexico by engaging it directly, as caravans traveled regularly to Chiapas in building global solidarity for the struggle against capitalism. At the same time, experiences in Mexico helped some organizers come to understand the importance of focusing

more of their efforts on the local communities from which they were coming. As Los Angeles-based organizer Eddie Torres[2] explains it, "We wanted to learn everything we could from them but at a certain point…I think in 2001, the leadership of the EZLN said to us…'We don't need solidarity… you need to do your own organizing where you are'" (Zugman, p. 331).

It would not be far-fetched to cite the surfacing of Zapatismo as a starting point for the GJM itself, but it is unclear how widespread the specific influence of locality was to GJM organizers within the US. In *Direct Action: An Ethnography*, anthropologist David Graeber provides an expansive study of several GJM anarchist groups, depicting their struggle in bringing local contexts to the forefront of their agendas. This depiction is in line with a popular criticism of the GJM as "summit hoppers" who tended to follow around powerful politicians and corporate leaders to protest their globally-focused negotiations, yet neglected work that needed to be done in their own communities. Finally, the GJM has also been criticized as being an extremely white phenomenon. A notable explanation for this is offered in an article published by *Colorlines* (2000), in which Elizabeth Betita Martínez points out that many organizers of color chose not to participate in the Battle in Seattle because they thought it more important to focus time and resources on the communities of color in which they lived.

Despite the efforts of the GJM and other currents of sociopolitical organization, it has been common for scholars to point out a "dead zone" of political activity around this time period. This point attempts to nullify the work of many organizers who continually organized in the undercurrents of mainstream political consciousness in the decades between the civil rights movement and the emergence of OWS—those who did not necessarily locate their work as a sect of the GJM first and foremost, but who continued to organize regardless. I do find it fair to mention a dead zone of *popular* activism during this period, where dissent from the US political system seems to have been less than trendy. And perhaps this explains the widespread excitement for OWS when it began to mobilize. Many organizers who came out of the GJM were among the first to begin working for and with OWS. So after several years of a waning GJM, activists in the US were quick to be inspired by uprisings across Europe and the Middle East that began early in the second decade of the 21st century.

Occupy exploded onto the scene in the late summer of 2011. In seeming contrast to the summit hopping associated with the GJM, Occupy attempted to localize its approach by encouraging cities and towns to organize their own version of the original encampment in New York City. By fall of the same year, somewhere around 1,500 encampments had established themselves around the world, though to varying degrees and predominantly within the US. Organizers of the first encampment had planned for months before their occupation began, but most of the encampments that followed were thrown together in a matter of weeks, or even days. The expediency with which OWS arose at first seemed to be a key vantage point, but a lack of infrastructure—any sort of strategy, sustained tactical analysis, community development, or overarching plan—was quickly exposed. Police began cracking down to wipe out the encampments, and there was little for Occupiers to fall back on after the occupations themselves were gone. Without the visibility the encampments provided, Occupy supporters began losing interest, and the OWS trend soon departed from the attention of the mainstream almost as voraciously as it had emerged.

For these reasons, it makes more sense to think of OWS as a "moment" than as a "movement." Those dedicated to movement building typically understand that movements happen over long periods of time, that they place an emphasis on long-term political education, and that they work to build sustainable infrastructures that are not heavily dependent on media coverage or a single

tactic, as was OWS. Referring to OWS as a moment is also a cordial recognition of those who have continued to build movements throughout the period of the political "dead zone" mentioned earlier. At the same time, it is important not to overlook the Occupy moment too quickly. It has been a telling exposure of mainstream political thought—a flash of insight—that can help us in building future coalitional forces in a healthier way, if not because of its successes, then because of its "failures."

More than anything else, what OWS needed in order to serve its own generalizable purposes was more intimate guidance from its elder social justice organizations. Southerners on New Ground (SONG), for example, became an appealing alternative for many former Occupiers in the south who wanted to organize against capitalism, because the organization has decades of experience doing just that. Instead of asking what OWS might have done differently in order to keep its cause going, it might be more helpful to redefine its "failure." OWS as pop activism may have died out almost completely, but the Occupy moment ushered hoards of energetic activists into organizations with more experience, strategy, and expertise. Waning interest in OWS might also be seen as part of our own collective filtration system in rejecting a moment that was perhaps too integrated with the technologies of capitalism to actually be anti-capitalist.

It is tempting to view the emergence of OWS as an organic human development, as it was a moment that developed very quickly and was very much about placing physical bodies into visible spaces. However, that moment was also highly reflective of the ways in which ICTs are organized—"separate" devices connected to a larger network of similar devices. Theoretically, each occupation had the capacity to build whatever sort of organizational infrastructure they saw fit, yet the vast majority of occupations seem to have been governed by nearly identical communicative and tactical designs—from the use of hand signals, to the structure of decision-making bodies, to the construction of a rhetoric dominated by single-axis concerns of economic inequality. It is no wonder, then, that while OWS created a national (or even transnational) sense of solidarity, it often had trouble addressing the unique localities in which each encampment was individually situated. This tension was evident in Virginia, for example, where Occupy Richmond often seemed at odds with sociopolitical groups who have been organizing across the state and region for decades. But how are people swept up into neglecting their own locality for the sake of broader feelings of solidarity? To unpack this question, it will help to look at some of the specific tactics used by OWS.

PERFORMING TECHNO-SEDUCTION

The heart of OWS has been its General Assembly (GA). This is where all formal decisions for the group are made, and where the most concretized manifestation of the group's consensus process can be found. Conversations within GA are structured by a complex and shifting set of rules aimed at making group discussion as inclusive as possible, and much time is often spent within these conversations debating varying interpretations of what the process calls for, making amendments to the process, and simply trying to keep the group focused on its own agenda. Along with the physical occupations, the GA is responsible for helping Occupiers to capture a sustained spotlight of media attention over a period of several months. While the vast majority of journalists seemed befuddled by the intentions of OWS, GA made one Occupy demand clear: the opportunity to participate.

The space created by GA attempts to reflect a particular kind of participation as well. In this space, everyone is encouraged to speak and have opinions heard. Its modified nine-tenths consensus model, requiring agreement from 90% of all members present in a given GA, is used with the intention of protecting extreme minorities from

domination by the majority. Finally, progressive stack is typically used in order to move the most marginalized voices to the center of the GA's conversation—people of color, queer folks, etc. are supposed to be allowed to speak before others. In these ways, GA attempts to create a horizontal political space that values the opinions of all members and places a special emphasis on including those who are underrepresented in business and government. In the following analysis, I am not so much concerned with explaining how Occupy spaces became unsafe and oppressive for many of its participants—this was clearly the case. I am more concerned with offering one particular explanation as to why many scholars, journalists, and occupiers have not seemed to pick up on the fact that these spaces became oppressive for a lot of people—the dynamics of techo-seduction.

To this end, it can be helpful to think of GA as a theatre. In this theatre there are performances of democracy, horizontalism, and consensus that allow us to experience these ideals without ever becoming the ideals themselves. We are confined to performance because we lack the political, economic, and social infrastructures that would allow us to break free from the need to interact with institutions of power that control our lives outside of the GA theatre. In order to put on a show, the theatre requires the use of technology to dramatize its performances; one particular technology of the GA theater is known as the people's mic. The people's mic has been a practical tool used to circumvent laws prohibiting electronic amplification, but it has also been a symbolic tool used to perform Occupy ideals with a call and response system that amplifies the voice of one with the voices of many. Viewing this as a performance of ideals, instead of ideals actualized, allows us to more soberly analyze the lure of the techo-seduction that inevitably accompanies the performances. The people's mic is a technology in so far as it is a tool used to transmit information (on both symbolic and concrete levels), and insofar as it allows the performance of ideals to be carried out. Whether or not these performances bring us closer to experiencing either consensus or democracy is suspect. In the present moment, the ideals of consensus, horizontalism, and democracy—terms which, for the purposes of this current discussion, can be considered synonymous—are experienced in fragments of potential futures; they are not yet actual, and are not determinants for actualization.

However, the people's mic is not exactly a new technology. It is a strange mixture of old technologies that has manifest in a new way, which some scholars have approached through a lens of electronic innovation and oral tradition. Ruby, for example, interprets the people's mic as a post-literate device, or a device situated within the electronic age that is somehow reminiscent of oral tradition. In his essay "On the People's Mic: Politics in a Post-Literate Age," (2012) Ruby contemplates the reasons for the emergence of ancient communication and social organization techniques in an era broadly defined by advances in communications technology. He asks, "Why is it precisely in technological civilization that the orgiastic erupts?" Ruby is not only referring to the people's mic when he asks this, but also to post-literate devices such as Twitter, Gchat, and other tools that similarly rely on oral tradition and electronic technology. "Orgiastic" (in this context) refers vaguely to what Ruby prefers to call "sacral orality," and what I have been calling *techno-seduction*. The unifying thread among these terms is the characterization of an object (broadly interpreting "object") as being enraptured by some powerful force of emotion or sacredness.

Answering his own question, Ruby argues that the orgiastic erupts precisely in technological civilization "because…technological civilization produces boredom…in the Heideggerean sense, as 'the ontological condition of humanity which has subordinated its life in everydayness and its anonymity' as a descent into inauthenticity and decadence." Transferring this response to our own

context, we could say that technological civilization had become bored with the performance of democratic ideals allowed by Internet devices, and techno-seduction provoked mass participation in a device that was even more reminiscent of oral tradition, the people's mic.

What is missing from Ruby's analysis is a consideration of how the people's mic is a not only situated within the electronic age, but how it also reflects definitive characteristics of electronically networked devices as well. The people's mic is an oral device in the sense that it relies on speech to be accomplished, but in another way its underlying process appears almost algorithmic.[3] In most call and response practices, an audience will typically repeat something different from what the original speaker has said. However, with the people's mic, the audience repeats back precisely what the original speaker has said. This computational dynamic also reflects the flow of information within popular social media where items posted by one person are shared and re-shared by a virtual audience—Tumblr might be the best example of this, with its emphasis on reblogging the content of others, as opposed to the blogging of user-created content. This, too, is the amplification of the voice of one with the voices of many.

In the 50-odd GAs I attended—primarily in Richmond, Virginia, but also in Portland, Oregon and Lansing, Michigan—the people's mic seemed to resonate in a ritualistic, or even spiritual, sense with Occupiers. The symbol of collectivism feels concretized when you are amidst that sea of voices, when you not only hear but feel the collective amplification of "democracy" in your own chest. This might be why Chris Garces draws a connection, in "Preamble to an Ethnography of the People's Mic," (2011) between the people's mic and eighteenth-century town hall frontier assemblies, where one spoke in public under the guidance of the holy spirit. Yet Garces himself seems to succumb to the seduction of this technology:

what I discovered upon arrival in Zucotti was the town hall "frontier assembly" par excellence, a radically heterogenous public gathering, cobbling together notion of the public good in a democratic process attentive to plurality and minority protections almost unimaginable unless you observed its public workings firsthand. (Garces, 2011)

It is most likely that by "minority protections" Garces is at least partially referring Occupy's use of *progressive stack*. I am an advocate of this device, though enacting it based on such identity markers can be problematic, but as Garces perceives this phenomena to be "unimaginable unless you observed its public workings firsthand," perhaps what is actually unimaginable (for some) is looking beyond the seduction of the people's mic to see the internal oppression at work within OWS. Most scholars seem to have visited Occupy sites only periodically, and only to observe a small number of GAs, or to deliver speeches. Few stuck around long enough to examine its internal oppression, instead allowing themselves to be captivated by the performance of consensus, and taking that experience home to write about. Finally, it is remarkable that, if unimaginable protections of minorities actually existed within OWS, no scholars have gone into greater detail about them. "Building a Complex Emancipatory Unity: Documenting Decolonial Feminist Interventions within the Occupy Movement" is one of the few scholarly works to address internal oppression within the group, but its work focuses—importantly—on documenting decolonial feminist interventions, not on explaining otherwise unimaginable dynamics of some advanced horizontalism, the existence of which Garces suggests (Talcott & Collins, 2012).

To return to the analogy of techno-seduction as a preacher of advanced capitalism, we can see ourselves—whether as journalists, activists, or scholars—amplifying with our own voices the preacher's rhetoric of technological determinism. Even within moments like OWS, which might seem to transcend the technological current presented to us by the preacher, we replicate digital-colonial mentalities while remaining largely oblivious to them. Techno-seduction is successful because it makes itself invisible, for if we are unaware of how colonialism functions in the digital age, then we have little hope of counteracting it.

FUTURE RESEARCH DIRECTIONS

More scholarship needs to be produced in relation to consensus. It has become all but the de facto form of leftist political organizing, yet remains largely undertheorized. In particular, the relation of consensus to the self-naturalizing imperial temporality remains undertheorized. I have attempted to point out here that techno-seduction relies heavily on speed and efficiency, and more scholarship addressing the relationship between imperial temporality and consensus will better inform our activism that has come to rely so heavily upon consensus.

In addition to philosophical approaches that deconstruct the impulse for ever greater speed and efficiency, there is an equally great need for a development of tangible practices that can be used to counteract the imperial temporality. Technology and time are issues rarely organized around by activists in a direct way, yet the colonial evolution of these issues set the parameters of our political participation in a very real way. This is deeply interwoven with our broad conceptualization and treatment of the DD, which assumes that further digitizing our communities is the only pathway to economic and cultural autonomy. Consensus is inherently antithetical to the imperial temporality, but it is not a determinant of the deconstruction of linear and velocity-obsessed applications of time and technology. Time, technology, and consensus should be integrated into our intersectional analyses if we aim to build economically and culturally autonomous communities.

Finally, more critical analyses of identity formation and influence in relation to the digital would also help us to re-conceptualize the impact emergent technologies are having on society discourse. Not only would such scholarship help us to better understand the digital, but also to better equip dissident movements to function within and outside of digital contexts. As I have tried to make clear, digital expansion continues to accelerate. This has resulted in a number of unexamined communities within the digital realm, as they continue to emerge and transform at greater rates than we are able to keep pace with.

CONCLUSION

At many points in this chapter, I have diverted attention away from the metaphor *digital is dead*. This metaphor is a conceptual approach that works to destabilize popular assumptions about what the digital is, what it does, and how it impacts both global and local communities. It is meant to parallel the mysticism and complexity of the digital as an idea that is as open-ended as it applicable to contemporary political and technological frameworks, functioning most aptly in the undercurrents of discourse and analysis when it remains invisible. Colonial-capitalism is always ready to impact while never exposing itself willingly. The point is to force this exposure and pull apart the exposed in order to examine its fragments and craft them into a new political consciousness—one that takes an intersectional approach in considering the interplay between all colonial identity categories, including digital.

REFERENCES

Baudrillard, J. (1994). *Simulacra and simulation.* Ann Arbor, MI: University of Michigan Press.

Chesneaux, J. (2000). Speed and democracy: An uneasy dialogue. *Social Sciences Information. Information Sur les Sciences Sociales, 39*(3), 407–420. doi:10.1177/053901800039003004

Crenshaw, K. W. (1989). Demarginalizing the intersection of race and sex: A black feminst critique of antidiscrimination doctrine, feminist theory and antiracist politics. *University of Chicago Legal Forum*, 139–167.

Esch, D. (2013, April 19). Of typewriters and masking tape: A media history of the Zapatistas. *AlJazeera*. Retrieved from http://www.aljazeera.com/indepth/opinion/2013/04/2013415112152991530.html

Garces, C. (2011). Preamble to an ethnography of the people's mic. *Somatosphere: Science, Medicine, and Anthropology*. Retrieved from http://somatosphere.net/2011/10/preamble-to-an-ethnography-of-the-people%E2%80%99s-mic.html

Golumbia, D. (2009). *The cultural logic of computation.* Cambridge, MA: Harvard University Press.

Graeber, D. (2004). *Direct action: An ethnography.* Oakland, CA: AK Press.

Greco, G. M., & Floridi, L. (2004). The tragedy of the digital commons. *Ethics and Information Technology, 6*, 73–81. doi:10.1007/s10676-004-2895-2

Hassan, R. (2009). *Empires of speed: Time and the acceleration of politics and society.* Boston, MA: Brill Publishers. doi:10.1163/ej.9789004175907.i-254

Jackson, L. A. et al. (2008). Race, gender, and information technology use: The new digital divide. *Cyberpsychology & Behavior, 11*(4), 437–442. doi:10.1089/cpb.2007.0157 PMID:18721092

Lugones, M. (2010). Toward a decolonial feminism. *Hypatia, 25*(4), 742–759. doi:10.1111/j.1527-2001.2010.01137.x

Martínez, E. B. (2000, March 10). Where was the color in Seattle? Looking for reasons why the great battle was so white. *Colorlines*. Retrieved from http://colorlines.com/archives/2000/03/where_was_the_color_in_seattlelooking_for_reasons_why_the_great_battle_was_so_white.html

Mignolo, W. (2000). *Local histories/global designs*. Princeton, NJ: Princeton University Press.

Mignolo, W. (2002). The Zapatista's theoretical revolution: Its historical, ethical, and political consequences. *Utopian Thinking, 25*(3), 245–275.

Muñoz, J. E. (2009). *Cruising utopia: The then and there of queer futurity*. New York, NY: New York University Press.

Norris, P. (2001). *Digital divide: Civic engagement, information poverty, and the internet worldwide*. Cambridge, UK: Cambridge University Press. doi:10.1017/CBO9781139164887

Pew Internet and American Life Project. (2002). *The digital disconnect: The widening gap between internet-savvy students and their schools*. Author.

Quijano, A. (2000). Coloniality of power, eurocentrism, and Latin America. *Nepantla: Views from the South, 1*(3), 533–580.

Ronfeldt, D. et al. (1998). *The Zapatista social netwar in Mexico*. Santa Monica, CA: RAND Corporation.

Ronfeldt, D., & Arquilla, J. (n.d.). *Networks and netwars: The future of terror, crime, and militancy*. Santa Monica, CA: RAND Corporation.

Ruby, R. (2012). On the people's mic: Politics in a post-literate age. *Journal for Occupied Studies*.

Ruecker, T. (2012). Exploring the digital divide on the U.S.-Mexico border through literacy narratives. *Computers and Composition, 29*, 239–253. doi:10.1016/j.compcom.2012.06.002

Talcott, M., & Collins, D. (2012). Building a complex emancipatory unity: Documenting decolonial feminist interventions within the occupy movement. *Feminist Studies, 38*(2).

Zugman, K. (2005). Autonomy in a poetic voice: Zapatistas and political organizing in Los Angeles. *Latino Studies, 3*(3), 325–346. doi:10.1057/palgrave.lst.8600157

ADDITIONAL READING

Anzaldúa, G. (1987). *Borderlands/la frontera*. Bloomington: In Indiana University Press.

Bayer, B. M. (2012). Enchantment in an age of occupy. *Women's Studies Quarterly, 40*(3 & 4), 27–50.

Butler, J. (2011). For and against precarity. *Tidal: Occupy Theory. Occupy Strategy, 1*, 12–13.

Cruz-Malave, A., & Manalansan, M. F. (2002). *Queer globalizations: Citizenship and the afterlife of colonialism*. New York, NY: New York University Press.

Gleason, B. (2013). #Occupy wall street: Exploring informal learning about a social movement on twitter. *The American Behavioral Scientist, XX*(X), 1–17.

Goldberg, D. T. (2010). Call and response. *Patterns of Prejudice, 44*(1), 89–106. doi:10.1080/00313220903507651

Hardt, M., & Negri, A. (2000). *Empire*. Cambridge, MA: Harvard University Press.

Hayles, K. M. (1999). *How we became posthuman: Virtual bodies in cybernetics, literature, and infomatics*. Chicago, IL: Chicago University Press. doi:10.7208/chicago/9780226321394.001.0001

Holloway, J. (2010). *Crack capitalism*. New York, NY: Pluto.

Keating, A. L. (2005). *Entre mundos/among worlds: New perspectives on Gloria Anzaldúa*. New York, NY: Palgrave Macmillan.

Loomba, Ania. (1998). *Colonialism/postcolonialism: New critical idiom*, New York, NY: Routlegde. Lothian, Alexis, & Phillips, Amanda. Can digital humanities mean transformative critique? *Journal of e-Media Studies, 3*(1), 25.

Lugones, M. (2006). On complex communication. *Hypatia*, *21*(3), 75–85. doi:10.1111/j.1527-2001.2006.tb01114.x

Nygon'o, T. (2012). The scene of occupation. *The Drama Review*, *56*(4), 136–149. doi:10.1162/DRAM_a_00219

Ong, Walter J. (1982). *Orality and literacy: the technologizing of the world.*

Penney, J., & Dadas, C. (2013). Re(T)weeting in the service of protest: Digital composition and circulation in the occupy wall street movement. *New Media & Society*, *0*(0), 1–17.

Pérez, E. (1999). *The Decolonial Imaginary: Writing Chicanas into History*. Bloomington: In Indiana University Press.

Picower, B. (2012). Education should be free! Occupy the DOE!: Teacher activists involved in the occupy wall street movement. *Critical Studies in Education*, *54*(1), 44–56. doi:10.1080/17508487.2013.739569

Said, E. (1979). *Orientalism*. New York, NY: Vintage.

Young, K., & Schwartz, M. (2012). Can prefigurative politics prevail? The implications for movement strategy in John Holloway's *Crack capitalism. Journal of Classical Sociology*, *12*(2), 220–239. doi:10.1177/1468795X12443533

KEY TERMS AND DEFINITIONS

Colonial Difference: Spaces in which the coloniality of power is enacted; an open-ended conceptual tactic for envisioning resistance to colonization.

Coloniality of Power: The process by which people are dehumanized and categorized; the process of colonization.

Consensus: A form of group deliberation and decision-making in which all members of a group must give their consent before the group itself puts a decision into action.

Digital Divide (DD): A framework that depicts a separation between people in relation to their access to (and literacy involving) ICTs.

Eurocentricism: A dominant lens that privileges history and analysis filtered through a European perspective.

Information and Communication Technology (ICT): Communication devices connected to a larger network of devices.

Intersectionality: A type of analysis that focuses on the multidimensional interplay between socially constructed categories; ie, race, gender, sexuality, digital.

Temporality: The condition of time; not necessarily a linear progression from past, present, to future.

ENDNOTE

[1] In their book, *Empire*, Michael Hardt and Antonio Negri argue that the age of Imperialism is over, and that we have entered into the age of Empire. Despite practical difference in our claims, I do not consider my argument here to be in contention with their idea of Empire, but in collaboration with it.

[2] In her essay, "Autonomy in a Poetic Voice: Zapatistas and Political Organizing in Los Angeles," Kara Zugman explains that Eddie is co-founder of Casa del Pueblo, a community center in Los Angeles that has worked closely with Zapatistas in Chiapas.

[3] David Golumbia (personal communication)

Chapter 14
The Spaces Between Us

Mohanalakshmi Rajakumar
Virginia Commonwealth University in Qatar, Qatar

ABSTRACT

Despite having one of the highest per-capita incomes of the world, social and political changes in Qatar have not kept pace with the country's economic development. The expatriate and national population of the small emirate have access to luxury brands and a variety of Western goods including food as well as hotels. The high level of commercialization, however, does not mean that cultural differences between the various nationalities have been erased. Online forums and social media have provided neutral public spaces where debate and dialogue about identity and values can take place in a way they do not occur in public. This chapter examines a variety of examples through comments by expats and nationals on a number of media sites as well as Twitter, Facebook, and Instagram.

INTRODUCTION

The oil-rich Arabian Gulf states are bustling with commercial activity, which accompanies globalization. Virtually every major North American or European brand is available for consumption. From the ubiquitous McDonald's arches, to the luxury logos of Mercedes, or screening of international movies and every range of product in between, the Gulf Cooperation Council (GCC) is a hotbed for the commodities of the world. The flow of material objects is mirrored by the symbolic exchange of ideas present in online spaces. Often consumption is mistaken for acquiescence to a western outlook, but examination of people's online behaviors reveals that these objects do not hold symbolic value as replacements for cultural values (Black, 2009, p. 397). Yet, as Allan Fromherz suggests in *Qatar: A Modern History* (2012), the modernization of the Qatari economy has not been associated with an accompanying significant shift in social or political practices.

DOI: 10.4018/978-1-4666-5150-0.ch014

Qatar, Fromherz (2012) argues, has managed to elude the tangle of social and political change assumed to be part and parcel of a developing economy (p. 8). With modernization, he explains, comes change, often descending into chaos before entering a stable period. Unlike other parts of the developing world, including Africa, Asia, or Latin America, Qatar has managed to remain socially and politically stable while simultaneously managing the world's largest economy. One need not look far for evidence supporting Fromherz's claims; consumer behavior has not changed the population's acceptance of rule by a monarchy, led by an Emir. Though the malls are full of western clothing brands, and the arms of customers in line at the cashier's counter piled with jeans, shorts, or dresses, the locals are still dressed in traditional clothing to wear when traveling or inside the home. Western outfits are reserved for travel or at home. Physical appearance still dictates many assumptions people make about one another in the public spaces of the city. In such rigidly defined public spaces, where dress, gender, nationality and occupation still dictate behavior, regardless of one's background, we find evidence of Fromherz's claims that social structure in Qatar has not kept apace with the development of the country's roads, buildings or economy. Resistance to cultural change persists in the social structure, particularly as applied to the roles of women as well as interactions between expats and nationals. Despite western products and influences, the government maintains a presence in the everyday lives of all the residents of the country.

Within such a context, the possibilities for debate and dialogue between people of different communities and viewpoints are limited; therefore, the relative freedom made possible by more egalitarian spaces like online forums, news sources, and social media, become critical. As Rebecca Black (2009) explains, "deterritorialized online spaces offer multiple points of social and cultural contact with individuals from diverse backgrounds" (p. 398). The additional layer of complication, however, is that in the continued acceptance by the national population of a benevolent, yet hyper, vigilante State apparatus, which monitors all mediums of communication by all its residents. The online interactions in Qatar have an ever-present audience.

The absence of testing the limits of the constitutional monarchy's restraint of internal criticism in print newspaper or online forums is another example of Qatar's divergence from the assumed interconnectedness of socio-economic development. The national telecom provider, Qtel, does not allow unrestricted access to technology, whether on the phones or computers. The word "Oops!" with a cartoon illustration of a man with kinky, frazzled black hair pops up if attempting to access sexual content. The continuation of traditional values and social rules—Qataris still have the obligations that governed the lives of their grandparents, including marrying within their family and socializing within their tribes—hints at a contradiction with the modern setting of the glittering capital city Doha, which is filled with five star hotels, shopping malls, and skyscrapers.

The rapid development of Qatar and the GCC has encouraged voluntary migration from expatriates across all levels of industry in order to provide the labor necessary for the ongoing building of infrastructure. Blue-collar construction workers and maids from Asia, as well as doctors, professors, and engineers from Europe and North America have been moving to the GCC to make their fortunes and contribute to infrastructure development.

At a time when few other countries in the Middle East had the resources to develop technological infrastructure, the GCC governments were investing heavily. The small nature of the countries, from Saudi Arabia, Oman, Kuwait, Qatar, Bah'rain, and the United Arab Emirates, as well as the relative affluence of their native populations, has made them technology innovators in the Middle East. The Internet and related media are not neutral concepts in the Middle East, malleable for a variety of purposes, determined by the user. Newspapers, social media and blogs are public arenas with severe political and social consequences. The contrast between the attitude of Middle Eastern governments towards the activities of residents and citizens online is carried over from their monitoring of activities in print. The region, which has been grappling with the affects of globalization against the rule of dictatorships, has recently experienced political upheaval in the "Arab Spring" often cited as having started on social media. Even so, sources of information, programs, and content made available by the Internet are often mistrusted. Fromherz's characterization of Qatar as the promoter of freedom abroad, while restrictive internally, is a reminder of the risks of online forums for all users who reside inside the country's borders. Despite the risks, including loss of employment or prison time, expats and nationals in Qatar do engage on a variety of online platforms. Within the boundaries drawn by the State there are spaces to contest and debate issues of daily lives, which take place over the Internet rather than in person.

In fact, in the Middle East, social media can be used to contest perceptions of the Other as defined by Edward Said who explained that in opposition to western centric notions of self, the idea of the Other was created as an exotic opposite, based on differences between western and eastern cultures. Said's work explored the practice of Orientalism, whereby the west marginalizes other cultures, including the Middle East, through stereotypes. Users of blogs, Twitter, and even YouTube, contest the depiction of the Middle East as a war-torn region as presented on nightly news broadcasts.

In daily life in Qatar, however, the Other has is a double meaning as the two communities, expats and nationals, define themselves in opposition. Otherness in Qatar works both ways and it is through platforms like Twitter, the normal barriers of hierarchical life in a society ruled by a constitutional monarchy, can be overridden. The population can be divided into two overarching categories: expats, or those non-native to the country, and nationals, also known as locals, or the citizens of the country. The socialization patterns of the two groups rarely overlap in physical spaces. Their online socialization, however, reflects the switching patterns outlined by Ken Miller, Frances Fabian and Shu-Jo Lin (2009). They explain that the Internet provides opportunities for online communities where people either:

1. Change an opinion as more participants are exposed more broadly to other opinions in the population or
2. Become entrenched and polarized perspectives, to the extent that individuals restrict their participation to communities with likeminded participants. (p. 309).

These two types of behaviors reflect heterophilous or homophilous connections. In the case of expats and nationals' usage of social media in Qatar, both types of affiliation patterns are present, pointing to the diverse nature of interactions between these two groups.

Nationals with large families and the extreme importance placed on maintaining kinship ties within the extended family often do not have time or the need for relationships with expatriates who leave after an average of three years in the country. Since the two groups don't spend much time together in person, social media becomes a way for people to establish relationships with those whom they would not otherwise interact. Online platforms allow nationals to vent their feelings about controversial topics, such as attitudes towards being a minority in their own country and being vastly outnumbered. As one respondent said on Twitter to a question about the Qatari opinion of expats, "What we think about expats, well they get paid more than us, triple, even though we studied abroad and we are in the same level." The anonymity of an online response allows for more honesty than if the interaction had taken place in person.

To balance their smaller ratio to the overall population in Qatar (locals represent 350,000 out of nearly 2 million), social media gives their word equal weight to that of the larger group of expats.

The tension between the two communities comes to the surface in the public space of social media. Unlike the discussions occurring in private homes or cocktail parties, these conversations have the opposing sides addressing concerns to each other. Another respondent commented: "I have lived in the UK for 20 years. They [expats] don't get the luxury they are getting here. Be real." In an honor based culture, where saving face is the ultimate goal, and projecting an affluent persona has been crucial for nationals in a cash rich state powered by oil and gas sales, admissions of being less than wealthy are made possible on social media: "You don't know the Qataris or what they go through. People think we are rich, but we are not. We live in two rooms in our mother-in-law's house and that's torture by itself." The idea that Qataris are living in shared rooms, rather than in palaces as projected by the stereotypes of a wealthy local population is counterintuitive, but admission is permissible via social media. These tweets amount to the exchange of ideas and perspectives between expats and Qataris, made possible via the anonymity of online screen names and the impersonal nature of Twitter interactions. Yet all interactions between expats and nationals on social media are not always so positive, unguarded, or self-revealing.

For example, Facebook, where friends can read, comment, share or like the posts of others, is an optimal space for discussion and debate, often with emotional reactions. One such example is in the reaction to the sharing of a *Global Voices* story on female athletes from Saudi Arabia in the 2012 London Olympics. *Global Voices*, an online media outlet made up largely of citizen journalists around the world, ran a piece titled "Saudi Arabia: Kingdom's First Female Olympic Athletes Called 'Prostitutes'." A Qatari woman responded to the poster, objecting to the characterization of the athletes as prostitutes:

This is absolutely ridiculous! Is it necessary for news to have "Saudi Arabia" in the title for it to be a headline? Seriously, one guy's ignorance should not be news, and the title is so misleading too! Many, if not all, twitter users protested this hashtag, but let's not care for the voice of reason. It's Saudi Arabia; let's bank on that! So ridiculous.

The expat, and owner of the wall, replied to the poster. Their tones are measured as they debate whether or not the piece counts as news:

I didn't see the Twitter protest Hind - and I wonder where the demographic breakdown happens - but I'm glad that they're being backed up and rooting for them like Emily said.

It is the two weeks of non-stop Olympics, so to be fair, if anyone said this about their female athletes, I'm sure someone would pick it up.

I know what you mean about the media—a pastor in my hometown a few years ago wanted to burn the Quran. Was on international media for days.

Yet the commenter was not satisfied. She continued to question the legitimacy of the article and the motives behind posting it when there are other stories to tell about female athletes from the GCC.

Honestly, I think a headline like this is so misleading. Qatar sent its first female athletes this year, but the media loves a story about Saudi Arabia. … Let's decide to reinforce a stereotype. That's what responsible media does, right?

The Qatari commentator was concerned not only with Qatar's position in regards to female athletes, but also how stereotypes paint other countries in the GCC with a negative brush. Her concern about the negative stories about Saudi Arabia could be related to the geographic proximity of the country and the shared southern border with Qatar. As well-established religious and political entities in Middle East politics, both Saudi and Egypt often overshadow the actions of the much more liberal Qatar. The commentator resists being painted with the same brush both by *Global Voices* and the Facebook account holder; for her both the image of Qatar and the greater GCC are at stake.

The expat attempted to steer the conversation away from the immediate post at hand and to a larger discussion of stereotyping, the media, and how to address concerns: "Stereotypes exist for a reason. And the way to combat them is to contribute to discourse. The mainstream never decides to change on its own because it's the right, moral or balanced thing to do."

As the conversation continued, the tone began to disintegrate. The breakdown in communication occurred as the national accused the expat of favoring negative stories about Saudi and thereby feeding the media:

Yes but it is our job not to allow it to grow, enforce it, or approve of it! Just because stereotypes exist doesn't mean they are right, or that somehow they should be used for something other than comic relief.

The expat countered, questioning the efficacy of posting such opinions on a Facebook wall. Sustaining such a conversation over the course of several hours demonstrates the extent to which Facebook is a forum in which to contest perceptions of the Middle East.

The exchange over a routine headline by *Global Voices* exposes the underlying tension between expats and locals, even in social media spaces. While there is room for positive interaction, and support by people of all nationalities, there is also an ongoing contention between them regarding values, ideologies, and motives behind the positing of articles, photos, and other material on social media sites. Therefore, in social media usage by expats and locals, we see the same contesting of

identities and the tension between the imagination of the individual versus the perceptions of the collective as Rebecca Black (2009) points to in her study about global identities and imagination online (p. 378).

The benefits and dangers of the Internet as a public space take on a different context given the gender segregation common in GCC countries. In addition, the limited amount of interactions between expatriates and nationals in physical public spaces means that social media provides other opportunities for socialization. The intangibility of one's physical appearance in online spaces allows for a greater range of self-defining behaviors than perhaps any other technological invention in the history of writing. In the Middle East context, this ability to exchange ideas, regardless of the social or political constraints in one's physical environment, make social media a key part of communication in everyday life.

In Syria, for example, Facebook is blocked via official Internet connections. If you enter any café, however, you'll see most of the screens are backlit by the blue glow of the Facebook homepage. This contrast demonstrates that Middle Eastern users of the Internet do not wholly subscribe to the restrictions of their governments. The opening of a door to the rest of the world is met with some anxiety about the ability of values to influence traditional Muslim culture.

In Qatar, the single service provider blocks any pages that might have pornographic content. This includes Websites of vendors that sell bathing suits or celebrity gossip columns with salacious articles or photos.

The worry that Deborah L. Wheeler (2001) raises, that cultural mores will be undermined by western assumptions implicit in the very makeup of the Internet itself, has not kept people from flocking to it on a variety of devices (p.200). What we see is that use of the Internet and attendant social media platforms is policed both by other users in the online space and also monitored by the government. For both expats and nationals in Middle East countries, these two circles of influence guide decisions about what to post and how to respond.

In GCC countries, the decisions about content are governed either by social convention for the nationals, or by employment considerations for the expatriates. Nationals risk alienation of their families, tribes, or larger kinship structures if they transgress against these rules. Expatriates risk termination or deportation by the immigration authorities if they cause offense to Islam or defame the Emir. The two categories vary greatly; the first is intangible and can be used to cover a variety of objectionable behaviors, which are subject to interpretation by civic authorities. While very different in nature, both groups have significant considerations when it comes to self-policing their online behaviors.

As Rebecca Black (2009) suggests, this "ongoing flow of information, people, and ideas in turn provides frameworks for permeable, networked, and transnational social structures" (p. 397). For expatriates, the use of social media is focused on friends and family at home who may never have the experience of daily life in the Middle East. Given the rhetoric of a post 9/11 era, their blogs, tweets, and Facebook posts bring a reality that that is not accessible via the mainstream media or nightly news into the homes of an otherwise disconnected population. For GCC nationals, many of whom love to travel, have studied for advanced degrees abroad, or grown up as children of parents working overseas, the online space allows them to maintain cosmopolitan interests and identities from the within their traditional lives.

The advent of the smartphone, plus the high percentage of youth in this demographic, means that presently many of them spend hours of time on the Internet across a range of social media sites including Facebook, Twitter, and Instagram. The primary use for the social media networks by nationals is to exchange information, but they also use these networks to augment their commercial and social activities.

This is not without complications, however, as residents and citizens who responded to a Social Media Usage survey indicated (M. Rajakumar, survey, June 6, 2012). Participants in the survey were asked how their usage of Facebook and Twitter compared with their in-person social circles. Whether expat or national, many of the comments related to the drawbacks of being a member of small, hyper status-conscious population. "I noticed that people use programs like Instagram to show off their stuff. (Eg., car, watch, etc.), whereas elsewhere it's pictures mostly of people!" The restriction against local women to post photographs of themselves may also contribute to the emphasis on objects that are more neutral and also testify to one's ability to enjoy a luxurious lifestyle whether in clothes, food, or travel. The other mishaps from being monitored by a small network include the universal problem of inadvertently divulging one's activities. The context for Qatari women is even more claustrophobic due to their relatively small number. Men comprise eighty percent of the population in comparison to 350,000 women.

Both expats and locals exhibit diverse identities in their online presence that they might not be able to exhibit within the somewhat rigid structures of everyday life in an environment defined by nationality. A naturalized citizen of a western country, for example, from any non-Caucasian heritage, will be assumed to hail from that country of origin. "Why are you happy?" someone remarked to a celebrating British citizen of Pakistani origin when London was awarded the summer 2012 Olympics. "Aren't you Pakistani?"

Both expats and nationals participated in a survey which asked a series of questions of how their online interactions compared with their in person exchanges. A respondent to the social media usage in a Qatar survey (M. Rajakumar, June 6, 2013) confirms Black's view. "Many people spend too much time on social media and less time talking or meeting up in person. Social media is often used to do things privately that isn't culturally appropriate here." The idea that time online replaces time spent in person is an interesting given the social nature of life in Qatar for all communities. People of all backgrounds spend time together, often sharing meals, but perhaps, as the respondent suggests, this time is spent in culturally homogenous groups.

Expatriates, the other segment of the population in these states, are equally active. The uses of online social spaces by expats are varied and involve one of two types of linked behaviors. The overarching category is that of information sharing. One respondent to the Social Media Usage survey (M. Rajakumar, survey, June 6, 2013) commented on the usefulness of social media in the local context: "I find that in Qatar online forums are quite popular and useful as well. I would be unlikely to use them in the US."

Far away from friends and family back home, expats rely on social media platforms to connect with others, disseminate and receive information, as well as for entertainment. As another respondent indicated: "Twitter was such an enormous help when I first moved to Qatar (2009) to find out current news and info. More recently it became a good source for entertainment." This behavior is so prevalent that there are specialty groups established to cater to the various information needs. A popular online network for moms, for example, allows members to post questions in a private forum. Within the members-only forum, no one is allowed to quote or share posts submitted by members of all ages, nationalities, and religions. They hold candid conversations about a range of topics—from how to get children to fall asleep, where to enroll them in schools, or whether or not to seek a divorce. In the absence of one's family and friends, western expats and Arabs from around the Middle East share their tips and trade information crucial to motherhood. Often there are debates about the effectiveness of certain techniques, such as child-led weaning, or questions about why children of some communities tend not to have fixed bed times. These types of questions, and the ability of women from various

backgrounds to respond, is another example of how mothers who may not opportunities to interact socially in physical spaces are able to do so at great depth online. Considering the ethno-centric nature of the country's social scene, and the nation based schooling system (only British passport holders can attend British schools, for example), the moms' network is another example of how an online space within Qatar provides an opportunity to build strong bonds with people outside one's standard professional or social sphere.

In a media landscape where there are six monitored, mainstream newspapers, three in English and three in Arabic, there is a critical need for a more balanced news source. The *Doha News* Website is one such non-traditional online news source for pieces that mainstream media often do not report. Established and editorially managed by two Western trained journalists, the site reports on everything from housemaid abuse, to weekend events, or stories behind national tragedies like the Villaggio Mall fire in 2012 in which 16 people were killed. *Doha News* has come under criticism by nationals for pointing out the negatives of life in Qatar instead of the positive changes occurring in the country. Others see it as a vital part of understanding events in Qatar and related stories throughout the Middle East. The case of a Doha resident reporting a sexual assault while traveling in Dubai, in the United Arab Emirates, is another example of a sensitive story not covered in print media, but picked up by *Doha News* and later featured in *The New York Times* as well as other international outlets. Whether reporting on maids who run away because of long hours during Ramadan or the massive traffic pattern changes occurring across the city, the articles posted garner comments from expats and nationals alike, often sparking heated debate.

The various uses of social media platforms nationals and expatriates means online spaces become an arena in which two groups that traditionally do not have much physical interaction in public are able to interact in meaningful ways.

Often these types of interactions are positive. Arabic language usage, either through Arabic script or in transliterated Roman letters, is another key feature of online presence in the GCC. The Arabic Twitter community in particular is a demonstrated vibrant community. Their hashtags are often the most popular, nationally, particularly when used to critique customer service experiences with airlines or telecommunications companies as has occurred in the past in Qatar.

GENDER AND SOCIAL MEDIA

In my earlier study about Qatari women's use of Facebook (Rajakumar, 2012, pg. 125), I explored the tendency to use social media within self-policed, communally established cultural constraints.

The Internet is one arena, perhaps because it is even inside the home, where women can both express themselves and yet restrain themselves because of social conventions around photography and dissemination of images of female citizens older than adolescents. Hence, social networking sites such as Facebook or even blogs are applied in different ways. The contrast is a marked one: while American college students are posting compromising photos of parties, relationships, or outings (perhaps unthinkingly from their smartphones at all hours of the day and night), female Qatari college students, and indeed Muslim women of all ages in Qatar, often do not use any images at all on their pages. This is not due to a lack of technology or ability as the populations are fairly similar in their degree of middle class affluence and technological savvy. Instead of a photo in a bathing suit or embracing a friend, a Qatari female user's profile photo is more often a younger relative, favorite celebrity, or object rather than an image of the user. Many women in Qatar do not use their full names or photos to identify themselves with their Facebook profiles, blogs, or Twitter accounts.

As Wheeler (2001) explains, "women and young people [had] the most to gain from finding an autonomous realm in which to voice their opinions" (p. 188). Due to consideration for families and traditional values, women do not directly challenge social norms through their online presence. This is in keeping with Wheeler's (2001) findings among Kuwaiti women: "Women in Kuwait were unlikely to use the Internet to publically challenge the political system or the patriarchal structure of daily life" (p. 198). Among Qatari women, the same is true. The overriding concern is for their role in protecting family honor. The secondary concern, equally important, is to support the tenets of the Muslim religion. Women use the Internet and social media platforms to further expand their existing relationships rather than to challenge or forge new ones. Their strategies, however, often do circumvent certain cultural prescriptions against identifying themselves in the public space, which has been a long-standing tenant of Muslim attitudes towards women. In societies where men customarily don't mention the names of their female relatives in public, women are now creating online accounts with their names, and posting the details of their everyday routines, which would have been unthinkable even thirty years ago.

While photography of local female women is a cultural taboo, female users of Instagram, for example, circumvent this by taking photos at an event of objects or even children as substitutes for their personal images. Profile photos on every platform of social media do not feature the best photos these women have of themselves, but rather photos of brands they like to purchase, elegant displays of food, jewelry, or clothing. Another popular feature are the photos of young children, often family members such as younger siblings or cousins, in various poses guaranteed to evoke an adoring response. Children who are captured behaving precociously, either mimicking adult behavior such as young girls wearing high heels or boys on cell phones, are the images of choice. As such, they replace personal images of the user and project either a wealthy persona or an attractive one by association. The management of profile photos is an intricate art, cultivated with as much care as an actual photo of the individual.

In this manner social media is a paradoxical mix of restraint and liberation, particularly for women in the GCC. An overwhelming eighty percent of respondents in Rajakumar's previous study, which focused exclusively on Qatari women's use of Facebook (2012) said no when asked if they had photos of themselves on Facebook.

When asked why, their responses echoed a common theme. In such a public forum, they were not sure where their photos would end up or by whom they would be seen. Even while veiled or appropriately dressed, the respondents felt uncomfortable with the thought of having their images floating on the Internet via their Facebook accounts. When the respondents tried to explain their choices, their theorizations pointed to the consequences of their actions and reputations on their larger familial and social circle (p. 127).

Here is a sampling of the Facebook survey responses (M. Rajakumar, survey, September 18, 2010):

It's kind of a rule here in Qatar; girls usually don't put up photos of themselves. I used to until my mom advised me to stop because lots of rumors go around in Doha and stuff.

It is a long story. Bottom line is that I do rarely post pictures of myself just to let people whom I am friends with from abroad know who are they friends with & trust me. But afterward I just take them off, as whenever pix are online, they are online! And we all know how creepy some people can be (talking from an experience!)

I am afraid of sharing my photos with others, even my friends. I don't imagine having my photos at half of the country's houses. I also don't [have a] guarantee [that] men [won't] look at my photos.

The consequences for these women are greater than compromised employment opportunities or judgment of their choices by others; they could be shunned by their friends, families, acquaintances and strangers for images they post of themselves online. Choosing not to put up photos on Facebook may seem ironic, but for them it is a form of protection against criticism. It is an active and conscious choice to circumvent any negative attention that may result in sanctions against their other social choices.

Yet for those who step outside the boundaries of acceptable social engagement, the consequences are clear. As one respondent of the Social Media Survey (M. Rajakumar, survey, June 7, 2013) indicated, family monitoring of social media can be as threatening for certain individuals as official sanction for others. "My dad reading my Arabic free writings on Twitter felt really embarrassing when he asked my Mom about my tweets. He was concerned. I understand but afterward I couldn't tweet anything random."

The self-policing mentioned here is a voluntary restraint due to the familial repercussions of the individual's use of Twitter. This type of hyper awareness is common for female users of social media in Qatar. Another person commented how her "family relatives dig through [my] timeline either on twitter or Facebook, and keep pinpointing some incidents and then discussing it with [my] parents and causing a big problem out of simple nothing" (M. Rajakumar, survey, June 7, 2013). In a more collectivist oriented society, the monitoring of public spaces, including the Internet, can for some individuals be as restricting as authorities preventing their physical presence in inappropriate locations. For others, who are bolder and step further into the public space through their Internet presence, the consequences are even more drastic.

A female comedian, the first of her kind from among the local population, experienced the policing of behavior and the crossover of traditional values into the social media realm. A video of her standup routine, including a joke she made about wearing a bikini, was sent around through BlackBerry messenger (BBM) along with phrases in Arabic denouncing her behavior. She referenced the abaya, the long black robe over clothing by GCC nationals, and having a bikini on underneath, while talking to some co-workers who were concerned she would feel left out when she heard their plans to go to the beach on the weekend. "I'll come in my bikini guys," is what she said on stage. In the presence of the live audience, this innocuous line received a few laughs. Through the YouTube video circulated to BlackBerry users, however, the line took a life of its own. She became an emblem of taking liberties too far. Veiled women were not supposed to show their bodies, much less talk about them in public. The ensuing outcry against her through these informal social networks was enough to discourage her from performing again. "I was scared for my life," she said. "I was afraid to leave my house." The fact that both the offending behavior and the discipline against her occurred through social media—not from civic authorities—is an interesting example of how social media and the Internet can both allow and prohibit local women's behaviors. In a setting where content is monitored by the state, this young woman stopped participating in comedy, not because of official pressure but because of social monitoring, demonstrating that while women may have the right to public speech, they may not always exercise them.

ONLINE CULTURE WARS

The converse is also true. Online spaces become a reflection of the tensions felt elsewhere in society. The relationships between expats and locals are complicated, overlaid with a variety of factors, including resentment over employment compensation and notions of favoritism. The Qatarization policy, whereby nationals are expected to participate in every level of the workforce, leaves many expatriates with colleagues who are not qualified

or motivated to perform. The minority status of locals within their own country, outnumbered several times over by the expatriates, leads to feelings of displacement and resentment. The tension between these two groups often boils over in online spaces.

Such was the case after National Day in 2009 when an expatriate professor posted her reaction to the antics by youth on Doha's Cornice. On National Day, young men can often be seen riding on the hoods of cars, doing tricks with their four wheel drive vehicles, such as driving them on two wheels, or dressing up, wearing masks to shock pedestrians and passersby. The woman was posting through an alias on the popular online forum, *Qatar Living*. Yet due to the small population, people were able to discover her real identity. Her post in the forum "Shame on Qatar on National Day" and on Facebook "Qatar National Day: A Day of Shameful Behavior" sparked a national dialogue about who had the right to criticize the country. The comments revealed the depth of the disagreement and the double-sided nature of the Internet as a space to debate social issues. The reactions to the original post are an example of social contagion, defined by Kent Miller, Frances Fabian., and Shu-Jou Lin (2009) as an incident when content garners a rapidly growing response from other users as more and more people join the conversation (p. 320). The post created a cascade effect among expats and nationals both on the original site and others who posted about it. The cascade in this sense affected the ways in which either group reacted to the post; the early adopters in both communities represented the tone for the rest of the group. A post by an expatriate university professor on the popular forum Qatar Living sparked a lively online debate between hundreds of participants from all sections of the community. Commenting on boys celebrating during Qatari National Day, the speaker juxtaposed the inability of an ambulance to get through a roundabout against youth revelers and draws a negative conclusion about the overarching values of the society in general:

It took an ambulance 20 minutes to get through a single roundabout with their lights flashing and sirens blasting, because these Qatari boys were so intent on showing off they blocked all traffic and couldn't hear the sirens with their music blasting. No problem if anyone died because the ambulance couldn't get to them; after all, it's more important to have a HUGE display for Qatar National Day!

The entire post sparked what many felt was the closest thing to a "culture" war that Qatar had ever seen. There was an intense response, with over 78 comments, on a popular blog hosted by another professor on an adjacent campus. Here the reactions were more measured with both expats and locals debating the nature of criticism (all spelling from the original post):

No one goes to people from a certain nationality, race, identity, or even a fan club and criticize them to their faces (especially on a special day for them) in a mean and arrogant manner, expecting them not to react.

The issues expanded to include notions of Qatarization, expat motivations for moving overseas, and impressions of both sides. Expats also chided Clayton for her post:

You have to agree with me that [expats] don't interfere in Qatar's customs, traditions, politics, etc. You only came to Qatar for a living, so don't hide behind this fact. If you are a citizen of Qatar, then you must make sure that expats residing in Qatar do not influence the demographic picture, even though their numbers are much more than the locals. To Lisa: I don't know your nationality but I am sure you did a big mistake by giving your opinion about your host country while you are in that country.

The discussion grew even more heated when Lisa herself came to comment on the blog. She described the result of her actions, after 10 years of living in Qatar:

I have repeatedly apologized on QL and on the Anti-Lisa Clayton FB group, as well as privately to many of my attackers. I have been banned from QL and can't write anymore. I am destroyed by my own poor choice of words and my life here is over. I have nothing left to give.

Ultimately her contract was not renewed at her institution and she moved on to another GCC country, Bahrain. The interactions about and around the National Day post are a microcosm of the disciplining aspect of social media in Qatar. The most interesting parts of this exchange circulate around the open discussion of the "Us Against Them" paradigm, an unspoken but understood given in everyday life in the country.

The urge to defend Qatar against insults on social media has been demonstrated on other platforms, including Instagram. As explained by Miller, Fabian and Lin (2009), no switching of membership in these instances occurs because "loyalty is high" and in this case, nationalist sentiments (p. 309). The defense of the country against perceived threats to its reputation or culture is a common practice by nationals in online forums. These behaviors speak both to the siege-like mentality, which many feel due to the population numbers as well as serve as an example of homophilous affiliation patterns by which the community defends itself against insults by foreigners. Even if people would agree in private that a comment might not be that threating, in public, or in this case the Internet, they may indicate otherwise.

A popular application is where users can post photos, using filters and cropping style options similar to Photoshop, and upload to followers. Photos can be marked with captions, commented on, and identified through hashtags. Unless a user's account is private, her photos are visible to the general public. Often expats' use of social media is to showcase those features that are unique to their host country. This can be tongue-in-cheek and take a humorous angle. One such post on Instagram of a Landcrusier with a BB Pin on the back, a unique number for BlackBerry handheld devices allowing access to a free messaging service, generated a volley of comments between the poster and nationals who felt the post was offensive because of the #sodoha hashtag. The primary criticism against the use of #sodoha was that it gave outsiders an unfavorable image of Qatar. There was no space for humor or sarcasm in dealing with the foibles of everyday life in the capital. In an honor-based, collectivist culture, like Qatari society, the importance of saving face overrides all other values including the assertion of an individual's humor or opinion if it could harm the reputation of the majority. During the course of the conversation, the expat and nationals debated the use of the hashtag. With the first commenter, the tone of the debate was about appropriateness of the hashtag, which responders felt was disrespectful, influencing outside perceptions of Qatar. At the core of this exchange are conflicting ideas about the use of humor as social commentary and respectful nationalism. The disagreement between the expat and the nationals demonstrates contrasting values of the nature of postings on social media.

moha_doha: *Anyone silly enough to still have a Blackberry may also be the kind of person who would add this guy... #bbpin #hilarious #sodoha*

__almannai: *#sodoha? I think this hashtag is #inappropriate to be said about "our" country:) @moha_doha*

Her use of quotes around "our" country allowed the expat to know that she is not to claim Qatar as her own since such distinctions are only for citizens. The smiley face emoticon keeps the tone friendly, perhaps to soften the blow. Their

conversation continued through the reply feature as the national and expat offered their interpretations of the caption below the posted photo, each asserting their original point. The national insisted on the negativity of the hashtag, saying that it was not applied to the positive pictures the user posted from Qatar. The expat contested the label of negative, asserting that the hashtag was intended to be humorous. Their exchange is an example of a semiotic situation made possible through the online platform of Instagram. With a photo and caption, the two conducted an in depth discussion about issues related to presentation, appropriateness, and humor. A few minutes later, however, they are reminded this exchange is not held in a vacuum. Another national did not feel the need to be so restrained.

Therealnoor: *BlackBerrys are smart phones! Owning one would make you technology advanced not "silly." Just because you can't afford one it doesn't mean you put your jealousy on those who can.*

Misconstruing the comment to be about the facility of the BlackBerry, the commentator returns the perceived insult with one of her own, an accusation that the poster cannot afford a BlackBerry, and hence her post. What happens next, however, is that the expat has had enough of these comments because of an exchange happening on another post elsewhere. The hashtag added, #iphone, informs the commenter that the user is in fact more than capable of owning a BlackBerry since she is posting from the more expensive iPhone. The back and forth between the expat and the national demonstrate many of the core identity issues at stake for these two groups even in an online setting.

moha_doha: *@therealnoor Can you please go hate on someone else whose sense of humor you don't get? #iphone*

Since the user has been blocked, another interesting turn happens in the conversation. Someone else, perhaps a friend of the original commenter, appears to take issue with the joke made in the caption.

___hessa: *@therealnoor She's not the one hating; you just have a horrible sense of humor.*

moha_doha: *@___hessa Guess that's an opinion and this is a public space so feel free to find something more to your taste somewhere else.*

The expat resists the nationals' attempts to define her humor as positive or negative interpretations of life in Qatar, or as a reflection of Qatar in general. She reminds the followers who take issue with the post that the Instagram is a voluntary public forum. In doing so, she rejects their attempts to police her behavior. This exchange on Instagram, with six likes and 12 comments, demonstrates the level of detail at which nationals take pride in their country and issue with expats posting their perspectives on Qatar in social media outlets. While other Qataris did like the original photo, they did not enter the conversation via the comments chain.

The same dynamic between a poster and commenters is exhibited in the comments section of another photo. This image is of a broken Gucci shoe, with the heel hanging off. The poster marks the photo with the @gucci tag, perhaps in the hopes that the retailer would respond to the fact it takes a long time to fix a shoe with only one outlet in Qatar. The only other solution is to send it Italy, which can take as long as three months. This post also had the accompanying hashtag #sodoha. The commenter from the previous post took issue with the limitations of Gucci shoe repair options in Doha as the problem:

Yes, this is how it should be fixed. If you can't afford that solution, don't buy it! Just as simple as that. The problem is not Doha or finding a

good shop in Doha. It's your problem. You had the solution but you threw it on Doha! So lame.

Here she directly defended the capital of the city-state against insult and once again, the question of cost reared its head. The affluence of the Qatari population is overstated in many cases, as not all families have the same degree of wealth. Yet the assumption that the problem is a financial one is undertaken by more than one commenter in this post: "No one told you to buy a fake and come look for a repair shop! See if it was real you'd just go to Gucci." The expat took umbrage here, as she did not in the original post, and asked her own questions about why there were repeated references to her purchasing power:

Wow. Feel better for having corrected lame old me. Do people keep assuming I can't "afford" X because my face is brown? The solution costs nothing but a ridiculous amount of time. And time is all we have. A luxury brand should offer much, much more for a faulty product. And yes you're right, it's a Gucci problem not a Doha one, though this is the second time it's happened to me here, and if there were more retailers here, they could have more solutions. Hope Doha appreciates the time spent defending it from hashtag lame-os on the Internet.

At that point she blocked both commenters so that they couldn't keep replying and the conversation ended. As her avatar is of an Indian woman, she concludes the nationals are relying on stereotypes about Indians in Qatar, which include the assumption that they are qualified only for menial jobs as maids, cooks, or drivers.

These exchanges are a few examples of the online reputation management through social media as a major concern for nationals, and the underlying cultural assumptions, which infuse every conversation. Expats, meanwhile, are trying to put forward their perspectives on life in Qatar, which often contrast with their memories of life in their home country.

GOVERNMENT MONITORING

Internet usage and communities in the Middle East occupy a more vexed space vis-à-vis the context of the user because of the monitoring policies of Arab governments. Words typically ascribed to Internet usage, including "democratic," may not have the resonance that they are assumed to have in the West. In fact, the lauded values of European or North American countries, free expression and exchange, may be harmful as demonstrated by recent arrests in the United Arab Emirates in 2012. Normal citizens are not the only ones using social media to discipline those who violate cultural norms; within the Ministry of Culture, the Department of Information and the Censorship Office screen all books that come into the country and give permission for any book or magazine printed within Qatar. The telecom provider, Qtel, performs a similar sorting of content on the Internet by in country users by key words related to sexuality.

The reminder that nationals are also subject to scrutiny was brought across when Qatari poet Mohammed Rashid Al Ajami was sentenced to life in prison for his poetry. His poem, written after the Arab Spring and recorded in Cairo, included the offending line, "We are all Tunisia in the face of the repressive elite." In equating himself and the people of Qatar with the protestors in Tunisia, Al-Ajami was eventually charged with "insulting the Emir" and "inciting the overthrow of the ruling regime" (Omarsc, Dec. 4, 2012). The extension of an honor culture, where saving face is very important, is heightened by the regime's sensitivity in managing any threats against it. Even this subdued line is read as a threat in a post-revolutionary climate when Arab governments have been toppled in Tunisia, Libya and Egypt. The state monitors the actions of citizens on social media as a form of reputation management.

The government has made arrests, as in the case of one self-defined Internet activist, Saleh al-Dhufairi, because of "of spreading ideas by speech, writing, and any other means that provoke strife,

hurt national unity, and social peace" (Messieh). The jailing of GCC nationals is a new step that demonstrates the anxiety governments have over the behaviors of their citizens and residents on social media networks. Many of the arrests in the GCC have been for what people have said on the their Twitter accounts.

Yet this is not the only platform that is being monitored, however, as a Facebook post about UAE Wikileaks documents demonstrates. Within minutes of a post about 7 twitter users being arrested, three of them UAE nationals, the link was broken. "403 Forbidden," was the message anyone who tried to click the link saw. The ensuing commentary on the post was as telling as the attempt to restrict access to the article. What followed exposes an interesting exchange of ideas between expats and residents of the UAE about the life and policies of the government.

"403 Forbidden in three minutes. Lol, and ppl [people] think we're crazy," someone posted. From commentary about the broken link itself, others reflected on the motives behind the action to block and the implications for greater UAE policies. An expat offered his perspective on the UAE's role on the global stage: "You guys have done so much for the world recently. What the hell is going on. You contribute so much to getting Islam out of the dark ages. Stay with the program please. Remember your roots—you were not meant to live like brutes."

Many did not share the idea that the decision to block the article about the tweets was based on Islamic motives. Others found the motive for the arrests more easily understood, through the lens of nationality: "Don't screw with a country that does not like you."

The two viewpoints, one that the government was cracking down on social media usage based on Islamic principles, and two, that expats were not welcome in the country and therefore should be careful of their actions, co-existed alongside other comments about 403 Forbidden and users asking for information on why the link wasn't working, demonstrating the multi-faceted nature of reactions to the Facebook wall post. The complicated nature of interactions between expats and nationals, and the constant presence of the government as intermediary of these exchanges, is an additional layer in the dynamics of online communities within Qatar and the GCC.

CONCLUSION

Social media in the GCC is a complex tool used in a variety of ways by expatriates and nationals. The various platforms present opportunities for individuals who would not normally interact to share, discuss, and debate ideas pertinent to the unique context of their everyday lives in Qatar. Given the limited opportunities for meaningful face-to-face communication between disparate groups, online platforms can play a key role in such contexts. Twitter, Facebook, and Instagram, among others, allow interpersonal exchange through continuous access, moderated at the discretion of the user. Nationals and expats can access others' opinions, evaluate and adjust their thoughts and actions. Social media usage in Qatar allows users to reaffirm their identities, which are often rooted in racial or national affiliations.

The nature of social relationships in such a small country, however, also presents a variety of limitations, given the concerns between expatriates and nationals about employment compensation and cultural mores. Pressure to behave within governmentally established limits applies to both expats and nationals. The most successful usage of social media in Qatar centers on knowledge and information sharing. As the country continues to grow and develop, her citizens and residents will continue to grapple with the terms of engagement around cultural critique.

REFERENCES

Black, R. (2009). Online fan fiction, global identities and imagination. *Research in the Teaching of English*, *43*(4), 397–425.

Dubai School of Government. (2011). *Arab social media report*. Retrieved from http://www.dsg.ae/LinkClick.aspx?fileticket=-WvgLGPQ9G0%3d&tabid=1163

Fabian, F., Miller, K.D., & Lin, S-J. (n.d.). Strategies for online communities. *Strategic Management Journal, 30* (3), 305-322.

Fromherz, A. J. (2012). *Qatar: A modern history*. Washington, DC: Georgetown University Press.

Ghareeb, E. (2000). New media and the information revolution in the Arab world: An assessment. *The Middle East Journal*, *54*(3), 395–418.

Joseph, S. (2000). *Gendering citizenship in the Middle East. Gender and Citizenship in the Middle East*. Syracuse, NY: Syracuse University Press.

League, R., & Chalmers, I. (2010). Degrees of caution: Arab girls unveil on Facebook. In S. R. Mazzarella (Ed.), *Girl wide web 2.0* (pp. 27–44). New York: Peter Lang Publishing.

Messieh, N. (2012, March 7). UAE citizen arrested for criticizing security forces on Twitter. *The Next Web*. Retrieved from http://thenextweb.com/me/2012/03/07/uae-citizen-arrested-for-criticizing-security-forces-on-twitter/

Miller, K. D., & Frances, F. (2008). Strategies for online communities. *Strategic Management Journal*, *30*, 305–322. doi:10.1002/smj.735

Omarsc. (2012, December 4). Lawyer: Qatari poet sentenced to life in prison is Gulf's Mandela. *Doha News*. Retrieved from http://dohanews.co/post/37109798863/lawyer-poet-sentenced-to-life-in-prison-is-qatars

Rajakumar, M. (2012). Faceless Facebook: Qatari women choose wisely. In *New media literacies and participatory popular culture across borders*. New York: Routledge.

Sefton-Green, J. (2006). Youth, technology, and media cultures. *Review of Research in Education*, *30*, 279–306. doi:10.3102/0091732X030001279

Wheeler, D. L. (2001). The internet and public culture in Kuwait. *Gazette*, *63*(2-3), 187–201.

KEY TERMS AND DEFINITIONS

Hashtag: A word indicated by the pound or hashkey # in social media to signify a particular topic, event, or person. Users employ hashtags to allow others to follow their thoughts on particular topics or themes.

Niqab: Face covering veil, usually black, which covers all but a woman's eyes. Worn by Muslim women in the Arabian Gulf.

Related References

To continue our tradition of advancing information science and technology research, we have compiled a list of recommended IGI Global readings. These references will provide additional information and guidance to further enrich your knowledge and assist you with your own research and future publications.

Acilar, A., & Karamasa, Ç. (2013). Factors affecting e-commerce adoption by small businesses in a developing country: A case study of a small hotel. In S. Chhabra (Ed.), *ICT influences on human development, interaction, and collaboration* (pp. 174–184). Hershey, PA: Information Science Reference.

Ahmed, N. U., Montagno, R., & Sharma, S. (2012). Strategy and structure in a virtual organization. In S. Sharma (Ed.), *E-adoption and technologies for empowering developing countries: Global advances* (pp. 34–45). Hershey, PA: Information Science Reference. doi:10.4018/978-1-4666-0041-6.ch003

Aikins, S. K., & Chary, M. (2013). Online participation and digital divide: An empirical evaluation of U.S. midwestern municipalities. In I. Association (Ed.), *Digital literacy: Concepts, methodologies, tools, and applications* (pp. 63–85). Hershey, PA: Information Science Reference.

Al-Nuaim, H. A. (2013). Developing user profiles for interactive online products in practice. In M. Garcia-Ruiz (Ed.), *Cases on usability engineering: Design and development of digital products* (pp. 57–79). Hershey, PA: Information Science Reference. doi:10.4018/978-1-4666-4046-7.ch003

Al-Shqairat, Z. I., & Altarawneh, I. I. (2013). The role of partnership in e-government readiness: The knowledge stations (KSs) initiative in Jordan. In A. Mesquita (Ed.), *User perception and influencing factors of technology in everyday life* (pp. 192–210). Hershey, PA: Information Science Reference.

Albers, M. J. (2012). How people approach finding information. In *Human-information interaction and technical communication: Concepts and frameworks* (pp. 398–427). Hershey, PA: Information Science Reference. doi:10.4018/978-1-4666-0152-9.ch012

Albers, M. J. (2012). How people approach graphical information. In *Human-information interaction and technical communication: Concepts and frameworks* (pp. 262–295). Hershey, PA: Information Science Reference. doi:10.4018/978-1-4666-0152-9.ch008

Albers, M. J. (2012). How people approach information. In *Human-information interaction and technical communication: Concepts and frameworks* (pp. 114–169). Hershey, PA: Information Science Reference. doi:10.4018/978-1-4666-0152-9.ch004

Albers, M. J. (2012). How people approach technology-based interactions. In *Human-information interaction and technical communication: Concepts and frameworks* (pp. 170–216). Hershey, PA: Information Science Reference. doi:10.4018/978-1-4666-0152-9.ch005

Albers, M. J. (2012). How people approach typography. In *Human-information interaction and technical communication: Concepts and frameworks* (pp. 241–261). Hershey, PA: Information Science Reference. doi:10.4018/978-1-4666-0152-9.ch007

Albers, M. J. (2012). How people interact with information presentation. In *Human-information interaction and technical communication: Concepts and frameworks* (pp. 330–365). Hershey, PA: Information Science Reference. doi:10.4018/978-1-4666-0152-9.ch010

Albers, M. J. (2012). How people make decisions and take action. In *Human-information interaction and technical communication: Concepts and frameworks* (pp. 428–458). Hershey, PA: Information Science Reference. doi:10.4018/978-1-4666-0152-9.ch013

Albers, M. J. (2012). How people perform a first glance evaluation. In *Human-information interaction and technical communication: Concepts and frameworks* (pp. 218–240). Hershey, PA: Information Science Reference. doi:10.4018/978-1-4666-0152-9.ch006

Albers, M. J. (2012). Information in the situation. In *Human-information interaction and technical communication: Concepts and frameworks* (pp. 31–60). Hershey, PA: Information Science Reference. doi:10.4018/978-1-4666-0152-9.ch002

Albers, M. J. (2012). What people bring with them. In *Human-information interaction and technical communication: Concepts and frameworks* (pp. 61–113). Hershey, PA: Information Science Reference. doi:10.4018/978-1-4666-0152-9.ch003

Albert, S., & Flournoy, D. (2012). Think global, act local: How ICTs are changing the landscape in community development. In E. Coakes (Ed.), *Technological change and societal growth: Analyzing the future* (pp. 101–116). Hershey, PA: Information Science Reference. doi:10.4018/978-1-4666-0200-7.ch007

Alexopoulos, G., Koutsouris, A., & Tzouramani, I. (2012). Adoption and use of ICTs among rural youth: Evidence from Greece. In S. Chhabra (Ed.), *ICTs for advancing rural communities and human development: Addressing the digital divide* (pp. 125–142). Hershey, PA: Information Science Reference. doi:10.4018/978-1-4666-0047-8.ch009

Alfaro, F., Molina, J. P., & Camacho, K. (2012). Public access ICT in Dominican Republic. In R. Gomez (Ed.), *Libraries, telecentres, cybercafes and public access to ICT: International comparisons* (pp. 184–200). Hershey, PA: Information Science Publishing.

Alhussain, T., & Drew, S. (2012). Employees' perceptions of biometric technology adoption in e-government: An exploratory study in the kingdom of Saudi Arabia. In S. Sharma (Ed.), *E-adoption and technologies for empowering developing countries: Global advances* (pp. 129–142). Hershey, PA: Information Science Reference. doi:10.4018/978-1-4666-0041-6.ch010

Alkhattabi, M., Neagu, D., & Cullen, A. (2012). User perceptions of information quality in e-learning systems: A gender and cultural perspective. In R. Pande, & T. Van der Weide (Eds.), *Globalization, technology diffusion and gender disparity: Social impacts of ICTs* (pp. 138–145). Hershey, PA: Information Science Reference. doi:10.4018/978-1-4666-0020-1.ch012

Amoretti, F., & Musella, F. (2013). Governing digital divides: Power structures and ICT strategies in a global perspective. In I. Association (Ed.), *Digital literacy: Concepts, methodologies, tools, and applications* (pp. 1256–1271). Hershey, PA: Information Science Reference.

Andacht, F. (2013). The tangible lure of the technoself in the age of reality television. In R. Luppicini (Ed.), *Handbook of research on technoself: Identity in a technological society* (pp. 360–381). Hershey, PA: Information Science Reference.

Anderson, C. S., Al-Gahtani, S., & Hubona, G. (2013). The value of TAM antecedents in global IS development and research. In A. Dwivedi, & S. Clarke (Eds.), *Innovative strategies and approaches for end-user computing advancements* (pp. 19–39). Hershey, PA: Information Science Reference.

Arifoglu, A., Afacan, G., & Er, E. (2013). Guidelines for successful public internet access points (PIAPs) implementation. In I. Association (Ed.), *Digital literacy: Concepts, methodologies, tools, and applications* (pp. 502–521). Hershey, PA: Information Science Reference.

Arning, K., & Ziefle, M. (2012). Ask and you will receive: Training novice adults to use a PDA in an active learning environment. In J. Lumsden (Ed.), *Social and organizational impacts of emerging mobile devices: Evaluating use* (pp. 20–47). Hershey, PA: Information Science Reference. doi:10.4018/978-1-4666-0194-9.ch002

Arpaci, I., & Gürbüz, T. (2013). Innovation in learning: Innovative tools and techniques for learning. In S. Sharma (Ed.), *Adoption of virtual technologies for business, educational, and governmental advancements* (pp. 117–125). Hershey, PA: Information Science Reference.

Asino, T. I., Wilder, H., & Ferris, S. P. (2012). Innovative use of ICT in Namibia for nationhood: Special emphasis on the Namibian newspaper. In R. Lekoko, & L. Semali (Eds.), *Cases on developing countries and ICT integration: Rural community development* (pp. 53–61). Hershey, PA: Information Science Reference.

Bainbridge, W. S. (2013). Ancestor veneration avatars. In R. Luppicini (Ed.), *Handbook of research on technoself: Identity in a technological society* (pp. 308–321). Hershey, PA: Information Science Reference.

Baker, P. M., Fairchild, A., & Pater, J. (2012). E-accessibility and municipal wi-fi: Exploring a model for inclusivity and implementation. In S. Chhabra (Ed.), *ICTs for advancing rural communities and human development: Addressing the digital divide* (pp. 109–124). Hershey, PA: Information Science Reference. doi:10.4018/978-1-4666-0047-8.ch008

Ballesté, F., & Torras, C. (2013). Effects of human-machine integration on the construction of identity. In R. Luppicini (Ed.), *Handbook of research on technoself: Identity in a technological society* (pp. 574–591). Hershey, PA: Information Science Reference.

Barker, R. (2013). Social networking and identity. In R. Luppicini (Ed.), *Handbook of research on technoself: Identity in a technological society* (pp. 474–501). Hershey, PA: Information Science Reference.

Barker, S., & Fiedler, B. (2013). Developers, decision makers, strategists or just end-users? Redefining end-user computing for the 21st century: A case study. In A. Dwivedi, & S. Clarke (Eds.), *Innovative strategies and approaches for end-user computing advancements* (pp. 61–76). Hershey, PA: Information Science Reference.

Barlach, A., Hertzum, M., & Simonsen, J. (2013). Pilot implementation driven by effects specifications and formative usability evaluation. In M. Garcia-Ruiz (Ed.), *Cases on usability engineering: Design and development of digital products* (pp. 221–254). Hershey, PA: Information Science Reference. doi:10.4018/978-1-4666-4046-7.ch010

Barón, L. F., & Valdés, M. (2012). Public access ICT in Colombia. In R. Gomez (Ed.), *Libraries, telecentres, cybercafes and public access to ICT: International comparisons* (pp. 169–183). Hershey, PA: Information Science Publishing.

Baum, S., & Mahizhnan, A. (2013). Public participation in e-government: Some questions about social inclusion in the Singapore model. In I. Association (Ed.), *Digital literacy: Concepts, methodologies, tools, and applications* (pp. 1044–1058). Hershey, PA: Information Science Reference.

Beedle, J., & Wang, S. (2013). Roles of a technology leader. In S. Wang, & T. Hartsell (Eds.), *Technology integration and foundations for effective leadership* (pp. 228–241). Hershey, PA: Information Science Reference.

Beklemishev, A. P. (2012). Public access ICT in Kazakhstan. In R. Gomez (Ed.), *Libraries, telecentres, cybercafes and public access to ICT: International comparisons* (pp. 330–343). Hershey, PA: Information Science Publishing.

Ben, E. R. (2012). Gendering professionalism in the internationalization of information work. In R. Pande, & T. Van der Weide (Eds.), *Globalization, technology diffusion and gender disparity: Social impacts of ICTs* (pp. 51–69). Hershey, PA: Information Science Reference. doi:10.4018/978-1-4666-0020-1.ch005

Bentley, C. M. (2013). Designing and implementing online collaboration tools in West Africa. In N. Azab (Ed.), *Cases on web 2.0 in developing countries: Studies on implementation, application, and use* (pp. 33–60). Hershey, PA: Information Science Reference.

Bentley, Y., & Clarke, S. (2013). Evaluation of information strategy implementation: A critical approach. In A. Dwivedi, & S. Clarke (Eds.), *Innovative strategies and approaches for end-user computing advancements* (pp. 1–18). Hershey, PA: Information Science Reference.

Beuschel, W. (2013). The net generation and changes in knowledge acquisition. In T. Takševa (Ed.), *Social software and the evolution of user expertise: Future trends in knowledge creation and dissemination* (pp. 201–226). Hershey, PA: Information Science Reference.

Bhaskar, S. (2012). Moving with time and strategy: India and Bangladesh's development in the era of ICTs. In R. Lekoko, & L. Semali (Eds.), *Cases on developing countries and ICT integration: Rural community development* (pp. 146–161). Hershey, PA: Information Science Reference.

Bielenia-Grajewska, M. (2013). Actor-network-theory in medical e-communication: The role of websites in creating and maintaining healthcare corporate online identity. In A. Tatnall (Ed.), *Social and professional applications of actor-network theory for technology development* (pp. 156–172). Hershey, PA: Information Science Reference.

Black, D. (2013). The digital soul. In R. Luppicini (Ed.), *Handbook of research on technoself: Identity in a technological society* (pp. 157–174). Hershey, PA: Information Science Reference.

Boelter, J., & Kaschub, C. (2013). Developing the intel® pair & share experience. In M. Garcia-Ruiz (Ed.), *Cases on usability engineering: Design and development of digital products* (pp. 171–194). Hershey, PA: Information Science Reference. doi:10.4018/978-1-4666-4046-7.ch008

Bonelli, S., & Napoletano, L. (2013). The usability evaluation of a touch screen in the flight deck. In M. Garcia-Ruiz (Ed.), *Cases on usability engineering: Design and development of digital products* (pp. 270–297). Hershey, PA: Information Science Reference. doi:10.4018/978-1-4666-4046-7.ch012

Bourgault, M., Drouin, N., Sicotte, H., & Daoudi, J. (2012). Moderating effect of team distributedness on organizational dimensions for innovation project success. In A. Mesquita (Ed.), *Human interaction with technology for working, communicating, and learning: Advancements* (pp. 216–235). Hershey, PA: Information Science Reference.

Bowe, B. J., Blom, R., & Freedman, E. (2013). Negotiating boundaries between control and dissent: Free speech, business, and repressitarian governments. In J. Lannon, & E. Halpin (Eds.), *Human rights and information communication technologies: Trends and consequences of use* (pp. 36–55). Hershey, PA: Information Science Reference.

Bricout, J. C., & Baker, P. M. (2012). Deploying information and communication technologies (ICT) to enhance participation in local governance for citizens with disabilities. In S. Chhabra (Ed.), *ICTs for advancing rural communities and human development: Addressing the digital divide* (pp. 91–108). Hershey, PA: Information Science Reference. doi:10.4018/978-1-4666-0047-8.ch007

Butcher, K. R., & Sumner, T. (2013). How does prior knowledge impact students' online learning behaviors? In R. Zheng (Ed.), *Evolving psychological and educational perspectives on cyber behavior* (pp. 97–115). Hershey, PA: Information Science Reference.

Bwalya, K. J. (2012). Botswana's novel approaches for knowledge-based economy facilitation: Issues, policies and contextual framework. In S. Chhabra (Ed.), *ICTs for advancing rural communities and human development: Addressing the digital divide* (pp. 45–56). Hershey, PA: Information Science Reference. doi:10.4018/978-1-4666-0047-8.ch004

Bwalya, K. J. (2012). Towards a knowledge-based economy – The case of Botswana: A discussion article. In E. Coakes (Ed.), *Technological change and societal growth: Analyzing the future* (pp. 117–127). Hershey, PA: Information Science Reference. doi:10.4018/978-1-4666-0200-7.ch008

Bwalya, K. J., Du Plessis, T., & Rensleigh, C. (2013). A snapshot overview of the digital divide: E-inclusion and e-government in the Zambian context. In I. Association (Ed.), *Digital literacy: Concepts, methodologies, tools, and applications* (pp. 1–19). Hershey, PA: Information Science Reference.

Byrd, T. A., & Byrd, L. W. (2012). Contrasting IT capability and organizational types: Implications for firm performance. In A. Dwivedi, & S. Clarke (Eds.), *End-user computing, development, and software engineering: New challenges* (pp. 1–24). Hershey, PA: Information Science Reference. doi:10.4018/978-1-4666-0140-6.ch001

Cabitza, F., & Simone, C. (2012). WOAD: A framework to enable the end-user development of coordination-oriented functionalities. In A. Dwivedi, & S. Clarke (Eds.), *End-user computing, development, and software engineering: New challenges* (pp. 127–147). Hershey, PA: Information Science Reference. doi:10.4018/978-1-4666-0140-6.ch006

Carofiglio, V., & Abbattista, F. (2013). BCI-based user-centered design for emotionally-driven user experience. In M. Garcia-Ruiz (Ed.), *Cases on usability engineering: Design and development of digital products* (pp. 299–320). Hershey, PA: Information Science Reference. doi:10.4018/978-1-4666-4046-7.ch013

Carpenter, J. (2013). Just doesn't look right: Exploring the impact of humanoid robot integration into explosive ordnance disposal teams. In R. Luppicini (Ed.), *Handbook of research on technoself: Identity in a technological society* (pp. 609–636). Hershey, PA: Information Science Reference.

Cartelli, A. (2013). A framework for digital competence assessment. In I. Association (Ed.), *Digital literacy: Concepts, methodologies, tools, and applications* (pp. 196–212). Hershey, PA: Information Science Reference.

Cartelli, A. (2013). Theory and practice in digital competence assessment. In I. Association (Ed.), *Digital literacy: Concepts, methodologies, tools, and applications* (pp. 1367–1383). Hershey, PA: Information Science Reference.

Carter, P. D. (2012). The emerging story of the machine. In A. Mesquita (Ed.), *Human interaction with technology for working, communicating, and learning: advancements* (pp. 1–12). Hershey, PA: Information Science Reference.

Chadwick, D. D., Fullwood, C., & Wesson, C. J. (2013). Intellectual disability, identity, and the internet. In R. Luppicini (Ed.), *Handbook of research on technoself: Identity in a technological society* (pp. 229–254). Hershey, PA: Information Science Reference.

Chaka, C. (2013). Digitization and consumerization of identity, culture, and power among gen mobinets in South Africa. In R. Luppicini (Ed.), *Handbook of research on technoself: Identity in a technological society* (pp. 399–418). Hershey, PA: Information Science Reference.

Chan, L., & Daim, T. (2012). High technology industrialization and internationalization: Exploring international technology transfer. In A. Cakir, & P. Ordóñez de Pablos (Eds.), *Social development and high technology industries: Strategies and applications* (pp. 70–98). Hershey, PA: Information Science Reference.

Chand, A. (2013). Reducing digital divide: The case of the 'people first network' (PFNet) in the Solomon Islands. In I. Association (Ed.), *Digital literacy: Concepts, methodologies, tools, and applications* (pp. 1571–1605). Hershey, PA: Information Science Reference.

Charnkit, P., & Tatnall, A. (2013). Knowledge conversion processes in Thai public organisations seen as an innovation: The re-analysis of a TAM study using innovation translation. In A. Tatnall (Ed.), *Social and professional applications of actor-network theory for technology development* (pp. 88–102). Hershey, PA: Information Science Reference.

Chary, M. (2013). Social equity, the digital divide and e-governance: An analysis of e-governance initiatives in India. In I. Association (Ed.), *Digital literacy: Concepts, methodologies, tools, and applications* (pp. 1321–1334). Hershey, PA: Information Science Reference.

Chary, M., & Aikins, S. K. (2013). Policy as a bridge across the global digital divide. In I. Association (Ed.), *Digital literacy: Concepts, methodologies, tools, and applications* (pp. 364–379). Hershey, PA: Information Science Reference.

Chase, N. M., & Clegg, B. (2013). Effects of email utilization on higher education professionals. In A. Mesquita (Ed.), *User perception and influencing factors of technology in everyday life* (pp. 233–247). Hershey, PA: Information Science Reference.

Chen, T., Harper, S., & Yesilada, Y. (2013). How do people use their mobile phones? A field study of small device users. In J. Lumsden (Ed.), *Developments in technologies for human-centric mobile computing and applications* (pp. 38–55). Hershey, PA: Information Science Reference.

Chen, W., & Xie, W. (2012). Cyber behaviors of immigrants. In Z. Yan (Ed.), *Encyclopedia of cyber behavior* (pp. 259–272). Hershey, PA: Information Science Reference. doi:10.4018/978-1-4666-0315-8.ch022

Chen, Y. (2012). The center for mobile communication studies. In Z. Yan (Ed.), *Encyclopedia of cyber behavior* (pp. 77–87). Hershey, PA: Information Science Reference. doi:10.4018/978-1-4666-0315-8.ch006

Chen, Y., Lee, B., & Kirk, R. M. (2013). Internet use among older adults: Constraints and opportunities. In R. Zheng, R. Hill, & M. Gardner (Eds.), *Engaging older adults with modern technology: Internet use and information access needs* (pp. 124–141). Hershey, PA: Information Science Reference.

Chilana, P. K., Fishman, E., Geraghty, E. M., Tarczy-Hornoch, P., Wolf, F. M., & Anderson, N. R. (2013). Characterizing data discovery and end-user computing needs in clinical translational science. In A. Dwivedi, & S. Clarke (Eds.), *Innovative strategies and approaches for end-user computing advancements* (pp. 301–313). Hershey, PA: Information Science Reference.

Choi, S. M., Chu, S., & Kim, Y. (2012). Culture-laden social engagement: A comparative study of social relationships in social networking sites among American, Chinese and Korean Users. In K. St.Amant, & S. Kelsey (Eds.), *Computer-mediated communication across cultures: International interactions in online environments* (pp. 1–16). Hershey, PA: Information Science Reference.

Chong, L., Mei, W., & Guang, A. W. (2013). Research and implementation of self-publishing website platforms for universities based on CMS. In T. Gao (Ed.), *Global applications of pervasive and ubiquitous computing* (pp. 166–178). Hershey, PA: Information Science Reference.

Chudoba, K. M., Watson-Manheim, M. B., Crowston, K., & Lee, C. S. (2013). Participation in ICT-enabled meetings. In A. Dwivedi, & S. Clarke (Eds.), *Innovative strategies and approaches for end-user computing advancements* (pp. 192–214). Hershey, PA: Information Science Reference.

Clark, E. (2013). Interaction and expertise in an Appalachian music archive. In T. Takševa (Ed.), *Social software and the evolution of user expertise: Future trends in knowledge creation and dissemination* (pp. 311–329). Hershey, PA: Information Science Reference.

Coakes, E., & Coakes, J. (2012). Exploring meaning: The implications of a hyphen for socio-technical theory and practice. In E. Coakes (Ed.), *Technological change and societal growth: Analyzing the future* (pp. 1–35). Hershey, PA: Information Science Reference. doi:10.4018/978-1-4666-0200-7.ch001

Colomo-Palacios, R., Ruano-Mayoral, M., Soto-Acosta, P., & García-Crespo, Á. (2012). Identifying competences in IT professionals through semantics. In E. Coakes (Ed.), *Technological change and societal growth: Analyzing the future* (pp. 88–99). Hershey, PA: Information Science Reference. doi:10.4018/978-1-4666-0200-7.ch006

Comunello, F. (2013). From the digital divide to multiple divides: Technology, society, and new media skills. In I. Association (Ed.), *Digital literacy: Concepts, methodologies, tools, and applications* (pp. 1622–1639). Hershey, PA: Information Science Reference.

Concha, A. S. (2012). Filipino cyborg sexualities, chatroom masculinities, self-ascribed identities, ephemeral selves. In R. Pande, & T. Van der Weide (Eds.), *Globalization, technology diffusion and gender disparity: Social impacts of ICTs* (pp. 211–224). Hershey, PA: Information Science Reference. doi:10.4018/978-1-4666-0020-1.ch018

Conway, J. (2013). Getting lost in the labyrinth: Information and technology in the marketplace. In B. Medlin (Ed.), *Integrations of technology utilization and social dynamics in organizations* (pp. 226–242). Hershey, PA: Information Science Reference.

Corbett, J., & Mann, R. (2012). Tlowitsis re-imagined: The use of digital media to build nation and overcome disconnection in a displaced aboriginal community. In S. Chhabra (Ed.), *ICTs for advancing rural communities and human development: Addressing the DIGITAL DIVIDE* (pp. 158–179). Hershey, PA: Information Science Reference. doi:10.4018/978-1-4666-0047-8.ch011

Cordella, A. (2013). Emerging standardization. In A. Tatnall (Ed.), *Social and professional applications of actor-network theory for technology development* (pp. 221–237). Hershey, PA: Information Science Reference.

Corrocher, N., & Raineri, A. (2013). The evolution of the digital divide across developing countries: Theoretical issues and empirical investigation. In I. Association (Ed.), *Digital literacy: Concepts, methodologies, tools, and applications* (pp. 1554–1570). Hershey, PA: Information Science Reference.

Coulton, P., & Bamford, W. (2013). Experimenting through mobile 'apps' and 'app stores. In J. Lumsden (Ed.), *Developments in technologies for human-centric mobile computing and applications* (pp. 277–293). Hershey, PA: Information Science Reference.

Cropf, R. A., Benmamoun, M., & Kalliny, M. (2013). The role of web 2.0 in the Arab spring. In N. Azab (Ed.), *Cases on web 2.0 in developing countries: Studies on implementation, application, and use* (pp. 76–108). Hershey, PA: Information Science Reference.

D'Andrea, A., Ferri, F., & Grifoni, P. (2013). Assessing e-health in Africa: Web 2.0 applications. In N. Azab (Ed.), *Cases on web 2.0 in developing countries: Studies on implementation, application, and use* (pp. 442–467). Hershey, PA: Information Science Reference.

DaCosta, B., Kinsell, C., & Nasah, A. (2013). Millennials are digital natives? An investigation into digital propensity and age. In I. Association (Ed.), *Digital literacy: Concepts, methodologies, tools, and applications* (pp. 103–119). Hershey, PA: Information Science Reference.

Dahms, M. (2013). Shifting focus from access to impact: Can computers alleviate poverty? In I. Association (Ed.), *Digital literacy: Concepts, methodologies, tools, and applications* (pp. 1743–1770). Hershey, PA: Information Science Reference.

Danihelka, J., Hak, R., Kencl, L., & Zara, J. (2013). 3D talking-head interface to voice-interactive services on mobile phones. In J. Lumsden (Ed.), *Developments in technologies for human-centric mobile computing and applications* (pp. 130–144). Hershey, PA: Information Science Reference.

Daugherty, J. L., Mentzer, N. J., Lybrook, D. O., & Little-Wiles, J. (2013). Philosophical perspectives on technology leadership. In S. Wang, & T. Hartsell (Eds.), *Technology integration and foundations for effective leadership* (pp. 42–56). Hershey, PA: Information Science Reference.

Dedeaux, T. (2013). An introduction to educational research. In S. Wang, & T. Hartsell (Eds.), *Technology integration and foundations for effective leadership* (pp. 319–340). Hershey, PA: Information Science Reference.

Deokar, A. V., Meservy, T. O., Helquist, J. H., & Kruse, J. (2013). Understanding collaboration success in context of cognitive and social presence. In B. Medlin (Ed.), *Integrations of technology utilization and social dynamics in organizations* (pp. 91–107). Hershey, PA: Information Science Reference.

DiMarco, J. (2013). Implementing a website portal using portfoliovillage.com to evaluate professional credentials. In S. Wang, & T. Hartsell (Eds.), *Technology integration and foundations for effective leadership* (pp. 308–317). Hershey, PA: Information Science Reference.

Doll, W. J., & Deng, X. (2013). Antecedents of improvisation in IT-enabled engineering work. In A. Dwivedi, & S. Clarke (Eds.), *Innovative strategies and approaches for end-user computing advancements* (pp. 242–264). Hershey, PA: Information Science Reference.

Doyle, J., Bertolotto, M., & Wilson, D. (2013). Towards multimodal mobile GIS for the elderly. In I. Association (Ed.), *Digital literacy: Concepts, methodologies, tools, and applications* (pp. 590–609). Hershey, PA: Information Science Reference.

Drigas, A., Kouremenos, D., & Vrettaros, J. (2013). Learning applications for disabled people. In I. Association (Ed.), *Digital literacy: Concepts, methodologies, tools, and applications* (pp. 1090–1103). Hershey, PA: Information Science Reference.

Dunn, H. S. (2013). Information literacy and the digital divide: Challenging e-exclusion in the global south. In I. Association (Ed.), *Digital literacy: Concepts, methodologies, tools, and applications* (pp. 20–38). Hershey, PA: Information Science Reference.

Dunn, R. A. (2013). Identity theories and technology. In R. Luppicini (Ed.), *Handbook of research on technoself: Identity in a technological society* (pp. 26–44). Hershey, PA: Information Science Reference.

Edenius, M., & Rämö, H. (2013). An office on the go: Professional workers, smartphones and the return of place. In A. Mesquita (Ed.), *User perception and influencing factors of technology in everyday life* (pp. 158–177). Hershey, PA: Information Science Reference.

Edwards, R. (2013). Pogo chat. In M. Garcia-Ruiz (Ed.), *Cases on usability engineering: Design and development of digital products* (pp. 378–404). Hershey, PA: Information Science Reference. doi:10.4018/978-1-4666-4046-7.ch016

Eijkman, H., Herrmann, A., & Savige, K. (2012). E-assessment as a driver for cultural change in network-centric learning. In S. Sharma (Ed.), *E-adoption and technologies for empowering developing countries: Global advances* (pp. 233–244). Hershey, PA: Information Science Reference. doi:10.4018/978-1-4666-0041-6.ch016

Eisenberg, M., Buechley, L., & Elumeze, N. (2012). Bits and pieces: Potential future scenarios for children's mobile technology. In J. Lumsden (Ed.), *Social and organizational impacts of emerging mobile devices: Evaluating use* (pp. 108–123). Hershey, PA: Information Science Reference. doi:10.4018/978-1-4666-0194-9.ch006

El Ali, A., Nack, F., & Hardman, L. (2013). Good times?! 3 problems and design considerations for playful HCI. In J. Lumsden (Ed.), *Developments in technologies for human-centric mobile computing and applications* (pp. 204–221). Hershey, PA: Information Science Reference.

Elias, N. (2013). Immigrants' internet use and identity from an intergenerational perspective: Immigrant senior citizens and youngsters from the former Soviet Union in Israel. In R. Luppicini (Ed.), *Handbook of research on technoself: Identity in a technological society* (pp. 293–307). Hershey, PA: Information Science Reference.

Encuentra, E. H., Fernández, M. P., & Gómez-Zúñiga, B. (2013). The internet and older adults: Initial adoption and experience of use. In R. Zheng, R. Hill, & M. Gardner (Eds.), *Engaging older adults with modern technology: Internet use and information access needs* (pp. 212–228). Hershey, PA: Information Science Reference.

Eslambolchilar, P., & Murray-Smith, R. (2012). A model-based approach to analysis and calibration of sensor-based human interaction loops. In J. Lumsden (Ed.), *Social and organizational impacts of emerging mobile devices: Evaluating use* (pp. 48–71). Hershey, PA: Information Science Reference. doi:10.4018/978-1-4666-0194-9.ch003

Evans, C., & Palacios, L. (2013). Interactive self-assessment questions within a virtual environment. In S. Sharma (Ed.), *Adoption of virtual technologies for business, educational, and governmental advancements* (pp. 218–227). Hershey, PA: Information Science Reference.

Fallery, B., Taddei, R., & Gerbaix, S. (2012). Acceptance and appropriation of videoconferencing for e-training: An empirical investigation. In A. Mesquita (Ed.), *Human interaction with technology for working, communicating, and learning: Advancements* (pp. 104–119). Hershey, PA: Information Science Reference.

Farmer, L. (2013). New perspectives of andragogy in relation to the use of technology. In I. Association (Ed.), *Digital literacy: Concepts, methodologies, tools, and applications* (pp. 1606–1621). Hershey, PA: Information Science Reference.

Fenley, S. (2013). Navigation and visualisation techniques in elearning and internet research. In I. Association (Ed.), *Digital literacy: Concepts, methodologies, tools, and applications* (pp. 636–667). Hershey, PA: Information Science Reference.

Fidler, C. S., Kanaan, R. K., & Rogerson, S. (2013). Barriers to e-government implementation in Jordan: The role of Wasta. In A. Mesquita (Ed.), *User perception and influencing factors of technology in everyday life* (pp. 179–191). Hershey, PA: Information Science Reference.

Fitzgibbons, M. (2013). Teaching political science students to find and evaluate information in the social media flow. In T. Takševa (Ed.), *Social software and the evolution of user expertise: Future trends in knowledge creation and dissemination* (pp. 180–200). Hershey, PA: Information Science Reference.

Flammia, M. (2012). Using the cultural challenges of virtual team projects to prepare students for global citizenship. In K. St.Amant, & S. Kelsey (Eds.), *Computer-mediated communication across cultures: International interactions in online environments* (pp. 328–343). Hershey, PA: Information Science Reference.

Folorunso, O. O., Vincent, R. O., Ogunde, A. A., & Agboola, B. (2012). Knowledge sharing adoption model based on artificial neural networks. In S. Sharma (Ed.), *E-adoption and technologies for empowering developing countries: Global advances* (pp. 46–58). Hershey, PA: Information Science Reference. doi:10.4018/978-1-4666-0041-6.ch004

Fors, A. C. (2013). The ontology of the subject in digitalization. In R. Luppicini (Ed.), *Handbook of research on technoself: Identity in a technological society* (pp. 45–63). Hershey, PA: Information Science Reference.

Franckel, S., Bonsignore, E., & Druin, A. (2012). Designing for children's mobile storytelling. In J. Lumsden (Ed.), *Social and organizational impacts of emerging mobile devices: Evaluating use* (pp. 90–107). Hershey, PA: Information Science Reference. doi:10.4018/978-1-4666-0194-9.ch005

Frobish, T. S. (2013). On pixels, perceptions, and personae: Toward a model of online ethos. In M. Folk, & S. Apostel (Eds.), *Online credibility and digital ethos: Evaluating computer-mediated communication* (pp. 1–23). Hershey, PA: Information Science Reference.

Furtmüller, E., Wilderom, C., & van Dick, R. (2012). Sustainable e-recruiting portals: How to motivate applicants to stay connected throughout their careers? In A. Mesquita (Ed.), *Human interaction with technology for working, communicating, and learning: Advancements* (pp. 66–86). Hershey, PA: Information Science Reference.

García-Gómez, A. (2013). Technoself-presentation on social networks: A gender-based approach. In R. Luppicini (Ed.), *Handbook of research on technoself: Identity in a technological society* (pp. 382–398). Hershey, PA: Information Science Reference.

Garofalakis, J., & Koskeris, A. (2013). Digital divide and rural communities: Practical solutions and policies. In I. Association (Ed.), *Digital literacy: Concepts, methodologies, tools, and applications* (pp. 698–720). Hershey, PA: Information Science Reference.

Gauzente, C. (2012). Does anybody read SMS-advertising? A qualitative and quantitative study of mobile users' attitudes and perceived ad-clutter. In A. Mesquita (Ed.), *Human interaction with technology for working, communicating, and learning: Advancements* (pp. 13–30). Hershey, PA: Information Science Reference.

Germaine-McDaniel, N. S. (2012). The emerging hispanic use of online health information in the United States: Cultural convergence or dissociation? In K. St.Amant, & S. Kelsey (Eds.), *Computer-mediated communication across cultures: International interactions in online environments* (pp. 251–265). Hershey, PA: Information Science Reference.

Goggins, S., Schmidt, M., Guajardo, J., & Moore, J. L. (2013). 3D virtual worlds: Assessing the experience and informing design. In B. Medlin (Ed.), *Integrations of technology utilization and social dynamics in organizations* (pp. 194–213). Hershey, PA: Information Science Reference.

Gomez, R. (2012). Success factors for public access computing: Beyond anecdotes of success. In R. Gomez (Ed.), *Libraries, telecentres, cybercafes and public access to ICT: International comparisons* (pp. 82–94). Hershey, PA: Information Science Publishing.

Gomez, R. (2013). Success factors in public access computing for development. In S. Chhabra (Ed.), *ICT influences on human development, interaction, and collaboration* (pp. 97–116). Hershey, PA: Information Science Reference.

Gomez, R., & Camacho, K. (2013). Users of ICT at public access centers: Age, education, gender, and income differences in users. In S. Chhabra (Ed.), *ICT influences on human development, interaction, and collaboration* (pp. 1–21). Hershey, PA: Information Science Reference.

Gong, W. (2012). Government monitoring of online media and its influence on netizens' language use in China. In K. St.Amant, & S. Kelsey (Eds.), *Computer-mediated communication across cultures: International interactions in online environments* (pp. 155–172). Hershey, PA: Information Science Reference.

Göritz, A. S., Singh, R. K., & Voggeser, B. J. (2012). Human behavior on the WWW. In Z. Yan (Ed.), *Encyclopedia of cyber behavior* (pp. 117-131). Hershey, PA: Information Science Reference. doi:10.4018/978-1-4666-0315-8.ch010

Gozza-Cohen, M., & May, D. (2012). Individuals with disabilities and internet use. In Z. Yan (Ed.), *Encyclopedia of cyber behavior* (pp. 242–258). Hershey, PA: Information Science Reference. doi:10.4018/978-1-4666-0315-8.ch021

Grant, A. A. (2013). Textperts: Utilizing students' skills in the teaching of writing. In T. Takševa (Ed.), *Social software and the evolution of user expertise: Future trends in knowledge creation and dissemination* (pp. 247–258). Hershey, PA: Information Science Reference.

Greenhow, C. (2013). Online social networking and learning: What are the interesting research questions? In R. Zheng (Ed.), *Evolving psychological and educational perspectives on cyber behavior* (pp. 15–31). Hershey, PA: Information Science Reference.

Gruich, M. R. (2013). Defining professional development for technology. In S. Wang, & T. Hartsell (Eds.), *Technology integration and foundations for effective leadership* (pp. 152–170). Hershey, PA: Information Science Reference.

Grundén, K. (2013). Internal digital divide in organizations. In I. Association (Ed.), *Digital literacy: Concepts, methodologies, tools, and applications* (pp. 1104–1117). Hershey, PA: Information Science Reference.

Gu, L., Aiken, M., Wang, J., & Wibowo, K. (2013). The influence of information control upon on-line shopping behavior. In A. Mesquita (Ed.), *User perception and influencing factors of technology in everyday life* (pp. 16–27). Hershey, PA: Information Science Reference.

Guechtouli, M. (2012). E-HRM's impact on an environmental scanning process: How can technology support the selection of information? In A. Mesquita (Ed.), *Human interaction with technology for working, communicating, and learning: Advancements* (pp. 120–133). Hershey, PA: Information Science Reference.

Guilloux, V., Laval, F., & Kalika, M. (2012). Theorizing HR intranets: Contextual, strategic and configurative explanations. In A. Mesquita (Ed.), *Human interaction with technology for working, communicating, and learning: Advancements* (pp. 87–103). Hershey, PA: Information Science Reference.

Guo, R. X. (2013). A case study of social interaction on ANGEL and student authoring skills. In I. Association (Ed.), *Digital literacy: Concepts, methodologies, tools, and applications* (pp. 890–908). Hershey, PA: Information Science Reference.

Hall, L. L., & Johnson, R. D. (2013). Preparing IS students for real-world interaction with end users through service learning: A proposed organizational model. In A. Dwivedi, & S. Clarke (Eds.), *Innovative strategies and approaches for end-user computing advancements* (pp. 119–133). Hershey, PA: Information Science Reference.

Han, D., & Braun, K. L. (2013). Promoting active ageing through technology training in Korea. In I. Association (Ed.), *Digital literacy: Concepts, methodologies, tools, and applications* (pp. 572–589). Hershey, PA: Information Science Reference.

Hanafizadeh, M. R., Hanafizadeh, P., & Saghaei, A. (2013). Perusing e-readiness and digital divide: From a critical view. In I. Association (Ed.), *Digital literacy: Concepts, methodologies, tools, and applications* (pp. 313–346). Hershey, PA: Information Science Reference.

Hanappi-Egger, E. (2012). Exclusiveness vs. inclusiveness in software development: The triple-loop-learning approach. In R. Pande, & T. Van der Weide (Eds.), *Globalization, technology diffusion and gender disparity: Social impacts of ICTs* (pp. 96–109). Hershey, PA: Information Science Reference. doi:10.4018/978-1-4666-0020-1.ch008

Harby, F. A., Qahwaji, R., & Kamala, M. (2012). End-users' acceptance of biometrics authentication to secure e-commerce within the context of Saudi culture: Applying the UTAUT model. In R. Pande, & T. Van der Weide (Eds.), *Globalization, technology diffusion and gender disparity: Social impacts of ICTs* (pp. 225–246). Hershey, PA: Information Science Reference. doi:10.4018/978-1-4666-0020-1.ch019

Hartsell, T., & Wang, S. (2013). Introduction to technology integration and leadership. In S. Wang, & T. Hartsell (Eds.), *Technology integration and foundations for effective leadership* (pp. 1–17). Hershey, PA: Information Science Reference.

Hawreliak, J. (2013). "To be shot at without result": Gaming and the rhetoric of immortality. In R. Luppicini (Ed.), *Handbook of research on technoself: Identity in a technological society* (pp. 531–553). Hershey, PA: Information Science Reference.

Heilesen, S. B. (2012). Human behaviors with podcasts. In Z. Yan (Ed.), *Encyclopedia of cyber behavior* (pp. 178–188). Hershey, PA: Information Science Reference. doi:10.4018/978-1-4666-0315-8.ch015

Heng, J., & Banerji, S. (2013). Low usage of intelligent technologies by the aged: New initiatives to bridge the digital divide. In I. Association (Ed.), *Digital literacy: Concepts, methodologies, tools, and applications* (pp. 135–153). Hershey, PA: Information Science Reference.

Henze, N., Pielot, M., Poppinga, B., Schinke, T., & Boll, S. (2013). My app is an experiment: Experience from user studies in mobile app stores. In J. Lumsden (Ed.), *Developments in technologies for human-centric mobile computing and applications* (pp. 294–315). Hershey, PA: Information Science Reference.

Hermeking, M. (2012). Culture, online technology and computer-mediated technical documentation: Contributions from the field of intercultural communication. In K. St.Amant, & S. Kelsey (Eds.), *Computer-mediated communication across cultures: International interactions in online environments* (pp. 77–90). Hershey, PA: Information Science Reference.

Hester, A. J. (2013). Examining the varying influence of social and technological aspects on adoption and usage of knowledge management systems. In B. Medlin (Ed.), *Integrations of technology utilization and social dynamics in organizations* (pp. 142–158). Hershey, PA: Information Science Reference.

Ho, V. (2013). The need for identity construction in computer-mediated professional communication: A Community of practice perspective. In R. Luppicini (Ed.), *Handbook of research on technoself: Identity in a technological society* (pp. 502–530). Hershey, PA: Information Science Reference.

Hoggan, E. (2012). Crossmodal audio and tactile interaction with mobile touchscreens. In J. Lumsden (Ed.), *Social and organizational impacts of emerging mobile devices: Evaluating use* (pp. 249–264). Hershey, PA: Information Science Reference. doi:10.4018/978-1-4666-0194-9.ch014

Hsu, C. (2012). Exploring the player flow experience in e-game playing. In A. Mesquita (Ed.), *Human interaction with technology for working, communicating, and learning: Advancements* (pp. 48–65). Hershey, PA: Information Science Reference.

Hsu, J., Wang, Z., & Hamilton, K. (2013). Developing and managing digital/technology literacy and effective learning skills in adult learners. In I. Association (Ed.), *Digital literacy: Concepts, methodologies, tools, and applications* (pp. 394–413). Hershey, PA: Information Science Reference.

Iannella, R. (2012). Towards e-society policy interoperability for social web networks. In S. Sharma (Ed.), *E-adoption and technologies for empowering developing countries: Global advances* (pp. 83–99). Hershey, PA: Information Science Reference. doi:10.4018/978-1-4666-0041-6.ch007

Iivari, N. (2012). Culturally compatible usability work: An interpretive case study on the relationship between usability work and its cultural context in software product development organizations. In A. Dwivedi, & S. Clarke (Eds.), *End-user computing, development, and software engineering: New challenges* (pp. 54–80). Hershey, PA: Information Science Reference. doi:10.4018/978-1-4666-0140-6.ch003

Ikolo, V. E. (2013). Gender digital divide and national ICT policies in Africa. In I. Association (Ed.), *Digital literacy: Concepts, methodologies, tools, and applications* (pp. 812–832). Hershey, PA: Information Science Reference.

Imran, A., & Gregor, S. (2013). A process model for successful e-government adoption in the least developed countries: A case of Bangladesh. In I. Association (Ed.), *Digital literacy: Concepts, methodologies, tools, and applications* (pp. 213–241). Hershey, PA: Information Science Reference.

Ionescu, A. (2013). Cyber identity: Our alter-ego? In R. Luppicini (Ed.), *Handbook of research on technoself: Identity in a technological society* (pp. 189–203). Hershey, PA: Information Science Reference.

Ionescu, A. (2013). ICTs and gender-based rights. In J. Lannon, & E. Halpin (Eds.), *Human rights and information communication technologies: Trends and consequences of use* (pp. 214–234). Hershey, PA: Information Science Reference.

Irune, A. A. (2013). Evaluating the visual demand of in-vehicle information systems: The development of a new method. In J. Lumsden (Ed.), *Developments in technologies for human-centric mobile computing and applications* (pp. 1–21). Hershey, PA: Information Science Reference.

Islam, A. N. (2013). Understanding the continued usage intention of educators toward an e-learning system. In S. Sharma (Ed.), *Adoption of virtual technologies for business, educational, and governmental advancements* (pp. 180–195). Hershey, PA: Information Science Reference.

Islam, M. N., & Tétard, F. (2013). Integrating semiotics perception in usability testing to improve usability evaluation. In M. Garcia-Ruiz (Ed.), *Cases on usability engineering: Design and development of digital products* (pp. 145–169). Hershey, PA: Information Science Reference. doi:10.4018/978-1-4666-4046-7.ch007

Ivanova, M., & Popova, A. (2013). Formal and informal learning flows cohesion in web 2.0 environment. In J. Wang (Ed.), *Information systems and modern society: Social change and global development* (pp. 1–16). Hershey, PA: Information Science Reference. doi:10.4018/978-1-4666-2922-6.ch001

Iyamu, T. (2013). Institutionalisation of the enterprise architecture: The actor-network perspective. In A. Tatnall (Ed.), *Social and professional applications of actor-network theory for technology development* (pp. 144–155). Hershey, PA: Information Science Reference.

Jahnke, I. (2012). A way out of the information jungle: A longitudinal study about a socio-technical community and informal learning in higher education. In E. Coakes (Ed.), *Technological change and societal growth: Analyzing the future* (pp. 180–201). Hershey, PA: Information Science Reference. doi:10.4018/978-1-4666-0200-7.ch012

James, T., & Louw, M. (2012). Public access ICT in Namibia. In R. Gomez (Ed.), *Libraries, telecentres, cybercafes and public access to ICT: International comparisons* (pp. 452–465). Hershey, PA: Information Science Publishing.

Janneck, M., & Staar, H. (2013). Playing virtual power games: Micro-political processes in inter-organizational networks. In B. Medlin (Ed.), *Integrations of technology utilization and social dynamics in organizations* (pp. 171–192). Hershey, PA: Information Science Reference.

Jensen, K. L. (2013). Remote and autonomous studies of mobile and ubiquitous applications in real contexts. In J. Lumsden (Ed.), *Developments in technologies for human-centric mobile computing and applications* (pp. 79–98). Hershey, PA: Information Science Reference.

Jin, L. (2013). A new trend in education: Technoself enhanced social learning. In R. Luppicini (Ed.), *Handbook of research on technoself: Identity in a technological society* (pp. 456–473). Hershey, PA: Information Science Reference.

Johnson, K. T., & Smith-Jackson, T. L. (2013). A human factors view of the digital divide. In I. Association (Ed.), *Digital literacy: Concepts, methodologies, tools, and applications* (pp. 1510–1532). Hershey, PA: Information Science Reference.

Johnson, M. (2012). Designing visionary leadership teams. In E. Coakes (Ed.), *Technological change and societal growth: Analyzing the future* (pp. 36–55). Hershey, PA: Information Science Reference. doi:10.4018/978-1-4666-0200-7.ch002

Johnson, N. (2013). Online credibility and information labor: Infrastructure reverberating through ethos. In M. Folk, & S. Apostel (Eds.), *Online credibility and digital ethos: Evaluating computer-mediated communication* (pp. 37–55). Hershey, PA: Information Science Reference.

Johnson, R. D. (2013). Gender differences in e-learning: Communication, social presence, and learning outcomes. In A. Dwivedi, & S. Clarke (Eds.), *Innovative strategies and approaches for end-user computing advancements* (pp. 175–191). Hershey, PA: Information Science Reference.

Johnston, A., & Warkentin, M. (2012). The influence of perceived source credibility on end user attitudes and intentions to comply with recommended IT actions. In A. Dwivedi, & S. Clarke (Eds.), *End-user computing, development, and software engineering: New challenges* (pp. 312–334). Hershey, PA: Information Science Reference. doi:10.4018/978-1-4666-0140-6.ch015

Joo, K. P. (2012). ICT-supported education for sustainable development of South Korean rural communities. In R. Lekoko, & L. Semali (Eds.), *Cases on developing countries and ICT integration: Rural community development* (pp. 174–191). Hershey, PA: Information Science Reference. doi:10.4018/978-1-4666-0882-5.ch408

Jumisko-Pyykkö, S., & Vainio, T. (2012). Framing the context of use for mobile HCI. In J. Lumsden (Ed.), *Social and organizational impacts of emerging mobile devices: Evaluating use* (pp. 217–248). Hershey, PA: Information Science Reference. doi:10.4018/978-1-4666-0194-9.ch013

Jyothi, P. (2012). Challenges faced by women: BPO sector. In R. Pande, & T. Van der Weide (Eds.), *Globalization, technology diffusion and gender disparity: Social impacts of ICTs* (pp. 147–155). Hershey, PA: Information Science Reference. doi:10.4018/978-1-4666-0020-1.ch013

Kafai, Y. B., Fields, D., & Burke, W. Q. (2012). Entering the clubhouse: Case studies of young programmers joining the online scratch communities. In A. Dwivedi, & S. Clarke (Eds.), *End-user computing, development, and software engineering: New challenges* (pp. 279–294). Hershey, PA: Information Science Reference. doi:10.4018/978-1-4666-0140-6.ch013

Kaiser, C., & Butcher, G. (2013). Exploring evaluation techniques for children's websites. In M. Garcia-Ruiz (Ed.), *Cases on usability engineering: Design and development of digital products* (pp. 1–25). Hershey, PA: Information Science Reference. doi:10.4018/978-1-4666-4046-7.ch001

Kamal, S., & Chu, S. (2012). Cultural differences in social media usage and beliefs and attitudes towards advertising on social media: Findings from Dubai, United Arab Emirates. In K. St.Amant, & S. Kelsey (Eds.), *Computer-mediated communication across cultures: international interactions in online environments* (pp. 123–141). Hershey, PA: Information Science Reference.

Karasavvidis, I. (2013). Rethinking expertise in the web 2.0 era: Lessons learned from project durian. In T. Takševa (Ed.), *Social software and the evolution of user expertise: Future trends in knowledge creation and dissemination* (pp. 330–353). Hershey, PA: Information Science Reference.

Kauppinen, J., Kivijärvi, H., & Talvinen, J. (2013). Committing to organizational change in IT industry. In B. Medlin (Ed.), *Integrations of technology utilization and social dynamics in organizations* (pp. 74–90). Hershey, PA: Information Science Reference.

Kawlra, A. (2013). From rural outsourcing to rural opportunities: Developing an ICT mediated distributed production enterprise in Tamil Nadu, India. In S. Chhabra (Ed.), *ICT influences on human development, interaction, and collaboration* (pp. 158–173). Hershey, PA: Information Science Reference.

Kaynak, M. S. (2013). The potentials and pitfalls of the information society project in Turkey: A critical assessment of policy paradigms regarding e-transformation and digital divide. In I. Association (Ed.), *Digital literacy: Concepts, methodologies, tools, and applications* (pp. 833–851). Hershey, PA: Information Science Reference.

Kelly, D. (2013). An analysis of process characteristics for developing scientific software. In A. Dwivedi, & S. Clarke (Eds.), *Innovative strategies and approaches for end-user computing advancements* (pp. 347–363). Hershey, PA: Information Science Reference.

Kettani, D., Moulin, B., & El Mahdi, A. (2013). Toward a roadmap to e-government for a better governance toward a roadmap to e-government for a better governance. In I. Association (Ed.), *Digital literacy: Concepts, methodologies, tools, and applications* (pp. 1771–1799). Hershey, PA: Information Science Reference.

Khan, G. F., & Moon, J. (2013). E-government issues in developing countries: An analysis from a digital divide, e-skills, and civil conflict theory approach. In I. Association (Ed.), *Digital literacy: Concepts, methodologies, tools, and applications* (pp. 1272–1288). Hershey, PA: Information Science Reference.

Klaus, T. (2013). Understanding user dissatisfaction: exploring the role of fairness in IT-enabled change. In A. Dwivedi, & S. Clarke (Eds.), *Innovative strategies and approaches for end-user computing advancements* (pp. 215–241). Hershey, PA: Information Science Reference.

Knight, M. L., Knight, R. A., Goben, A., & Dobbs, A. W. (2013). Theory and application: Using social networking to build online credibility. In M. Folk, & S. Apostel (Eds.), *Online credibility and digital ethos: Evaluating computer-mediated communication* (pp. 285–301). Hershey, PA: Information Science Reference.

Knoche, H., Rao, P. S., & Huang, J. (2013). Human-centered design for development. In J. Lumsden (Ed.), *Developments in technologies for human-centric mobile computing and applications* (pp. 155–167). Hershey, PA: Information Science Reference.

Korpelainen, E., Vartiainen, M., & Kira, M. (2012). Self-determined adoption of an ICT system in a work organization. In A. Dwivedi, & S. Clarke (Eds.), *End-user computing, development, and software engineering: New challenges* (pp. 148–167). Hershey, PA: Information Science Reference. doi:10.4018/978-1-4666-0140-6.ch007

Korres, G. M., & Kokkinou, A. (2012). Reviewing the European innovation activities and industrial competitiveness. In A. Cakir, & P. Ordóñez de Pablos (Eds.), *Social development and high technology industries: Strategies and applications* (pp. 176–186). Hershey, PA: Information Science Reference. doi:10.4018/978-1-4666-0882-5.ch209

Kumar, M., & Sareen, M. (2013). Impact of technology-related environment issues on trust in B2B e-commerce. In S. Chhabra (Ed.), *ICT influences on human development, interaction, and collaboration* (pp. 22–42). Hershey, PA: Information Science Reference.

Kumar, M., Sareen, M., & Chhabra, S. (2013). Technology related trust issues in SME B2B E-Commerce. In S. Chhabra (Ed.), *ICT influences on human development, interaction, and collaboration* (pp. 243–259). Hershey, PA: Information Science Reference.

Kumari, B. R. (2012). Gender, culture, and ICT use. In R. Pande, & T. Van der Weide (Eds.), *Globalization, technology diffusion and gender disparity: Social impacts of ICTs* (pp. 36–50). Hershey, PA: Information Science Reference. doi:10.4018/978-1-4666-0020-1.ch004

Kunal,. (2013). Innovation in financing mechanism of information and communication technology (ICT). In I. Association (Ed.), *Digital literacy: Concepts, methodologies, tools, and applications* (pp. 1152-1191). Hershey, PA: Information Science Reference. doi:10.4018/978-1-4666-1852-7.ch061

Kvasny, L., & Hales, K. D. (2013). The evolving discourse of the digital divide: The internet, black identity, and the evolving discourse of the digital divide. In I. Association (Ed.), *Digital literacy: Concepts, methodologies, tools, and applications* (pp. 1350–1366). Hershey, PA: Information Science Reference.

L'Abate, L. (2013). Of paradigms, theories, and models: A conceptual hierarchical structure for communication science and technoself. In R. Luppicini (Ed.), *Handbook of research on technoself: Identity in a technological society* (pp. 84–104). Hershey, PA: Information Science Reference.

Langran, E. (2013). Caste, class, and IT in India. In I. Association (Ed.), *Digital literacy: Concepts, methodologies, tools, and applications* (pp. 976–994). Hershey, PA: Information Science Reference.

Larsen, J. E., & Stopczynski, A. (2013). A festival-wide social network using 2D barcodes, mobile phones and situated displays. In J. Lumsden (Ed.), *Developments in technologies for human-centric mobile computing and applications* (pp. 168–185). Hershey, PA: Information Science Reference.

Lawrence, H. R. (2013). Women's roles: Do they exist in a technological workforce? In S. Wang, & T. Hartsell (Eds.), *Technology integration and foundations for effective leadership* (pp. 57–69). Hershey, PA: Information Science Reference.

Laxman, K., & Chin, Y. K. (2012). Emergent technologies and social connectedness in learning. In A. Cakir, & P. Ordóñez de Pablos (Eds.), *Social development and high technology industries: Strategies and applications* (pp. 25–37). Hershey, PA: Information Science Reference.

Lee, J., & Rethemeyer, R. K. (2012). Virtual interactions via smartphones. In Z. Yan (Ed.), *Encyclopedia of cyber behavior* (pp. 189–198). Hershey, PA: Information Science Reference. doi:10.4018/978-1-4666-0315-8.ch016

Lee, T., Shen, P., & Tsai, C. (2012). Enhance students' computing skills via web-mediated self-regulated learning with feedback in blended environment. In A. Mesquita (Ed.), *Human interaction with technology for working, communicating, and learning: Advancements* (pp. 149–166). Hershey, PA: Information Science Reference.

Leichsenring, C., Tünnermann, R., & Hermann, T. (2013). feelabuzz: Direct tactile communication with mobile phones. In J. Lumsden (Ed.), Developments in technologies for human-centric mobile computing and applications (pp. 145-154). Hershey, PA: Information Science Reference. doi: doi:10.4018/978-1-4666-2068-1.ch009

Lekoko, R., Modise-Jankie, J., & Busang, C. (2012). Libraries as portal for knowledge driven rural community development cases from Botswana. In R. Lekoko, & L. Semali (Eds.), *Cases on developing countries and ICT integration: Rural community development* (pp. 34–41). Hershey, PA: Information Science Reference.

Leung, L., & Zheng, C. P. (2012). The net generation. In Z. Yan (Ed.), *Encyclopedia of Cyber behavior* (pp. 200–211). Hershey, PA: Information Science Reference. doi:10.4018/978-1-4666-0315-8.ch017

Lewandowski, D. (2013). Credibility in web search engines. In M. Folk, & S. Apostel (Eds.), *Online credibility and digital ethos: Evaluating computer-mediated communication* (pp. 131–146). Hershey, PA: Information Science Reference.

Li, G., Zhang, X., Wang, Z., & Gao, T. (2013). Coordination performance evaluation of supply logistics in JIT environment. In T. Gao (Ed.), *Global applications of pervasive and ubiquitous computing* (pp. 17–30). Hershey, PA: Information Science Reference.

Li, X., & Leong, A. M. (2012). Model analysis and development strategy on building an industrial research and development (R&D) centre: Shanghai's practice and inspiration. In A. Cakir, & P. Ordóñez de Pablos (Eds.), *Social development and high technology industries: Strategies and applications* (pp. 1–14). Hershey, PA: Information Science Reference.

Li, Y., & Chang, K. (2013). Exploring the dimensions and effects of computer software similarities in computer skills transfer. In A. Dwivedi, & S. Clarke (Eds.), *Innovative strategies and approaches for end-user computing advancements* (pp. 99–118). Hershey, PA: Information Science Reference.

Light, A., Kleine, D., Holloway, R., & Vivent, M. (2012). Performing charlotte: A technique to bridge cultures in participatory design. In E. Coakes (Ed.), *Technological change and societal growth: Analyzing the future* (pp. 219–236). Hershey, PA: Information Science Reference. doi:10.4018/978-1-4666-0200-7.ch014

Linares, K., Subrahmanyam, K., Cheng, R., & Guan, S. A. (2013). A second life within second life: Are virtual world users creating new selves and new lives? In R. Zheng (Ed.), *Evolving psychological and educational perspectives on cyber behavior* (pp. 205–228). Hershey, PA: Information Science Reference.

Lind, L., Berglund, A., Berglund, E., Bång, M., & Hägglund, S. (2013). Effortless data capture for ambient e-services with digital pen and paper technology. In I. Association (Ed.), *Digital literacy: Concepts, methodologies, tools, and applications* (pp. 522–540). Hershey, PA: Information Science Reference.

Loewen, S., & Wang, J. (2012). Human behavior in chatrooms. In Z. Yan (Ed.), *Encyclopedia of cyber behavior* (pp. 148–156). Hershey, PA: Information Science Reference. doi:10.4018/978-1-4666-0315-8.ch012

Low, R., Jin, P., & Sweller, J. (2013). Instructional design in digital environments and availability of mental resources. In R. Zheng, R. Hill, & M. Gardner (Eds.), *Engaging older adults with modern technology: Internet use and information access needs* (pp. 81–104). Hershey, PA: Information Science Reference. doi:10.4018/978-1-4666-4422-9.ch059

Lukaitis, S. (2013). Applying hermeneutic phenomenology to understand innovation adoption. In A. Tatnall (Ed.), *Social and professional applications of actor-network theory for technology development* (pp. 103–116). Hershey, PA: Information Science Reference.

Luppicini, R. (2013). The emerging field of technoself studies (TSS). In R. Luppicini (Ed.), *Handbook of research on technoself: Identity in a technological society* (pp. 1–25). Hershey, PA: Information Science Reference.

Mabry, S. (2012). Driving IT architecture innovation: The roles of competing organizational cultures and collaborating upper echelons. In S. Sharma (Ed.), *E-adoption and technologies for empowering developing countries: Global advances* (pp. 15–33). Hershey, PA: Information Science Reference. doi:10.4018/978-1-4666-0041-6.ch002

Mahatanankoon, P. (2012). The impact of personal electronic communications on work-life balance and cognitive absorption. In S. Chhabra (Ed.), *ICTs for advancing rural communities and human development: Addressing the digital divide* (pp. 1–14). Hershey, PA: Information Science Reference. doi:10.4018/978-1-4666-0047-8.ch001

Maidel, V., & Epstein, D. (2013). The query is just the beginning: Exploring search-related decision-making of young adults. In M. Folk, & S. Apostel (Eds.), *Online credibility and digital ethos: Evaluating computer-mediated communication* (pp. 95–113). Hershey, PA: Information Science Reference.

Malleus, R. (2013). Whose news can you trust? A framework for evaluating the credibility of online news sources for diaspora populations. In M. Folk, & S. Apostel (Eds.), *Online credibility and digital ethos: Evaluating computer-mediated communication* (pp. 186–214). Hershey, PA: Information Science Reference.

Mano, R. S., & Mesch, G. S. (2012). E-mail and work performance. In Z. Yan (Ed.), *Encyclopedia of cyber behavior* (pp. 106–116). Hershey, PA: Information Science Reference. doi:10.4018/978-1-4666-0315-8.ch009

Marmura, S. (2013). The mediation of identity: Key issues in historic perspective. In R. Luppicini (Ed.), *Handbook of research on technoself: Identity in a technological society* (pp. 137–156). Hershey, PA: Information Science Reference.

Martin, I., Kear, K., Simpkins, N., & Busvine, J. (2013). Social negotiations in web usability engineering. In M. Garcia-Ruiz (Ed.), *Cases on usability engineering: Design and development of digital products* (pp. 26–56). Hershey, PA: Information Science Reference. doi:10.4018/978-1-4666-4046-7.ch002

Martin, J., & McKay, E. (2013). Mental health, post-secondary education, and information communications technology. In J. Lannon, & E. Halpin (Eds.), *Human rights and information communication technologies: Trends and consequences of use* (pp. 196–213). Hershey, PA: Information Science Reference. doi:10.4018/978-1-4666-4422-9.ch063

Martin, J. N., & Cheong, P. H. (2012). Cultural considerations of online pedagogy. In K. St.Amant, & S. Kelsey (Eds.), *Computer-mediated communication across cultures: International interactions in online environments* (pp. 283–311). Hershey, PA: Information Science Reference.

Mattingly, D. J. (2012). Indian women working in call centers: Sites of resistance? In R. Pande, & T. Van der Weide (Eds.), *Globalization, technology diffusion and gender disparity: Social impacts of ICTs* (pp. 156–168). Hershey, PA: Information Science Reference. doi:10.4018/978-1-4666-0020-1.ch014

McColl, D., & Nejat, G. (2013). A human affect recognition system for socially interactive robots. In R. Luppicini (Ed.), *Handbook of research on technoself: Identity in a technological society* (pp. 554–573). Hershey, PA: Information Science Reference. doi:10.4018/978-1-4666-4607-0.ch015

McDonald, A., & Helmer, S. (2013). A comparative case study of Indonesian and UK organisational culture differences in IS project management. In A. Mesquita (Ed.), *User perception and influencing factors of technology in everyday life* (pp. 46–55). Hershey, PA: Information Science Reference.

McGrady, R. (2013). Ethos [edit]: Procedural rhetoric and the Wikipedia project. In M. Folk, & S. Apostel (Eds.) Online credibility and digital ethos: Evaluating computer-mediated communication (pp. 114-130). Hershey, PA: Information Science Reference. doi: doi:10.4018/978-1-4666-2663-8.ch007

McLay, A. (2012). Realising virtual reality: A reflection on the continuing evolution of new media. In E. Coakes (Ed.), *Technological change and societal growth: Analyzing the future* (pp. 144–161). Hershey, PA: Information Science Reference. doi:10.4018/978-1-4666-0200-7.ch010

McMillan, D., Morrison, A., & Chalmers, M. (2013). A comparison of distribution channels for large-scale deployments of iOS applications. In J. Lumsden (Ed.), *Developments in technologies for human-centric mobile computing and applications* (pp. 222–239). Hershey, PA: Information Science Reference.

Melson, G. F. (2013). Building a technoself: Children's ideas about and behavior toward robotic pets. In R. Luppicini (Ed.), *Handbook of research on technoself: Identity in a technological society* (pp. 592–608). Hershey, PA: Information Science Reference. doi:10.4018/978-1-4666-4607-0.ch068

Mendoza-González, R., Rodríguez, F. Á., & Arteaga, J. M. (2013). A usability study of mobile text based social applications: Towards a reliable strategy for design evaluation. In M. Garcia-Ruiz (Ed.), *Cases on usability engineering: Design and development of digital products* (pp. 195–219). Hershey, PA: Information Science Reference. doi:10.4018/978-1-4666-4046-7.ch009

Michikyan, M., & Subrahmanyam, K. (2012). Social networking sites: Implications for youth. In Z. Yan (Ed.), *Encyclopedia of cyber behavior* (pp. 132–147). Hershey, PA: Information Science Reference. doi:10.4018/978-1-4666-0315-8.ch011

Mitra, A. (2013). Collective narrative expertise and the narbs of social media. In T. Takševa (Ed.), *Social software and the evolution of user expertise: Future trends in knowledge creation and dissemination* (pp. 1–12). Hershey, PA: Information Science Reference.

Modise, O. M., Lekoko, R., & Thobega, J. M. (2012). Socio-economic empowerment through technologies: The case of tapestry at Lentswe La Oodi Weavers in Botswana. In R. Lekoko, & L. Semali (Eds.), *Cases on developing countries and ICT integration: Rural community development* (pp. 75–82). Hershey, PA: Information Science Reference.

Moloi, T. (2012). Linking mathematical literacy to ICT: A good mix for community development in South Africa. In R. Lekoko, & L. Semali (Eds.), *Cases on developing countries and ICT integration: Rural community development* (pp. 202–210). Hershey, PA: Information Science Reference.

Moore, J. E., & Love, M. S. (2013). An examination of prestigious stigma: The case of the technology geek. In B. Medlin (Ed.), *Integrations of technology utilization and social dynamics in organizations* (pp. 48–73). Hershey, PA: Information Science Reference.

Mørch, A. I., & Andersen, R. (2012). Mutual development: The software engineering context of end-user development. In A. Dwivedi, & S. Clarke (Eds.), *End-user computing, development, and software engineering: New challenges* (pp. 103–125). Hershey, PA: Information Science Reference. doi:10.4018/978-1-4666-0140-6.ch005

Moreau, R. A., & Hershorn, H. R. (2012). Children's internet safety websites. In Z. Yan (Ed.), *Encyclopedia of cyber behavior* (pp. 96–104). Hershey, PA: Information Science Reference. doi:10.4018/978-1-4666-0315-8.ch008

Moser, S., Bruppacher, S. E., & de Simoni, F. (2013). Public representation of ubiquitous ICT applications in the outpatient health sector. In A. Mesquita (Ed.), *User perception and influencing factors of technology in everyday life* (pp. 212–232). Hershey, PA: Information Science Reference.

Mosindi, O., & Sice, P. (2013). An exploratory theoretical framework for understanding information behaviour. In A. Mesquita (Ed.), *User perception and influencing factors of technology in everyday life* (pp. 1–8). Hershey, PA: Information Science Reference.

Mousten, B., Humbley, J., Maylath, B., & Vandepitte, S. (2012). Communicating pragmatics about content and culture in virtually mediated educational environments. In K. St.Amant, & S. Kelsey (Eds.), *Computer-mediated communication across cultures: International interactions in online environments* (pp. 312–327). Hershey, PA: Information Science Reference.

Muir, S. A. (2013). The gloss and the reality of teaching digital natives: Taking the long view. In I. Association (Ed.), *Digital literacy: Concepts, methodologies, tools, and applications* (pp. 1697–1719). Hershey, PA: Information Science Reference.

Mulcahy, D. (2013). Performativity in practice: An actor-network account of professional teaching standards. In A. Tatnall (Ed.), *Social and professional applications of actor-network theory for technology development* (pp. 1–16). Hershey, PA: Information Science Reference.

Murphy, J., Lee, R., & Swinger, E. (2013). Student perceptions and adoption of university smart card systems. In A. Mesquita (Ed.), *User perception and influencing factors of technology in everyday life* (pp. 142–157). Hershey, PA: Information Science Reference.

Mushi, R. T., & Chilimo, W. (2013). Contribution of information and communication technologies to malaria control in Tanzania. In S. Chhabra (Ed.), *ICT influences on human development, interaction, and collaboration* (pp. 132–141). Hershey, PA: Information Science Reference.

Mutaza, S., & Sami, L. K. (2012). Gender aspects in the use of ICT in information centres. In R. Pande, & T. Van der Weide (Eds.), *Globalization, technology diffusion and gender disparity: Social impacts of ICTs* (pp. 129–137). Hershey, PA: Information Science Reference. doi:10.4018/978-1-4666-0020-1.ch011

Mutula, S. M. (2012). E-government's role in poverty alleviation: Case study of South Africa. In R. Lekoko, & L. Semali (Eds.), *Cases on developing countries and ICT integration: Rural community development* (pp. 104–122). Hershey, PA: Information Science Reference.

Myers, B. A., Jeong, S. Y., Xie, Y., Beaton, J., Stylos, J., & Ehret, R. … Busse, D. K. (2012). Studying the documentation of an API for enterprise service-oriented architecture. In A. Dwivedi, & S. Clarke (Eds.) End-user computing, development, and software engineering: New challenges (pp. 81-102). Hershey, PA: Information Science Reference. doi: doi:10.4018/978-1-4666-0140-6.ch004

Nepali, R. K., & Bista, B. (2012). Public access ICT in Nepal. In R. Gomez (Ed.), *Libraries, telecentres, cybercafes and public access to ICT: International comparisons* (pp. 267–282). Hershey, PA: Information Science Publishing.

Nezlek, G., & DeHondt, G. (2013). Gender wage differentials in information systems: 1991–2008 a quantitative analysis. In B. Medlin (Ed.), *Integrations of technology utilization and social dynamics in organizations* (pp. 31–47). Hershey, PA: Information Science Reference.

Ng, W. (2013). Empowering students to be scientifically literate through digital literacy. In I. Association (Ed.), *Digital literacy: Concepts, methodologies, tools, and applications* (pp. 1219–1239). Hershey, PA: Information Science Reference.

Nhlekisana, R. O. (2012). Music as a catalyst for improved livelihood: The case of culture spears, a traditional music dance group in Botswana. In R. Lekoko, & L. Semali (Eds.), *Cases on developing countries and ICT integration: Rural community development* (pp. 83–90). Hershey, PA: Information Science Reference.

Nicholls, M. G., & Cargill, B. J. (2012). Achieving best practice manufacturing involving tacit knowledge through the cautious use of mixed-mode modelling. In E. Coakes (Ed.), *Technological change and societal growth: Analyzing the future* (pp. 237–256). Hershey, PA: Information Science Reference. doi:10.4018/978-1-4666-0200-7.ch015

Nordin, K., & Berglund, U. (2012). Children's maps in GIS: A tool for communicating outdoor experiences in urban planning. In S. Chhabra (Ed.), *ICTs for advancing rural communities and human development: Addressing the digital divide* (pp. 57–72). Hershey, PA: Information Science Reference. doi:10.4018/978-1-4666-0047-8.ch005

Nørgaard, M., & Hornbæk, K. (2012). Working together to improve usability: Exploring challenges and successful practices. In A. Mesquita (Ed.), *Human interaction with technology for working, communicating, and learning: Advancements* (pp. 167–187). Hershey, PA: Information Science Reference.

O'Hanlon, S., Bourke, A., & Power, V. (2013). E-health for older adults. In R. Zheng, R. Hill, & M. Gardner (Eds.), *Engaging older adults with modern technology: Internet use and information access needs* (pp. 229–248). Hershey, PA: Information Science Reference.

Oiry, E., Ologeanu-Taddeï, R., & Bondarouk, T. (2012). The role of the organizational structure in the IT appropriation: Explorative case studies into the interaction between IT and workforce management. In A. Mesquita (Ed.), *Human interaction with technology for working, communicating, and learning: Advancements* (pp. 236–251). Hershey, PA: Information Science Reference.

Olaniran, B. A., Burley, H., & Chang, M. (2013). Social issues and web 2.0: A closer look at culture in e-learning. In I. Association (Ed.), *Digital literacy: Concepts, methodologies, tools, and applications* (pp. 1456–1471). Hershey, PA: Information Science Reference.

Olaniran, B. A., Rodriguez, N., & Williams, I. M. (2012). Social information processing theory (SIPT): A cultural perspective for international online communication environments. In K. St. Amant, & S. Kelsey (Eds.), *Computer-mediated communication across cultures: International interactions in online environments* (pp. 45–65). Hershey, PA: Information Science Reference.

Ololube, N. P., Amaele, S., Kpolovie, P. J., & Egbezor, D. E. (2013). The issues of digital natives and tourists: Empirical investigation of the level of IT/IS usage between university students and faculty members in a developing economy. In I. Association (Ed.), *Digital literacy: Concepts, methodologies, tools, and applications* (pp. 1384–1401). Hershey, PA: Information Science Reference.

Orange, E. (2013). Understanding the human-machine interface in a time of change. In R. Luppicini (Ed.), *Handbook of research on technoself: Identity in a technological society* (pp. 703–719). Hershey, PA: Information Science Reference.

Ouwehand, K., van Gog, T., & Paas, F. (2013). The use of gesturing to facilitate older adults' learning from computer-based dynamic visualizations. In R. Zheng, R. Hill, & M. Gardner (Eds.), *Engaging older adults with modern technology: Internet use and information access needs* (pp. 33–58). Hershey, PA: Information Science Reference.

Owen, H. (2013). Intelligent m-learning frameworks: Information and communication technology applied in a laptop environment. In I. Association (Ed.), *Digital literacy: Concepts, methodologies, tools, and applications* (pp. 414–436). Hershey, PA: Information Science Reference.

Oye, N. D., Iahad, N. A., & Rahim, N. Z. (2013). An application of the UTAUT model for understanding acceptance and use of ICT by Nigerian university academicians. In S. Chhabra (Ed.), *ICT influences on human development, interaction, and collaboration* (pp. 214–229). Hershey, PA: Information Science Reference.

Özpinar, A., & Yavuz, E. (2013). E-commerce training with virtual commerce simulation. In S. Sharma (Ed.), *Adoption of virtual technologies for business, educational, and governmental advancements* (pp. 37–43). Hershey, PA: Information Science Reference.

Papadopoulos, F., Dautenhahn, K., & Ho, W. C. (2013). Behavioral analysis of human-human remote social interaction mediated by an interactive robot in a cooperative game scenario. In R. Luppicini (Ed.), *Handbook of research on technoself: Identity in a technological society* (pp. 637–665). Hershey, PA: Information Science Reference.

Paravati, G., Sanna, A., Lamberti, F., & Ciminiera, L. (2012). On quality of experience in remote visualization on mobile devices. In J. Lumsden (Ed.), *Social and organizational impacts of emerging mobile devices: Evaluating use* (pp. 1–19). Hershey, PA: Information Science Reference. doi:10.4018/978-1-4666-0194-9.ch001

Parker, D. (2013). Implementing the professional development program. In S. Wang, & T. Hartsell (Eds.), *Technology integration and foundations for effective leadership* (pp. 190–205). Hershey, PA: Information Science Reference.

Pee, L., Kankanhalli, A., & Show, V. O. (2013). ICT for digital inclusion: A study of public internet kiosks in Mauritius. In I. Association (Ed.), *Digital literacy: Concepts, methodologies, tools, and applications* (pp. 477–501). Hershey, PA: Information Science Reference.

Peevers, G., Douglas, G., & Jack, M. A. (2013). Multimedia technology in the financial services sector: Customer satisfaction with alternatives to face-to-face interaction in mortgage sales. In A. Mesquita (Ed.), *User perception and influencing factors of technology in everyday life* (pp. 92–106). Hershey, PA: Information Science Reference.

Peevers, G., Douglas, G., Jack, M. A., & Marshall, D. (2013). A usability comparison of SMS and IVR as digital banking channels. In A. Mesquita (Ed.), *User perception and influencing factors of technology in everyday life* (pp. 76–91). Hershey, PA: Information Science Reference.

Pereira da Silva, H., & Loureiro da Silva, L. D. (2013). Digital inclusion and electronic government: Looking for convergence in the decade 1997-2008. In I. Association (Ed.), *Digital literacy: Concepts, methodologies, tools, and applications* (pp. 1192–1218). Hershey, PA: Information Science Reference.

Pettitt, M., & Burnett, G. (2012). Visual demand evaluation methods for in-vehicle interfaces. In J. Lumsden (Ed.), *Social and organizational impacts of emerging mobile devices: Evaluating use* (pp. 265–278). Hershey, PA: Information Science Reference. doi:10.4018/978-1-4666-0194-9.ch015

Phipps, L. C., Wise, A., & Amundsen, C. (2013). The university in transition: Reconsidering faculty roles and expertise in a web 2.0 world. In T. Takševa (Ed.), *Social software and the evolution of user expertise: Future trends in knowledge creation and dissemination* (pp. 93–111). Hershey, PA: Information Science Reference.

Polifroni, J., Kiss, I., & Seneff, S. (2013). Speech for content creation. In J. Lumsden (Ed.), *Developments in technologies for human-centric mobile computing and applications* (pp. 114–129). Hershey, PA: Information Science Reference.

Popescu, E., & Badica, C. (2013). Creating a personalized artificial intelligence course: WELSA case study. In J. Wang (Ed.), *Information systems and modern society: Social change and global development* (pp. 31–48). Hershey, PA: Information Science Reference. doi:10.4018/978-1-4666-2922-6.ch003

Prakash, N. (2012). ICT and women empowerment in a rural setting in India. In R. Pande, & T. Van der Weide (Eds.), *Globalization, technology diffusion and gender disparity: Social impacts of ICTs* (pp. 15–24). Hershey, PA: Information Science Reference. doi:10.4018/978-1-4666-0020-1.ch002

Prescott, J., & Bogg, J. (2013). Self, career, and gender issues: A complex interplay of internal/external factors. In *Gendered occupational differences in science, engineering, and technology careers* (pp. 79–111). Hershey, PA: Information Science Reference.

Prescott, J., & Bogg, J. (2013). Stereotype, attitudes, and identity: Gendered expectations and behaviors. In *Gendered occupational differences in science, engineering, and technology careers* (pp. 112–135). Hershey, PA: Information Science Reference.

Prescott, J., & Bogg, J. (2013). The computer games industry: New industry, same old issues. In *Gendered occupational differences in science, engineering, and technology careers* (pp. 64–77). Hershey, PA: Information Science Reference.

Pure, R. A., Markov, A. R., Mangus, J. M., Metzger, M. J., Flanagin, A. J., & Hartsell, E. H. (2013). Understanding and evaluating source expertise in an evolving media environment. In T. Takševa (Ed.), *Social software and the evolution of user expertise: Future trends in knowledge creation and dissemination* (pp. 37–51). Hershey, PA: Information Science Reference.

Quesenberry, J. L. (2012). Re-examining the career anchor model: An investigation of career values and motivations among women in the information technology profession. In R. Pande, & T. Van der Weide (Eds.), *Globalization, technology diffusion and gender disparity: Social impacts of ICTs* (pp. 169–183). Hershey, PA: Information Science Reference. doi:10.4018/978-1-4666-0020-1.ch015

Quinlan, A., Quinlan, E., & Nelson, D. (2013). Performing actor-network theory in the post-secondary classroom. In A. Tatnall (Ed.), *Social and professional applications of actor-network theory for technology development* (pp. 56–66). Hershey, PA: Information Science Reference.

Radu, R. G. (2012). From drift to draft: International institutional responses to the global digital divide. In R. Pande, & T. Van der Weide (Eds.), *Globalization, technology diffusion and gender disparity: Social impacts of ICTs* (pp. 83–94). Hershey, PA: Information Science Reference. doi:10.4018/978-1-4666-0020-1.ch007

Raeth, P., & Smolnik, S. (2013). Towards a model of employee weblog usage: A process-oriented analysis of antecedents and consequences. In B. Medlin (Ed.), *Integrations of technology utilization and social dynamics in organizations* (pp. 125–141). Hershey, PA: Information Science Reference.

Ragusa, A. T., & Steinke, E. (2012). Studying locally, interacting globally: Demographic change and international students in Australian higher education. In K. St.Amant, & S. Kelsey (Eds.), *Computer-mediated communication across cultures: International interactions in online environments* (pp. 344–368). Hershey, PA: Information Science Reference.

Rahman, H., & Ramos, I. (2013). Empowerment of SMEs through open innovation strategies: Life cycle of technology management. In S. Chhabra (Ed.), *ICT influences on human development, interaction, and collaboration* (pp. 185–202). Hershey, PA: Information Science Reference.

Raihan, A. (2012). Public access ICT in Bangladesh. In R. Gomez (Ed.), *Libraries, telecentres, cybercafes and public access to ICT: International comparisons* (pp. 249–266). Hershey, PA: Information Science Publishing.

Rajesh, M. N. (2012). Virtual tourism as a new form of oppression against women. In R. Pande, & T. Van der Weide (Eds.), *Globalization, technology diffusion and gender disparity: Social impacts of ICTs* (pp. 200–209). Hershey, PA: Information Science Reference. doi:10.4018/978-1-4666-0020-1.ch017

Ratan, R. (2013). Self-presence, explicated: Body, emotion, and identity extension into the virtual self. In R. Luppicini (Ed.), *Handbook of research on technoself: Identity in a technological society* (pp. 322–336). Hershey, PA: Information Science Reference.

Reeves, T. C., & Herrington, J. (2013). Authentic tasks: The key to harnessing the drive to learn in members of "generation me". In I. Association (Ed.), *Digital literacy: Concepts, methodologies, tools, and applications* (pp. 1240–1255). Hershey, PA: Information Science Reference.

Resta, P., & Kalk, D. (2013). An ecological approach to instructional design: The learning synergy of interaction and context. In I. Association (Ed.), *Digital literacy: Concepts, methodologies, tools, and applications* (pp. 872–889). Hershey, PA: Information Science Reference.

Ribeiro, J. C., & Silva, T. (2013). Self, self-presentation, and the use of social applications in digital environments. In R. Luppicini (Ed.), *Handbook of research on technoself: Identity in a technological society* (pp. 439–455). Hershey, PA: Information Science Reference.

Rienties, B., Tempelaar, D., Pinckaers, M., Giesbers, B., & Lichel, L. (2012). The diverging effects of social network sites on receiving job information for students and professionals. In E. Coakes (Ed.), *Technological change and societal growth: Analyzing the future* (pp. 202–217). Hershey, PA: Information Science Reference. doi:10.4018/978-1-4666-0200-7.ch013

Rimpiläinen, S. (2013). Knowledge in networks: Knowing in transactions? In A. Tatnall (Ed.), *Social and professional applications of actor-network theory for technology development* (pp. 45–55). Hershey, PA: Information Science Reference.

Rive, P., & Thomassen, A. (2012). International collaboration and design innovation in virtual worlds: Lessons from Second Life. In K. St.Amant, & S. Kelsey (Eds.), *Computer-mediated communication across cultures: International interactions in online environments* (pp. 429–448). Hershey, PA: Information Science Reference.

Rössler, T. (2012). Electronic voting using identity domain separation and hardware security modules. In S. Sharma (Ed.), *E-adoption and technologies for empowering developing countries: Global advances* (pp. 100–114). Hershey, PA: Information Science Reference. doi:10.4018/978-1-4666-0041-6.ch008

Rothblatt, M. (2013). Mindclone technoselves: Multi-substrate legal identities, cyber-psychology, and biocyberethics. In R. Luppicini (Ed.), *Handbook of research on technoself: Identity in a technological society* (pp. 105–122). Hershey, PA: Information Science Reference.

Rozengardt, A., & Finquelievich, S. (2012). Public access ICT in Argentina. In R. Gomez (Ed.), *Libraries, telecentres, cybercafes and public access to ICT: International comparisons* (pp. 114–133). Hershey, PA: Information Science Publishing.

Sabone, M. B., Mogobe, K. D., & Sabone, T. G. (2012). ICTS and their role in health promotion: A preliminary situation analysis in selected Botswana rural communities. In R. Lekoko, & L. Semali (Eds.), *Cases on developing countries and ICT integration: Rural community development* (pp. 1–15). Hershey, PA: Information Science Reference.

Saleh, A. I. (2013). A novel strategy for managing user's locations in PCS networks based on a novel hot spots topology. In S. Chhabra (Ed.), *ICT influences on human development, interaction, and collaboration* (pp. 43–77). Hershey, PA: Information Science Reference.

Samiei, A., & Laitsch, D. A. (2012). The concerns of elementary educators with the diffusion of information and communication technology. In S. Chhabra (Ed.), *ICTs for advancing rural communities and human development: Addressing the digital divide* (pp. 193–207). Hershey, PA: Information Science Reference. doi:10.4018/978-1-4666-0047-8.ch013

Sandulli, F. D. (2013). Solving the paradoxes of the information technology revolution: Productivity and inequality. In I. Association (Ed.), *Digital literacy: Concepts, methodologies, tools, and applications* (pp. 1440–1455). Hershey, PA: Information Science Reference.

Santana, P. C., Ahumada, A. C., & Magaña, M. A. (2013). Usability testing of an education management information system: The case of the University of Colima. In M. Garcia-Ruiz (Ed.), *Cases on usability engineering: Design and development of digital products* (pp. 80–93). Hershey, PA: Information Science Reference. doi:10.4018/978-1-4666-4046-7.ch004

Schäler, R. (2012). Information sharing across languages. In K. St.Amant, & S. Kelsey (Eds.), *Computer-mediated communication across cultures: International interactions in online environments* (pp. 215–234). Hershey, PA: Information Science Reference.

Schleicher, R., Shirazi, A. S., Rohs, M., Kratz, S., & Schmidt, A. (2013). WorldCupinion: Experiences with an android app for real-time opinion sharing during soccer world cup games. In J. Lumsden (Ed.), *Developments in technologies for human-centric mobile computing and applications* (pp. 240–257). Hershey, PA: Information Science Reference.

Schott, G., & Selwyn, N. (2013). Game literacy: Assessing its value for both classification and public perceptions of games in a New Zealand context. In I. Association (Ed.), *Digital literacy: Concepts, methodologies, tools, and applications* (pp. 347–363). Hershey, PA: Information Science Reference.

Schulmeister, R. (2013). Students, internet, elearning and web 2.0. In I. Association (Ed.), *Digital literacy: Concepts, methodologies, tools, and applications* (pp. 1720–1742). Hershey, PA: Information Science Reference.

Scolari, C. A., Romaní, C. C., & Kuklinski, H. P. (2013). Should we take disintermediation in higher education seriously? Expertise, knowledge brokering, and knowledge translation in the age of disintermediation. In T. Takševa (Ed.), *Social software and the evolution of user expertise: Future trends in knowledge creation and dissemination* (pp. 72–92). Hershey, PA: Information Science Reference.

Segal, J., & Morris, C. (2013). Scientific end-user developers and barriers to user/customer engagement. In A. Dwivedi, & S. Clarke (Eds.), *Innovative strategies and approaches for end-user computing advancements* (pp. 333–346). Hershey, PA: Information Science Reference.

Selg, H. (2013). Swedish students online: An inquiry into differing cultures on the internet. In I. Association (Ed.), *Digital literacy: Concepts, methodologies, tools, and applications* (pp. 735–756). Hershey, PA: Information Science Reference.

Shen, J., & Eder, L. B. (2013). An examination of factors associated with user acceptance of social shopping websites. In A. Mesquita (Ed.), *User perception and influencing factors of technology in everyday life* (pp. 28–45). Hershey, PA: Information Science Reference.

Sidhu, M. S., & Kang, L. C. (2012). New trends and futuristic information communication technologies for engineering education. In S. Chhabra (Ed.), *ICTs for advancing rural communities and human development: Addressing the digital divide* (pp. 251–262). Hershey, PA: Information Science Reference. doi:10.4018/978-1-4666-0047-8.ch017

Sierra, W., & Eyman, D. (2013). "I rolled the dice with trade chat and this is what i got": Demonstrating context-dependent credibility in virtual worlds. In M. Folk, & S. Apostel (Eds.), *Online credibility and digital ethos: Evaluating computer-mediated communication* (pp. 332–352). Hershey, PA: Information Science Reference.

Sintoris, C., Stoica, A., Papadimitriou, I., Yiannoutsou, N., Komis, V., & Avouris, N. (2012). MuseumScrabble: Design of a mobile game for children's interaction with a digitally augmented cultural space. In J. Lumsden (Ed.), *Social and organizational impacts of emerging mobile devices: Evaluating use* (pp. 124–142). Hershey, PA: Information Science Reference. doi:10.4018/978-1-4666-0194-9.ch007

Slegers, K., & van Boxtel, M. P. (2013). Actual use of computers and the internet by older adults: Potential benefits and risks. In R. Zheng, R. Hill, & M. Gardner (Eds.), *Engaging older adults with modern technology: Internet use and information access needs* (pp. 161–190). Hershey, PA: Information Science Reference.

Smith, P. (2012). Affective factors for successful knowledge management. In E. Coakes (Ed.), *Technological change and societal growth: Analyzing the future* (pp. 79–87). Hershey, PA: Information Science Reference. doi:10.4018/978-1-4666-0200-7.ch005

Söderström, S. (2013). Assistive ICT and young disabled persons: Opportunities and obstacles in identity negotiations. In R. Luppicini (Ed.), *Handbook of research on technoself: Identity in a technological society* (pp. 337–358). Hershey, PA: Information Science Reference. doi:10.4018/978-1-4666-4422-9.ch056

Sone, Y. (2013). Robot double: Hiroshi Ishiguro's reflexive machines. In R. Luppicini (Ed.), *Handbook of research on technoself: Identity in a technological society* (pp. 680–702). Hershey, PA: Information Science Reference.

Sørensen, B. H., & Levinsen, K. T. (2013). School in the knowledge society: A local global school. In I. Association (Ed.), *Digital literacy: Concepts, methodologies, tools, and applications* (pp. 959–975). Hershey, PA: Information Science Reference.

Spence, E. (2012). Luciano Floridi's metaphysical theory of information ethics: A critical appraisal and an alternative neo-Gewirthian information ethics. In A. Mesquita (Ed.), *Human interaction with technology for working, communicating, and learning: Advancements* (pp. 134–148). Hershey, PA: Information Science Reference.

Stam, K., Guzman, I. R., & Thoryk, D. (2012). Studying online communication features on international and cross-cultural web pages using websphere analysis methodology. In K. St.Amant, & S. Kelsey (Eds.), *Computer-mediated communication across cultures: International interactions in online environments* (pp. 187–199). Hershey, PA: Information Science Reference.

Stephens, R. T. (2013). Usability impact analysis of collaborative environments. In M. Garcia-Ruiz (Ed.), *Cases on usability engineering: Design and development of digital products* (pp. 94–116). Hershey, PA: Information Science Reference. doi:10.4018/978-1-4666-4046-7.ch005

Sterbini, A., & Temperini, M. (2013). SocialX: An improved reputation based support to social collaborative learning through exercise sharing and project teamwork. In J. Wang (Ed.), *Information systems and modern society: Social change and global development* (pp. 66–85). Hershey, PA: Information Science Reference. doi:10.4018/978-1-4666-2922-6.ch005

Stevens, G., Pipek, V., & Wulf, V. (2012). Appropriation infrastructure: Mediating appropriation and production work. In A. Dwivedi, & S. Clarke (Eds.), *End-user computing, development, and software engineering: New challenges* (pp. 254–278). Hershey, PA: Information Science Reference. doi:10.4018/978-1-4666-0140-6.ch012

Strömberg-Jakka, M. (2013). Social assistance via the internet: The case of Finland in the European context. In J. Lannon, & E. Halpin (Eds.), *Human rights and information communication technologies: Trends and consequences of use* (pp. 177–195). Hershey, PA: Information Science Reference.

Subrahmanyam, K., & Manago, A. (2012). The children's digital media center @ Los Angeles. In Z. Yan (Ed.), *Encyclopedia of cyber behavior* (pp. 64–76). Hershey, PA: Information Science Reference. doi:10.4018/978-1-4666-0315-8.ch005

Suki, N. M. (2013). Modelling factors influencing early adopters' purchase intention towards online music. In A. Mesquita (Ed.), *User perception and influencing factors of technology in everyday life* (pp. 298–314). Hershey, PA: Information Science Reference.

Sweet, C. (2013). Wikipedia's success and the rise of the amateur-expert. In T. Takševa (Ed.), *Social software and the evolution of user expertise: Future trends in knowledge creation and dissemination* (pp. 13–36). Hershey, PA: Information Science Reference.

Swindell, R., Grimbeek, P., & Heffernan, J. (2013). U3A online and successful aging: A smart way to help bridge the grey digital divide. In I. Association (Ed.), *Digital literacy: Concepts, methodologies, tools, and applications* (pp. 1640–1657). Hershey, PA: Information Science Reference.

Sylaiou, S., White, M., & Liarokapis, F. (2013). Digital heritage systems: The ARCO evaluation. In M. Garcia-Ruiz (Ed.), *Cases on usability engineering: Design and development of digital products* (pp. 321–354). Hershey, PA: Information Science Reference. doi:10.4018/978-1-4666-4046-7.ch014

Tai, Z., & Zhang, Y. (2013). Online identity formation and digital ethos building in the Chinese blogosphere. In M. Folk, & S. Apostel (Eds.), *Online credibility and digital ethos: Evaluating computer-mediated communication* (pp. 269–284). Hershey, PA: Information Science Reference.

Taiwo, R. (2012). Discursive manipulation strategies in virtual scams in global contexts. In K. St.Amant, & S. Kelsey (Eds.), *Computer-mediated communication across cultures: International interactions in online environments* (pp. 143–154). Hershey, PA: Information Science Reference.

Tchouakeu, L. N., Maldonado, E., Zhao, K., Robinson, H., Maitland, C., & Tapia, A. (2013). Exploring barriers to coordination between humanitarian NGOs: A comparative case study of two NGO's information technology coordination bodies. In J. Wang (Ed.), *Information systems and modern society: Social change and global development* (pp. 87–112). Hershey, PA: Information Science Reference. doi:10.4018/978-1-4666-2922-6.ch006

Tella, A., Mutula, S. M., Mutshewa, A., & Totolo, A. (2012). An evaluation of WebCT course content management system at the university of Botswana. In S. Sharma (Ed.), *E-adoption and technologies for empowering developing countries: Global advances* (pp. 205–232). Hershey, PA: Information Science Reference. doi:10.4018/978-1-4666-0041-6.ch015

Thatcher, A., & Ndabeni, M. (2013). A psychological model to understand e-adoption in the context of the digital divide. In I. Association (Ed.), *Digital literacy: Concepts, methodologies, tools, and applications* (pp. 1402–1424). Hershey, PA: Information Science Reference.

Todd, P. M., Rogers, Y., & Payne, S. J. (2013). Nudging the trolley in the supermarket: How to deliver the right information to shoppers. In J. Lumsden (Ed.), *Developments in technologies for human-centric mobile computing and applications* (pp. 99–113). Hershey, PA: Information Science Reference.

Tojib, D. R., & Sugianto, L. (2013). Construct validity assessment in IS research: Methods and case example of user satisfaction scale. In A. Dwivedi, & S. Clarke (Eds.), *Innovative strategies and approaches for end-user computing advancements* (pp. 134–159). Hershey, PA: Information Science Reference.

Tregeagle, S. (2012). Participation in child welfare services through information and communication technologies. In S. Chhabra (Ed.), *ICTs for advancing rural communities and human development: Addressing the digital divide* (pp. 73–90). Hershey, PA: Information Science Reference. doi:10.4018/978-1-4666-0047-8.ch006

Truong, Y. (2013). Antecedents of consumer acceptance of mobile television advertising. In A. Mesquita (Ed.), *User perception and influencing factors of technology in everyday life* (pp. 128–141). Hershey, PA: Information Science Reference.

Truyen, F., & Buekens, F. (2013). Professional ICT knowledge, epistemic standards, and social epistemology. In T. Takševa (Ed.), *Social software and the evolution of user expertise: Future trends in knowledge creation and dissemination* (pp. 274–294). Hershey, PA: Information Science Reference.

Tsai, C. (2013). How much can computers and internet help? A long-term study of web-mediated problem-based learning and self-regulated learning. In A. Mesquita (Ed.), *User perception and influencing factors of technology in everyday life* (pp. 248–264). Hershey, PA: Information Science Reference.

Tsai, C., & Shen, P. (2013). Improving students' computing skills and attitudes toward learning via web-mediated self-regulated learning with feedback in an online problem-solving environment. In S. Sharma (Ed.), *Adoption of virtual technologies for business, educational, and governmental advancements* (pp. 162–179). Hershey, PA: Information Science Reference.

Unsal, F., Komaromi, K., & Erickson, G. S. (2013). Trust in e-commerce: Social networks vs. institutional credibility. In S. Sharma (Ed.), *Adoption of virtual technologies for business, educational, and governmental advancements* (pp. 44–57). Hershey, PA: Information Science Reference.

van de Sande, C. (2012). Free, open, online help forums: convenience, connection, control, comfort, and communication. In E. Coakes (Ed.), *Technological change and societal growth: Analyzing the future* (pp. 162–179). Hershey, PA: Information Science Reference. doi:10.4018/978-1-4666-0200-7.ch011

van der Weide, T. (2012). A digital (r)evolution to the information age. In R. Pande, & T. Van der Weide (Eds.), *Globalization, technology diffusion and gender disparity: Social impacts of ICTs* (pp. 1–14). Hershey, PA: Information Science Reference. doi:10.4018/978-1-4666-0020-1.ch001

van Dijck, J. (2013). Google scholar as the co-producer of scholarly knowledge. In T. Takševa (Ed.), *Social software and the evolution of user expertise: Future trends in knowledge creation and dissemination* (pp. 130–146). Hershey, PA: Information Science Reference.

Varga-Atkins, T., Prescott, D., & Dangerfield, P. (2012). Cyber behavior with wikis. In Z. Yan (Ed.), *Encyclopedia of cyber behavior* (pp. 164–177). Hershey, PA: Information Science Reference. doi:10.4018/978-1-4666-0315-8.ch014

Veil, S. R. (2012). Adoption barriers in a high-risk agricultural environment. In A. Mesquita (Ed.), *Human interaction with technology for working, communicating, and learning: Advancements* (pp. 31–47). Hershey, PA: Information Science Reference.

Walczak, S., & Mann, R. (2012). Utilization and perceived benefit for diverse users of communities of practice in a healthcare organization. In A. Dwivedi, & S. Clarke (Eds.), *End-user computing, development, and software engineering: New challenges* (pp. 25–53). Hershey, PA: Information Science Reference. doi:10.4018/978-1-4666-0140-6.ch002

Wallgren, L. G., Leijon, S., & Andersson, K. M. (2013). IT managers' narratives on subordinates' motivation at work: A case study. In A. Mesquita (Ed.), *User perception and influencing factors of technology in everyday life* (pp. 282–297). Hershey, PA: Information Science Reference.

Walton, A. L., DeVaney, S. A., & Sandall, D. L. (2013). Graduate students' perceptions of privacy and closed circuit television systems in public settings. In A. Mesquita (Ed.), *User perception and influencing factors of technology in everyday life* (pp. 107–127). Hershey, PA: Information Science Reference.

Wang, J., Doll, W. J., & Deng, X. (2012). A model of system re-configurability and pedagogical usability in an e-learning context: A faculty perspective. In A. Dwivedi, & S. Clarke (Eds.), *End-user computing, development, and software engineering: New challenges* (pp. 168–184). Hershey, PA: Information Science Reference. doi:10.4018/978-1-4666-0140-6.ch008

Wang, J., Zhou, B., & Hsu, J. (2012). Assessment and contrast of the effects of information and communication technology. In S. Chhabra (Ed.), *ICTs for advancing rural communities and human development: Addressing the digital divide* (pp. 15–32). Hershey, PA: Information Science Reference. doi:10.4018/978-1-4666-0047-8.ch002

Wang, Y., Wang, X., Qian, Y., Luo, H., Ge, F., Yang, Y., & Xia, Y. (2013). Residential load pattern analysis for smart grid applications based on audio feature EEUPC. In T. Gao (Ed.), *Global applications of pervasive and ubiquitous computing* (pp. 107–121). Hershey, PA: Information Science Reference.

Wang, Y. K., & Datta, P. (2012). Investigating technology commitment in instant messaging application users. In A. Dwivedi, & S. Clarke (Eds.), *End-user computing, development, and software engineering: New challenges* (pp. 227–252). Hershey, PA: Information Science Reference. doi:10.4018/978-1-4666-0140-6.ch011

Was, C. A., & Woltz, D. J. (2013). Implicit memory and aging: Adapting technology to utilize preserved memory functions. In R. Zheng, R. Hill, & M. Gardner (Eds.), *Engaging older adults with modern technology: Internet use and information access needs* (pp. 1–19). Hershey, PA: Information Science Reference.

Watson, J. M., Lambert, A. E., Cooper, J. M., Boyle, I. V., & Strayer, D. L. (2013). On attentional control and the aging driver. In R. Zheng, R. Hill, & M. Gardner (Eds.), *Engaging older adults with modern technology: Internet use and information access needs* (pp. 20–32). Hershey, PA: Information Science Reference.

Watson, S. L., & Mulvihill, T. (2013). Exploring the notion of 'technology as a public good': Emerging characteristics and trends of the digital divide in East Asian education. In I. Association (Ed.), *Digital literacy: Concepts, methodologies, tools, and applications* (pp. 1472–1488). Hershey, PA: Information Science Reference.

Watts, C. (2013). Connection, fragmentation, and intentionality: Social software and the changing nature of expertise. In T. Takševa (Ed.), *Social software and the evolution of user expertise: Future trends in knowledge creation and dissemination* (pp. 52–70). Hershey, PA: Information Science Reference.

Watts, J. D., Kanyasone, V., & Vongkhamsao, V. (2012). Pathways to participatory landscape governance in northern Laos: The role of information and communication technologies. In S. Chhabra (Ed.), *ICTs for advancing rural communities and human development: Addressing the digital divide* (pp. 143–157). Hershey, PA: Information Science Reference. doi:10.4018/978-1-4666-0047-8.ch010

Weber, R. H. (2013). ICT policies favouring human rights. In J. Lannon, & E. Halpin (Eds.), *Human rights and information communication technologies: Trends and consequences of use* (pp. 21–35). Hershey, PA: Information Science Reference.

Wei, Z., & Kramarae, C. (2012). Women, big ideas, and social networking technologies: Hidden assumptions. In R. Pande, & T. Van der Weide (Eds.), *Globalization, technology diffusion and gender disparity: Social impacts of ICTs* (pp. 70–82). Hershey, PA: Information Science Reference. doi:10.4018/978-1-4666-0020-1.ch006

Whiteside, A. L., & Dikkers, A. G. (2012). Maximizing multicultural online learning experiences with the social presence model, course examples, and specific strategies. In K. St.Amant, & S. Kelsey (Eds.), *Computer-mediated communication across cultures: International interactions in online environments* (pp. 395–413). Hershey, PA: Information Science Reference.

Widyanto, L., & Griffiths, M. (2013). An empirical study of problematic internet use and self-esteem. In R. Zheng (Ed.), *Evolving psychological and educational perspectives on cyber behavior* (pp. 82–95). Hershey, PA: Information Science Reference.

Wiebelhaus-Brahm, E. (2013). Truth-seeking at a distance: Engaging diaspora populations in transitional justice processes. In J. Lannon, & E. Halpin (Eds.), *Human rights and information communication technologies: Trends and consequences of use* (pp. 72–85). Hershey, PA: Information Science Reference.

Wilhelmson, L., Johansson, P., & Döös, M. (2013). Bridging boundaries: Middle managers' pedagogic interventions as technology leaders. In S. Wang, & T. Hartsell (Eds.), *Technology integration and foundations for effective leadership* (pp. 278–292). Hershey, PA: Information Science Reference.

Wilson, C., & Dunn, A. (2013). Contingency and hybridity in the study of digital advocacy networks: Implications of the Egyptian protest movement. In J. Lannon, & E. Halpin (Eds.), *Human rights and information communication technologies: Trends and consequences of use* (pp. 100–121). Hershey, PA: Information Science Reference.

Wilson, S., & Haslam, N. (2013). Reasoning about human enhancement: Towards a folk psychological model of human nature and human identity. In R. Luppicini (Ed.), *Handbook of research on technoself: Identity in a technological society* (pp. 175–188). Hershey, PA: Information Science Reference.

Woodfield, R. (2012). Gender and employability patterns amongst UK ICT graduates: Investigating the leaky pipeline. In R. Pande, & T. Van der Weide (Eds.), *Globalization, technology diffusion and gender disparity: Social impacts of ICTs* (pp. 184–199). Hershey, PA: Information Science Reference. doi:10.4018/978-1-4666-0020-1.ch016

Yan, Z., & Zheng, R. Z. (2013). Growing from childhood into adolescence: The science of cyber behavior. In R. Zheng (Ed.), *Evolving psychological and educational perspectives on cyber behavior* (pp. 1–14). Hershey, PA: Information Science Reference.

Yang, P. (2012). Knowing through asynchronous time and space: A phenomenological study of cultural differences in online interaction. In K. St.Amant, & S. Kelsey (Eds.), *Computer-mediated communication across cultures: International interactions in online environments* (pp. 108–122). Hershey, PA: Information Science Reference.

Yi, M. (2012). Minimizing cultural differences using ontology-based information retrieval system. In K. St.Amant, & S. Kelsey (Eds.), *Computer-mediated communication across cultures: International interactions in online environments* (pp. 200–214). Hershey, PA: Information Science Reference.

Yocom, H. (2013). Implementation of the technology plan. In S. Wang, & T. Hartsell (Eds.), *Technology integration and foundations for effective leadership* (pp. 102–123). Hershey, PA: Information Science Reference.

Yoo, J., Hwang, W., Seok, H., Park, S. K., Kim, C., Choi, W. H., & Park, K. (2012). Cocktail: Exploiting bartenders' gestures for mobile interaction. In J. Lumsden (Ed.), *Social and organizational impacts of emerging mobile devices: Evaluating use* (pp. 186–199). Hershey, PA: Information Science Reference. doi:10.4018/978-1-4666-0194-9.ch011

Zaman, M., Simmers, C. A., & Anandarajan, M. (2013). Using an ethical framework to examine linkages between "going green" in research practices and information and communication technologies. In B. Medlin (Ed.), *Integrations of technology utilization and social dynamics in organizations* (pp. 243–262). Hershey, PA: Information Science Reference.

Zhang, L., & Jones, M. C. (2013). A social capital perspective on IT professionals' work behavior and attitude. In A. Dwivedi, & S. Clarke (Eds.), *Innovative strategies and approaches for end-user computing advancements* (pp. 160–174). Hershey, PA: Information Science Reference.

Zheng, R. Z. (2013). Effective online learning for older people: A heuristic design approach. In R. Zheng, R. Hill, & M. Gardner (Eds.), *Engaging older adults with modern technology: Internet use and information access needs* (pp. 142–159). Hershey, PA: Information Science Reference.

Zolfaghar, K., Khoshalhan, F., & Rabiei, M. (2012). User acceptance of location-based mobile advertising: An empirical study in Iran. In S. Sharma (Ed.), *E-adoption and technologies for empowering developing countries: Global advances* (pp. 59–71). Hershey, PA: Information Science Reference. doi:10.4018/978-1-4666-0041-6.ch005

Compilation of References

@ev and @biz. (2011, Feb 16). #Jan25: One tweet, one story. [blog post]. *Hope140*. Retrieved from http://hope140.org/blog/?p=127

Aday, S., Farrell, H., Lynch, M., Sides, J., Kelly, J., & Zuckerman, E. (2010). *Blogs and bullets: New media in contentious politics*. Retrieved from http://www.usip.org/files/resources/pw65.pdf

Aday, S., Farrell, H., Lynch, M., Sides, J., & Freelon, D. (2012). *Blogs and bullets II: New media and conflict after the Arab spring. PeaceWorks, 80*. Washington, DC: The American Institute.

Adler, P., & Kwon, S.-W. (2002). Social capital: Prospects for a new concept. *Academy of Management Review, 27*, 17–40.

AdvTeamMadman. (2013). *The sandbox glossary: A rosetta stone for joe-heads*. Retrieved from http://www.beegeeks.com/atmadman/joeglossary.html

Agha, A., & Naveen, N. (2011, Jul 12). *Social media activist Mohamed Ibrahim talks to gawaahi.com*. Retrieved from http://www.youtube.com/watch?v=w4Rh497KJ4c

Arinc. (2012, December 28). *Internethaber*. Retrieved from http://www.internethaber.com/arinc-universitelerde-tehlike-var-489378h.htm

Arnheim, R. (2004). *Visual thinking*. Berkeley, CA: University of California Press.

Arola, K. (2010). The design of web 2.0: The rise of the template, the fall of design. *Computers and Composition, 27*, 4–14. doi:10.1016/j.compcom.2009.11.004

Au, W. J. (2012, July 2). *Will the well survive?* [Web log post]. Retrieved from http://nwn.blogs.com/nwn/2012/07/will-the-well-survive-members-pledge-to-buy-from-salon.html

Autonomy. (2010). *Aurasma*. Retrieved from http://www.aurasma.com/

Bakhtin, M. (1984). *Problems of Dostoevsky's poetics*. Minneapolis, MN: University of Minnesota Press.

Bakhtin, M. (1984). *Rabelais and his world* (H. Iswolsky, Trans.). Bloomington, IN: Indiana University Press.

Balloon Juice. (n.d.). Retrieved from http://www.balloon-juice.com/

Banksy (Director). (2010). *Exit through the gift hop*. [Motion Picture]. United Kingdom: Paranoid Pictures.

Banksy. (2006). *Wall and piece*. London: Century.

Banksy. (n.d.). *Banksy*. Retrieved from http://banksy.co.uk

Barnes, J. (2001, February 10). Where did you go, Raggedy Ann? Toys in the age of electronics. *The New York Times*. Retrieved from http://www.nytimes.com

Barnes, S. (2000). Developing a concept of self in cyberspace communities. In S. B. Gibson, & O. O. Oviedo (Eds.), *The emerging cyberculture* (pp. 169–201). Cresskill, NJ: Hampton Press.

Baudrillard, J. (1994). *Simulacra and simulation*. Ann Arbor, MI: University of Michigan Press.

Baym, N. (2010). *Personal connections in the digital age*. Cambridge, UK: Polity Press.

Baym, N. K., & Boyd, D. (2012). Socially mediated publicness: An introduction. *Journal of Broadcasting & Electronic Media*, *56*(3), 320–329. doi:10.1080/08838151.2012.705200

Bealer, A. H. (2012). Eco-performance in the digital RPG gamescape. In *Dungeons, dragons, and digital denizens: The digital role-playing game* (Vol. 1, pp. 27–47). New York: The Continuum International Publishing Group.

Beard, A. (2007). *How to find the Digg friends you never knew you had*. Retrieved April 16, 2013 from http://andybeard.eu/730/digg-friends.html

Behm-Morawitz, E., & Mastro, D. (2009). The effects of the sexualization of female video game characters on gender stereotyping and female self-concept. *Sex Roles*, *61*(11-12), 808–823. doi:10.1007/s11199-009-9683-8

Bennett, W. L. (2003). Communicating global activism: Strengths and vulnerabilities of networked politics. *Information Communication and Society*, *6*(2), 143–168. doi:10.1080/1369118032000093860a

Bennett, W. L. (2012). The personalization of politics: Political identity, social media, and changing patterns of participation. *The Annals of the American Academy of Political and Social Science*, *644*(20), 20–39. doi:10.1177/0002716212451428

Bennett, W. L., Breunig, C., & Givens, T. (2008). Communication and political mobilization: Digital media and the organization of anti-Iraq war demonstrations in the U.S. *Political Communication*, *25*, 269–289. doi:10.1080/10584600802197434

Bhat, C. S., Chang, S.-H., & Linscott, J. A. (2010). Addressing cyberbullying as a media literacy issue. *New Horizons in Education*, *58*(3), 34–43.

Biel, E. (n.d.). The guerilla cartoonist of Rio. *The Cairo Review of Global Affairs*. Retrieved from http://www.aucegypt.edu/gapp/cairoreview/pages/articleDetails.aspx?aid=157#

BioWare. (2009). *Dragon age: Origins*. DRPG, Electronic Arts.

BioWare. (2010). *Dragon age: Awakening*. DRPG, Electronic Arts.

BioWare. (2011). *Dragon age II*. DRPG, Electronic Arts.

Black, R. (2009). Online fan fiction, global identities and imagination. *Research in the Teaching of English*, *43*(4), 397–425.

Boellstorff, T. (2008). *Coming of age in Second Life*. Princeton, NJ: Princeton University Press.

Bogost, I. (2008). *Unit operations: An approach to videogame criticism*. Cambridge, MA: MIT Press.

Booker, C. (2006). *The seven basic plots: Why we tell stories*. New York: Continuum Books.

Borriello, G., Breit, N., Brunette, W., Chaudhri, R., Dell, N., & Sundt, M. (2010). *Open data kit*. Retrieved from http://mobileactive.org/

boyd, d., Golder, & Lotan. (2010). *Tweet, tweet, retweet: Conversational aspects of retweeting on twitter*. Retrieved from http://www.danah.org/papers/TweetTweetRetweet.pdf

Boyd, D. (2008). Can social network sites enable political action? *International Journal of Media and Cultural Politics*, *4*(2), 241–244. doi:10.1386/macp.4.2.241_3

Boyd, D. M., & Ellison, N. B. (2008). Social network sites: Definition, history and scholarship. *Journal of Computer-Mediated Communication*, *13*, 210–230. doi:10.1111/j.1083-6101.2007.00393.x

Brabham, D. C. (2008). Crowdsourcing as a model for problem solving: An introduction and cases. *Convergence: The International Journal of Research into New Media Technologies*, *14*(1), 75–90. doi:10.1177/1354856507084420

Brown, A. (2011). Relationships, community, and identity in the new virtual society. *The Futurist*, *45*(2), 29–34.

Brown, P., & Levinson, S. (1987). *Politeness: Some universals in language use*. Cambridge, UK: Cambridge University Press.

Brown, S. D., & Capdevila, R. (1999). Perpetuum mobile: Substance, force, and the sociology of translation. In J. Law, & J. Hassard (Eds.), *Actor network theory and after* (pp. 26–50). Malden, MA: Blackwell Publishing.

Bryce, J., & Rutter, J. (2002, June). *Killing like a girl: Gendered gaming and girl gamers' visibility*. Paper presented at the Computer Games and Digital Culture Conferences. Tampere, Finland.

Bryce, J., & Rutter, J. (2003). Gender dynamics and the social and spatial organization of computer gaming. *Leisure Studies*, *22*, 1–15. doi:10.1080/02614360306571

Building Digital Communities, The Institute of Museum and Library Services, together with the University of Washington and the International City/County Management Association. (2012). Retrieved from http://www.imls.gov/about/building_digital_communities.aspx

Call, J., Whitlock, K., & Voorhees, G. (2012). From dungeons to digital denizens. In *Dungeons, dragons, and digital denizens: The digital role-playing game* (Vol. 1, pp. 11–24). New York: The Continuum International Publishing Group.

Callon, M. (1986). Some elements of a sociology of translation domestication of the scallops and the fishermen of St. Brieux Bay. In J. Law (Ed.), *Power action and belief: A sociology of knowledge* (pp. 197–220). London: Routledge & Kegan Paul.

Callon, M. (1999). Actor network theory--The market test. In J. Law, & J. Hassard (Eds.), *Actor network theory and after* (pp. 181–185). Oxford, UK: Wiley-Blackwell.

CapEff. (2013, January 13). *I normally respect artist, but that dude @banksy is a fucking lame. He's just mad he couldn't make it in the graffiti world.* [Twitter post]. Retrieved from https://twitter.com/CapEff/status/290610859053572096.

Carlson, C. (2011). The playing field: Attitudes, activities, and the conflation of play and games. *Journal of the Philosophy of Sport*, *38*(1), 74–87. doi:10.1080/009487 05.2011.9714550

Carpenter, R. (2012). Virtual places in the physical world: Geographies of literacy and (national) identity. In B. Williams, & A. A. Zenger (Eds.), *New media literacies and participatory popular culture across borders* (pp. 193–212). New York, NY: Routledge.

Carr, D. (2005). Contexts, gaming pleasures, and gendered preferences. *Simulation & Gaming*, *36*(4), 464–482. doi:10.1177/1046878105282160

Cassell, J., & Jenkins, H. (1998). Chess for girls? Feminism and computer games. In J. Cassell, & H. Jenkins (Eds.), *From Barbie to Mortal Kombat: Gender and computer games* (pp. 2–45). London: MIT Press.

Cassidy, S. B. (2011). The videogame as narrative. *Quarterly Review of Film and Video*, *28*(4), 292–306. doi:10.1080/10509200902820266

Castronova, E. (2007). *Exodus to the virtual world: How online fun is changing reality*. New York: Palgrave Macmillan.

Chesneaux, J. (2000). Speed and democracy: An uneasy dialogue. *Social Sciences Information. Information Sur les Sciences Sociales*, *39*(3), 407–420. doi:10.1177/053901800039003004

Clift, P. (2012). *Virgin's handbook on virtual relationships*. Createspace Independent Publishing Platform.

Cole, J. (2011, February 7). *Christians, Muslims one hand in Egypt's youth revolution*. [web log post]. Retrieved from http://www.juancole.com/2011/02/christians-muslims-one-hand-in-egypts-youth-revolution.html

Collin, P. (2008). The internet, youth participation policies, and the development of young people's political identities in Australia. *Journal of Youth Studies*, *11*(5), 527–542. doi:10.1080/13676260802282992

Collins, L. (2007). Banksy was here: The invisible man of graffiti art. *The New Yorker*. Retrieved from http://www.newyorker.com/reporting/2007/05/14/070514fa_fact_collin

Connelly, R., & Ghodsee, K. (2011). *Professor mommy: Finding work-family balance in academia*. Lanham, MD: Rowman & Littlefield.

Conover, M., Ratkiewicz, J., Francisco, M., Gonçalves, B., Flammini, A., et al. (2011). Political polarization on twitter. In *Proceedings of the 5th Intl. Conference on Weblogs and Social Media*. AAAI. Retrieved from http://www.aaai.org/ocs/index.php/ICWSM/ICWSM11/paper/download/2847/3275

Consalvo, M., & Harper, T. (2009). The sexi(e)st of all: Avatars, gender, and online games. In N. Panteli (Ed.), *Virtual social networks: Mediated, massive and multiplayer sites* (pp. 98–113). New York: Palgrave Macmillan.

Consalvo, M., & Paasonen, S. (Eds.). (2002). *Women & everyday uses of the internet: Agency & identity*. New York, NY: Peter Lang Publishing.

Corbett, S. (2009). Portrait of an artist as an avatar. *New York Times Magazine*. Retrieved April 17, 2013 from http://www.nytimes.com/2009/03/08/magazine/08fluno-t.html?pagewanted=all&_r=1&

Costanza-Chock, S. (2003). Mapping the repertoire of electronic contention. In A. Opel, & D. Pompper (Eds.), *Representing resistance* (pp. 173–191). Westport, CT: Praeger Publishers.

Cottle, S., & Lester, L. (2011). *Transnational protests and the media*. New York, NY: Peter Lang.

Crawford, C. (1982). *The art of computer game design*. Vancouver, WA: Washington State University. Retrieved from http://www.google.com/url?sa=t&rct=j&q=&esrc=s&source=web&cd=3&ved=0CDoQFjAC&url=http%3A%2F%2Fwww-rohan.sdsu.edu%2F~stewart%2Fcs583%2FACGD_ArtComputerGameDesign_ChrisCrawford_1982.pdf&ei=oAWUUebBOOnD4AOH9YCYBA&usg=AFQjCNEsgNzqFHKmE6Ca_l7c8jgHxBtF9w&sig2=MdrYFyAFB8gDIAye5nKfzA&bvm=bv.46471029,d.dmg

Crenshaw, K. W. (1989). Demarginalizing the intersection of race and sex: A black feminst critique of antidiscrimination doctrine, feminist theory and antiracist politics. *University of Chicago Legal Forum*, 139–167.

Crovitz, L. G. (2011, February 14). Egypt's revolution by social media: Facebook and twitter let the people keep ahead of the regime. *The Wallstreet Journal*. Retrieved from http://online.wsj.com/article/SB10001424052748703786804576137980252177072.html

Cucciarre, C., Morris, D. E., Nickoson, L., Owens, K., & Sheridan, M. P. (2011). Mothers' ways of making it--Or making do? Making (over) academic lives in rhetoric and composition with children. *Composition Studies*, *39*(1), 41–61.

Darrah, M. (2013). An open letter from Mark Darrah, executive producer. *Dragon Age III: Inquisition*. Retrieved from http://dragonage.bioware.com/inquisition/

Day, D. V., & Antonakis, J. (2012). Leadership: Past, present, and future. In D. V. Day, & J. Antonakis (Eds.), *The nature of leadership* (pp. 3–25). Los Angeles, CA: Sage.

Dekker, P., & Uslaner, E. (2001). Introduction. In E. Uslaner (Ed.), *Social capital and participation in everyday life* (pp. 1–8). London: Routledge.

DeLanda, M. (2006). *New philosophy of society: Assemblage theory and social complexity*. Retrieved from www.amazon.com

DeLanda, M. (1997). *A thousand years of nonlinear history*. Brooklyn, NY: Zone Books.

Denton, D. W., & Wicks, D. (2013). Implementing electronic portfolios through social media platforms: Steps and student perceptions. *Journal of Asynchronous Learning Networks*, *17*(1), 123–133.

DePew, K. E., & Miller-Cochran, S. (n.d.). Social networking in a second language: Engaging multiple literate practices through identity composition. In M. Cox, J. Jordan, C. Ortmeier-Hooper, & G. Schwartz (Eds.), *Inventing identities in second language writing* (pp. 273–295). Urbana, IL: NCTE.

Dery, M. (1993). Flame wars. *The South Atlantic Quarterly*, *92*(4), 559–568.

Dibbell, J. (1993, December 21). A rape in cyberspace. *Village Voice*, pp. 36-42.

Dickey, M. D. (2006). Girl gamers: The controversy of girl games and the relevance of female-oriented game design for instructional design. *British Journal of Educational Technology*, *37*(5), 785–793. doi:10.1111/j.1467-8535.2006.00561.x

Digital, N. Y. C. (2012). *Digital RoadMap: The city of New York*. Retrieved from http://www.nyc.gov/html/digital/html/roadmap/roadmap.shtml

Dill, K. E., & Burgess, M. C. (2012). Influence of Black masculinity game exemplars on social judgments. *Simulation & Gaming*. Retrieved December 19, 2012, from http://sag.sagepub.com/content/early/2012/07/24/1046878112449958.abstract?rss=1

Dragon Age, I. I. (2013). *Dragon age wiki*. Retrieved from http://dragonage.wikia.com/wiki/Dragon_Age_Wiki

Dubai School of Government. (2011). *Arab social media report*. Retrieved from http://www.dsg.ae/LinkClick.aspx?fileticket=-WvgLGPQ9G0%3d&tabid=1163

Duncan, S. C., & Hayes, E. R. (2012). Expanding the affinity space: An introduction. In E. R. Hayes, & S. C. Duncan (Eds.), *Learning in video game affinity spaces.* New York, NY: Peter Lang.

Economist. (2011, December 3). More than just digital quilting. *The Economist.* Retrieved from http://www.economist.com/node/21540392/

Elbow, P. (1977). *Writing without teachers.* Oxford, UK: Oxford University Press.

Erikson, E. H. (1995a). Late adolescence. In S. Schlein (Ed.), *A way of looking at things: Selected papers from 1930 to 1980* (pp. 631–643). New York, NY: Norton.

Erikson, E. H. (1995b). Psychoanalysis and ongoing history: Problems in identity, hatred and nonviolence. In S. Schlein (Ed.), *A way of looking at things: Selected papers from 1930 to 1980* (pp. 481–496). New York, NY: Norton.

Erikson, E. H. (1997). *The life cycle completed.* New York, NY: Norton.

Esch, D. (2013, April 19). Of typewriters and masking tape: A media history of the Zapatistas. *AlJazeera.* Retrieved from http://www.aljazeera.com/indepth/opinion/2013/04/2013415112152991530.html

Essid, J. (2011). *A failure to disrupt: Why second life failed.* [Web log post]. Retrieved from http://www.vwer.org/2011/01/14/a-failure-to-disrupt-why-second-life-failed/

Essid, J. (2011). Playing in a new key: In a new world: virtual worlds, millennial writers, and a 3D composition. In *Teaching and learning in virtual worlds: Pedagogical models and constructivist approaches.* Hershey, PA: IGI Global. doi:10.4018/978-1-60960-517-9.ch010

Essid, J. (2014). Internet past tense: Trolls, sock-puppets, and good Joes in the sandbox newsgroup. In D. J. Hickey, & J. Essid (Eds.), *Identity and leadership in virtual communities: Establishing credibility and influence.* Hershey, PA: IGI Global.

Fabian, F., Miller, K.D., & Lin, S-J. (n.d.). Strategies for online communities. *Strategic Management Journal, 30* (3), 305-322.

Fauziah, A., Kee, C. P., Normah, M., & Ibrahim, F., Mahmud & Dafrizal, W. A. (2012). Information propagation and the forces of social media in Malaysia. *Asian Social Science, 8*(5), 71–76.

Feng, J., Spence, I., & Pratt, J. (2007). Playing an action video game reduces gender differences in spatial cognition. *Psychological Science, 18*(10), 850–855. doi:10.1111/j.1467-9280.2007.01990.x PMID:17894600

Fenton, N., & Barassi, V. (2011). Alternative media and social networking sites: The politics individuation and political participation. *Communication Review, 14*(3), 179–196. doi:10.1080/10714421.2011.597245

Fenwick, T., & Edwards, R. (Eds.). (2012). *Researching education through actor-network theory.* Malden, MA: Wiley-Blackwell. doi:10.1002/9781118275825

Firedoglake. (n.d.). Retrieved from http://www.firedoglake.com

Flanagan, M. (2009). *Critical play: Radical game design.* Cambridge: MIT Press.

Fleischer, D. (2003). The guardian (paranormal adventures). Port Town Publishing. Fleischer, D. (2007). Altar of freedom. Port Town Publishing.

Fleischer, D. (2007). *Deadly reservations.* Port Town Publishing.

Fogg, B. J. (2008). Mass interpersonal persuasion: An early view of a new phenomenon. In *Proceedings of Third International Conference on Persuasive Technology.* Retrieved from http://www.bjfogg.com/mip.html

Fromherz, A. J. (2012). *Qatar: A modern history.* Washington, DC: Georgetown University Press.

Fron, J., Fullerton, T., Morie, J. F., & Pearce, C. (2007). The hegemony of play. In *Proceedings of DiGRA (Digital Games Research Association) 2007: Situated Play.* DiGRA.

Gagnon, D. (2011). ARIS. Retrieved from http://aris-games.org/

Gaider, D. (2011). *To the op... dragon age II official campaign quests and story (SPOILERS).* Retrieved from http://social.bioware.com/forum/1/topic/304/index/6661775&lf=8

Garces, C. (2011). Preamble to an ethnography of the people's mic. *Somatosphere: Science, Medicine, and Anthropology.* Retrieved from http://somatosphere.net/2011/10/preamble-to-an-ethnography-of-the-people%E2%80%99s-mic.html

Gates, B. (2011, November). *A report by Bill Gates to G20 leaders.* Retrieved from http://www.gatesfoundation.org/What-We-Do/Global-Policy/G20-Report

Gee, J. P. (2004). *Situated language and learning: A critique of traditional schooling.* London: Routledge.

Gee, J. P. (2007). *Good video games + good learning: Collected essays on video games, learning, and literacy.* New York, NY: Peter Lang.

Gerbaudo, P. (2012). *Tweets and the streets: Social media and contemporary activism.* New York, NY: Pluto.

Ghareeb, E. (2000). New media and the information revolution in the Arab world: An assessment. *The Middle East Journal, 54*(3), 395–418.

Ghonim, W. (2012). *Revolution 2.0.* Retrieved from www.amazon.com

Goffman, E. (1967). *Interaction rituals: Essays on face-to-face behavior.* Garden City, NY: Anchor.

Golumbia, D. (2009). *The cultural logic of computation.* Cambridge, MA: Harvard University Press.

Goode, J. (2010). The digital identity divide: How technology knowledge impacts college students. *New Media & Society, 12*(3), 497–513. doi:10.1177/1461444809343560

Graeber, D. (2004). *Direct action: An ethnography.* Oakland, CA: AK Press.

Grandin, T. (2006). *Thinking in pictures.* New York: Vintage Books.

Grant, S. (2013, March 19). *A citizen-led crowdsourcing roadmap for the CI-BER big data project.* Retrieved from http://www.hastac.org/blogs/slgrant/2013/03/19/citizen-led-crowdsourcing-roadmap-ci-ber-%E2%80%9Cbig-data%E2%80%9D-project

Gray, K. L. (2012). Intersecting oppressions and online communities: Examining the experiences of women of color in Xbox live. *Information Communication and Society, 15*(3), 411–428. doi:10.1080/1369118X.2011.642401

Greco, G. M., & Floridi, L. (2004). The tragedy of the digital commons. *Ethics and Information Technology, 6,* 73–81. doi:10.1007/s10676-004-2895-2

Greenfield, P. M. (1994). Video games as cultural artifacts. *Journal of Applied Developmental Psychology, 15*(1), 3–12. doi:10.1016/0193-3973(94)90003-5

GrumpyCiara. (2011, November 8). *I love how @banksy follows nobody and has tweeted nothing and still has 372 followers #respect.* [Twitter post]. Retrieved from https://twitter.com/GrumpyCiara/status/132239489262292992

Gustin, S. (2011, February 11). Social media sparked, accelerated Egypt's revolutionary fire. *Wired.* Retrieved from http://www.wired.com/business/2011/02/egypts-revolutionary-fire/

Halstead. (1999). A politics for generation X. *Atlantic Monthly, 284* (2), 33-42.

Hartmann, T., & Klimmt, C. (2006). Gender and computer games: Exploring females' dislikes. *Journal of Computer-Mediated Communication, 11*(4), 910–931. doi:10.1111/j.1083-6101.2006.00301.x

Harvard University, Institute of Politics. (2006). *Youth survey.* Retrieved from http://www.iop.harvard.edu/fall-2006-youth-survey

Hassan, R. (2009). *Empires of speed: Time and the acceleration of politics and society.* Boston, MA: Brill Publishers. doi:10.1163/ej.9789004175907.i-254

Hawisher, G., & Selfe, C. L. (1993). Tradition and change in computer-supported writing environments: A call for action. In P. Kahaney (Ed.), *Theoretical and critical perspectives on teacher change* (pp. 155–186). Norwood, NJ: Ablex.

Hawisher, G., & Selfe, C. L. (Eds.). (1991). *Evolving perspectives on computers and composition studies: Questions for the 1990s.* Urbana, IL: National Council of Teachers of English.

Head_Fish. (2011). Dragon age 2 companion guide. *Bone Fish Gamer.* Retrieved from http://www.bonefishgamer.com/2011/06/dragon-age-2-companion-guide/

Helguera, P. (2011). *Education for socially engaged art: A materials and techniques handbook*. New York, NY: Jorge Pinto Books. hooks, b. (1995). *Art on my mind: Visual politics*. New York, NY: New Press.

Henton, A. (2012). Game and narrative in dragon age: Origins: Playing the archive in digital rpgs. In *Dungeons, dragons, and digital denizens: The digital role-playing game* (Vol. 1, pp. 66–87). New York: The Continuum International Publishing Group.

Herring, S. (2004). Slouching toward the ordinary: Current trends in computer-mediated communication. *New Media & Society, 6*(1), 26–36. doi:10.1177/1461444804039906

Hesford, W., & Schell, E. (2008). Introduction: Configurations of transnationality: Locating feminist rhetorics. *College English, 70*(5), 461–470.

Hickey, D. J. (2014). Firedogs at the lake: Ties that bind until they don't. In D. J. Hickey, & J. Essid (Eds.), *Identity and leadership in virtual communities: Establishing credibility and influence*. Hershey, PA: IGI Global.

Hjarvard, S. (2008). The mediatization of society. *Nordicom Review, 29*, 105–134.

Hofstede, G., Hofstede, G. J., & Minkov, M. (2010). *Cultures and organizations*. New York: McGraw-Hill.

Howard, M. (2011). *Transnationalism and society*. Jefferson, NC: McFarland and Company, Inc.

Howard, P., & Hussain, M. (2013). *Democracy's fourth wave? Digital media and the Arab spring*. Oxford, UK: Oxford University Press. doi:10.1093/acprof:oso/9780199936953.001.0001

Howard, T. (1997). *A rhetoric of electronic communities*. Greenwich, CT: Ablex.

Howe, N., & Strauss, W. (2000). *Millennials rising: The next great generation*. New York, NY: Vintage.

Huizinga, J. (1955). *Homo ludens: A study of the play-element in culture*. Beacon Press.

Hum, N. J., Chamberlin, P. E., Hambright, B. L., Portwood, A. C., Schat, A. C., & Bevan, J. L. (2011). A picture is worth a thousand words: A content analysis of Facebook profile photographs. *Computers in Human Behavior, 27*, 1828–1833. doi:10.1016/j.chb.2011.04.003

Jackson, L. A. et al. (2008). Race, gender, and information technology use: The new digital divide. *Cyberpsychology & Behavior, 11*(4), 437–442. doi:10.1089/cpb.2007.0157 PMID:18721092

Jamieson, H. V. (2008). *Adventures in cyberformance experiments at the interface of theatre and the internet*. (Unpublished master's thesis). Queensland University of Technology.

Jamieson, H. V. (n.d.). *Cyberformance*. Retrieved from http://creative-catalyst.com/cyberformance/

Jenkins, H. (2006). *Confronting the challenges of participatory culture: Media education for the 21st century*. White paper for the MacArthur Foundation. Retrieved on December 4, 2011, from www.digitallearning.macfound.org

Jenkins, H. (1998). Complete freedom of movement: Video games as gendered play spaces. In J. Cassell, & H. Jenkins (Eds.), *From Barbie to Mortal Kombat: Gender and computer games* (pp. 262–297). London: MIT Press.

Jensen, J., & de Castell, S. (2011). Girls@Play: An ethnographic study of gender and digital gameplay. *Feminist Media Studies, 11*(2), 167–179. doi:10.1080/14680777.2010.521625

Joseph, S. (2000). *Gendering citizenship in the Middle East. Gender and Citizenship in the Middle East*. Syracuse, NY: Syracuse University Press.

Juul, J. (2001). Games telling stories? A brief note on games and narratives. *Game Studies, 1*(1).

Kafai, Y. B. (1996). Gender differences in children's constructions of video games. In P. Greenfield, & R. Cocking (Eds.), *Interacting with video* (pp. 39–66). Norwood, NJ: Ablex.

Kafai, Y. B. (1998). Video game designs by girls and boys: Variability and consistency of gender differences. In J. Cassell, & H. Jenkins (Eds.), *From Barbie to Mortal Kombat: Gender and computer games* (pp. 90–114). London: MIT Press.

Kafai, Y. B., Heeter, C., Denner, J., & Sun, J. Y. (2008). Pink, purple, casual, or mainstream games: Moving beyond the gender divide. In Y. B. Kafai, C. Heeter, J. Denner, & J. Y. Sun (Eds.), *Beyond Barbie and Mortal Kombat: Perspectives on gender and gaming*. Cambridge, MA: MIT Press.

KeithCore88. (2013, April 11). *It would make sense for @ banksy to be on twitter, but would @banksy be @banksy or would being @banksy be too obvious? Or would it not?* [Twitter post]. Retrieved from https://twitter.com/KeithCore88/status/322332524175048706

Kelm, O. R. (2011). Social media: It's what students do. *Business Communication Quarterly*, *74*(4), 505–520. doi:10.1177/1080569911423960

Kemp, S. (2011). Banksy request to appear at the Oscars in disguise rejected. *Hollywood Reporter*. Retrieved from http://www.hollywoodreporter.com/news/banksy-request-at-oscars-disguise-159736

Kiesler, S., Sproull, L., & Eccles, J. S. (1985). Pool halls, chips, and war games: Women in the culture of computing. *Psychology of Women Quarterly*, *9*(4), 451–462. doi:10.1111/j.1471-6402.1985.tb00895.x

Kimmel, M. (2008). *Guyland: The perilous world where boys become men*. New York, NY: Harper Collins.

Kittelstrom, A. (2010). The academic-motherhood handicap. *The Chronicle of Higher Education*. Retrieved from http://chronicle.com/article/The-Academic-Motherhood/64073

Knobloch-Westerwick, S., Glynn, C. J., & Huge, M. (2013). The Matilda effect in science communication: An experiment on gender bias in publication quality perceptions and collaboration. *Science Communication*. Retrieved online on May 7, 2013 from http://scx.sagepub.com/content/early/2013/01/24/1075547012472684

KONDA. (2010). *Law and justice – Perceptions and expectations*. Retrieved from http://www.konda.com.tr/tr/raporlar.php?tb=2

KONDA. (2011). *Turkish youth survey*. Retrieved from http://www.konda.com.tr/tr/raporlar.php

Kozlowski, L. (2011, February 1). *Egypt: Capturing voices with Twitter and a cellphone*. [web log post]. Retrieved from http://latimesblogs.latimes.com/babylon-beyond/2011/02/egypt-twitter-voices-jan25-cell-phones-egyptians.html

Kushin, M. J., & Yamamoto, M. (2010). Did social media really matter? College students' use of online media and political decision making in the 2008 election. *Mass Communication & Society*, *13*, 608–630. doi:10.1080/15205436.2010.516863

Kuznekoff, J. H., & Rose, L. M. (2013). Communication in multiplayer gaming: Examining player responses to gender cues. *New Media & Society*, *15*(4), 541–556. doi:10.1177/1461444812458271

Lacy, S., Roth, M., & Mey, K. (2010). *Leaving art: Writings on performance, politics, and publics, 1974-2007*. Durham, NC: Duke University Press. doi:10.1215/9780822391227

Latour, B. (2008). *Reassembling the social: An introduction to actor-network-theory*. New York, NY: Oxford University Press.

Lave, J., & Wenger, E. (1991). *Situated learning: Legitimate peripheral participation*. Cambridge, UK: Cambridge University Press. doi:10.1017/CBO9780511815355

Lave, J., & Wenger, E. (2002). Legitimate peripheral participation in communities of practice. In M. R. Lea, & K. Nicholl (Eds.), *Distributed learning, social and cultural approaches to practice*. London: Routledge.

League, R., & Chalmers, I. (2010). Degrees of caution: Arab girls unveil on Facebook. In S. R. Mazzarella (Ed.), *Girl wide web 2.0* (pp. 27–44). New York: Peter Lang Publishing.

Lebanc, L. (1999). *Pretty in punk: Girls' gender resistance in a boys' subculture*. New Brunswick, NJ: Rutgers University Press.

Lebduska, L. (2013). Profession of letters. *College Composition and Communication*, *65*(1), 40–42.

Leech, G. (1983). *Principles of pragmatics*. London: Longman.

Lee, J. E. R., & Park, S. G. (2011). Whose second life is this? How avatar-based racial cues shape ethno-racial minorities' perception of virtual worlds. *Cyberpsychology, Behavior, and Social Networking*, 14(11), 637–642. doi:10.1089/cyber.2010.0501 PMID:21486164

Legewie, J., & DiPrete, T. A. (2011). *High school environments, stem orientations, and the gender gap in science and engineering degrees.* Unpublished Working Paper. Retrieved from http://www.ssc.wisc.edu/soc/faculty/docs/diprete/paper_pathway_06062011.pdf

Liebowitz, M. (2012, May 31). *Huge spike expected in employer Facebook snooping.* Retrieved from http://www.nbcnews.com/id/47636375/ns/technology_and_science-security/t/huge-spike-expected-employer-facebook-snooping/https://twitter.com/quotemyroomies/status/303074529842974720

Lugones, M. (2010). Toward a decolonial feminism. *Hypatia*, 25(4), 742–759. doi:10.1111/j.1527-2001.2010.01137.x

Mackey, R. (2011, January 27). *Video chat interview with Gigi Ibrahim.* Retrieved from http://thelede.blogs.nytimes.com/2011/01/27/interview-with-an-egyptian-blogger/

Madlena, C. (2011, July 7). Telecomix: Tech support for the Arab spring. *The Gaurdian*. Retrieved from http://www.theguardian.com/technology/2011/jul/07/telecomix-arab-spring

Malanek999. (2011). *The worst was when I. dialogue wheel mishaps.* Retrieved from http://social.bioware.com/forum/1/topic/304/index/6757005/1

Manago, A. M., Graham, M. B., Greenfield, P. M., & Salimkhan, G. (2008). Self-presentation and gender on MySpace. *Journal of Applied Developmental Psychology*, 29(6), 446–458. doi:10.1016/j.appdev.2008.07.001

Markoff, J. (2005). *What the dormouse said: How the sixties counterculture shaped the personal computer industry.* New York, NY: Penguin.

Marquez, L. (2011). Narrating our lives: Retelling mothering and professional work in composition studies. *Composition Studies*, 39(1), 73–85.

Marshall, J. (2012, January 22). Online gamers achieve first crowd-sourced redesign of protein. *Scientific American*. Retrieved from http://www.scientificamerican.com/article.cfm?id=victory-for-crowdsourced-biomolecule2&page=2

Martínez, E. B. (2000, March 10). Where was the color in Seattle? Looking for reasons why the great battle was so white. *Colorlines*. Retrieved from http://colorlines.com/archives/2000/03/where_was_the_color_in_seattlelooking_for_reasons_why_the_great_battle_was_so_white.html

Massey, D. (2005). *For space.* Los Angeles, CA: Sage.

Matthew, E. (2012, September 6). *Sexism in video games: There is sexism in gaming.* Retrieved from: http://blog.pricecharting.com/2012/09/emilyami-sexism-in-video-games-study.html

McCabe, B. (2010). Blurring the lines between real and virtual, art and work. *CityPaper*. Retrieved April 29, 2013 from http://www2.citypaper.com/news/story.asp?id=20086

McDowell, Z. (2012). Postcards from the other side: Interactive revelation in post-apocalyptic rpgs. In *Dungeons, dragons, and digital denizens: The digital role-playing game* (Vol. 1, pp. 174–193). New York: The Continuum International Publishing Group.

McGarty, C., Bliuc, A.-M., Thomas, E., & Bongiorno, R. (2009). Collective action as the material expression of opinion-based group membership. *The Journal of Social Issues*, 65(4), 839–857. doi:10.1111/j.1540-4560.2009.01627.x

McGonigal, J. (2011). *Reality is broken: why games make us better and how they can change the world.* New York: The Penguin Press.

McNair, W. (1993). *My brother running and other poems.* Boston, MA: David R. Godine Press.

Messieh, N. (2012, March 7). UAE citizen arrested for criticizing security forces on Twitter. *The Next Web*. Retrieved from http://thenextweb.com/me/2012/03/07/uae-citizen-arrested-for-criticizing-security-forces-on-twitter/

Mignolo, W. (2000). *Local histories/global designs.* Princeton, NJ: Princeton University Press.

Mignolo, W. (2002). The Zapatista's theoretical revolution: Its historical, ethical, and political consequences. *Utopian Thinking, 25*(3), 245–275.

Miller, K. D., & Frances, F. (2008). Strategies for online communities. *Strategic Management Journal, 30*, 305–322. doi:10.1002/smj.735

Miller, M. K., & Summers, A. (2007). Gender differences in video game characters' roles, appearances, and attire as portrayed in video game magazines. *Sex Roles, 57*(9-10), 733–742. doi:10.1007/s11199-007-9307-0

Molloy, J. T. (1988). *New dress for success*. New York, NY: Warner Books.

Moran, C. (1995). We write, but do we read? *Computers and Composition, 8*(3), 51–61.

Morin, J. L. (2009a). SAZZAE. Hollywood, CA: Harvard Square Ed.s.

Morin, J. L. (2009b). Above ground. Hollywood, CA: Harvard Square Ed.s.

Morin, J. L. (2011). Traveling light. Hollywood, CA: Harvard Square Ed.s.

Morin, J. L. (2012). Trading dreams. Hollywood, CA: Harvard Square Ed.s.

Mr. Scott. (2013, February 28). *Roll call for old time...* [Online newsgroup post]. Retrieved from http://groups.google.com/group/alt.toys.gi-joe

Muñoz, J. E. (2009). *Cruising utopia: The then and there of queer futurity*. New York, NY: New York University Press.

Nakamura, L. (2009). Don't hate the player, hate the game: The racialization of labor in World of Warcraft. *Critical Studies in Media Communication, 26*(2), 128–144. doi:10.1080/15295030902860252

Nelson, M. E., Hull, G. A., & Roche-Smith, J. (2008). Challenges of multimedia self-presentation. *Written Communication, 25*(4), 415–440. doi:10.1177/0741088308322552

Ng, W. (2012). Can we teach digital natives digital literacy? *Computers & Education, 59*, 1065–1078. doi:10.1016/j.compedu.2012.04.016

Norman, J. (1997). *Tarnsman of Gor*. Masquerade Books.

Norris, P. (2001). *Digital divide: Civic engagement, information poverty, and the internet worldwide*. Cambridge, UK: Cambridge University Press. doi:10.1017/CBO9781139164887

nranola. (2011). *Oh boy, the dialogue wheel: Dialogue wheel mishaps*. Retrieved from http://social.bioware.com/forum/1/topic/304/index/6757005/2

Omarsc. (2012, December 4). Lawyer: Qatari poet sentenced to life in prison is Gulf's Mandela. *Doha News*. Retrieved from http://dohanews.co/post/37109798863/lawyer-poet-sentenced-to-life-in-prison-is-qatars

Oravec, J. A. (2012). Bullying and mobbing in academe: Challenges for distance education and social media applications. *Journal of Academic Administration in Higher Education, 8*(1), 48–58.

Otnes, M. (2012, July 26). *The sandbox is dead: Long live the sandbox! The Joe report*. [Web log post]. Retrieved from http://patchesofpride.wordpress.com/2012/06/26/the-sandbox-is-dead-long-live-the-sandbox/

Ovide, S. (2012, June 12). Tapping big data to fill potholes. *The Wall Street Journal*. Retrieved from http://online.wsj.com/article/SB10001424052702303444204577460552615646874.html

Pandora's Mighty Soliders (PMS). (2011a). *Homepage*. Retrieved on December 1, 2011 from http://www.pmsclan.com/index.html

Pandora's Mighty Soliders (PMS). (2011b). *About us*. Retrieved on December 1, 2011 from http://www.pmsclan.com/page.php?page=About%20Us

Pandora's Mighty Soliders (PMS). (2012). *Handbook*. Retrieved on January 25, 2012 from http://www.pmsclan.com/forum/showthread.php?t=30905

Pest Control Office. (n.d.). *What is pest control?* Retrieved from http://www.pestcontroloffice.com/whatispco.html

Pew Internet and American Life Project. (2002). *The digital disconnect: The widening gap between internet-savvy students and their schools*. Author.

Pew Research Center. (n.d.). *Social networking popular across globe: Arab publics most likely to express political views online*. Retrieved from http://www.pewglobal.org/files/2012/12/Pew-Global-Attitudes-Project-Technology-Report-FINAL-December-12-2012.pdf

Philipsen, M. I., & Bostic, T. (2008). *Challenges of the faculty career for women*. San Francisco, CA: Jossey-Bass.

Pike, G. H. (2011). Fired over Facebook. *Information Today, 28*(4), 26.

Pinchot, J. L., Douglas, D., Paullet, K. L., & Rota, D. R. (2011). Talk to text: Changing communication patterns. In *Proceedings of Conference for Information Systems Applied Research*. Wilmington, NC: EDSIG.

Plackett, B. (2013, March 27). Citizen scientist: Eyewire's call to game. *The Connectivist*. Retrieved from http://www.theconnectivist.com/2013/03/citizen-scientist-eyewires-call-to-game/

Post, W. (2007). *Timeline: The criminal investigation*. Retrieved from http://www.washingtonpost.com/wpdyn/content/custom/2007/03/06/CU2007030600916.html

Potts, L., & Jones, D. (2011). Contextualizing experiences: Tracing the relationships between people and technologies in the social web. *Journal of Business and Technical Communication, 23*(3), 338–358. doi:10.1177/1050651911400839

Pristin, T. (2003, January 15). Graying, and playing with trains. *The New York Times*. Retrieved from http://www.nytimes.com/2003/01/15/nyregion/graying-playing-with-trains-2-midtown-hobby-shops-struggle-customers-dwindle.html

Pronin, E., Steele, C. M., & Ross, L. (2004). Identity bifurcation in response to stereotype threat: Women and mathematics. *Journal of Experimental Social Psychology, 40*(2), 152–168. doi:10.1016/S0022-1031(03)00088-X

Puar, J. K. (2007). *Terrorist assemblages: Homonationalism in queer times*. Durham, NC: Duke UP. doi:10.1215/9780822390442

Quijano, A. (2000). Coloniality of power, eurocentrism, and Latin America. *Nepantla: Views from the South, 1*(3), 533–580.

quotemyroomies. (2013, February 17). @*Banksy just show your face dude! You're not even a prolific in the gallery world. Trust me you're dead in the street art world. #Usedtobegood*. [Twitter post]. Retrieved from https://twitter.com/quotemyroomies/status/303074529842974720

Rajakumar, M. (2012). Faceless Facebook: Female Qatari users choosing wisely. In B. Williams, & A. A. Zenger (Eds.), *New media literacies and participatory popular culture across borders* (pp. 125–134). New York, NY: Routledge.

Raoof, R. (2011, May 4). *About the media tent in Tahrir Square*. Retrieved from http://ebfhr.blogspot.com/2011/05/media-tent-in-tahrir-square.html

Rheingold, H. (2001). Look who's talking. *Wired, 7*(1).

Richard, G. T. (2012b). *On the periphery of video game culture: Understanding urban Latino gamers' experiences*. Paper presented at Meaningful Play 2012. East Lansing, MI.

Richard, G. T. (2013). *Understanding gender, context and game culture for the development of equitable digital games and learning environments*. (Doctoral Dissertation). New York University, New York, NY.

Richard, G. T. (2013a). Designing games that foster equity and inclusion: Encouraging equitable social experiences across gender and ethnicity in online games. In G. Christou, E. L. Law, D. Geerts, L. E. Nacke, & P. Zaphiris (Eds.), *Proceedings of the CHI'2013 Workshop: Designing and Evaluating Sociability in Online Video Games*. ACM Press.

Richard, G. T. (2013b). The interplay between gender and ethnic harassment in game culture and its implications for play and learning. In *Proceedings of DiGRA (Digital Games Research Association) 2013: Defragging Game Studies*. DiGRA.

Richard, G. T. (2012a). Gender and game play: Research and future directions. In B. Bigl, & S. Stoppe (Eds.), *Playing with virtuality, theories and methods of computer game studies*. Frankfurt, Germany: Peter Lang.

Richard, G. T., & Hoadley, C. M. (2013). Investigating a supportive online gaming community as a means of reducing stereotype threat vulnerability across gender. In *Proceedings of Games, Learning & Society 2013*. Academic Press.

Roberts, L., & Parks, M. R. (1999). The social geography of gender-switching in virtual environments on the internet. *Information Communication and Society*, *2*, 521–540. doi:10.1080/136911899359538

Roiphe, K. (2012, August). Disappearing mothers. *Financial Times Magazine*. Retrieved from http://www.ft.com/intl/cms/s/2/0bf95f3c-f234-11e1-bba3-00144feabdc0.html#axzz26UO8WkoC

Ronfeldt, D., & Arquilla, J. (n.d.). *Networks and netwars: The future of terror, crime, and militancy*. Santa Monica, CA: RAND Corporation.

Ronfeldt, D. et al. (1998). *The Zapatista social netwar in Mexico*. Santa Monica, CA: RAND Corporation.

Rouzie, A. (2001). Conversation and carrying-on: play, conflict, and serio-ludic discourse in synchronous computer conferencing. *College Composition and Communication*, *53*(2), 251–299. doi:10.2307/359078

Rowan, L., & Bigum, C. (Eds.). (2012). *Transformative approaches to new technologies and student diversity*. New York City, NY: Springer. doi:10.1007/978-94-007-2642-0

Rowe, J. C. (2002). *The new American studies*. Minneapolis, MN: University of Minnesota Press.

Ruby, R. (2012). On the people's mic: Politics in a post-literate age. *Journal for Occupied Studies*.

Ruecker, T. (2012). Exploring the digital divide on the U.S.-Mexico border through literacy narratives. *Computers and Composition*, *29*, 239–253. doi:10.1016/j.compcom.2012.06.002

Schillinger, R. (2011, October 20). *Social media and the Arab spring: What have I learned?* [Blog Post]. Retrieved from http://www.huffingtonpost.com/raymond-schillinger/arab-spring-social-media_b_970165.html

Schlenker, B., & Pontari, B. (2000). The strategic control of information: Impression management and self-presentation in daily life. In A. Tesser, R. Felso, & J. Suls (Eds.), *Psychological perspectives on self and identity* (pp. 199–232). Washington, DC: American Psychological Association. doi:10.1037/10357-008

Schott, G., & Horrell, K. (2000). Girl gamers and their relationship with gaming culture. *Convergence*, *6*(4), 36–53. doi:10.1177/135485650000600404

Sefton-Green, J. (2006). Youth, technology, and media cultures. *Review of Research in Education*, *30*, 279–306. doi:10.3102/0091732X030001279

Settles, I. H., Jellison, W. A., & Pratt-Hyatt, J. S. (2009). Identification with multiple social groups: The moderating role of identity change over time among women-scientists. *Journal of Research in Personality*, *43*(5), 856–867. doi:10.1016/j.jrp.2009.04.005

Shaw, A. (2012). Do you identify as a gamer? Gender, race, sexuality, and gamer identity. *New Media & Society*, *14*(1), 28–44. doi:10.1177/1461444811410394

Sherman, A. (2009). *6 tips for better branding using avatars*. Retrieved April 16, 2003 from http://gigaom.com/2009/07/16/6-tips-for-better-branding-using-avatars/

Shirky, C. (2010). *Cognitive surplus: How technology makes consumers into collaborators*. New York: Penguin.

Shirky, C. (2011). The political power of social media: Technology, the public sphere, and political change. *Foreign Affairs*, 1.

Shute, V. J. (2007). Tensions, trends, tools and technologies: Time for an educational sea change. In C. A. Dwyer (Ed.), *The future of assessment: Shaping teaching and learning* (pp. 139–187). New York: Lawrence Earlbaum / Taylor & Francis.

Sicart, M. (2009). *The ethics of computer games*. Cambridge, MA: MIT Press. doi:10.7551/mitpress/9780262012652.001.0001

Siibak, A. (2009). Constructing the self through the photo selection: Visual impression management on social networking websites. *Cyberpsychology*, *3*(1), 1–9.

Silius, K., Kailanto, M., & Tervakari, A. M. (2011). Evaluating the quality of social media in an educational context. *International Journal of Emerging Technologies in Learning*, *6*(3), 21–27.

Simon, B. (2004). *Identity in modern society: A social psychological perspective*. Oxford, UK: Blackwell. doi:10.1002/9780470773437

Simon, B., & Klandermans, B. (2001). Politicized collective identity: A social psychological analysis. *The American Psychologist*, *56*(4), 319–331. doi:10.1037/0003-066X.56.4.319 PMID:11330229

Spencer-Oatey, H. (2007). Theories of identity and the analysis of face. *Journal of Pragmatics*, *39*(4), 639–656. doi:10.1016/j.pragma.2006.12.004

Sponcil, M., & Gitimu, P. (n.d.). Use of social media by college students: Relationship to communication and self-concept. *Journal of Technology Research, 4*, 1-13.

Squire, K. (2005). Changing the game: What happens when video games enter the classroom. *Innovate: Journal of Online Education, 1* (6).

Squire, K. (2003). Video games in education. *International Journal of Intelligent Simulations and Gaming*, *2*(1), 49–62.

Squire, K. (2011). *Video games and learning: Teaching and participatory culture in the digital age*. New York: Teachers College Press.

Steele, C. M. (1997). A threat in the air: how stereotypes shape intellectual identity and performance. *The American Psychologist*, *52*, 613–629. doi:10.1037/0003-066X.52.6.613 PMID:9174398

Steele, C. M., & Aronson, J. (1995). Stereotype threat and the intellectual test performance of African Americans. *Journal of Personality and Social Psychology*, *69*(5), 797–811. doi:10.1037/0022-3514.69.5.797 PMID:7473032

Steffgen, G., König, A., Pfetsch, J., & Melzer, A. (2011). Are cyberbullies less empathic? Adolescents' cyberbullying behavior and empathic responsiveness. *CyberPsychology. Behavior & Social Networking*, *14*(11), 643–648. doi:10.1089/cyber.2010.0445

Stephenson, N. (2000). *Snow crash*. New York: Bantam Spectra.

Stockdell-Giesler, A., & Ingalls, R. (2007). Faculty mothers. *Academe*, *93*(4).

Strano, M. M. (2008). User descriptions and interpretations of self-presentation through Facebook profile images. *Cyberpsychology*, *2*(2), 1–11.

Subrahmanyam, K., & Greenfield, P. M. (1994). Effect of video game practice on spatial skills in girls and boys. *Journal of Applied Developmental Psychology*, *15*, 13–32. doi:10.1016/0193-3973(94)90004-3

Sullivan, R. (2010). The problem with WHOIS. *Spectator: The University of Southern California Journal of Film & Television*, *30*(2), 57–64.

Sunden, J., & Sveningsson, M. (2012). *Gender and sexuality in online game cultures*. New York, NY: Routledge.

Talcott, M., & Collins, D. (2012). Building a complex emancipatory unity: Documenting decolonial feminist interventions within the occupy movement. *Feminist Studies*, *38*(2).

Tarrow, S. (2009). *The new transnational activism*. New York: Cambridge UP.

Tatnall, A. (2010). *Actor-network theory and technology innovation: Advancements and new concepts*. Hershey, PA: IGI Global. doi:10.4018/978-1-60960-197-3

Taylor, T. L. (2003). Multiple pleasures: Women and online gaming. *Convergence*, *9*(1), 21–46. doi:10.1177/135485650300900103

Taylor, T. L. (2006). *Play between worlds: Exploring online game culture*. Cambridge, MA: MIT Press.

Taylor, T. L. (2008). Becoming a player: Networks, structure and imagined futures. In Y. B. Kafai, C. Heeter, J. Denner, & J. Y. Sun (Eds.), *Beyond Barbie and Mortal Kombat: Perspectives on gender and gaming* (pp. 51–66). Cambridge, MA: MIT Press.

Theocharis, Y. (2013). The wealth of (occupation) networks? Communication patterns and information distribution in a Twitter protest network. *Journal of Information Technology & Politics*, *10*(1), 35–56. doi:10.1080/1933 1681.2012.701106

Thomas, D., & Brown, J. S. (2011). *A new culture of learning: Cultivating the imagination for a world of constant change*. Lexington, KY: CreateSpace.

TJG. (2012). *Generation jones*. Retrieved from http://www.generationjones.com/

Toma, C. L., & Hancock, J. T. (2013). Self-affirmation underlies Facebook use. *Personality and Social Psychology Bulletin, 39*(3), 321–331. doi:10.1177/0146167212474694 PMID:23359086

Tomilson, J. (1999). *Globalization and culture*. Chicago, IL: University of Chicago Press.

Travis, R. (2012). Epic style: Re-compositional performance in the bioware digital RPG. In *Dungeons, dragons, and digital denizens: The digital role-playing game* (Vol. 1, pp. 235–255). New York: The Continuum International Publishing Group.

Trottier, D. (2012). Policing social media. *Canadian Review of Sociology, 49*(4), 411–425. doi:10.1111/j.1755-618X.2012.01302.x

Tunisia Attacks Al-Jazeera and the Protests Expand all over the Country. (2010, December 28). Retrieved from http://www.aljazeera.net

Turkle, S. (1995). *Life on the screen: Identity in the age of the internet*. New York, NY: Simon and Schuster.

Turkle, S. (1995). Taking things at interface value. In S. Turkle (Ed.), *Life on the screen* (pp. 102–124). New York, NY: Touchstone.

Turkle, S. (1997). *Life on the screen*. New York, NY: Simon and Schuster.

Turkle, S. (2011). *Alone together: Why we expect more for technology and less from each other*. New York, NY: Basic Books.

Turkle, S. (2011). *Alone together: Why we expect more from technology and less from each other*. New York, NY: Basic Books.

Twitter Help Center. (n.d.). *FAQs about verified accounts*. Retrieved from https://support.twitter.com/groups/31-twitter-basics/topics/111-features/articles/119135-about-verified-accounts

Urban Dictionary. (n.d.). Retrieved from http://www.urbandictionary.com/

Uslaner, E. (2001). Volunteering and social capital: How trust and religion shape civic participation in the United States. In E. Uslaner (Ed.), *Social capital and participation in everyday life* (pp. 104–117). London: Routledge. doi:10.4324/9780203451571_chapter_8

Utz, S. (2009). The (potential) benefits of campaigning via social network sites. *Journal of Computer-Mediated Communication, 14*, 221–243. doi:10.1111/j.1083-6101.2009.01438.x

Utz, S. (2010). Show me your friends and I will tell you what type of person you are: How one's profile, number of friends, and type of friends influence impression formation on social network sites. *Journal of Computer-Mediated Communication, 15*, 314–335. doi:10.1111/j.1083-6101.2010.01522.x

Utz, S., Tanis, M., & Vermeulen, I. (2012). It is all about being popular: The effects of need for popularity on social network site use. *Cyberpsychology, Behavior, and Social Networking, 15*(1), 37–42. doi:10.1089/cyber.2010.0651 PMID:21988765

Valenzuela, S., Namsu, P., & Kee, K. F. (2009). Is there social capital in a social network site? Facebook use and college students' life satisfaction, trust, and participation. *Journal of Computer-Mediated Communication, 14*, 875–901. doi:10.1111/j.1083-6101.2009.01474.x

Van House, N. A. (2011). Feminist HCI meets Facebook: Performativity and social networking sites. *Interacting with Computers, 23*, 422–429. doi:10.1016/j.intcom.2011.03.003

Vargas, R. (2007). Are you going to the March? How Mexican-American youth in Oakland and Richmond California became politically active on May 1st. In *Proceedings of American Sociological Association*. American Sociological Association.

Veletsianos, G. G. (2012). Higher education scholar's participation and practices on twitter. *Journal of Computer Assisted Learning, 28*(4), 336–249. doi:10.1111/j.1365-2729.2011.00449.x

Verclas, K. (2005). *MobileActive*. Retrieved from http://mobileactive.org/

Vertovec, S. (1999). Transnationalism and identity. *Journal of Ethnic and Migration Studies*, 27(4), 573–582. doi:10.1080/13691830120090386

Vitak, J., Zube, P., Smock, A., Carr, C. T., Ellison, N., & Lampe, C. (2011). It's complicated: Facebook users' political participation in the 2008 election. *Cyberpsychology, Behavior, and Social Networking*, 14(3), 107–114. doi:10.1089/cyber.2009.0226 PMID:20649449

Voice of America. (2010, March 9). *World Bank online game invites youth to solve global problems.* [Video file]. Retrieved from http://www.voanews.com/content/world-bank-computer-game-invites-youth-to-be-creative--87240387/113855.html

Volmar, P. (2010). How to use social media to forge corporate identity. *Public Relations Tactics*, 17(6), 20.

Wang, Z., Tchernev, J. M., & Solloway, T. (2012). A dynamic longitudinal examination of social media use, needs, and gratifications among college students. *Computers in Human Behavior*, 28, 1829–1839. doi:10.1016/j.chb.2012.05.001

Wark, M. (2007). *Gamer theory.* Cambridge, MA: Harvard University Press.

Well. (n.d.). *About the well.* Retrieved from http://www.well.com/aboutwell.html

Wheeler, D. L. (2001). The internet and public culture in Kuwait. *Gazette*, 63(2-3), 187–201.

Whitlock, K. (2012). Traumatic origins: Memory, crisis, and identity in digital RPGs. In *Dungeons, dragons, and digital denizens: The digital role-playing game* (Vol. 1, pp. 135–152). New York: The Continuum International Publishing Group.

Williams, D., Martins, N., Consalvo, M., & Ivory, J. D. (2009). The virtual census: Representations of gender, race and age in video games. *New Media & Society*, 11(5), 815–834. doi:10.1177/1461444809105354

Wilson, C., & Dunn, A. (2011). Digital media in the Egyptian revolution: Descriptive analyses from the Tahrir data set. *International Journal of Communication*, 5, 1248–1272.

Wu, T. (2010). *The master switch: The rise and fall of information empires.* New York, NY: Alfred A. Knopf.

Yancey, K. B. (2004). Made not only in words: Composition in a new key. *College Composition and Communication*, 56(2), 297–328. doi:10.2307/4140651

Yee, N. (2008). *Characters and main character.* The Daedalus Project. Retrieved from http://www.nickyee.com/daedalus/archives/001634.php

Yee, N. (2008). Maps of digital desires: Exploring the topography of gender and play in online games. In Y. B. Kafai, C. Heeter, J. Denner, & J. Y. Sun (Eds.), *Beyond Barbie and Mortal Kombat: Perspectives on gender and gaming* (pp. 83–96). Cambridge, MA: MIT Press.

yourfriendmitch. (2010, February 26). *You know we're ALL Banksy, right?.* [Twitter post].

Yukl, G. (2013). *Leadership in organizations* (8th ed.). Boston: Pearson.

Zizek, S. (1999). *The cyberspace real.* Retrieved from http://www.egs.edu/faculty/slavoj-zizek/articles/the-cyberspace-real/

Zook, K. (2012). In the blood of dragon age: Origins: Metaphor and identity in digital RPGs. In *Dungeons, dragons, and digital denizens: The digital role-playing game* (Vol. 1, pp. 219–234). New York: The Continuum International Publishing Group.

Zugman, K. (2005). Autonomy in a poetic voice: Zapatistas and political organizing in Los Angeles. *Latino Studies*, 3(3), 325–346. doi:10.1057/palgrave.lst.8600157

About the Contributors

Dona J. Hickey, Professor of English at the University of Richmond, teaches courses in rhetoric and composition and in modern and contemporary American literature. A native of Wisconsin, she earned her M.A. and Ph.D. at the University of Wisconsin-Milwaukee. She is the author of *Developing a Written Voice* (1993) and *Figures of Thought for College Writers* (1999) and co-editor (with Donna Reiss) of *Learning Literature in an Era of Change: Innovations in Teaching* (2000). Dona's articles have appeared in a variety of chapbooks, journals, and collections, both in print and online. She created the WAC program at the University of Richmond in 1992 and served as senior associate dean of the School of Arts and Sciences, 2003-2011. Outside of the academy, she enjoys spending time with her granddaughter, Olivia, and riding their spoiled rotten Arabian pony, Ryder, at Four Seasons Horse Center in Chester, VA.

Joe Essid directs the Writing Center at the University of Richmond, where he teaches courses in writing pedagogy, literature, and cyberculture. He is a Richmond native who did his undergraduate work at the University of Virginia, then earned a Master's and Ph.D. at Indiana University. His research interests include technology in the writing-intensive classroom, virtual worlds and their development, and the history of technology. His academic writing has appeared in *Computers and Humanities*, *The Writing Lab Newsletter*, and anthologies about technology and writing. He freelances as a science-fiction writer, with recent work in the anthology *Catastrophia* and forthcoming in *Hagerty Magazine*. He writes op-ed pieces about energy, localism, homesteading, transportation, and education for *Style Weekly*, *Eighty One*, and *RVA*. When not being an academic, he can be found keeping bees and learning the trade of an organic farmer.

* * *

Kristin Bezio is an Assistant Professor of Leadership Studies in the Jepson School of Leadership Studies at the University of Richmond. She teaches courses on theater, film, critical thinking, and gaming. Her background is in technical theater and early modern drama, with a Ph.D. from Boston University in English Literature. Her research interests include (but are not limited to) gaming, gender studies, theater and film, Shakespeare, and leadership. She has published in a variety of journals, including the *Early Modern Studies Journal*, *Shakespeare*, and *Leadership in the Humanities*, and has chapters appearing in *Macbeth: A Critical Anthology*, *Leadership and Elizabethan Culture*, and *The Joker: Critical Essays on the Clown Prince of Crime*. She contributes regularly to the online critical blog, *The Learned Fangirl*, on games and gaming, and has written on gaming and violence for the *Christian Science Monitor*. In addition to her academic and videogame-related interests, she is a board member of the Unorthodox Arts Foundation and a technician and performer for Richmond's Host of Sparrows Aerial Dance Company.

Katherine Bridgman is a doctoral student at Florida State University in Rhetoric and Composition. Her dissertation examines the use of social media by protesters in the Egyptian Revolution of 2011. This dissertation is part of a broader inquiry into social media and the ways in which digital authors claim agency through their visual-discursive interventions into the interface as a way of motivating supportive responses from audiences around the globe. Katherine also enjoys teaching a variety of courses addressing both print and digital composing practices.

Tüge T. Gülşen holds the degrees of B.A. in Foreign Languages Education (Middle East Technical University), M.A. in Learning and Teaching of English and Literacy (Institute of Education, University of London), and M.A. in Cultural Studies (Istanbul Bilgi University). She is currently completing a Ph.D. in Communication at Istanbul Bilgi University. Her main areas of interest are critical discourse and genre analysis, popular culture, academic literacies and media literacy. She has been teaching academic skills and Medicine ESP courses with a major contribution to curriculum and materials design in Istanbul Bilgi University. She has also taught the MA course "Discourse Analysis in Language Teaching" in Bahçeşehir University in Istanbul.

Elizabeth Hodges, Ph.D., is an Associate Professor of English at Virginia Commonwealth University in Richmond, Virginia. She teaches courses in composition studies, sociolinguistics, creative nonfiction, nature writing, the history of the essay, and Joan Didion. Collaborating with two physicians from the Medical College of Virginia, Elizabeth has designed a course in medicine and literature as part of VCU's developing program in medical humanities. Her publications include scholarship in the field of Composition Studies and essays in the genre of creative nonfiction. Her first book, *What the River Means* (1999), was published by Duquesne University Press in its Emerging Writers in Creative Nonfiction series and was one of four finalists in 2000 for the Library of Virginia Book Award in nonfiction. Her current book-in-progress, about caretaking, is *Keeping Folks Alive*. Beyond teaching, reading, and writing, her passions include estuaries, kayaking, and swimming.

Karen Keifer-Boyd, Ph.D., is professor of art education and women's studies at The Pennsylvania State University, where she teaches: *Visual Culture & Educational Technologies*; *Gender, Art & STEM*; *Artistic Creations & Theories of Knowing*; *Action Research*; *Art as Public Pedagogy*; *Including Difference*. She is co-founder and co-editor of *Visual Culture & Gender*, a cutting-edge online journal. Her leadership and teaching awards include two Fulbright Awards (2006 in Finland and 2012 in Austria). Her writings on feminist pedagogy, visual culture, cyberNet activism art pedagogy, action research, and identity are in more than 50 peer-reviewed research publications, and translated into several languages. She co-authored *InCITE, InSIGHT, InSITE* (NAEA, 2008), *Engaging Visual Culture* (Davis, 2007), co-edited *Real-World Readings in Art Education: Things Your Professors Never Told You* (Falmer, 2000), and served as editor of the *Journal of Social Theory in Art Education* and as guest editor for *Visual Arts Research*.

Wanda B. Knight is Associate Professor of Art Education and Women's Studies at the Pennsylvania State University. Her academic and research interests related to cultural competence and culturally competent teaching stem from her diverse life experiences as parent, university supervisor of preservice teachers, professor, public school teacher, school principal, and associate curator of an art museum. She is former president of the United States Society for Education through Art (USSEA) and past chair of the National Art Education Association's (NAEA) Committee on Multi-Ethnic Concerns. A previous editor of the *Journal of Social Theory in Art Education,* her work regarding teacher education, visual culture, cultural studies, professional learning, and issues of difference (race, class, gender) is published widely and her research presentations span national and international borders. Dr. Knight's professional achievements have been recognized through various honors and teaching awards including "teacher of the year," the Eugene Grigsby Award for outstanding contribution to the field of art education, and the Kenneth Marantz Distinguished Alumni Award from The Ohio State University.

Aaron Knochel is the Graduate Coordinator of Art Education at the State University of New York at New Paltz. He completed his doctorate in Art Education at The Ohio State University in 2011, focused on critical media literacy, software studies, and art education. He has worked in a variety of visual arts learning spaces including schools, museums, and nonprofit community arts programs both domestically and internationally. Publications include articles in *Visual Arts Research, The International Journal of Education through Art*, and *Kairos*. Generally, he tries to live up to his @artisteducator twitter bio: artist-teacher-visual culture researcher-digital media flaneur-novice hacker and pixel stacker.

Christine Liao, Ph.D, is an Assistant Professor in Watson College of Education at University of North Carolina Wilmington, where she teaches Arts Integration in Elementary Curriculum. She received her Ph.D. in art education with a minor in science, technology, and society from The Pennsylvania State University. After receiving her Bachelors and Masters degrees from National Hsinchu University of Education, she was an elementary school art teacher in Taiwan, where she originates. Her research interest focuses on new media pedagogy, identity, gender and technology, and STEAM education.

Mary Elizabeth Meier is Assistant Professor of Art and Program Director of Art Education at Mercyhurst University in Erie, PA. Mary Elizabeth holds B.S. and M.S. degrees in art education from The Florida State University, and a Ph.D. in art education from the Pennsylvania State University. Mary Elizabeth Meier is President of the Pennsylvania Art Education Association, a professional organization with 900 members who are committed to advancing art education through professional development, leadership, and service. Mary Elizabeth's narrative inquiry research is focused on the professional learning of arts teachers as they study their own teaching practice in technology-infused, inquiry-oriented, professional learning communities.

Thomas Mowbray is Chief Enterprise Architect of The Ohio State University where he leads information technology standardization and strategic technology initiatives. While currently in Columbus, Ohio, Dr. Mowbray is a long-time consultant in the Washington D.C. area, having recently consulted for the Chief Architect of the Center for Medicaid and Medicaid Services and served as Chief Enterprise Architect of the District of Columbia government. He did his undergraduate work at University of Illinois Champaign Urbana, Masters at Stanford, and Ph.D. at the University of Southern California. He served on the VWBPE Program Committee in 2013 and currently serves on the Editorial Board of the *Journal of Enterprise Architecture*. Dr. Mowbray has six professional books, including the new Wiley title *Cybersecurity: Managing Networks, Conducting Tests, and Investigating Intrusions*. His extracurricular activities include producing a major new MOOC on Cyber Security.

Nahla Nadeem is an Assistant Professor at Cairo University where she teaches courses in applied linguistics. Her M.A. focused on pragmatics and drama; her Ph.D. from Cairo University focused on translation studies and contrastive analysis. Her research interests are pragmatics, TEFL, gender and narrative studies. Her academic writing has appeared in the proceedings of academic conferences in Turkey, Egypt, and Austria. Her recent publication is a narrative analysis of Hadith in a story telling e-book by Interdisciplinary.net.

Ryan M. Patton is an Assistant Professor of Art Education at Virginia Commonwealth University. As part of his research in new media art education, Dr. Patton co-created an augmented reality game called CitySneak that explores disrupting conventions of public space and surveillance with smart phone devices, and he designed and produced a set of modular electronic switches intended for youth to design video game controllers. His academic writing has appeared in several publications including *Studies in Art Education*, *Journal of Social Theory in Art Education*, and *Visual Arts Research*. Dr. Patton's current research interests include technology in art education, new media, games-based pedagogy, physical computing, data visualization, visual culture, and urban education. When he's not working, Ryan enjoys being with his wonderful, amazing wife, Julianne, and their two dogs, Maggie and Brando.

Mohanalakshmi Rajakumar is Assistant Professor of English at Virginia Commonwealth University in Qatar. She holds a Ph.D. in Literature from the University of Florida. Her research interests include gender and postcolonial literature. Mohana has published articles and chapters in a variety of academic journals, including *The South Asian Review* and *The Annals of Urdu Studies*. Her first book, *Haram in the Harem* (2009, Peter Lang), is a study of subversive use of Indian and Algerian women's domestic fiction by female writers. Her fictional work: *Love Comes Later* (2012 Amazon) is the first novel in English set in Qatar, and it was named the 2013 Best Indie Book in the Romance category. Her non-fiction work has been published in *Variety Arabia*, *Brownbook Middle East*, *AudioFile Magazine*, *Explore Qatar*, *Woman Today*, *The Woman*, *Writers and Artists Yearbook*, *QatarClick*, and *Qatar Explorer*. Mohana teaches writing and literature courses in Doha, Qatar. You can read more about her work on her Website: www.mohanalakshmi.com.

Santos Felipe Ramos holds an M.A. in Writing and Rhetoric from Virginia Commonwealth University, where his research focused on the digitization of social movements and public discourse, Indigenous identity formation, and the mapping of global colonial world systems. He has presented this work and taught internationally—most recently as an English Instructor at the American University of Phnom Penh. His current research examines the function of English as a global colonial language deeply tied to the proliferation of computer technology over the past three decades.

Gabriela T. Richard just completed her Ph.D. from the Educational Communication and Technology program at New York University and is a Postdoctoral Fellow for Academic Diversity at the University of Pennsylvania in the Graduate School of Education. Her research focuses on understanding the intersections between culture, experience, media, and learning. Her dissertation work centered on gender and ethnic experiences with games and within game culture to help inform the design of equitable educational games and learning environments. Gabriela has received research funding from the National Science Foundation and the American Association of University Women. She has a master's degree in interactive and embodied design and she has taught instructional design, educational technology integration, and game design for learning to youth, educators and at the undergraduate and graduate levels at the City University of New York and New York University.

Ryan Shin is an associate professor in the School of Art at the University of Arizona. He received his Ph.D. in Art Education from Florida State University in 2002. His research interests include issues of the representation and appropriation of Asian popular media and visual culture, critical discourse on minority visual culture, and studies of Asian cultural performances and folk traditions. Furthermore, he is interested in applying new media technologies to the art classroom and museum settings, exploring new Web 2.0 technologies and creative endeavors in traditional and non-traditional educational contexts. His articles have appeared in *Studies in Art Education, Art Education, Visual Arts Research, Journal of Cultural Research in Art Education*, and *International Journal of Education through Art*. He has authored numerous scholarly book chapters and has given presentations at national and international levels.

Sarah R. Spangler is a doctoral student in the English Department at Old Dominion University. She researches the rhetorics of digital identity composing on social networking sites, students' composing practices on social media, community building in digital spaces, and the pedagogical uses and implications of digital tools and platforms in the composition classroom. She also teaches writing courses at Old Dominion University and assists the graduate program director for the English Ph.D. program. Her writing has appeared in *MediaCommons* (http://mediacommons.futureofthebook.org), and she has a forthcoming chapter in *Emerging Pedagogies in the Networked Knowledge Society: Practices Integrating Social Media and Globalization.*

Cheri Lemieux Spiegel is Assistant Professor of English and Program Head of Credit English at Northern Virginia Community College's Annandale Campus. She is also a doctoral candidate at Old Dominion University. Her dissertation synthesizes guerrilla warfare and rhetorical concepts to develop and, test, using punk rock and graffiti art as case studies, a theory of guerrilla rhetoric. She has published articles in *Computers and Composition Online* and *Teaching English in the Two-Year College.*

Robert W. Sweeny is Associate Professor of Art and Art Education at Indiana University of Pennsylvania (USA) and the author of *Dysfunction and Decentralization in New Media Art Education* (forthcoming), published by Intellect Press. He is the editor of *Inter/Actions/Inter/Sections: Art Education in a Digital Visual Culture* (2011), published by NAEA Press. He is the editor of *The Journal of the National Art Education Association*. He publishes and presents widely on the topic of digital visual culture, including the relationship between art educational practices and complexity theory, videogames, social and locative media, and surveillance technologies.

Index